D1382662

To

Marshall Baily

In appreciation of
your many kindnesses
to the improvement of
the Salem Public Library

Nellie L. Glass

Also by Joseph Kerman

OPERA AS DRAMA (*1956*)

This is a Borzoi Book published by Alfred A. Knopf in New York

THE BEETHOVEN QUARTETS

EETHOVEN IN 1815, BY CHRISTOPH HECKEL

The Beethoven Quartets

JOSEPH KERMAN

ALFRED · A · KNOPF

NEW YORK · 1967

This is a Borzoi Book published by Alfred A. Knopf, Inc.

FIRST EDITION

 Distributed by Random House, Inc. Published simultaneously in Toronto, Canada, by Random House of Canada Limited.
Library of Congress Catalog Card Number: 66-19383
Manufactured in the United States of America

To Lucy, Jonathan, and Peter

ACKNOWLEDGMENTS

Quotations from Sir Donald Tovey are reprinted with the permission of the Oxford University Press.

To Mrs. Jane Imamura and Christopher Macie I am grateful for assistance in preparing the manuscript of this book. David Lewin and John Roberts were good enough to read some chapters, and made valuable comments and corrections, but of course they must not be implicated in remaining infelicities.

The frontispiece, a portrait of Beethoven by Christoph Heckel, is reproduced with the kind permission of the owner, Mr. Robert Owen Lehman. Daniel Heartz drew my attention to this portrait, which until recently seems to have been known only in badly distorted black-and-white reproductions and engravings. It has been assigned to the year 1815: between the composition and the publication of the *Quartetto serioso* in F minor, Op. 95.

CONTENTS

BOOK I

BOOK II

BOOK III

BOOK I

1

BEETHOVEN IN 1798

Quartet in D Major, Op. 18, No. 3

Beethoven had come to Vienna six years before, at the end of 1792. "Dear Beethoven!" his first patron, Count Waldstein, wrote in his album at Bonn, "You are going to Vienna in fulfillment of your long-frustrated wishes. The Genius of Mozart is mourning and weeping over the death of her pupil. She found a refuge but no occupation with the inexhaustible Haydn; through him she wishes to form a union with another. With the help of assiduous labor you shall receive *Mozart's spirit from Haydn's hands. . . .*"[1]

It was an age that could entertain such a prediction with complete, innocent sincerity: an age that had already begun building novels around the artist as hero, and would see him soon as the unacknowledged legislator of mankind. This image Beethoven himself was to fix indelibly into the Western consciousness. It was an age of rapid transition in the social order, at some stage of which a young Knight of the Teutonic Order could befriend a half-educated sub-organist whose improvisations promised to excite the world. Not many young composers setting out for a musical metropolis—not Handel or Mozart in earlier times, nor Brahms or Stravinsky in theirs—have been so heartened by idealistic aristocrats predicting great conquests and mapping out ahead, with sufficient accuracy, the future course of musical history.

Better simply to bless Count Waldstein for having helped Beethoven, and to envy him for his contact with the composer; one need not defer to his accuracy in prediction. The remark, after all, was a facile one, as facile

[1] Thayer, *Life of Beethoven*, p. 115. The full titles of works from which quotations have been taken are given in the Bibliography, pp. 383–6.

as the generalization appears to us from our quite different vantage point nearly two centuries later. We find ourselves drawn to the historical prophecy because history is our instinct, perhaps—because a sense of history is what we have left. Not having been there, with Waldstein, we can only establish contact by imposing upon people, art, and events a retrospective order that is quite another thing than the rich disorder of involvement. History for us has whitened actuality into abstraction. The immediacy of artistic struggle becomes a set of trends, points of contact, and lines of development relating works of art which grow more and more isolated; isolation may make them appear more impressive, yet the impressiveness is lonely, and the price inexorably in flesh and blood. It can be repaid only by an effort of historical imagination, and then only in small part. We can hardly recapture the living quality of that time and place, the chaos that Waldstein knew.

What was it like to write a symphony or a string quartet in the city of Mozart and Haydn? What was it to make a musical career—to be a composer?

The death of Mozart was the memory of less than a year. Beethoven, who had been introduced to Mozart as a boy, would certainly have gravitated towards him now, had he been alive; as it was, Mozart remained a standard —already whitening, at once pathetic, stringent, and ironic. Viennese musical opinion, which seems never to have been in doubt as to the extraordinary nature of Mozart's genius, made no mistake about Beethoven either. His talent was surpassing, and plain to everybody. His success was assured. Unlike Mozart, Beethoven knew how to make success stick.

Joseph Haydn, at the age of sixty, had just returned to Vienna from his first tour to London, where he had earned much adulation, much money, and a new sense of his position in the musical life of his era. To Haydn, inevitably, the young musician from the provinces first went for lessons. He felt the instruction was perfunctory, and neither then nor later was Beethoven one to make allowances because of hero-worship or any appreciation of the cleft in generations. But after a year Haydn went off on his second London tour, and Beethoven went to Johann Georg Albrechtsberger, a painstaking theorist who ran him through the old-fashioned contrapuntal curriculum. The record of Beethoven's indeed assiduous (if not always exemplary) labor is preserved in dozens of exercises, which he clung to until his death, along with literally hundreds of sketchbooks, notebooks, and conversation tablets. For the secrets of *bel canto* and vocal declamation he also studied sporadically with the leading opera composer in Vienna, the Court *Kapellmeister* Antonio Salieri, whose name also haunts the biographies of Mozart and Schubert. Salieri's method seems to have been simply to correct finished compositions; there exists a respectable Italian aria by Beethoven, to words by Metastasio, with Salieri's dry annotations. It is unlikely that Beethoven suffered such instruction frequently.

But Haydn and Salieri were important connections. As compared with Mozart, Beethoven seems to have been infinitely energetic or skillful in courting influence and financial preferment. Through Count Waldstein he already brought with him from Bonn an entrée to Viennese society, a matter of the first importance for the making of a musical career. As things stood at that time, unless one worked in opera—which was largely Italian—one had to gain a foothold in the homes of the Viennese nobility. There was no public concert life worth mentioning, and publishing was a secondary consideration. Private persons, on the other hand, cultivated instrumental music with a passion, and it was possible for a brilliant pianist, composer, and improviser to maintain himself very well from one soirée to the next. There were even several full orchestras in the homes of princes. The first steps of Beethoven's rising career, then, cannot be traced in the public sphere. During 1793 and 1794 he laid the foundation for his hold on the international aristocracy of Vienna which was to maintain him all his life. He played and improvised; he accepted gifts and commissions; he even taught. On his list of patrons were such names as Prince Lichnowsky, Prince Lobkowitz, Count Apponyi, Count Browne, Countess Thun, Countess Keglevics, and the formidable old connoisseur who had introduced Haydn and Mozart to the music of Bach, Baron von Swieten.

Soon Beethoven came into the public eye. Through Salieri, apparently, he was introduced in 1795 at the Easter Benefit Concerts of the *Tonkünstlergesellschaft*, which were among the few established public concerts in Vienna. Beethoven gave the premiere of his Piano Concerto in B♭, and thereafter appeared frequently as performer and composer in these twice-yearly events. On the day after the Easter Benefit Concerts, he played a Mozart concerto at a concert performance of *La Clemenza di Tito* which Mozart's widow had arranged. And late in the year, when Haydn returned and gave a concert introducing three of his last London symphonies, Beethoven played the B♭ Concerto once again. He was also commissioned to write minuets and *Teutsche* for the annual Artists' Ball—a signal honor, according to the historians of Viennese musical manners.

Publication was the next step, and in the middle of 1795 Beethoven issued his Opus 1, the three impressive piano trios. Previously he had published a few smaller pieces, one of them at Artaria's in Vienna, but he dignified with opus numbers only works that he took entirely seriously. The trios had been played in Haydn's presence as early as 1793, and there is no way of knowing whether they were now appreciably revised or for that matter whether drafts of them may not date back to Bonn. The pieces were dedicated to Prince Lichnowsky, Beethoven's chief supporter in the early years, and gained the composer a good profit. He was now keeping a horse and servant.

After Op. 1 came Beethoven's first group of piano sonatas, Op. 2, inscribed dutifully to his teacher Joseph Haydn; his first String Trio, Op. 3; and his first String Quintet, Op. 4. None of this music, again, was entirely new. The three piano sonatas had been heard at least a year earlier than their publication—and very curiously, each one of them incorporates sections out of old piano quartets written at the age of fifteen. The String Quintet was a definitive rewriting of a composition from Bonn, a wind octet. It appears that 1794 is the latest possible date for the String Trio, which is a work in six movements, like a divertimento, recalling Mozart's single String Trio, K. 563, of 1788 (also in the key of E♭). By a strange set of circumstances a manuscript of Beethoven's trio turned up in England during the early 1790's and made a sensation. "This composition, so different from anything I had ever heard, awakened in me a new sense, a new delight, in the science of sounds. . . ." So writes a certain William Gardiner many years later, in the full awareness of Beethoven's then towering position in musical affairs; and Gardiner was never quite sure whether the revelation took place in 1793, 1794, 1795, or 1796. If we do not entirely discount the story, it may serve to alert us to signs of heady novelty even in Beethoven's so-called "imitative" period of composition.

Flushed by all this activity, perhaps, in 1796 the composer took off to Prague with his patron Lichnowsky. Records of Beethoven's early years are sparse, but it appears that the trip developed into a highly successful concert tour. Glowing reports are preserved of his playing and improvising. In Berlin, he wrote a pair of cello sonatas for Frederick William II of Prussia, the cellist king who had commissioned Mozart's three quartets with the prominent cello parts (the "Prussian" Quartets) only six years earlier. The sonatas are almost miniature concertos. In December Beethoven probably played them again at public concerts in Vienna.

1797 was another year for publication. After the cello sonatas appeared as Op. 5, they were followed by the little four-hand Piano Sonata, Op. 6; the *Grande Sonate* in E♭ for Piano, Op. 7; the Serenade for String Trio, Op. 8; as well as quite a few unnumbered smaller works, including the once-popular song *Adelaide*. It is clear enough from this rush of publication that not everything was brand new when it went to the printers; and around 1802, at any rate, we are specifically informed that most of Beethoven's music was commissioned by amateurs, who received exclusive rights to the manuscripts for "a half year, a year, or even longer." Only after such a period was the author free to publish. Next, in July 1798, were published the three String Trios, Op. 9 (genuine trios, not serenades), described in Beethoven's dedication as "*la meilleure de ses œuvres.*" As the three important Sonatas, Op. 10, had not yet appeared, this was probably a just claim. Probably, though, these sonatas were already completed by then, along with the famous *Sonate Pathétique*, Op. 13, two smaller Sonatas, Op. 14, and three violin sonatas that were to be dedicated to Beethoven's other teacher, Salieri, as Op. 12.

With this music behind him, in the middle of 1798, Beethoven turned his attention to the composition of string quartets. The task was to preoccupy him for about two years.

As a matter of fact, the suggestion to write quartets had come some time before, from a certain Count Apponyi in 1795. This information comes from Beethoven's old friend and first biographer Dr. Franz Wegeler, the husband of the first of many ladies with whom the composer's name has been associated, Eleonore von Breuning of Bonn. Wegeler followed Beethoven from Bonn to Vienna in 1794 and stored away in his mind many suggestive memories of those early years. (He reports, for instance, that the finale of the Concerto in B♭ was written—or written out?—two days before its premiere at the Easter Benefit Concert in 1795. No wonder Beethoven later came to feel that the piece could stand revision; sketches for this revision are found together with those for the quartets, in 1798.) Apponyi, says Wegeler,

> asked Beethoven to compose a quartet for him for a given compensation, Beethoven not yet having written a piece in this genre. The Count declared that contrary to custom he did not want to have exclusive possession of the quartet for half a year before publication, nor did he ask that it be dedicated to him, etc. In response to repeated urgings by me, Beethoven twice set about the task, but the first effort resulted in a grand violin Trio (Op. 3), the second in a violin Quintet (Op. 4).[2]

Count Apponyi's interest appears natural enough, in view of the fact that he had recently commissioned Haydn's six Quartets, Op. 71 and 74. (In a similar sequence Prince Lobkowitz commissioned Haydn's Op. 77

[2] Thayer (Krehbiel edn.), II, 187.

in 1799 and Beethoven's Op. 18 in 1801.) As a heavy subscriber to the Piano Trios, Op. 1, in 1795—along with Prince Lichnowsky, Countess Thun, and half a dozen other devotees—Apponyi was presumably much impressed with the young composer. That Op. 3 or Op. 4 had anything to do with the case seems unlikely, for as has already been mentioned, both of these works had been composed in main outline long before this time. However there are small signs that Beethoven did not at once reject Apponyi's quite handsome proposition. Several preludes and fugues for string trio and string quartet were written in this period, as an outcome of the contrapuntal studies with Albrechtsberger; they were never intended for publication, of course, but the genre has significance, as we shall see. A small Minuet in A♭ for string quartet may also stem from 1795; it is written on a blank page from the early (1795) version of the B♭ Concerto. Together with sketches for this concerto, Gustav Nottebohm found sketches for the Piano Sonata in E, Op. 14, No. 1, which he claimed showed signs of an original conception for string quartet. (Nottebohm, the great nineteenth-century expert on the Beethoven sketches, is still cited as an authority.) The point here is that in 1802 Beethoven actually published this sonata in an arrangement for string quartet, commenting in a letter as follows:

> The *unnatural mania*, now so prevalent, for transferring even *pianoforte compositions* to string instruments, instruments which in all respects are so utterly different from one another, should really be checked. I firmly maintain that only *Mozart* could arrange for other instruments the works he composed for the pianoforte; and *Haydn* could do this too . . . I have arranged only one of my sonatas for string quartet, because I was so earnestly implored to do so; and I am quite convinced that nobody else could do the same thing with ease.[3]

Was this exceptional arrangement made in memory of an original intention to cast this music for strings? Nottebohm's early dating for the sonata sketches has been doubted but never disproved. Beethoven may well have played with the idea of quartet composition in 1795.

However this may be, Apponyi's proposal bore no direct fruit. Beethoven must have received a more attractive commission for string trios, for in the dedication to Op. 9, in July 1798, Count Browne is called his "first Mæcenas" (a reference which was less than fair to Lichnowsky, who however put up with this and worse from Beethoven). And by 1798 the quar-

[3] *Letters,* No. 59.

tets were evidently designed not for Apponyi but for Prince Lobkowitz. After their publication Lichnowsky settled on the composer a splendid annual stipend of 600 florins. This was about equal to Schubert's average annual income during the last dozen years of his life.

Beethoven was twenty-seven (though thanks to an old advertising fraud perpetrated by his father, he seems to have believed that he was two years younger). He was to work intensively on quartet composition for nearly two years. By a rather striking coincidence, Mozart was also twenty-seven, and not yet two years in Vienna, when he started composing a set of six quartets which was later published with a famous, moving dedication to Joseph Haydn. This job too was spread out over two years, and from evidence both external and internal it is known that Mozart devoted uncommon care and trouble to the work. Indeed the six "Haydn" quartets are true "watershed works" for Mozart: together with *Le Nozze di Figaro* they mark the decisive turn into the period of his full maturity, his last ten years. The composition of Mozart's quartets was begun in 1782 —only sixteen years before Beethoven embarked on a parallel project of parallel importance to his career. And in 1785, when Mozart's quartets were published, the child organist at Bonn was making his first imitations of Mozart, in the same piano quartets that were later robbed of material for the first sonatas. Beethoven was soon to look searchingly at Mozart once again.

His own care and industry and worry and high seriousness in writing the six Op. 18 Quartets, as well as their chronology, is evidenced by his sketchbooks. Early in his career he settled on a regular routine of composition, keeping a series of large workbooks in which he sketched the music that occupied him. He also carried pocket-sized books on his walks around Vienna and into the countryside; the material in these interlocks with that found in the larger books. If all of these volumes were extant, an almost daily record of his compositional process would be available for study. Thanks to Beethoven's compulsion not to throw anything away, and thanks to the enthusiasm of souvenir hunters after his death, quite a number of these books have been preserved—though typically mutilated by the same souvenir hunters. Luckily enough for the present purpose, the earliest full books that are known happen to be a continguous pair containing extensive, laborious sketches for the first four of the quartets. In order, these are the Quartets in D major, F major, G major, and A major, which were published as Op. 18, Nos. 3, 1, 2, and 5. Nothing analogous—in fact, very little of anything—is known about the composition of the Quartets in C minor and B♭, Nos. 4 and 6.

The books date from the middle of 1798 to the end of 1799; and the interesting fact is that next to nothing else of any size is sketched along with the quartets. At the end, work begins on the Septet, Op. 20, but otherwise there are no major compositions in sonata form, only some songs and piano variations. For eighteen months or more, then, Beethoven seems to have concentrated on the four quartets. The task was essentially uninterrupted by other big projects.

· 2 ·

The composition of string quartets was important in several ways to Beethoven in 1798. It meant first of all, as Wegeler noted, entry upon a major musical genre which he had not yet tried. This entry itself may be seen as a step in his steady apprenticeship in all branches of composition. There can be little doubt that at this period of his life Beethoven had embarked on a more or less planned assault on the entire territory of music. The dogged studies in the old counterpoint with Albrechtsberger marked a beginning, and the extended work on the quartets an important stage. Almost from the start new areas opened up under the pressure of Beethoven's campaign. Assault was discovery; the Ninth Symphony, the *Missa solemnis*, and the Great Fugue completed an unmapped and unimagined conquest.

So far he had written only in certain genres. He had composed a few songs, and many piano variations, which contain besides trivia some exceedingly interesting things. The form that he had rapidly made his own was the piano sonata. It has often been observed that Beethoven worked most comfortably and flexibly in this medium, and as it were most consciously. Compositional problems were attacked and provisionally solved in sonatas, right under the fingers, years before they were broached in symphonies and chamber music. A clear sequence can be traced—has many times been traced—from the Sonatas in F minor, A major, and C major of Op. 2, with their relics of Bonn, to the impressive *Grande Sonate* in E♭, Op. 7, to the three Sonatas, Op. 10 (C minor, F, and D), and the *Sonate Pathétique*. Slightly off the central line stand the two smaller Sonatas, Op. 14 (E and G), and the pair of sonatinas later published as Op. 49. The sequence soon came to a head in another *Grande Sonate*, that in B♭, Op. 22, of 1800. The next sonatas—Op. 26, 27, 28, and 31—are the first works that press forward tentatively to the style of Beethoven's "second period."

Though Beethoven had sketched copiously at a symphony, all that he had completed for orchestra was a pair of concertos, in B♭ and C—for piano, for his own personal performance. In chamber music he had done a good deal of miscellaneous work for wind instruments. But it was never his best work, and he soon lost interest in winds, after the Septet of 1800. For strings, as we have seen, there were the Piano Trios, Op. 1; some sonatas for violin and for cello; and no fewer than five pieces for string trio —the early trio which sent William Gardiner into such raptures, the Serenade in D, and the recent three Trios, Op. 9. Now, in 1798, Beethoven moved to the string quartet. In 1800 he would produce his First Symphony, following it up with five more in the next eight years. Also in 1800 came his first work for the Viennese stage, the ballet *Prometheus*. In 1803 he dashed off an oratorio, *Christus am Ölberge*, and in 1805 he brought forth, after long labors, preliminary trials, exasperations, and exceptional problems, an opera. The C-major Mass appeared in 1807.

This march through the genres was inevitably a competitive one. As Malraux has observed, an artist paints a picture not because he has seen a tree, but because he has seen another picture of a tree. A quartet is written in response to another quartet. In so sophisticated and dense a musical environment as Vienna in the 1790's, no one composed for himself in a vacuum, let alone a musician as jealous of his status as Beethoven was. As a virtuoso pianist and a virtuoso improviser he easily established mastery and originality in the sonata, the variations, and the concerto for piano; he "surpassed" Haydn and Mozart in a certain sense by finding a place in the sun which they did not occupy. His piano trios also took a quite new view of the possibilities of the form. It seems significant, indeed, that with the one prominent (and inevitable) exception of the piano concerto, all the genres that Beethoven first controlled were those not specially favored by the other two Viennese masters. Their piano trios and variations, and even their sonatas, are on the whole secondary works. They scarcely wrote at all for string trio, the combination by which Beethoven first broke free of the piano. But with the string quartet, the symphony, the Mass, oratorio, and opera—here he moved into formidable competition with Haydn and Mozart in the forms they had cultivated with full responsibility and artistic intensity.

In the string quartet the towering examples by Mozart were the six quartets of 1785 dedicated to Haydn, and the "Prussian" Quartets of 1790; and by Haydn—innumerable. During the few years that Beethoven had been living in Vienna, he had seen the publication of Haydn's most powerful works: the Quartets, Op. 71 and 74 (for Apponyi) in 1793, and Op. 76 in 1797. These twelve great quartets include the "Emperor" and the "Sunrise"; two compositions in minor keys, the "Horseman" and the "*Quinten*"; and other masterpieces which have escaped the half-ritualistic, half-patronizing fixing by nickname. Might not Beethoven, after all, have experienced some hesitation in presenting himself as a quartet composer in 1795? Knowing the man, one hesitates to say so. All the same, his early output reveals a certain instinctive circumspection in what he tried and in what he broadcast.

By 1798 Beethoven could rest easy enough about the individuality of his quartets, for all that they reveal some clear traces of Haydn and some remarkably strong traces of Mozart. That he paid the least attention to any other Viennese quartet composers is heartily to be doubted. In the older musicological literature the name of Emanuel Aloys Förster was always mentioned in connection with the Op. 18 Quartets; this composer, who was twenty years Beethoven's senior, is said to have earned his friendship and his respect as a pedagogue. Certain it is that he published quartets in the 1790's; and so long as these were not easily available, one could always hint at Förster's having taught Beethoven. But when finally some of his chamber music was published in the Austrian *Denkmäler* series, in 1928, the worthy editor burst out with commendable heat:

> What would Beethoven have had to learn from Förster? As if he had not already with Op. 1—works of genius which seemed problematic even to a Haydn—left all the Försters of this world far behind him! . . . There remains only the possibility that at certain soirees and rehearsals the young master may have picked up one tip or another from Förster in respect to minor technical details. It really will not do to push this able but always rather philistine eclectic into the company of the great men of his time. . . .[4]

A glance at the music shows how apt this estimate is of Förster's ability; and of all the lesser Viennese composers, he is said to be infinitely the closest in style to Beethoven.

From a technical point of view, the writing of string quartets offered Beethoven a new challenge in the matter of texture. And much more was involved than picking up one or two tricks of the trade. Doubtless it will be obvious enough that a musical conception for four string instruments demands more contrapuntal control than one for piano or for piano and instruments. All good classic music exhibits a strong sense of line, in the progress of the single voice and in the relationship of parts. But piano music and orchestral music, each in its own way, can to some extent properly subordinate linearity in a "wash" of sonority—symbolized, in the extreme case,

[4] Förster, p. vi.

by the use of the sustaining pedal of the piano and by the standard treatment of the brass as harmonic underpinning in classical orchestration. The four instruments of the quartet, on the other hand, are always individuals, always sensitive, always exposed. They are limited in coloristic or even dynamic variety, and feeble in grand vertical effects; all they have is their relentless mutual confrontation. If—*pace* Förster—they are to be used with any sense of their true potentiality, the problem of linear integrity has to be met head on.

It may be slightly less obvious that the string quartet posed the problem a great deal more sharply than the string trio. A glance at Beethoven's Op. 9, or even at Mozart's Trio in E♭, K. 563, shows that this was indeed the case. The resources of the trio are just a little short of comfort, a circumstance which proved to be less a stimulus to ingenuity than a temptation to compromise. A usual expedient was to delegate one instrument (usually the viola) to fill in broken-chord figuration; whereupon the problem reduced itself to the handling of two voices in a rather simple-minded duet. But with four strings the texture is full enough so that broken chords are a free resource rather than a necessity. With four voices all available the task for the contrapuntist is of an appreciably higher order. This is a way of seeing why, given the eighteenth-century harmonic system, it was the quartet rather than the trio or the quintet which established itself as the chamber-music norm.

Now, Beethoven had revealed himself from the start as a formidable contrapuntist. Even before his work with Albrechtsberger, one is inclined to say, he had more natural instinct for counterpoint than any of his immediate contemporaries. His earliest music contains no brilliant polyphonic displays; but the control of large linear direction, the dynamic polarity of bass and soprano, and the taut manipulation of inner parts when they appropriately stand out of the texture—all this was excellently handled from the start. He experienced little trouble in manipulating the light classical *obbligato* counterpoint which Haydn and Mozart had developed as a life-giving force within the bland harmonic idiom of the late eighteenth-century style. This is clear in the Op. 18 Quartets; but it is also clear that Beethoven was looking for something more.

As is well known, Haydn's development of this classic contrapuntal style came after an extraordinary series of strictly fugal finales in his Op. 20 Quartets of 1772. They were instantly copied by the child Mozart. After these impressive studies in archaic counterpoint, Haydn gradually lightened and sophisticated a polyphonic idiom poised perfectly to the aesthetic of high comedy that Tovey pointed out as the essence of the high classic style. It is characteristic that Beethoven seems to have felt a need to live through in reverse, as it were, Haydn's own evolution. And so it happens strikingly that, starting with the six Quartets, Op. 18, Beethoven experiments again and again with the old counterpoint in its most scholastic forms: canons, stiff double-counterpoint inversions, *fugati*, even fugues. These exercises jostle smoother counterpoint in the facile classic style, which was something he could manage perfectly easily. Too easily, perhaps. The search for character, which is to say the search for power, sent him back to a more abstract contrapuntal ideal.

Experiments with formal contrapuntal devices are to be heard occasionally in the early piano trios, not at all in the string trios, and only very rarely in the first ten piano sonatas, for all their brilliant variety of effect. The mock-fugal *scherzoso* finale of the Sonata in F, Op. 10, No. 2, is an exception; this movement, even though it is a *presto*, belongs in the same complex with the *Andante scherzoso quasi allegretto* of the Quartet in C minor, Op. 18, No. 4, and the *Andante* of the First Symphony. Beethoven's intensification of these contrapuntal experiments in Op. 18 looks back directly to the fugue exercises for string trio and string quartet written with Albrechtsberger in 1795. It looks forward to impressive structures in the "Razumovsky" Quartets: to the huge *fugato* in the F-major first movement, the violent fugal Finale in the C-major, and the hair-raising canons on the Russian tune in the E-minor. Ultimately it sustains the contrapuntal obsession of the last period, which played itself out in the Great Fugue and the Quartet in C♯ minor.

In addition to a problem of texture, Beethoven found himself facing a problem of movement or pace, one that he had already met in writing string trios. In this regard, trio and quartet stand together in distinction from the piano sonata. There the problem of movement had been brilliantly solved; indeed, the sonatas include experiments with all kinds of virtuoso effects in the larger aspects of musical form, the scope and balance of the movements, and in the smaller aspects of phraseology and period structure. In detail, the sonatas are full of striking fits and starts, nervous transitions, ellipses, abrupt contractions and expansions. What is more, the form as Beethoven conceived it could embrace both the terseness of the Sonatas in F minor and E major (Op. 2, No. 1 and Op. 14, No. 1) and the breadth of the *Grande Sonate* in E♭, Op. 7—whose first movement is twice as long as either of theirs. Beethoven's mastery of improvisation must have had something to do with the variety of flow of the first ten piano sonatas. The piano sonata lay under his fingers. He could caress it and mold it and distort it to unprecedented effect.

The trio or the quartet for strings was inevitaby something more remote. Only in the last quartets was Beethoven to develop the same astonishing flexibility, the same extempore quality that seems to belong in writing for a single instrument. In the large, it is clear that during the 1790's Beethoven never imagined that a piece of chamber music should be concise. More is at issue than the general feeling that once four players are brought together, they need something substantial to make it worth their trouble; Haydn had written witty miniatures for quartet, but Haydn's epigrammatic style was the last thing that interested the younger composer. If the little Piano Sonata in E was really first intended for quartet, as Nottebohm hinted, one sure reason for its recasting would have been Beethoven's realization that the material was evolving so modestly. "*2. Theil. ohne das Thema durchzuführen,*" he wrote on an early sketch for the first movement. That is a possible prescription for a piano sonata, but to avoid serious development of first-movement material would have been unthinkable in a quartet.

On the smaller level, there are clear signs of a relatively monolithic conception of musical structure in Beethoven's string trios and early quartets. Phrases tend to be long and bland; they may link together skillfully, but they tend to repeat themselves, to recur, or to range themselves sequentially with solemn regularity. Formal procedures are prolix, formal balances are stiff, and the flow is generally ponderous. In fact, much of this music bespeaks evident technical problems—which Beethoven was soon to solve. He was going to solve them, however, in a different way than that adopted in the piano sonatas, and I believe it is a mistake to see only the negative aspect of the leisurely, sometimes sleepy momentum of the early chamber music. The nervous brilliance of the piano sonatas does not last in Beethoven's practice, but while it does, he capitalizes on it as an aesthetic quality in its own right. Similarly in the chamber music, a desire for great scope seems to have formed the basis of an aesthetic idea. For from the start, as has been said, the chamber music was big-boned. The Piano Trios, Op. 1, are overblown, and the quartets go through a monumental stage which would be grotesque in any other work than the F-major "Razumovsky" before Beethoven felt able to afford conciseness of expression, such as that of the Quartet in F minor, Op. 95. Weighty, impressive structure was integral to Beethoven's conception of chamber music, in contradistinction to the piano sonata. We shall not much understand the early quartets if we regard this solemnity, in the light of the piano sonatas, merely as awkwardness of technique.

· 3 ·

What has been sketched so far may be of use in setting an exterior context for a consideration of Beethoven's first quartet, the Quartet in D major, Op. 18, No. 3. Nothing yet has been said about what might be described as the interior context: the unspoken private principles of order and expression germane to the individual work of art. The interior context had better not be predefined, but allowed to grow out of our study of the work itself —by definition, if the definition be accepted.

Mehr Beethoven, als Quartett: the old epigram by A. B. Marx, the first to write an exhaustive German study of the composer, more than a hundred years ago, has stuck in the memory of every student of the D-major Quartet. Yet as Marx instantly observed, the work could only have been cast in the medium of string quartet. By the time Beethoven was through with it—Op. 18 went to the printer in 1800—the piece was flaunting brilliance of instrumental technique and texture; it certainly stands up and walks like a quartet, not like a trio or a piano sonata. Some other commentators to the contrary, it does not even remotely suggest comparison to Haydn, any more than it recognizes the very existence of a Pleyel, a Koželuch, or an Emanuel Aloys Förster. The piece shows signs both delicate and rude of Beethoven's determination to spike his quartet style with formal contrapuntal devices. In the first movement it makes out a good case for his early aesthetic of simple weight. This first movement is neither fast on its feet nor subtle in its gestures, but the determined march of its phrases and periods is on the whole excellently realized. Instead of contrast or drama Beethoven worked for solidity and continuity here, at the expense of momentary interest in inflection. The result is music with more easy momentum than spirit—quite the reverse of the typical early Beethoven experience.

The character of the movement grows directly out of the main theme, and in this respect the piece represents an advance in conception over his earlier works of the same general quality. It opens with a genuine, essentially indivisible 10-bar phrase, unusually broad and bland:

Example 1

Allegro.

In construction, the phrase is interesting, with its almost languid 2-bar dominant upbeat on the 7th leap, its exhaustive recouping from this leap with scale figures, and its dragging harmonic rhythm at the cadence. Underneath is a rising scale in the bass, firm but as yet unobtrusive. Whenever the theme occurs later, the dragging cadence is changed so as to move on ahead, as might be expected. But the slow upbeat was integral to Beethoven's conception; it is preserved and strengthened as the piece proceeds. The String Trio in D, Op. 9, No. 2, had tried for breadth with something similar but weaker:

Example 2

The 10-bar phrase of the quartet is answered by a 16-bar consequent—again practically an indivisible unit, with brilliant cascading runs in the first violin. One does not hear such openings in Haydn or Mozart. However, the placid emphasis on the subdominant chord which follows recalls Mozart more than Beethoven, as the theme develops a pair of 4-bar phrases in its own image, introducing *strettos* on the initial motif without much ruffling the steady flow. The bridge also keeps the leisurely pace, though otherwise making an utter contrast with the prior material. This bridge is perhaps the one decidely awkward element in the movement.

A peculiarity in the treatment of the second group seems also to relate to Beethoven's commanding idea of smooth momentum. Once the bridge has settled on a new dominant (the E triad), this harmony is prolonged by arpeggiation—note the 7th in the violin—for another solid phrase. The process sounds dull enough, as does also the punctual resolution to the new tonic, A major. But this turns out to be abortive. Instead of starting new material, Beethoven drops the tonic instantly and makes as though to repeat its prolonged dominant; a real element of doubt has been introduced, which deepens halfway through the phrase when it extends itself and defects steadily toward C (♭III of A). Here, when a marchlike "second subject" turns up, it has the unusual air of needing to get home as soon as decently possible. Instead of loitering, like so many of Beethoven's early second subjects, it has a somewhat urgent and welcome purpose in life which drives it in only eight bars to its cadence. The second group, in short, has been undercut in this movement. The sense of flow is all-important.

At the abortive resolution to A major, Beethoven allows himself the one serious irregularity in phrasing in the entire piece: 7 bars, 10 bars, then 8 into the cadence. Ultimately, the exposition winds up with Mozartian cadence figures sounding quite clipped by the standards set up by this piece or by the standards of Beethoven's other music. Usually he liked spicy cadence material. The tameness here was probably meant to set in relief this final gesture of transition:

Example 3

In this transition, the bold 9th in the violin and the bold chromatic scale in the cello link perfectly into the opening 7th and the bass of the main theme. (The repetition of the exposition, prescribed at this point, should definitely *not* be skipped.) As the most dramatic event yet in a piece that has been emphasizing regularity of pace, this transition sets up expectations. The cello has pushed up a strong C♯ (the leading-tone of the key, the 3rd of the dominant-7th) to support the slow dominant upbeat of the theme.

Beethoven duly returns to the C♯ at the end of the development section, just prior to the recapitulation. Now he stresses the note in a characteristic way, by dignifying it with its own triad—splashed out noisily over five octaves and eight full bars:

Example 4

What is characteristic is the *harmonic* intensification of a *melodic* element: the critical melodic step C♯–D (7–8) supported by a C♯ triad leading to a D triad. As often in such cases, there is a sense of paradox, because a C♯ triad does not lead properly to a D triad, and the intervening chord is not designed for more than grammatical plausibility. I take it that the sense of great solidity that tempers the paradox is due to the fact that the C♯ has been heard previously (twice, if the repetition was not skipped) leading to the theme in a purely melodic, unambiguous manner. Also, that grammatical convenience happens to coincide with the opening harmony of the recapitulating theme itself, the dominant chord under the slow upbeat 7th.

Besides the climactic establishment of the C♯, not much of interest happens in the development section. It follows a very old-fashioned stereotype: a series of long, even phrases modeled closely on specific phrases of the exposition. Such a section makes no stirring contrasts and opens no new vistas; it scarcely breaks step. It gives the impression of a loose run-through of selected highlights from the exposition, in some new modes and keys, rather than of "development" in any deeper sense. Beethoven had written developments of this general sort previously, in the trios, but this one is certainly no beauty, and would have seemed archaic to Haydn fifteen years earlier. I doubt that Beethoven was unaware of this, or that he found himself technically out of his depth. His judgment may have been wrong, but presumably he planned such a development in order to concentrate on large goals and on steady motion at the deliberate sacrifice of developmental detail. It cannot be denied that the loud stately canons in the concluding phrases, though strangely faceless, establish C♯ with a splendid sense of mass.

The recapitulation, at all events, succeeds well, and again the success depends on broad, simple, solid linkings of long phrases. After the initial 10-bar phrase, Beethoven ducks the consequent phrase directly to the subdominant and, with an unsuspected show of power, marches that unobtrusive bass scale up through fourteen steps, from low subdominant to high dominant. This 14-bar phrase is so strong that he can afford to eliminate his pair of 4-bar phrases and the entire bridge, and enter at once upon the second group. This was fine strategy on several counts. The stiff-jointed bridge had overstayed its welcome in the development and would have seemed merely pettifogging here. The half-canonic 4-bar phrases can now make a fresh impact when they reappear in the coda. The extension of the scale helps compensate for general developmental reticence in the development proper. Besides, the whole scheme of a placid succession of long phrases, however well Beethoven could control them, was in danger of falling out of the dramatic necessities of the sonata style; tactful and at the same time interesting pruning was exactly what was required to get tautness into the form. The recapitulation is shortened by 26 bars, something like 25 per cent by the clock, but certainly nothing seems to rush.

A more or less expected move to the subdominant, and an unexpected further move to the Neapolitan tonality (♭II, E♭), repay this loss in the coda. As an excellent concluding stroke, the coda resumes for the first time the cascading runs that had emerged in the original 16-bar consequent of the main theme. So at the end, the theme appears to encompass the whole action, and with more power than might have been anticipated at the start.

The very last bars are beholden to the conclusion of the first movement of Mozart's "Prussian" Quartet in D, K. 575. It was Mozart's "Hunt" Quartet in B♭, K. 458, I believe, that suggested the series of rhetorical diminished-7th chords in whole-notes at the main cadence of Beethoven's second group (the whole-notes also relate to the opening motif). In any case, this idea recurs in such works as the Second Symphony and even the Quartet in F, Op. 59, No. 1. The symphony, which is also in D major, recalls the quartet even more strongly through its retransition employing the very same paradoxical C♯ triad going to D. But where the quartet is serious and architectural, the symphony is humorous, more genuinely Haydnesque.

The interrelationship and the quality of the sequence among the movements of the classic cyclic work was the subject of one of Beethoven's most far-reaching reinterpretations of the Haydnesque or Mozartian conception. This is a well-known fact, which the reader may fairly expect to see traced extensively in any account of the Beethoven quartets. His earliest music, however, is not the place to study this tendency. In the sonatas, it first becomes a matter of aesthetic importance after 1800; in the symphonies, tentatively with the Second; and in the quartets, only after the Op. 18 series. The four movements of the Quartet in D show little sense of any intimate facing, little deepening of the sense of sequence beyond the conventional classic model. Thus the third movement, an *allegro*—Beethoven does not call it a minuet or a scherzo—is a spotlessly groomed little piece whose one interest seems to be in making itself inconspicuous. As a quartet movement, it automatically extends itself more broadly than any sonata minuet, such as that of the recent D-major Sonata, Op. 10, No. 3; but of the two, the latter would actually appear to be conceived more idiomatically for string quartet. The second movement, *Andante con moto*, has more personality, but does not attempt more than to set an appropriate lyric center into the structure of the whole piece. Long, serious, and very carefully worked, it is the densest of all the slow movements of Op. 18, with the exception of the pathetic D-minor *Adagio* of the Quartet in F which was composed next in order (and leave *La Malinconia* out of the account). Solemn weight in the lyric slow movement was Beethoven's early way, in piano sonatas and trios as well as in the first two of his quartets.

This *Andante*, warmly poised in B♭, is blessed and obsessed by one of the happiest lyric ideas of Beethoven's early period. For once he seems

Example 5

relaxed in slow melodic utterance, warm, simple, sentimental, neither intimidated by Haydn and Mozart nor tediously marking out his independence of them. But as a matter of fact a formal contrapuntal idea, not sheer lyricism, is basic to the conception. When after four bars the phrase repeats itself, the second violin adds a sixteenth-note scale-figure derived from the material of the half-cadence in bar 4. (The importance of this detail is suggested by the upside-down scoring at the start: Beethoven begins his tune in the second violin so that it will know where the sixteenth-note figure comes from.) The little double counterpoint which is established in this way recurs many times during the movement. It inverts contrapuntally, it works itself out in 3rds, it goes in the minor mode, it even inverts melodically and pretends to canon. Perhaps Beethoven rather overestimated the fresh interest he could give to his theme by these contrapuntal means. But as always with slow polyphony, the inherent attractiveness of the material counts for a great deal.

One cannot say that there is much music of distinction besides the theme and its quietly learned evolutions. The chromatic inflections in the second group are flatulent, all the more so because they relate back so obviously to the melodic motif of bars 1–3. The development is extremely long. The form is stiff, but stiffness allows Beethoven to extend his coda greatly: it can serve as an early example of his "liquidation" technique, by which a tune or theme is successively chipped away to motivic nothings. The treatment is still simple, the effect quite moving.

From the sketchbook Nottebohm was able to tell that the *presto* Finale was begun appreciably later than the other three movements, a fact that accords well with its virtuosity in instrumental and contrapuntal technique and with its general cleverness and *brio*. The original sketch, drab and conventional as it was, already expressed the basic notion of a *perpetuum mobile*. After changes of heart and a great deal of labor, the result was the most complicated finale that Beethoven had yet composed.

The main theme is certainly interesting; once again, from the qualities of the theme the rest of the movement derives both its momentum and its direction. Also, in this case, its motivic saturation. It is one of those Beethoven themes that seem to have been conceived schematically, more in abstract than in sonorous terms, as though the composer were working out some theoretical "precompositional assumption." Four descending 3rds are recouped by four ascending 4ths:

Example 6

(The end recalls a little the Finale of the Sonata in E, Op. 14, No. 1, of 1798—another half-schematic conception, in which a frustrated series of mounting 4ths draws away from an astonishing long scale in the bass.

This sonata, as has been mentioned, Beethoven transcribed as a quartet; in the quartet version—moved up to F—the scale is positively droll:

Example 7

Later on, the B♭ which gets stuck in the first violin seems to require the irregular return of the first rondo episode in the key of B♭, the subdominant.)

In the quartet, harmonic uncertainty is immediately established as the driving force for the whole machine. Within the theme, which is initially presented without accompaniment, we might hear I–vi in bar 1, IV–ii in bar 2, and then V_7 throughout bars 3–4, during the scale A–G. But during bars 2–4 an underlying suggestion of ii–V–I–IV obtrudes; the high G sits very strangely. (At this speed we might even settle lazily for ii_7 all the way through.) Ambiguity is not helped when the phrase at once repeats itself in 3rds, ending now on B plus G, in bar 8. Then a consequent phrase moves sequentially from A up to G plus B (once again) with underpinning that holds carefully to ii and IV, the latter harmony even being supported by its own subdominant. Only in the repetition of this phrase, contrapuntally inverted, are we sharply reminded that B plus G must be heard as a dominant-9th chord rather than as a subdominant (bars 22–4). This is unnatural emphasis on the subdominant degree, hedged around by vi and ii. No wonder Beethoven felt for once relieved of the necessity of inserting further subdominant sounds within the recapitulation.

The rest of the exposition whirls along with intense—too intense—inflections of all kinds. It prophesies of the tarantella finales that Schubert was to like so well. In complete contrast to the development of the first movement, this development really develops material, busily and imaginatively. Its chief harmonic centers, significantly, are IV, ii, and vi; even the return passage stresses ii on its curious chromatic path from IV to the penultimate dominant.

Formal counterpoint comes into its own in this movement. To be sure, the show of *fugato* near the beginning of the development is pretty slight, particularly by contrast with the free gossamer sequences that emerge from it:

Example 8

But presently furious, stiff canons are driving the music with excellent force. A more foolish canon, in four parts, is used to vary the bridge in the recapitulation, with the ostensible function of stabilizing the shaky key by means of dominant answers. The big guns are saved for the coda. Here a remarkable cadential idea develops, only vaguely related to the

Example 9

fugato, consisting of a forceful new *obbligato* added to the first strain of the theme—which is presented off rhythm! This combination Beethoven displays proudly as a double counterpoint at the octave and the tenth, though it is to be doubted that Albrechtsberger would have passed even the simple form, let alone the three inversions. As one of the first examples of Beethoven's celebrated rough-grained counterpoint, if not the very first, this may do violence to tender ears; so will its progeny up unto the Great Fugue. But it does clarify, at last, one harmonic solution for the cryptic theme, and its doublings in 3rds grow appropriately out of the doubling of the theme in 3rds at the very start of the movement (bars 4–8).

Conceptually this is one of the most ingenious and impressive movements in the entire Op. 18 series. Yet velocity, cleverness, and strain do not add up to genuine brilliance, or even, one feels, to a very sharp sense of character. Something in the idea has not been matched in realization; to see how Beethoven would later manage a strong thematic subdominant —in a rather different form, admittedly—one can consider a related series of compositions in E♭: the Sonata, Op. 31, No. 3, the Sonata, Op. 81a (*Les Adieux*), and the wonderful late Quartet, Op. 127. In Beethoven's first quartet there is technique to burn, but the theme works too hard and, in some ultimate sense, lacks conviction. A further point: Beethoven seems definitely to have arranged reflections of the first movement in this Finale. Both main themes feature the rising 7th A–G prominently, and make play with ambiguous *unisono* beginnings. Both expositions end with rising chromatic scales up to C♯ in the bass; both make their principal modulation by means of the step F♮–E, and once this has infected the second group, both cancel the step in the recapitulation. There is an imprecise family resemblance between the big canons within the two developments. Yet none of this ingenious hinting at "unity" seems to count. Beethoven has not found a way out of the classical scheme of essentially independent movements within the four-movement form. It is not even certain that he yet fully appreciated the need to get out.

· 4 ·

At this point we should be in a position to say something about the interior context of a work such as the Quartet in D, its inner postulates of eloquence and coherence. Discussing it, we have found a certain amount clarified by an examination of the exterior context, that is, by such means as measuring the work against its historical predecessors and siblings. The attraction of this approach for the present writer will be sufficiently indicated by its use in the chapters to come; but the approach has its distinct limitations. Historical analogy can go only so far in capturing the immediacy of actual artistic involvement. The aesthetic means created by great artists, furthermore, tend to be new and proper to the individual work of art—this with "early" works, written at the age of thirty, as well as with late ones. In the last analysis, every composition deserves to be granted its own private consistency, and considered as much as possible without preconception, to hear what it uniquely offers as expressive logic. Somewhere our ear has to meet the composer's; it ought therefore to be just as flexibly responsive as his has been inventive.

In the D-major Quartet we have encountered, perhaps as the chief aesthetic principle, a main theme dominating, permeating, or generating each of the three main movements of the work to a striking degree. The actual technique varies. It may be as simple as obsessive recurrences of the theme in new contrapuntal guises, in the second movement; as subtle as an attitude of gait, in the first; or as shadowy as a nervous uncertainty of harmonic implication, in the Finale. Motivic development is always involved, but whereas this plays a major role in the last movement, and a very impressive one, it plays a relatively small role in the early ones. In the matter of motivic play, the Finale is highly sophisticated, the *Andante* less so but already strongly expressive, during the long concluding passage of thematic liquidation. The means of thematic permeation are imaginative and free, as witness especially the large formal junctures of the first movement. Beethoven's superb obsession for coherence —his invention, it might be said, of whole new modes of coherence—is already yielding artistic dividends in his first quartet.

On a smaller level, it already appears that harmonic areas are being chosen with great deliberation. Often the large key-areas reflect local details of melodic articulation. In the first movement, a strong C♯, the seventh degree of the scale, may be "developed" from a simple element in the dominant-7th chord of D major into a triad in its own right, C♯ major, and the crux turned to expressive power. A finale theme which is subdominant-ridden may forecast a development section framed by the same subdominant stretched out as a key-area of some size. The choice of the unusual relationship ♭VI (B♭) for the slow movement may be traced to episodes on the "flat" side within the first movement. It may even be reflected in the D-minor tonality of the trio of the third movement.

Individual phrases link together firmly and powerfully, but Beethoven does not, in this work, construct any single really large period of commanding character and force. In the first movement, all the same, the quality of the form as a whole—the sweep of the exposition; the dumb, heavy arch of the development; the stiffening response of the recapitulation; the sense of potential and control in the coda—all this grows impressive enough to put some failures of detail into the background. In other movements, the large balances of the formal blocks are rather blank, adequate but inexpressive.

We have also encountered the problem that often comes up in the effort to comprehend interior context—the characteristic problem of "analysis," to employ the ordinary term for this effort in musical usage. ("Contextual criticism" is a corresponding term in literary usage, for the attempt to consider a poem in its own self-defined interior consistency, as much as possible without reference outside.) A number of technical aspects of the quartet are very likely to leave the listener cold—internal patterns and relationships which the composer certainly appears to have intended, but which seem to result in no appreciable aesthetic effect. Such, for example, are the details of parallelism between the first and last movements. By no means all of these aspects are to be dismissed as a young composer's crudeness, and in any case the same problem exists more generally—and more acutely—with mature works too. Something is amiss either with intention, or observation, or intuition, or at the very least with artistic economy. What stand is to be taken when observation and intuition of a work of art conflict?

A word on this standard critical question will not be out of place here; indeed the reader can quite properly ask to know the author's line of procedure in such cases. In brief, he would say, three obvious moves are possible in dealing with the problem. The first follows the instinctive tendency of the analyst, which is to instruct himself (and others) to experience as aesthetic fact what begins merely as observed fact. This tries to bring intuition around. The opposite move is to call the observed data into question on grounds of error, irrelevance, taking out of context, and so on. This tries to bring observation around. Only if these do not meet the situation should an aesthetic breach be conceded between ends and means within the work of art itself. This can feel like a failure of sensitivity on the listener's part; but the failure might be on the composer's part too. He could have tried for something and not succeeded.

Perhaps this last point needs no stressing, with an early work such as the Quartet in D. But with later works, it is striking how many serious writers on music would appear to deny or at least to shun it. They often seem to proceed on the unspoken premise that everything in the composition they happen to be examining makes aesthetic sense. That may be so, of course, if you choose your pieces carefully enough; the scope of the present study does not happen to allow such choosing. As we learn from listening to contemporary music, not everything a composer does works, a lesson that must be cautiously extrapolated even to Beethoven, even at the height of his powers. The problem is rendered circular and exquisite by the fact that the only sure standard of aesthetic sense—of things "working"—comes out of our expanding experience of actual pieces of music. The ear must be led by Beethoven's always extraordinary practice, but that is not to say that it must accept everything he does.

Analysis, given its head, can light upon data of every possible kind.

The fourth movement of the Quartet in D, for instance, contains just twice as many bars as the third. Clearly, a beautiful fact; but how may we gauge its significance? There has to be a standard of relevance, and a priori standards are open to the gravest difficulties, both theoretical and practical. The right standard is aesthetic, and the critic's role is constantly to return to feeling as a touchstone for analytical relevance. The inevitable ploy of the analyst is to coerce data into feeling. But critic and analyst exist in the same person; Sir Donald Tovey was simply referring to an inner dialectic when he wrote: "The line between the technical and the aesthetic is by no means easy to draw, and is often, even by musicians themselves, drawn far too high, so as to exclude as merely technicalities many things which are of purely aesthetic importance. . . . The process miscalled by Horace the concealment of art is the sublimation of technique into aesthetic results." [5] Indeed this line is by no means easy to draw, or sure in the drawing. Tovey's particular achievement was drawing it so cleanly a hundred times, and drawing it so low.

The issue, as has been suggested, may not strike anyone as very urgent in reference to the Quartet in D. However, it will come up at every stage in an examination of the Beethoven quartets, often more urgently, and too frequently to be discussed or even signaled on every occasion. Furthermore, this will appear to be the major critical problem that disturbs and animates the present writer. The reader will be able to watch him making each of his three moves in one situation or another—and may certainly look forward to registering some disagreement on each of the three counts. In certain interior technical details, I shall most probably discover aesthetic effects which others find they do not recognize. Analytical data which some analysts consider important I shall miss, or make light of, or even specifically repudiate as irrelevant. Worst of all, I shall see Beethoven fail where others see him succeed, and vice versa. All this the reader has surely been expecting, even if he had not formulated things in this particular way. We may as well understand one another early.

The critic hopes to persuade, of course, and he writes in the assumption that his sensibility is going to make contact with at least some section of the reading musical public. But he does not suppose that his statements are eternally right (though he cannot preface every one of them with the proviso that it represents merely his own best judgment in the matter). To deal with art is to deal with fact and feeling, and to deal closely is to discover more and more that each is problematic—fact as well as feeling.

[5] *Essays*, pp. 164–5.

Not to speak of their interrelationship. Our response to art is various and always partial, and therefore open to infinite instruction, so that provisional illumination can be brought to bear from many points of view. It is in this spirit that the present study of the Beethoven quartets is being conducted, and, I hope, being read.

2

TECHNIQUE AND EXPRESSION

Quartet in F Major, Op. 18, No. 1
Quartet in G Major, Op. 18, No. 2

Beethoven placed his second quartet, in F, at the head of the published Op. 18 series, on the advice of his friend the first violinist Ignaz Schuppanzigh, it is said, and for reasons that are not hard to guess. They are probably the same reasons that have made this work perennially the best-known and best-liked of the six. The Quartet in F is the biggest and in obvious ways the most impressive. Its first and last movements, besides lasting appreciably longer than corresponding movements in the other quartets, make a more brilliant effect—the first by means of thematic manipulation, the last by proliferating form. The second movement, if not quite the longest slow movement, is the only one in the minor mode and by far the most emotional. The Scherzo runs the fastest, and runs the farthest in harmonic range. Louis Spohr considered Beethoven's Quartet in F to be the ideal model in its genre; as an academic classicist par excellence, Spohr holds little interest for musicians today, but he was no mean connoisseur of the classic style, and something of a specialist in formal models.

Size in this Quartet, however, has not much to do with the steady progression of level phrases that serves to create the sense of breadth in the early trios and in the Quartet in D which precedes it. Within the work of a single man over the space of a few months, one would hardly anticipate so sharp a difference as that between these first two string quartets, particularly as regards their opening movements. The F-major

Quartet moves flexibly and nervously, like one of the early piano sonatas. Instead of emphasizing momentum, it emphasizes contrast. Its length results, simply, from an unusual amount of material, and its mood owes much to the perilous effort of holding all this material together.

Two features of this movement are commonly pointed out as significant heralds of things to come: its bold exploitation of contrast and, even more, its motivic single-mindedness. Indeed, as a herald the first movement of the Quartet in F serves more faithfully than any other member of the Op. 18 series—one might almost say, to the point of some personal self-sacrifice. The historical aspect need not be discussed now; the rest of this study will have much to do with Beethoven's development of these cardinal resources. The whole matter of musical contrast, in particular, has to be treated extensively in connection with the last quartets.

The movement is impregnated by its opening motif, which builds tautly from a single turn-figure. Actually, the motivic work in the Finale of the Quartet in D is as extensive and in its way just as ingenious; a similar technical impetus inspires both movements, however much they may differ in character. A fundamental distinction, I believe, lies in the fact that the turn-motif of the D-major Finale whirls by unobtrusively, whereas the turn-motif of the F-major *Allegro* catches attention. One motif is brief, the other long, one smooth, the other jagged. Beethoven insists on motivic play in this piece; the technique is meant to show—and has in consequence been widely noticed. The idea had not yet come to him of running a single motif all through his second subject, and so on, as in the Fifth Symphony or in the Finale of the Sonata in D minor, Op. 31, No. 2. But otherwise he saturated the connective tissue at every opportunity. After sparking the main theme and its successive phrases, the turn-motif appears as a backdrop to the bridge—which on this account does not comprise an essentially independent idea (as in the D-major and G-major Quartets). At the end of the second subject, the motif helps lead in the grand dominant cadence. It is not long absent from the lengthy, well-characterized cadential phrases thereafter. The motif monopolizes the development section, and in the coda, develops afresh in two surprising new aspects.

The autographs of all six numbers of Op. 18 have vanished. However, we are more than fortunate in possessing an early manuscript copy of the F-major work,[1] sent by Beethoven to his friend Karl Amenda in June 1799. It is a fair copy, bearing an affectionate inscription; obviously Beethoven thought of the piece as completed. But two years later he pointedly asked Amenda not to circulate this copy, for he had made

[1] Published in the new complete *Werke*, *Abt.* 6, Vol. III, 124–50.

many improvements: "I have just learned how to write quartets properly." By this he meant that he had now learned how to score properly for quartet, or so at least one would assume after comparing the final piece with the Amenda copy. The two versions differ mainly in matters of detail—extremely interesting detail—and only rarely in real compositional idea. But the early version is decidedly more extreme in momentary musical inflection; the later version seems able to afford less than maximum intensity for every statement. The famous turn-motif, to take the most striking instance, has been counted no fewer than 130 times in the Amenda version. For publication, Beethoven relented; the motif appears on only 104 occasions.

The published version is also noticeably less jumpy than the original. To mention a small index of this, *sf* signs are systematically softened into *fp* or <> or nothing. The quartet as we know it remains, nonetheless, a striking study in rapid modulations, divergent rhythms, and the juggling of highly individualized melodic material. This aspect of the work as a whole goes back to the irregular, volatile, abrupt theme itself. Within it, the motif behaves like a coiled spring, ready to shoot off in all directions—three already during the first phrase. Soon it is picking out successive diminished-7th chords:

Example 10

This is pretty intense stuff. In the development, Beethoven wanted to play with such intensity:

Example 11

The passage extends to a total of 22 bars. Something that was only hinted at in the Finale of the Quartet in D comes into its own here: a formal contrapuntal episode occupying the very heart and center of the development section. From now on such episodes occur frequently, for instance in the Finale of the present F-major Quartet and in the first movements of the G-major and B♭-major works, to look no farther than Op. 18.

The contrapuntal episode is improved over the Amenda version, in which (1) the four canonic imitations came absolutely regularly, on the first beat of each bar; (2) the passage was somewhat shorter; and (3) the harmony centered on three diminished-7th chords, as is true later, but on three different ones. So it would appear that (1) the composer was still perfecting his contrapuntal technique to advantage, as well as his instrumentation; (2) he grew more convinced of the centrality of the contrapuntal passage and extended it—though in general the later version is abbreviated, not extended; and (3) he cared not about the specific harmonic function of the diminished-7ths, but about their characteristic sonority per se. In the coda, Beethoven meant to exorcise this rather nervous-making sonority:

Example 12

A variety of sharply-defined rhythms jostle in the exposition. Again, what is striking is not so much their variety or sharpness, but the way they have of insisting on themselves. Or is that a sign of still inadequate technique? In his revision Beethoven worked to soften or rationalize rhythmic contrast, as for instance here:

Example 13

Chez Amenda the sixteenth-notes had been jolted by loud chords on the off-beats.

Harmonic contrast is possibly even more striking. A second subject that fluctuates harmonically is common practice in early Beethoven, as appears from the previous quartet; this second subject darts from V_7 to V to the minor tonic of C before settling clearly in C major. In terms of harmonic interest, the treatment of the bridge stands out as one of the finest single details in all the early quartets. It deflects boldly to a romantic-sounding ♭VI before preparing the emphatic dominant; and in the recapitulation, more boldly and more richly yet, it turns to the Neapolitan tonality ♭II. A harmonic shock introduces the development, too. Here Beethoven was imitating a typical Mozartian gesture (he would have known it from the Symphony in E♭, for instance, which was no more than ten years old at the time). After the standard full cadence in V ending an exposition, Mozart often leaps directly to the major III triad —probably with a paradoxical touch of cadence-theme material—and then leads III rapidly to IV, compounding abruptness. Appropriately, Beethoven remembered this idea in this quartet, which seeks to make a virtue out of sudden effects of every description. The same general harmonic plan, but handled less interestingly, comes up in the most Mozartian of the Op. 18 Quartets, No. 5 in A.

Very fine is the imaginative reflection of this harmonic shock at the beginning of the coda. Beethoven had the presumption to introduce a new scale-motif at this late date, new at least in this clear form, and develop it a bit:

Example 14

In fact the entire coda makes a particularly interesting herald.

The movement, then, is full of fits and starts, based on heady thematic, rhythmic, and harmonic contrast. In the hope of cementing some of this divergence, presumably, Beethoven planned a monolithic treatment of the recapitulation: twelve bars of scales on the dominant, sweeping in his recapitulated main theme *fortissimo*. Whatever the hopes, the effect is blatant, and no less so for being thoroughly typical of the man. The *fortissimo* recapitulation of Op. 18, No. 2, seems a great deal more intelligent, not to speak of a case like that of the E-minor "Razumovsky" Quartet. The present recapitulation has points of ingenuity, but it provides no true outcome for the frenetic, rather silly preparation.

An intrinsically explosive piece, the quartet works for control by means of unusual motivic "unity," and by the use of such blunt catchall strokes as the *fortissimo* recapitulation. It is rich fare, all a little undigested (though chewed over at least twice), more than a little too clever, advanced and at the same time not entirely sure in technique. Certainly it is a notably cold composition; somehow its gestures lack the natural conviction produced by that 14-bar rising-scale passage, for instance, in the D-major Quartet. Even the bridge, in spite of its sophisticated, powerful construction, seems more a deflection than a preparation in any relevant sense, so in the last analysis an elegant fuss over nothing. If the piece is looked at from a historical point of view, it instantly falls into line, palpitating with potential, heralding later Beethovenian attitudes and accomplishments very clearly. It poses itself so much more mature problems than those of the Quartet in D. But it does not really solve them as well; something here is not realized, and wisdom after the event will not blind us to the immediate shortcoming.

The stress of technique and expression in this movement has been widely felt, and has not unnaturally tended to interest commentators more than Beethoven's clearer success in music less consciously conceived. "*Im Gegensatz zum D-Quartett*," wrote A. B. Marx gloomily, "*ist hier mehr Quartett, als Beethoven.*" But I do not know what could be more characteristic of Beethoven, or of any other great original creator, than the compulsion to push technique past its expressive necessities. That is how unknown expressive horizons are arrived at. An artist does not start out with a beautiful idea or emotion clearly in mind, which he then labors to project through cut-and-dried technical means. The idea becomes known only through the very process of its exploration; the most we can postulate is an inchoate dialectic between ends and means, between technique and expression—a dialectic which can be strongly sensed, but scarcely plumbed, in Beethoven's sketchbooks. But it would be absurd to assume that every technical exploration finds its sure correlative in feeling. This movement is neither the first nor the last instance of such disparity within Beethoven's output.

· 2 ·

When a composer does start out with too clearly formed an emotional image, and holds to the preconception stubbornly, bending even an impressive technique to its service—what happens in such a case is a different kind of failure. The result is not sentiment but sentimentality, or at any rate, one of the things meant by sentimentality. This is a typical difficulty with Romantic music below the very highest rank, and it is one that manifests itself in the second movement of the Quartet in F.

Most of Beethoven's early *adagios* and *largos* bear qualifying inscriptions which seem to testify to an anxiety for greater expressive attentions on the part of the players. *Adagio cantabile*, *Largo e mesto*, *Adagio molto espressivo*, *Largo appassionato*, *Adagio con gran' espressione*, we are told; and in the slow movement of this Quartet, *Adagio affettuoso ed appassionato.* As it happens, there is concrete evidence about the "affect" that grounded this passionate *Adagio.* According to Amenda, Beethoven said that he composed the piece with the vault scene of *Romeo and Juliet* in mind. Sure enough, Nottebohm was able to read "*les derniers soupirs*" over an early sketch for the end of the movement, a sketch which already stresses the characteristic pathetic interval of the diminished 7th.

What Beethoven's conception of Shakespeare's play might have been, in 1799, rather staggers the imagination. Something like this quartet movement, only too probably. However, we scarcely need hints of representationalism to understand that he felt he was trafficking with raw exterior emotion here. Emotionality would be the better word; the piece is full of grand melodramatic gestures, which the composer appears to have manipulated with gusto as well as with great skill. The main theme ends with a lowering, mournful 4-bar dominant prolongation; then the theme reappears in flamboyant disguises—in the development, with the dynamics changed from *piano* to *forte;* in the recapitulation, with the surprising addition of *subito fortes;* and in the coda, with these plus an operatic *tremolo* (see p. 41). A great *coup de théâtre* prepares the recapitulation, as evocative rests punctuate the members of a drawn-out Neapolitan cadence marked down from *f* to *p* to *pp* to *ppp* (a rare dynamic mark at the time). In the coda, parallel dramatics culminate in a two-and-a-half-octave plunge down to the penultimate cadence.

All this was duly appreciated by the old commentators such as Marx, who dwelt further on the spiritual kinship between this *Adagio* and the *Largo e mesto* movement, also in D minor, of the Piano Sonata in D, Op.

Example 15

10, No. 3. Beethoven would have been seeing this opus through the press at the time he was sketching Op. 18. The sources of inspiration are certainly close, and in the absence of information about the sonata, enthusiasts have not failed to endow it with melancholy subject matter which might have inspired so somber a lament. Like the quartet *Adagio*, the sonata *Lento* exploits with power the traditional arsenal of the minor mode: semitones and diminished intervals, strongly resolving minor 3rds and 6ths, Neapolitan cadences and intense inflections throughout. If it is the less gaudy piece, perhaps that is simply because of less virtuosity in the handling of the musical materials.

In addition to the once-popular sonata movement, some other works may be set against the quartet *Adagio* in the hope of supplying what I have called the exterior context. The thematic structure is mirrored by some slightly later sonata themes, notably that of the *Adagio con molto espressione* in the *Grande Sonate* in B♭, Op. 22. (We shall return to this piece in connection with the Quartet, Op. 18, No. 6, its twin in key and its close contemporary.) The sonata theme lies in the major mode, and the "affect" sought is delicate languor, it would seem, rather than tragedy. Still, technical parallels abound: the throbbing accompaniment in $\frac{9}{8}$ chords; the preparatory beats of accompaniment figuration; the innocent harmonic skeleton I–V(or vii)–I–ii–V; the florid *cantabile* decorations; and, after eight bars, the static ending section of four more. Both themes are plainly operatic. With the sonata we almost stand in the wings at a performance of the *Casta diva*.

A third work to consider in conjunction with the quartet movement is the *Adagio ma non troppo* [for once!] *e cantabile* of the String Trio in G, Op. 9, No. 1, of 1796. The parallel here is not in mood or in thematic structure, but in the larger form—this despite the fact that the trio ranges itself not as a sonata-form movement but as a somewhat distended binary structure. To see the expansions or prolongations that Beethoven felt necessary to convert a large binary period into a true sonata-form exposition is rather instructive. Forgoing extensive musical quotations, we can perhaps make do with a summary account and outline of the musical progress in the two sections involved.

The trio begins with an 8-bar theme (still in $\frac{9}{8}$ meter, though far in character from that of the quartet). The theme starts to repeat itself at once, in the lower register, but soon drifts into a modulating sequence of a very familiar type, a circle of 5ths with expressive canonic $^{7}_{4-3}$ suspensions. Then a bar-by-bar alternation of tonic and dominant harmonies serves as the second subject. There follows a spacious cadential phrase involving sextuplet turn-figures and rich secondary harmonies. When this phrase too starts to repeat itself, it grows from 6 bars to 10, with imitations and doublings in 6ths:

Example 16

Somewhat remote harmonies are touched upon, including ♭VII of the new key V. As this amounts to IV of the original tonic key, the 10-bar phrase can run directly into the tonic and therewith into the second large period of the binary form.

The quartet movement is simply an expansion of this same scheme, with long interpolations to prolong and thus stress the main harmonic areas. The theme (after its vacant preparatory bar) is really 8 bars long, but it ends on the dominant and the dominant is prolonged for 4 bars more. The repetition of the theme, in the lower register again, drifts into canonic sequences of just the same type as those of the trio; but after they modulate to the new dominant, a 6-bar prolongation-phrase establishes that dominant properly. Then the second subject alternates tonic and dominant bars, as before. The cadential phrase that follows uses a sextuplet turn-figure very similar to that in the trio, as well as rich secondary harmonies; and in the repetition, imitations, doublings in 10ths, and further harmonic excursions, one of them to ♭VII (E♭):

Example 17

After 4 bars of the repetition Beethoven again felt the need to cement the harmony, which he managed by means of a final 8-bar phrase prolonging the new tonic. A strong, formal stop can then precede the next section, a real development.

The comparison between the two movements can be put in a diagram:

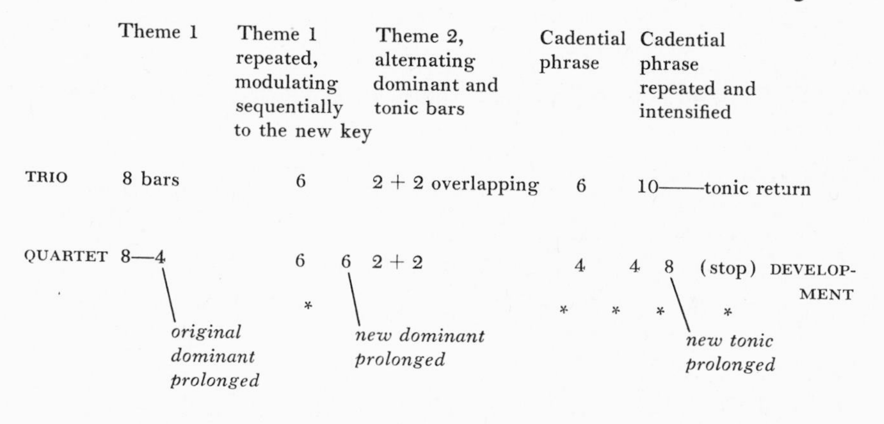

* = *full cadence in the new tonic*

A similarity in dimensions and in certain details once grasped, characteristic differences stand out as though in relief. A certain innocence of bearing in the trio, reminiscent of the Quartet in D, jars against the consciousness that everywhere informs the present quartet. The presence of five full cadences in the new key (*)—there are none at all in the trio—decisively changes the formal emphasis in the quartet, and makes it weightier, more self-serious, and more prolix. And to compare the two similar cadential phrases is to take a measure of Beethoven's technical progress in the two-year period. The phrase in the trio is interesting but pale and awkward; that in the quartet is astonishingly rich, almost overrich, in harmonic involvement and contrapuntal action. Harmony and counterpoint can appropriately expand at this point, of course, in order to make a contrast with the first group; but the contrast is bound in melodically by means of firm, inevitable descending steps. Perhaps it is this larger binding function that makes the Neapolitan cadence so excellent here, and so little stagey (bar 37, p. 39). This cadence brings to mind Chopin's beautiful Etude in E♭ minor.

A Neapolitan cadence employs a descending step in its most "affective" location; indeed this melodic interval permeates the second movement as thoroughly as, and more subtly than, the famous turn-motif dominates the first. Within the florid *cantabile* of the main theme itself, the steps D–C♯, E–D, and F–E stand out. Underneath D–C♯ comes an ostensible passing harmony of vii^{6}_{5}, a diminished-7th chord; this sonority too plays an important role in the movement (as was forecast by the *soupirs* sketch). There is something ominous in the way this chord declines to "pass," but simply maintains itself for two bars; the melody finds itself arpeggiating the diminished 7th, from C♯ up to high B♭ (bar 6; see p. 37). This note, although standing a full 9th above the low beginning of the melody, does not resolve at once, but waits three bars until caught by the repeated A's in the dominant prolongation which follows. Then Beethoven dilates upon the resolving step B♭–A: as though to proclaim how it grows out of the theme proper and reaches into the movement as a whole.

The bridge, second group, and cadential phrases all feature descending steps. A fine touch comes at the recapitulation, where the free repetition of theme 1 (see the diagram, page 39) is cut out entirely, so that theme 2 (in D major) arrives directly after the 4-bar prolongation. The effect of this compression is one of economy and relief—for theme 1 is shot through with new *subito fortes* which are quite harrowing. But the effect is also of a dramatic new relationship of parts: the high violin B♮–A of theme 2 links in the ear to the harping B♭–A steps heard just previously.

Still the B♭ grates in the mind, or at least in Beethoven's mind. He disposes of it finally only in the coda, moving the B♭ up instead of down in a very strong piece of thematic manipulation. Already a 9th above the floor of the tune, the cello B♭ (bar 100) is picked up by the violin (bar 102) and clutches its way up another 5th (bar 105), with octave transposition thrown in for good measure. The terrain had been laid bare a little earlier by magnesium flashes in the first violin (bars 96–8). From high F—compare bar 4—comes the almost hysterical cadential collapse, on yet another diminished-7th chord. And at last, the thematic material is contracted or distilled or liquidated, echoing the diminished 7th B♭–C♯ strikingly in the final cascade.

Example 18

This D-minor *Adagio affettuoso ed appassionato* is one of the most accomplished things that Beethoven had yet written, one of the very best things. Few movements among the Op. 18 Quartets so reward study, and testify so strongly to his now formidable ability in melodic draughtsmanship, his control of form, his mastery of the string quartet medium—well advanced over the previous quartet—and much else. Also very strongly to his expressive vision; but to his expressive achievement, I should not say. To sound the true note of tragedy which he seems clearly to have thought he wanted here, Beethoven had to feel differently, not only to write differently. He stayed too close to a sentimental image of the star-crossed lovers of Verona, I have hazarded, but I am not suggesting that the image served him as anything more than as a sort of externalization or excuse. The essential trouble had to do not with representation but with his own expressive resource. It was not external but internal, not literary or mythic but—need it be said?—musical.

Each of the grandiose gestures in the music can doubtless be supplied with an analytical "justification"—as climax to a line here, fulfillment of a rhythm there, completion of this large pattern or that design, and so on. Considerations of this kind have been suggested in the above paragraphs, and they could be carried much further. But they would only stress even more the same problem in criticism that occupied us at the close of the previous chapter: the crux of observation and intuition. One feels a disparity between ends and means, between technique and expression. In this case, it is hard not to come to the conclusion that when a composer's sensibility goes wrong, technical prowess merely allows him to go wrong irrevocably.

On another patently sentimental work of just the same period, the *Sonate Pathétique*, Tovey wrote: "In actual depth of idea, and even in pathos, this sonata does not surpass, if it equals, Mozart's in the same key. . . . The *Sonata Pathétique*, like the *Kreutzer Sonata* (a less consistent work, akin to it in many ways), begins with a magnificent piece of Homeric fighting; but if we overestimate the tragic quality of such fighting we shall end, like Tolstoy, in crassly underrating the rest." [2] Yet "nothing so powerful and so full of tragic passion had hitherto been dreamt of in pianoforte music." It was Tovey's way to resort to evasive epigram in a critical clutch of this kind. We, I think, are bound to see that Beethoven himself was overestimating his potential for tragedy at this time of his life. In the quartet the problem poses itself more sharply than in the sonata, for here the ideas are certainly deep and the working-out is admirable. The trouble with the piece does not lie in a stammering technique, but elsewhere: Beethoven lacked the tact of Mozart and Haydn in pathetic expression. Nothing so powerful and so full of tragic passion, doubtless, had been attempted in a quartet slow movement, nor anything buttressed with so sophisticated and integral a technical command. Beethoven had learned or taught himself amazing things by 1799. What he had not yet gained was the full resource of feeling needed to justify the full, raw employment of the traditional rhetoric of the minor mode. The problem remained with him up to the 1820's, to the time of the Piano Sonata in C minor, Op. 111, the Ninth Symphony, and the Quartet in A minor.

---

[2] *Beethoven's Piano Sonatas*, p. 68.

The last two movements of the Quartet in F risk less, on the whole, and gain less than the earlier two—though in flexibility of technique and consciousness of design, they evidence further advances over the D-major Quartet. Once again, there can be little doubt that links were intended between the movements. Diminished-7th sonorities characterize both the opening *Allegro* and the *Adagio*. Key-centers on the flat side (♭III, ♭VI, and ♭VII) constitute the sole harmonic digressions in the *Scherzo* and the most striking ones in the Finale; the most forceful moves in the first movement—those of the bridge—and the Neapolitan coloring of the second are likewise on the flat side. Turn-motifs are prominent not only in the first movement, but also in each of the last two.

The *Scherzo: Allegro molto* resembles the *Allegro* of the Quartet in D in a number of obvious points of physiognomy. (One resemblance, that the trio is a *minore*, the key-signature obscures.) Being a confirmed scherzo—the earlier movement was not even so christened—it behaves a little less palely, employing *scherzoso* dynamic effects and affecting the very fast $\frac{3}{4}$ meter of the misnamed *Menuetto* of the First Symphony, which is its twin. In the symphony, the main section makes radical modulations and keeps its trio harmonically bland, perhaps by way of compensation. The quartet modulates less, and so perhaps it can better afford to indulge in harmonic and thematic reflections of some interest between scherzo and trio. In spite of these, however, the piece is overshadowed by its very lively orchestral sibling. The instrumental contrast between the antecedent repeated chords (winds) and the consequent rustling scales (strings) in the symphony trio illuminates the conception in the quartet, and demonstrates unkindly the limitations of the chamber-music medium.

The Finale develops into a very large sonata-rondo, presumably in an effort to match the scope of the opening movements; but the effort is not much of a success. The level progression of long phrases mentioned in connection with the Quartet in D forms the basis of the motion, which hardly suits the intensity of the material. The piece bristles with remarkable ideas: 8 bars of the second subject appearing in V of V before 8 in V; the cadence theme (or something like it) trooping through the development in D♭, C, D♮, and E♭, the keys often prepared by strange crawling modulations; a 16-bar period in the coda built on *five* successive diminished-7th chords; and this fine idiosyncratic bridge phrase, which is only dimly relatable to anything else:

Example 19

(Is it supposed to recall the *Adagio?*) Too many ideas, in fact; the total effect seems forced and even arbitrary. The lengthy development section lacks focus, but it does not lack a central episode in double counterpoint, one that sounds conscientious rather than tense (like the episode in the first movement) or truly dramatic (like that in the first movement of the Quartet in G). The coda includes a peculiar reflection of this episode, joining the two main themes of the piece in unwilling counterpoint.

The rushing *Scherzo* will certainly serve, after the intense, nervous first movement, and the intense, pathetic slow movement. The Finale though is a disappointment, as Beethoven must have seen. In the next quartets one can trace a definite struggle to achieve a more viable balance among the various movements of the cyclic work. For some years the struggle would center about the finale; but in his next composition, the Quartet in G major, Op. 18, No. 2, Beethoven was not yet quite ready for radical remedies.

· 3 ·

The Quartet in G is Beethoven's wittiest composition in the genre. As such, it immediately recalls Haydn, and in view of the almost deferential bow to Mozart in the next quartet, the A-major, Op. 18, No. 5, it may be tempting to interpret this one as a parallel, prior act of homage to the older composer. The first movement is Beethoven's clearest attempt to press his personality into the comedy of manners which Haydn had discerned as the potential essence of the classic style. The third movement breathes more genuine *scherzoso* feeling than any other of the early quartet scherzos. The Finale cracks violent jokes which depend squarely on Haydn's language for their understanding. It would hardly be surprising to see Beethoven in his first quartets seriously influenced by the one great master who was steadily flooding Vienna with such pieces—fourteen of them, it will be remembered, in the decade of the 1790's (Op. 71, 74, 76, and 77).

But there is a real distinction between Beethoven's stance toward Haydn in this piece and his relationship to Mozart in the other. None of the movements appears to be modeled on a specific work by the other composer, as is the case with the A-major, and no passages could really pass for Haydn's work, as some could pass for Mozart in the A-major. The relationship is more original and more searching, more a matter of idea than of material or even of stylistic detail. It is as though Beethoven were deliberately exhuming an older, alien manner: a procedure that is certainly not unknown in the history of music, and that becomes more and more important in Beethoven's maturity. Think of such widely divergent works as *Die Meistersinger*, Stravinsky's *Pulcinella*, and the Minuet from *Don Giovanni;* to equate the style assumed by the composer with the actual style of the model which he chose to reinterpret would surely be an error of perception. No one would claim that Beethoven in this quartet reached a style-synthesis as secure as Wagner's, as clever as Stravinsky's, or as excellently appropriate to the occasion as Mozart's. His effort, however, cannot be understood by simply writing it off as anxious student imitation. Even ten years earlier, that was not Beethoven's way.

Nevertheless, the rigorous succession of 2-bar members at the start of this quartet, all of them bound to tonic and dominant, seems irresistibly to summon up images of courtly bowing and scraping in some never-never-land of rococo fantasy. German quartet players are said to call the piece the *Komplimentierungsquartett*, a name matched in idiocy only by English quartet players' title "How d'you do" for Haydn's Quartet in G, Op. 33, No. 5—a work which may conceivably have planted the original seed for Beethoven's conception. But if Beethoven was dealing with formalized and simplistic material here, more than likely he had some special purpose or some special inquiry in mind. This would have been, first of all, the exploration of subtle distinctions between his 2-bar thematic members as far as the distribution of weight within them is concerned. Such investigations had scarcely come up in the D-major Quartet, and only peripherally in the F-major.

Unambiguous, the first 2-bar fragment of the theme bears its main stress on the first beat of the first bar:

Example 20

The lower instruments simply hold a chord across the barline, while the violin returns upon itself in bar 2. But the next 2-bar fragments are so delicately poised that they can blow in either direction, or hover in between. The fragment in bars 3–4 experiences a slight bump on its second bar. So it is with the next pair of bars; and the fragment in bars 7–8 comes close to reversing accents. It comes closer yet when bars 5–8 return to conclude the exposition:

Example 21

Here—a fine point—the first bar carries even less stress than it did in bar 5, for instead of striking a new note (G after D), now it merely prolongs the $\frac{6}{4}$ chord asserted in the preceding passage. We also feel and want to feel more weight on the fourth bar of the phrase, since it is acting as a paradoxical final cadence—paradoxical, because a neat fragment of the main theme is reinterpreted so as to end the exposition, in place of fresh, leisurely cadence material as is ordinarily the case. The effect is Haydnesque, of course, and the most obviously "witty" detail in Beethoven's piece. Something similar had concluded Haydn's E♭ Quartet in the Op. 33 set, to look no further than that very influential publication of the early 1780's.

Beethoven fools with reversed accents most harshly at the recapitulation, where the original quiet first-theme material returns in a resounding *forte*, as in the F-major Quartet and many other compositions. Thanks to an off-beat pattern derived from the bridge, and clarified beyond any doubt by marked *sforzandi* D's, the original 2-bar "bow" backs into a kick in the rear:

Example 22

A new bass line contributes to the indignity; and when a moment later little one-bar canons emerge, confusion is raucously normalized. So much for Beethoven's concern for musical etiquette in an age of periwigs and powder.

The recapitulation which has begun so remarkably continues even more remarkably. But, to return to the theme as quoted from the exposition (p. 46): underneath the *agréments*, this proves to be one of Beethoven's obsessively triadic themes. Perhaps its second period is already insisting slightly on the 3rd of the tonic triad, B, in both soprano and bass—see bars 9, 11, 13, 15, and 19. At all events, B keeps turning up during the later periods of the exposition, and in the recapitulation positively flowers. In this recapitulation, as has just been remarked, D is hammered for a long time; the excess energy expands the initial phrase of 8 bars (bars 1–8) to exactly 16. Then in due order the high B returns with its 4-bar phrase, as in bars 9–12. What follows starts like a *pianissimo* repeat (of bars 13–16?), then works its way upward in canons to a rich and seemingly remote dominant chord. Only now is B properly resumed —but as the 5th, not the 3rd, of a triad, which is E major (VI):

Example 23

This is another instance of the harmonic intensification of a melodic detail, comparable in kind and in excellence to the climactic support of the leading-tone C♯ in the D-major Quartet by its own C♯-major triad. Beethoven uses the technique in the present case to single out the notes D, B, and G as the functional skeleton of his original ornate theme. D is the ordinary dominant (though hammered in no ordinary fashion). B is stressed as a strangely modulated 5th of an E-major triad, VI. G is safely home again in the second group.

In the coda of the F-major Quartet, Beethoven restated his set of three diminished-7th chords in a way calculated to exorcize their functional magic for the movement as a whole. In the brief coda of the present quartet, he does something similar with the three steps of the triad:

Example 24

He also makes sure that the reversed accent in the first two bars of the theme is quite forgotten. The phrase of bars 5–8, of course, can conveniently end the comedy.

There has been nothing comic, however, about the digression to VI in the recapitulation, one of the boldest and most effective instinctive strokes in Beethoven's early music. The development was also first-rate —once it got over its initial bowing and scraping; for rather like the development of the very first quartet, the D-major, this one begins with an even segment of the main theme in a minor key, and then trudges along with bridge material. A development of the old-fashioned "run-through" type seems to be in the making, but in the nick of time it switches to a complex contrapuntal study of elements freely derived from the opening thematic material. This contrapuntal center is more extensive than those in the first and last movements of the F-major Quartet, and more impressive, largely because of the successive addition of new counterpoints. Rather oddly, and I think sadly, this fertile idea is cut off—by the dull bridge theme again. The rhythm of the bridge was wanted to prepare the off-beat reinterpretation of the main theme in the *fortissimo* recapitulation; all the same, the strategy was a mistaken one. The bridge is too trivial in essence, and remains too trivial in its version here, to ground the high potential generated by those excellently irregular and passionate contrapuntal sequences.

Already at the very first entrance of the bridge theme, in the exposition, things had begun to sound wrong (see p. 50). It is not a case of a composer running out of ideas; if anything, he probably had too many ideas. For instance, he may have specially wanted the bridge to introduce an earthy jocular note after the refinement of the main theme itself. It links forward importantly to the Finale, as we shall see. And a central idea seems to have been to carry forward into the rest of the movement the obsessive regularity of phrasing established by the main theme; thus not only the bridge, but also the whole second group consists of an unusually long series of regular phrases, the tedium of which is tempered only faintly by harmonic gestures toward B. It is not even that this was a bad idea. The same idea—with others—came to serene fruition in another Beethoven quartet, his last: the Quartet in F major, Op. 135. Here, if you like, is another *Komplimentierungsquartett*, another retrospective evocation of classical symmetry and grace, though now from quite another standpoint of consciousness. Like the Quartet in G, Op. 135 has a questioning-and-answering dynamic in its theme; a sharply formal bridge; a *fortissimo* recapitulation; some witty reversals of accent; and an unusually long series of balanced phrases throughout. What can one say in comparison? The balanced phrases in Op. 135 are light and fluent and marvelously controlled; those in Op. 18, No. 2, are crude and rather ugly.

Maybe Beethoven already had an inchoate idea of some new ascendancy over the classic style, in 1799; that possibility makes a study of the G-major Quartet fascinating. Certainly he was still too close to that style to plumb it and turn it as he could in 1826. Despite powerful elements surpassing anything in the two earlier quartets, the first movement of the Quartet in G flounders on the cardinal point of technique which they had struggled to control: phraseology. Wit, furthermore, is a dangerous game—Haydn's game, not Beethoven's. His sense of humor is not far to be trusted at this time of his life.

In the G-major Quartet, interrelationships among the movements are more obvious than in the earlier (or, for that matter, the later) members of the Op. 18 series. Not until the Quartet in C♯ minor of 1826 will Beethoven draw so lucid an analogy between a finale theme and a theme from the opening movement:

Example 25

The theme referred to in the opening movement is that of the bridge—which had been short-changed in the recapitulation by the digression to VI. Almost everything corresponds, from the *unisono* effect, the melodic and harmonic direction, the heavy double mock-upbeat, the rhythm, and even the time-signature, down to the relentless multiplication of balanced end-stopped fragments.

And even before the Finale, the droll triadic limitation of the *Scherzo* theme had recalled, more subtly, the basic thematic cast of the opening movement. Meanwhile, this theme all but duplicates the beginning of the *Adagio* tune. This *Scherzo* is perhaps the cleverest that Beethoven had

Example 26

yet written, as well as one of the most amusing, in accordance with the dominant "affect" of the composition as a whole. The humor grows almost kittenish in places. Contrasting material is handled masterfully within a very short space; the one striking harmonic gesture stresses B, no doubt significantly, in view of the action in the opening movement. The opening phrase of the trio seems to mock another solemn detail of the *Adagio*, but after airy passage work the phrase evaporates as innocently as may be.

As compared to the first-movement bridge, the Finale theme is of course melodically freer and more developed in structure, with its functional move to vi, its fatuous 4-bar middle section, and its noisy, abrupt return. All this is funny; obviously the movement was designed to resume, prolong, and at the same time exaggerate the mood established in the first movement and in the *Scherzo*. Gross canons and inversions are the order of business, in great quantity. At the end of the second group, in D, an insistent B♭ promotes a more or less conventional deflection to F, and prepares ahead the sudden E♭ at the start of the development section. (Perhaps Beethoven even meant a link back to the strong E♭ in the first-movement development. Both keys accommodate the main themes.) There follows an exaggerated chromatic scale line in the bass; an exaggerated subdominant preparation; and at the retransition, exaggerated deflections toward E♭ and worse. The movement makes a brutal, highly intelligent extension of Haydn's aesthetic; yet strangely, the total effect is rather neutral.

Strangest of all, in this quartet, is the aspect and the history of the *Adagio cantabile*, the second movement. Beethoven decided on one of the most conventional ideas available to him: a heavy ternary melody in $\frac{3}{4}$ time similar to many in the early piano sonatas. Even the key, C major, rings a familiar bell. The genre is hardly an endearing one; the present example is diffuse, pretentious, and rather pointlessly ornate, featuring a good deal of chromatic inflection culminating in a raw augmented-6th chord near the cadence. Ordinarily these melodies make their cadences and then proceed at a leisurely pace to some sort of contrasting material in the dominant or another bright key. A certain amount of development may take place; then the tune returns at full length to close a simple *A B A* arch, possibly strung out with coda material.

Instead, after the *A* section here the tempo changes abruptly. A mousy little *Allegro* dance movement appears in (of all places) the subdominant, drastically simple, perfectly tooled. It is in fact one of the earliest of Beethoven's dance "parodies," a parody *contredanse* in $\frac{2}{4}$ time, of a type that will come up again and again in the later quartets. In the

Example 27

present work the result is a more or less irresponsible juncture of disparate styles—a gesture of weariness or desperation, it almost seems, with a type of slow thematic material that no longer satisfied the composer. After the dance has squared off its couplets, the *Adagio* begins stiffly a *da capo* in variation. Although renewed chromatic inflections seem at first to promise intensification, the variation lapses into the merely figural.

Precedent for so whimsical an insertion of a fast dance into an *Adagio* is hard to find. Haydn was capable of such a move, but the closest he seems to have come to it was in a finale, in his Quartet in C, Op. 54, No. 2; nor does the *Adagio–Scherzo* alternation in Beethoven's own Serenade-Trio in D, Op. 8, of 1796, seem comparable. The interesting fact is that, according to Nottebohm, the *Allegro* is absent from the main body of the sketches, and therefore must be assumed to have been added later than the time of composition of the rest of the piece. In other words, it was composed at the time of the last three quartets of Op. 18—works which show repeated experiments with new types of movement to incorporate into the over-all cyclic form. Beethoven tried *La Malinconia* in the B♭-major Quartet, the novel minuet in the A-major, and the *Andante scherzoso quasi allegretto* which does service as a slow movement in the C-minor. The B♭ Quartet, furthermore, contains as its Finale another dance "parody," an *alla Tedesca,* though not so named. From this piece and from the *Allegro* of the G-major Quartet, a line can be traced through the Sixth Symphony and the short Sonata in G, Op. 79, to the *Alla danza Tedesca* of the Quartet in B♭, Op. 130, and many other pieces in the last period.

The three later quartets of Op. 18 are best considered separately, as a group. Though not much later in actual time than the earlier three, they reveal in many ways a decisive break in Beethoven's mood; in his attitude toward the problem of quartet composition. At the stage of the Quartet in G, however, he does not appear to have clarified his dissatisfaction with the *status quo* even to the provisional point marked by the later Op. 18 compositions. Yet the more obvious and conventional dynamic of the F-major Quartet—not to speak of the D-major—has been left behind once and for all. The G-major Quartet is a transitional work par excellence, marking a point of transition between a momentary stability on the one hand and a brief new transitional phase on the other.

Its technical experiments are extremely interesting, and extremely earnest; in this respect the piece really makes a meaningful pair with the Quartet in F. (I cannot agree with B. H. Haggin, who once placed the G-major Quartet in the category "Uninteresting or Unimportant Works" while shunting the other Op. 18 quartets into the category "Good Early Works.") Something of the same disparity between technique and expression affects both compositions, certainly—though to say this is to admit the vagueness of such a formulation, so different are their individual aspects and ambitions. In one work the composer was looking for vehemence and passion, in the other for sustained humor, and in each the expressive focus is slightly off, or more than slightly off. What is very evident in each is a new boldness of invention, a surer grasp of the medium, and a deepening sophistication about musical means. These qualities are not the same as expressive clarification, but they form the only basis on which clarification can and will take place, in Beethoven's subsequent—though not yet immediately subsequent—compositions.

3

DISRUPTION

Quartet in A Major, Op. 18, No. 5
Quartet in C Minor, Op. 18, No. 4
Quartet in B♭ Major, Op. 18, No. 6

The first three quartets of Op. 18 were published by the Vienna firm of T. Mollo and Company in June 1801. The last three waited until October. They had been at the printer's for a rather long time, at least since December of the previous year, when Beethoven mentioned them in a letter to the publisher-composer Franz Anton Hoffmeister in Leipzig. He wrote again to Hoffmeister, more disquietingly, in April 1802: "Herr Mollo recently published my quartets again, but full of mistakes and errata—on a large scale and on a small scale. They swarm like little fishes in water, that is to say, ad infinitum.—*Questo e un piacere per un autore* —that I do call *engraving*, to tell the truth, my skin is quite full of pricks and scratches—thanks to the beautiful edition of my quartets. . . ." [1] Beethoven's expression *hat wieder neuerdings* would seem to limit his scathing reference to the second installment only, Op. 18, Nos. 4–6. It does not appear that the little fishes were ever caught. Probably they are still swimming through all present-day editions, performances, and recordings.

The division of the opus into two *cahiers* could have been occasioned by nothing more than a publishing convenience, but there is a certain sense to the separation, whether accidental or not, that strikes deeply into the quality of the works. For all their great variety and their even greater invention, the first three quartets of Op. 18 hold in principle

[1] *Letters*, No. 57.

to the standard design; they are serious, intense works in a more or less conventional dynamic. With the later three quartets, in A major, C minor, and B♭, Beethoven seems suddenly to have thrown the classical framework in doubt. These pieces all entertain experiments with different types and arrangements of movements. They show signs of perfunctory composition, of odd retrospective tendencies, even (it has been surmised, with a good show of reason) of the re-use of quite ancient material. The Quartet in A, Op. 18, No. 5, actually models itself on a composition by Mozart, in certain respects quite closely. Disruptive forces of all kinds are at work in these quartets, and from the standpoint of final aesthetic coherence the results leave a good deal to be desired.

That the later three quartets also incorporate the most interesting proleptic flashes will scarcely come as a surprise. The *Eroica* Symphony, that great turning point in Beethoven's career, and in the history of modern music, was conceived in 1802–3. From 1800 on, the compositions of each new month show his imagination racing in more and more extraordinary fashion. The road from Beethoven's so-called "first period" to his second is not altogether simple to trace—since, after all, the very concept of such periodization has been hewn roughly from the rich forest of an artist's creative activity. But the last three quartets of Op. 18 mark an important stage on this road, even though it may be one that is obscured by a certain amount of dead wood.

· 2 ·

The most palpable general novelty in the three quartets has to do with interrelationship and balance among the movements, a matter to which Beethoven will in later years direct very searching attention. He begins to tamper with the accepted weight, role, and style of each of the movements in the conventional cyclic form. He may have realized for the first time that he did not have to be bound by convention; or more likely he knew—with the Quartet in G incomplete, an unanswered question—that he simply could no longer hold to convention. Of the four movements, doubtless the first was the one to suffer the least radically—for the moment. Nevertheless, changes in the aspect of the first movement should not be overlooked. They amount to a rather new conception of the opening statement of the quartet form.

Evidently the general idea was to lighten this opening statement. Previous first movements had been intellectual and dense, staking much on a considerable adventure in the development and a consequent new ascendency over old material in the recapitulation and coda. This stems explicitly from the work of Haydn and Mozart. But the first movement of Beethoven's Quartet in A, Op. 18, No. 5, is positively bland; that of the Quartet in B♭, Op. 18, No. 6, is only slightly less so, despite high velocity and a fine froth worked up in the middle. As a pair, these two first movements depart in important details from the formal pattern of Op. 18, Nos. 1–3. Both movements lack a coda (with the trivial exception of six bars of tonic *crescendo* ending the A-major). In compensation, both prescribe a full-scale repetition of each of their halves—not only of the exposition, as in the earlier quartets and in all other music of this time, but also of the development plus recapitulation. In their recapitulations, both eschew the radical reinterpretation of the bridge section which was a cardinal feature of the early works—the 14-bar scale in the D-major, the Neapolitan expansion in the F-major, the sudden turn to major VI in the G-major. In fact, both movements do without a contrasting bridge passage entirely, running the first group into the second with a minimum of ceremony in the exposition, and with the simple addition of a subdominant phrase or two in the recapitulation. In both movements this particular addition sounds like a clumsy afterthought.

All these changes in the formal plan of the first movement tend in a single direction: they stress the symmetrical or architectural aspects of sonata form at the expense of the progressive or dramatic aspects. Beethoven was trying to write an easy-going opening, and succeeding only too well, perhaps: he is likely to strike us as perfunctory. Much of the time, these movements are content to cover space. The earlier movements fill space.

On the matter of the large repeats, incidentally, the composer did not always feel sure of his ground. Amenda's early copy of the Quartet in F, Op. 18, No. 1, directed both repeats—which at the rate of Beethoven's own metronome marking would have run the first movement eleven and a half minutes long! For publication, the second repeat was cut out. The second repeat stands only in the Quartets in A and B♭, in which the number of written bars is relatively low. Without repetition, indeed, these movements sound too small.

All in all, there is just less stuff in these movements than in the earlier ones. Not only is a characteristic bridge omitted from the expositions, as has just been remarked; all the other sections are composed less densely, more like Förster than Haydn (but not much like Förster), more like Mozart in the "Prussian" Quartets than in the six quartets dedicated to Haydn (but less densely than Mozart in the "Prussian" Quartets). The Quartet in A is also one of the very few Beethoven compositions that can be said to admit a vacuous development section. Almost a third of it is taken up by the final dominant preparation, and almost another quarter by a literal restatement of the theme, twelve bars in the most placid possible key, the subdominant. The conclusion of this development on a $^{6-5}_{4-3}$ progression—highly formal, curiously archaic in sound—would be hard to find duplicated in the work of Haydn or Mozart later than the 1770's. Such genuine development as this movement allows itself is of an elementary, unexciting sort.

Grace and ease the movement does possess; in places it betrays a strongly Mozartian flavor. The principal theme itself, save for tiny details, could have been written by Mozart, who would have come upon the soaring subdominant in bars 5 and 9 more naturally than Beethoven. But a run-through of Mozart's themes in the Köchel Catalogue does not suggest any model so close as Beethoven's own Violin Sonata, Op. 12, No. 2, in the same key and in the same $\frac{6}{8}$ time-signature. (This had just been published, in January 1799.) It is perhaps not necessary to mention the numerous similarities between the two movements in formal plan and in thematic detail. The essential point lies in the very fact of analogy. For Beethoven, as for Mozart, the violin sonata was never a very solemn form, certainly nothing comparable to the quartet. But Beethoven's A-major Violin Sonata has a more individual opening movement than the A-major Quartet, and, with its lively coda, also a more dynamic one.

Whitening the opening movement of this quartet was probably planned in relation to the placement of the minuet second in order, rather than third, after the slow movement, the traditional position. Perhaps this placement was promoted, in turn, by the choice of an especially lengthy, cumulative form for the slow movement, a theme and variations. In any case, the whole arrangement followed Mozart's Quartet in A major, K. 464, Beethoven's immediate model. The reversal of the two inner movements was not uncommon in the chamber music of Mozart and Haydn, though in the quartets of the 1790's Haydn resorts to it in only one composition, and Beethoven does so only in the present work.

Again: the minuet is starkly simple, by comparison with the scherzos of the earlier quartets. But it would be a mistake to equate its fragility with innocence, crudity, or anything elementary in conception. This is a pensive essay in classic grace, with a sophistication of its own, and most astonishing of all, with a delicacy that matches Mozart without at all following him in spirit. Reminiscences of the *Teutsche*—Beethoven's favorite dance *alla Tedesca*, forefather of the *Ländler* and the waltz—creep into the second section, as does also a touch of iron in a strongly reiterated *fortissimo* C♯. (This harks back to a reiterated C♯ at the start of the development of the first movement, I believe; at all events, C♯ provides the one point of harmonic tension in each of these movements. Only two dynamic marks are used in the whole minuet, *piano* and this single *fortissimo*.) The return of the original melody branches into a charming three-part canon in the subdominant—another instance of the use of formal counterpoint in

Example 28

the quartets, this one lightly worn. The canon is far from strict, but the countersubject makes up for this by multiplying itself elegantly in the viola.

Then the trio, with its positively Schubertian lilt, is the most mature and individual trio in the Op. 18 Quartets. It is also the simplest, once again.

This movement derives nothing from the minuet of Mozart's Quartet in A, unless one chooses to see kinship in the fact that both minuets are completely out of the ordinary—in different ways. (And perhaps, after all, that would be a more profound "influence" of one composer on another than the modeling of themes, formal schemes, and so on. Yet very curiously, a much later quartet of Beethoven's, in the same key but in the minor mode, *will* adopt actual ideas from Mozart's wonderful minuet: the Quartet in A minor, Op. 132, a quarter of a century later.) It is the third and fourth movements of Op. 18, No. 5, which borrow directly from the corresponding movements of Mozart's composition, movements which Beethoven is known to have copied out in full.

Now the fact of this Mozart imitation has been well known since at least the time of Theodor Helm's book of 1885, but it seems never to have astonished commentators sufficiently. Beethoven had written two dozen pieces in Vienna, three of them quartets, and while these pieces are certainly less beautiful than Mozart's, they certainly move far ahead of his aesthetic. That Beethoven copied Mozart at the age of fifteen, writing his childish piano quartets, is one thing; it is quite another to find him so interrupting the preparation of a set of string quartets featuring movements like *La Malinconia*, and the first and second movements of the Quartet in F. Daniel Gregory Mason's passing remark about a "tyro evidently at times imitating the finished practitioner" stems from a small understanding of Beethoven's already tremendous accomplishment. The man was no timid beginner; he was, however, facing a really serious artistic problem—perhaps for the first time in his career. I take this Mozart imitation as the most dramatic sign of his uncertainty and sense of disruption at this particular stage of the quartet project. Beethoven, who was capable of filling page after page of a notebook with compulsive sketches of a single melody, was also capable of threshing around at Mozart, in an inchoate effort to find some way out of a momentary impasse.

Why this particular quartet of Mozart's? Beethoven seems to have made it a special favorite, to judge from the copy and from a report by Carl Czerny: "Once Beethoven came across the score of Mozart's six quartets in my house. He opened the fifth, in A [K. 464], and said: 'That's what I call a work! In it, Mozart was telling the world: "Look what I could do if you were ready for it!" ' "[2] A patrician choice: the Quartet in A is Mozart's most serious and troubled composition in the genre, less "available" and more learned than the others. It stands out as one of Mozart's most chromatic compositions, though this aspect of the matter did not interest Beethoven at this point. Of the six quartets dedicated to Haydn, this one probably owes him the most; yet Haydn must have found the Finale unusually dense for a chamber-music work—a full-scale, intellectual sonata-form movement in spite of its nonchalant, fleet surface. It may be this very combination of qualities that fascinated Beethoven, at the present juncture.

Back of his interest in the slow movement, furthermore, may have been a feeling of circumspection in planning a serious theme and variations as the center of gravity in a quartet. With late Beethoven in our ears, we tend to feel it quite natural for a piece in this weighty form to belong in a quartet or a sonata. But the Beethoven of 1800 would have felt rather differently. Though he had written and improvised many such pieces for piano, within larger works he had placed only the innocent variations in the Piano Trio in C minor and the Violin Sonata in D; the stupid ones in the Piano Sonata in G; and the brilliant variations on somebody else's tune

[2] Czerny, p. 14; cf. Hamburger, p. 224.

in the Finale of the Clarinet Trio, Op. 11 (a distant and, I am afraid, a rather contemptuous nod to Mozart's Clarinet Quintet). Only occasionally had Mozart and Haydn built slow movements of real weight in variation form. The idea was a fairly novel one, novel anyhow to Beethoven. He could scarcely have looked to a finer model than the third movement of Mozart's Quartet in A.

Mozart found his own model in Haydn's Quartet in D, Op. 20, No. 4—another excellent choice. It is to be doubted that the entire decade of the 1770's yielded a more impressive composition. Haydn's piece being in D minor, the ♭VI degree B♭ can be stressed throughout quite naturally; intense pathos, rare in Haydn's later music, animates the theme and also the entire movement. There are only four variations, and the last of them really returns to the theme in its original state, "rounding" the form before running into a long, free concluding passage or coda. This highly expressive outgrowth lasts for as long as 34 bars without modulation or even clear articulation. Haydn marked his movement *Un poco adagio affettuoso*, by the way. Echoes of its rhetorical ♭VI sounds and diminished-7th chords are still to be heard in the *Adagio affettuoso ed appassionato* (also in D minor) of Beethoven's Quartet in F, Op. 18, No. 1.

Mozart's variations are in the major mode; he had done duty by D-minor variations at the end of his famous quartet in that key. His form is larger and more varied: six variations, the fourth of them an expanded *minore* paying due attention to the ♭VI degree, B♭. The concluding passage or coda reaches a passionate climax in a plunge down to B♭, and this leads at once to a 10-bar compressed return of the original theme. This provides Mozart with a rounding effect comparable to that achieved by Haydn's last "variation." A new idea is the *ostinato* figure in the final variation, which continues well into Mozart's concluding section, pulsing up from the cello into all the other instruments.

Beethoven has five variations, and no *minore*, though Variation 4 grows chromatic and touches upon strange (indeed, clumsy) minor harmonies. B♭ is just barely indicated. But when Variation 5 is done, a sudden modulation occurs to this key. Only after an intervening episode in the subdominant (G major) may the piece return to its tonic key, D major; modulation was Beethoven's personal contribution to the formal plan laid down by Haydn and Mozart. Very much like Mozart, Beethoven concludes with a fragment of his theme, in variation—preceded by an analogous, but less successful rhetorical plunge involving (once again) the B♭. From Mozart he also took the idea of linking the conclusion back to the final variation proper by means of a striking low *ostinato* rhythm. This is more self-consciously handled than in Mozart, and soon drops out. In dimensions, Beethoven's concluding section comes very close to Mozart's (44 bars as against 41). Among his variations, the first is notable for its contrapuntal try, and the last for an unprecedented driving orchestral style which forecasts a late variation in the Quartet in C♯ minor, Op. 131.

That Beethoven would go out of his way to modulate, even in variations, one could perhaps have predicted, just knowing the man. One could certainly have predicted it on the basis of his other essays in the form. In another set of D-major variations, for example, a favorite old piano showpiece on Righini's *Venni Amore*, which he was rewriting around this time, the coda moves to the same ♭VI and IV (but also to ♭V) before coming home triumphantly with a half-variation in the tonic. The inconsequential D-major variation movement in the Serenade-Trio, Op. 8, pulls B♭ out of the air for an analogous conclusion:

Example 29

This is very like the quaint contrapuntal excursus which diverted the composer in the modulatory passages of the coda in the quartet:

Example 30

A sketch for this idea is dated back in 1794–5.

It is well known that Beethoven loved a drastically simple variation theme—well known from the *Appassionatta* Sonata, the Violin Concerto, and the Sonata in G, Op. 14, No. 2, not to speak of the "Diabelli" Variations. There is no more naïve outcome of this love than the present piece. Rhythmically, the theme slices its sixteen bars with machinelike rigor. Harmonically, it clings to four and only four chords, I, IV, V, and V of V. Melodically, it marches up and down the scale like the noble duke of York:

Example 31

Haydn's theme is pure emotion; Mozart's is an impressive, subtle melodic invention; Beethoven's is not a tune at all, but an abstract construction. (An early sketch for the theme printed by Nottebohm is more, not less tuneful.) The idea does shed some light on the contrapuntal excursus of the conclusion: the scale spawning a mirror image of itself in double time. It does not much warm the movement as a whole, however, which for all its points of interest certainly stands inferior to the variations of Haydn and Mozart in practically every way. If Beethoven had been quite sure how to write as good a variation movement as Mozart's, there would presumably have been less need to model on him.

Beethoven's need to model in the Finale is more obscure—because his success is so much clearer. But the impulse was strong enough to have him lift one of Mozart's themes, only superficially modified, as well as the

Example 32 *Mozart*

Beethoven

scale idea for its development. Mozart's theme first appears toward the end of the development—a great surprise. Beethoven's is simply the second subject, though it does return with an analogous function at the end of his development too. Probably it was the change of pace that attracted him; and in Mozart's principal theme, he was probably attracted by the quality of swift, highly articulate simplicity. In the whole matter of plotting a last movement, I believe, Beethoven found himself faced with a problem similar to that of the first movement. He wanted to lighten the Finale; his earlier ones had made a good effect, but only by means of frantic effort, by working too hard and showing it. So now in the C-minor Quartet he tried a gypsy rondo, all clatter and no substance whatsoever. In the B♭ Quartet he wrote an *alla Tedesca* which omits a development section entirely, and which in any case makes its point in relation to an extra *Adagio* movement, *La Malinconia*. In the present quartet he still clung to the idea of brilliance in conjunction with some measure of density—not the tense brilliance of his own previous work, however, but a glossy, easy, relaxed brilliance. And this, Beethoven may have thought, could be learned from Mozart.

Beethoven learned; if the slow movement of the Quartet in A seems to remain baffled by Mozart, the Finale matches him excellently well. So much the better, if one of Mozart's themes could help. In fact, the composer here courted the logical defect of success: the piece is so Mozartian as to lack, very strangely, individual profile. As Daniel Gregory Mason remarked, the light concluding epigram is exactly in Mozart's spirit. So is the delicate pout of the retransition:

Example 33

Nothing could be less "Beethovenian" than this, not even the stiff $\begin{smallmatrix}6-5\\4-3\end{smallmatrix}$ cadence at the analogous point in the first movement. Formal contrapuntal devices are entirely absent, but light classic counterpoint is everywhere, managed with a fluidity and charm that surpasses even Beethoven's very considerable technique with this kind of thing in the earlier quartets. Let us not talk about tyros:

Example 34

Thus the bridge, as it comes in the recapitulation, with the last four bars added in order to shift around to the subdominant. We have seen how Beethoven worried about this particular shift in the early quartets, turning the whole form about this point; we have mentioned the self-conscious subdominant apologies for a lack of similar responsibility in the first movements of the Quartets in A and B♭. Here a perfectly simple Mozartian move suffices. The freedom of counterpoint, the new diatonic dissonances over the pedal, the attenuation of the texture—all this gives the violin just the fillip it needs to climb effortlessly to a new vantage point and take easy control of the tonic. One can think already of the fantastic, airy transformations in the Finale of the Quartet in E♭, Op. 127.

Effortlessness—that is a key term, maybe, for Beethoven's most imponderable and unruffled quartet. It must also be counted the least personal of the quartets: pursuing again and again the will-o'-the-wisp of Mozart, Beethoven blunders into blankness in the first movement and (just as bad!) happens upon Mozart in the Finale. The minuet, only, is a small gem. As for the slow movement, look at it as the starting point of a journey leading through the *Appassionata* Sonata and the "Archduke" Trio to the Ninth Symphony and the last piano sonatas and quartets, to Op. 127 and Op. 131. As a work in its own right, this theme and variations has had too much claimed for it, by Helm and Marliave, D'Indy and Mason. But it would take hard insensitivity toward the adventure of musical history to remain altogether unmoved by its earnest, rather stolid tentative effort.

· 3 ·

One reason why Beethoven preserved sketches so carefully was in order to look back over them in times of need or in times of doubt. This was such a time; many signs point to this conclusion. As Beethoven studied his fair copy of the Mozart quartet, a copy that had probably been made years previously, he is not likely to have neglected his accumulated backlog of juvenilia, half-finished pieces, sketches, drafts, and notions of every kind.

There is at least one suggestion of a return to old material in the composition of the A-major Quartet. With the C-minor Quartet, Op. 18, No. 4, the situation seems to be more complex. In default of external evidence pointing to an earlier origin, the case was argued from internal evidence by Hugo Riemann, the most formidable of the musical historians in the great German tradition prior to the first World War. Riemann's *Anmerkung* on this matter in his revised edition of Thayer's *Life of Beethoven* is worth reproducing here.[3]

> The complete absence of sketches for the Quartet in C minor is curious and brings to mind the possibility that we may have before us an older piece of work. To be sure, fragments for one movement or another are perhaps still to be found in the sketchbooks. . . . For the first movement, however, it is possible at this point to trace, if not perhaps a model or a sketch, an altogether undeniable relationship: with the "Duet for a Pair of Obbligato Eyeglasses" [so reads the comic title of an unfinished composition in E♭ destined, evidently, for a short-sighted pair of Beethoven's friends, viola and cello, and evidently never completed past one and a half movements.[4] The work has not been dated more closely than in the period 1795–8]. A figure which is also very important in the Duet (bars 2–4 of its opening theme)—

Example 35

> meets us in the first movement of the quartet with such remarkable frequency, in all possible ranges and in all the instruments, that it is not possible to overlook the similarity. In the quartet, the figure

[3] Pp. 188–90.
[4] *Supplemente zur Gesamtausgabe*, VI, 7–17.

starts the consequent phrase of the second subject, which in full runs as follows:

Example 36

Indeed this theme betrays a Mannheim physiognomy so strong as to point back directly to Cannabich or Karl Stamitz. Further examination reveals that the first theme too is constructed in the same fashion, and has in fact already terminated in the bars which are common to the duet:

Example 37

This is highly suspect; such identity between a first and second subject is known only in the early Bonn compositions. The inability to shake free of a strong dominating motif indicates without any doubt an earlier period for this movement.

It is of course quite another question whether in its original version the piece was written for quartet. But further relationships with the duet press upon our attention: once interest in the comparison is aroused, we have little difficulty recognizing the second subject of the duet in the bridge leading to two themes of the quartet movement:

Example 38

The "dying fall" of the Mannheim composers, which turns up as early as bars 7–8 of the duet—

Example 39

appears twice just before the end of the quartet movement:

Example 40

. . . I take the "Duet for a Pair of Obbligato Eyeglasses" to be the later work, written after the first movement of the C-minor Quartet; for the former shows an essential step forward in power of organization and in the differentiation of contrasting elements.

In his monograph on the Beethoven quartets, Riemann summed up the matter a little more cautiously, proposing that both pieces used material from some unknown *Jugendwerk*, more of which is preserved in the quartet than in the duet. That is about as specific as one had better get, in view of Vincent d'Indy's shrewd observation of similarities between the first movements of the quartet and the Septet (in E♭) written in 1800.

That the Quartet in C minor includes very old material, predating the first known quartet sketches and extending back to Bonn—this theory by his reviser would have much pleased Alexander Wheelock Thayer. Thayer in his determined way always believed that Beethoven must have brought a sizable portfolio of music from Bonn to Vienna, and must have dipped into it frequently during the course of subsequent years. Riemann himself had a bee in his bonnet about the "Mannheim School" of composers, whom he considered to have fathered everything of virtue in the classic symphonic style. However this may be, it cannot be denied that the younger generation of composers attached to the Bavarian elector palatine at Mannheim—Mozart's friend Christian Cannabich, Toëschi, Beck, and Karl Stamitz—were famous all over Europe in the 1780's and 1790's, and that some of their wretched orchestral mannerisms were dignified by Mozart in the "Paris," "Linz," and "Prague" Symphonies, as well as by Beethoven and even Haydn. On Mannheim matters, Riemann is always a biased authority, but that is not to say that he is always wrong. In this case his insight seems to me just, as far as it goes.

Riemann's argument exemplifies both the fruitful application of musicological method and its characteristic limitations. A scholar's interest in influence and chronology can operate to the exclusion of any other kind of judgment; Riemann just barely mentions, in his last half-sentence, facts of considerable moment to a critical approach to the quartet as a work of art. We are left with a brusque vague statement about "power of organization" and "differentiation of contrasting elements." In the abstract, influence and chronology are neutral data—just as neutral as analytical data in the abstract. It may be—in fact, it is—important to understand that the heady expressive means employed in this first movement of the Quartet in C minor were widely known conventions of the time, indeed clichés. However, this composer was eminently capable of dignifying cliché into aesthetic bullion; it is important to take the further step and point out that in this case he did not. The passion that later commenators (Helm, Hadow, Mason—not Riemann) have admired in this piece can strike other modern listeners as trumped up—and though the piece made a success in the 1800's, I should suppose that certain connoisseurs of that time were also struck unpleasantly. The coarse rhetoric which the late eighteenth-century composers used as an easy source of pathos has scarcely been refined at all.

For the C-minor first movement is more crudely written than anything in the other Op. 18 Quartets. Transitions such as the bridge, the retransition, and the move into the development are less pithy—as Beethoven probably intended—than brutal, and the ideas themselves seem to me second rate, with one or two exceptions: the first theme itself, perhaps, and the coda, in spite of Riemann's Mannheim "dying fall." In the exposition, the first and second themes are too similar and the remaining material is much too various. The development section, like that of the Quartet in D, holds to the old-fashioned "run-through" type: theme 1 *in extenso* in the dominant; then some helpless contrapuntal developments; then the *forte* double-stop chords which preceded the bridge; then theme 2, complete, in the major subdominant with continuations still to come in the minor. In the D-major movement, this tedious scheme at least builds to an impressive climax at the retransition, before the recapitulation. But in the C-minor the retransition seems quite aimlessly tacked on. Duplication in the recapitulation of a dramatic development idea—the sequence from the *forte* chords to theme 2—would be hard to match for feebleness in any of Beethoven's important music, early or late.

"Regarding the later movements"—now Riemann is choosing his words carefully— "it must remain an open question whether they too may be based on earlier drafts. Certainly this is not unlikely. The Minuet as well as the *scherzoso* still reveal signs of a beginner's hand; and the fragmented aspect of the final Rondo does not rule out an early origin. The sense of large line is conspicuously absent from the whole quartet." The minuet is well enough constructed, though, and neither an unquestionably old-fashioned gait nor reminiscences of Mozart's Symphony in G minor seem to hurt its sober strength or its impression of muted passion. In this movement, Beethoven was working consistently and just within the expressive limits of a certain style, even if it was a style that his own more adventurous music had left behind some years previously. Moreover, the *Andante scherzoso quasi allegretto*, the second movement, reveals quite an original conception, even though as a work of art it is likely to strike us as trifling and frigid. Like the faster-moving Finale of the Sonata in F, Op. 10, No. 2, and like the slower-moving *Andante* of the First Symphony, this sonata-form movement features a fugal opening which, in the recapitulation, is to return with ostentatious new countersubjects weaving through its *fugato* exposition. Formal counterpoint appears methodically in the bridge, second subject, cadence theme, and development. The

Andante of the symphony overshadows this movement, however, just as the symphony minuet seems to realize better the basic notion of the *Scherzo* of the Quartet in F.

It would help if we knew the date of the First Symphony. The premiere performance was at Beethoven's first *Academie* in April 1800, but the sketches are hard to date, and they may go all the way back to 1795. My own thought is that the contrapuntal ostentation of this movement would not precede 1798–1800, the period of work of the six quartets, and that the idea of using a *scherzoso* in place of the lyric slow movement would not have come up before this particular point in the project: the point of disruption marked by the Mozart imitation of the Quartet in A and by other features. Within this half fast, half slow movement there are passages similar not only to the First Symphony but also to other recent works (compare bars 102–10 of the *scherzoso* with bars 30–8 in the minuet of the A-major Quartet, and bars 131–45 with bars 143–52 and 185–92 in the Finale of the F-major). In the latter comparison, to be sure, the C-minor Quartet once again appears the more elementary in conception; but it is likely that Beethoven was working for droll simplicity of procedure here, in the *scherzoso* humor. Such was surely the case when the fugue subject returns in the coda, now throwing in its lot with the *Teutsche* of the Viennese ballrooms, and rattling itself away to nothing—in something of the same spirit as will animate the Mälzel-metronome movement of the Eighth Symphony:

Example 41

The last movement, as a rondo without any admixture of sonata-form elements, strikes a much lighter intellectual pose than an ordinary quartet finale. Perhaps the crudities of construction do suggest an early origin, as

Riemann thought. Mainly the piece plays for effect—and it makes a certain effect, with its gypsy tune for the violin and its whirling *prestissimo* concluding section. But it remains one of the most vapid finales in any ostensibly first-line Beethoven composition.

Riemann's concluding thrust—that a sense of large line is conspicuously absent from the quartet as a whole—is the point of commanding interest here, rather than the details of dating; for after all, if we were out to disqualify compositions on account of early origin, we should according to a long view have long since disqualified all of Op. 18. Once again, Riemann shows little interest in supporting his stylistic judgment. But chronological investigation (that archetype of scholarly endeavor) is not necessarily all removed from aesthetic substance, and it would be idiotic to scorn this or any other tool that offers help in the matter of aesthetic discrimination. One further point stemming directly out of the chronological study has not yet been broached, namely, Beethoven's own conduct in patching together a quartet out of—perhaps—very old, two-year-old, and quite new material. Obviously he wanted one composition in the minor mode for his set of six, as was the custom (the D-minor Quartet in Haydn's Op. 76, the D-minor in Mozart's set dedicated to Haydn, and so on. Beethoven even liked to have one minor-mode piece in his sets of three: an F-minor Sonata in Op. 2, C-minor Sonatas in Op. 10 and Op. 30, C-minor Trios in Op. 1 and Op. 9). Factors that we can scarcely even conjecture—convenience, cynicism, despair, impatience—caused Beethoven to abandon his settled mode of composition at this particular point. The contrast with the earnest aesthetic tone manifested by the Quartets, Op. 18, Nos. 1–3, is striking. One thing does seem beyond conjecture: the whole attitude fits in a time of doubt and transition, a period of the break-up of norms.

Almost always, it will be seen, C minor was the minor key that Beethoven chose. His affection for this tonality in the early years amounted to a mania, one that was not really played out until the Sonata in C minor, Op. 111, in 1822. Back of all these pieces lay an expressive vision of Mozart's, in such compositions as the great C-minor Concerto, the C-minor Quintet, and especially the Fantasy and Sonata for Piano in C minor. This latter work (or pair of works) was published in 1785. What an effect it must have made on the emotional boy at Bonn! But the "C-minor mood" in early Beethoven, the mood of the *Sonate Pathétique*, is one that has dated most decisively and dishearteningly over the years. Even Tovey saw through it, reluctantly. In this familiar emotional posture, Beethoven seems to be an unknowing prisoner of some conventional image of passion, rather than his own passion's master.

And in this particular drawer, the quartet counts as one of the least attractive items. The C-minor String Trio of 1798 (not to speak of the *Sonate Pathétique*) surpasses it in polish and true passion, and one would be hard pressed not to agree with Riemann that the first movement of the trio must have been written later than the quartet, or at least later than an Urquartet. Some vague memory of the two C-minor compositions must underlie the not uncommon opinion that the trios of Op. 9 outshine the quartets of Op. 18 "in certain ways" (or however the qualification happens to be expressed). Apart from this one comparison, which is certainly damaging to the quartet, the opinion seems to me incomprehensible. And the Quartet in C minor, surely, is the exceptional work in the Op. 18 series; exceptional, by its weakness, in the entire corpus of the Beethoven quartets.

· 4 ·

For the Quartet in B♭, Op. 18, No. 6, at least a few sketches have been discovered and described by Nottebohm in an approximate way. They occur not in the main sketchbooks containing work on Op. 18, Nos. 3, 1, 2, and 5 (in that order), but on some other sheets together with traces of the *Grande Sonate* in B♭, Op. 22. (Incidentally, an early sketch for the sonata *Rondo* looks like the *Allegro* that was inserted at a late date into the slow movement of the Quartet in G.) The proximity of sketches for Op. 18, No. 6, and Op. 22 suggests that this quartet was indeed the last written of the six—as one would think anyway from the advanced style of the ending, *La Malinconia* with its connected *Allegretto quasi allegro*, not to speak of various more refined signs. It also immediately suggests a comparison between the two compositions.

The first movement of the B♭ Sonata turns out to be a twin for that of the B♭ Quartet—and a more highly developed and more revealing twin than, for instance, the A-major Violin Sonata in relation to the A-major Quartet. The main themes show interesting similarities and even more interesting dissimilarities. Not to labor the comparison, we might sum it up by picturing the quartet theme as a stiff early draft for the sonata, the powerful dynamic variety of which seems not yet to have evolved from the quartet's blank symmetry and mere galvanic action. In contrast to the sonata, the entire quartet movement is cut in flat swaths, four or six rapid bars in length.

Still, the quartet theme does not have the mien of a very early Beethoven melody, something dredged up from a sketchbook. An Italian critic, Ippolito Valetta, claimed it as Italianate, perhaps remembering an *opera buffa* tune by Salieri on which Beethoven wrote a very good set of variations at this period, *La stessa, la stessissima;* there are some striking points of contact with the quartet. Or perhaps Förster deserves another look. Probably, though, Beethoven was after something of his own here. Was he perhaps already groping for the type of drawn-out flat first subject that appears in the F-major "Razumovsky" Quartet and in the "Archduke" Trio? If so, he was going much too fast, for he clocked his *Allegro con brio* at 𝅗 = 80, a pace allowing for little leisure. (In the sonata, the same tempo description, *Allegro con brio*, could imply precisely the same rate—the beat being a quarter-note here, rather than a half.) Many of the metronome marks for the B♭ Quartet tend to extremes. This one is fast; the *Adagio* very slow in spite of the qualification *ma non troppo;* and the Finale so fast (♩. = 88) that *Allegretto quasi allegro* should have been *piùtosto allegro* or plain *Allegro* to achieve the desired effect. When Beethoven came to issue metronome marks for the early and middle quartets, around 1819, it may be that his ear had grown impatient with some of his old music.

The simplification of form in this movement and in the first movement of the Quartet in A has already been pointed out. Both expositions noticeably skimp on material. As in the A-major Quartet, an independent bridge passage is lacking; a blunt repetition of the long opening theme runs directly into a rather fatuously emphatic passage of dominant preparation for the second subject. (In the sonata, an analogous repetition is suggested, but only suggested, and the emphatic preparatory passage sounds formal, terse, or funny, not fatuous.) The final cadential phrase of the exposition uses the scale material of this passage of dominant preparation, joined contrapuntally to a fragment of the first theme. The handling is not very adept.

The development, however, begins to crackle in real Beethovenian fashion. Here similarity of plan with the A-major Quartet ends, and similarity of detail with the B♭ Sonata becomes quite close. The opening is first rate, as motivic elements of the theme and its accompaniment are unexpectedly dissociated and fragmented (the sonata uses something rather similar, also in the dominant). Spooky sounds churn up to a powerful rhetorical pause on V of vi (the sonata has the same modulation, without the pause). The main action of the development consists once again of a formal double-counterpoint episode, built on the scale figure of the dominant preparation plus a figure similar to one out of the main theme. This episode is the largest and most central of all the many contrapuntal essays in the Op. 18 Quartets. But unfortunately the idea itself is too feeble, and too uniform, and the circle-of-5ths modulation much too predictable, to keep up interest. The idea had already tried our patience in the cadential passage of the exposition. (The sonata treats an excellent, much more concise contrapuntal idea at this point, also moving through a circle of 5ths.)

At last the counterpoint merges into a sweeping scale landing on the dominant of B♭. There follow 36 bars of new dominant prolongation

Example 42

which look far ahead in Beethoven's activity, to retransitions such as that in the first movement of the "Archduke" Trio. Gone is the dutiful motivic fuss which animates the analogous passage in the F-major Quartet, for instance. Here everything breathes freedom and flexibility; quite new figures sprout, leisurely dialogues develop, and the instruments carry on a sort of debate about dominant harmony—first inventing V_9, then investigating its relationship to vii_7, then finally agreeing on a hollow 5th. Almost a little development of its own in minature, this concluding passage works into a grand *diminuendo* and *allargando* culminating in a *fermata* just prior to the recapitulation. (In the sonata, after another development episode, there is a concluding passage of a very similar sort, also ending with a *fermata*, and this time yielding to the quartet in imaginative quality.)

This dominant conclusion to the development of the quartet is admirable, but it exists almost in isolation. From the point of view of the movement as a whole, the passage overprepares the recapitulation, which comes as a definite anticlimax (and comes twice, remember: the second repeat is obligatory). There is a disappointing lack of integral variation, the regular phrases sounding foolish after the show of power in the development. As in the opening movement of the Quartet in A, the one appreciable change in the recapitulation consists of a clumsy subdominant passage injected before the second group (where the sonata makes short but imaginative additions). No coda is forthcoming; there is really nothing more to be said.

It presents a strange mixture, this *Allegro con brio*. One is tempted to say that it is a movement that could have stood some more sketching. Certain things in it seem advanced over the other quartets, but crudities of composition also abound; only its second subject, however, may be suspected of harking back to early material. From Sir W. H. Hadow, it drew a rather terrible rebuke: "To pry into the weak moments of genius is an impiety from which we may well desire to shrink: it is enough to say that no part of this first movement is on Beethoven's customary levels of thought, and that the greater part is far below them." [5] The composer, it seems indicated, was facing a problem in how to map out a first movement for a string quartet, from his particular new point of disturbance in 1800. Perhaps it was just as well that no more quartets had to be written just then. The problem waited for the quartets of Op. 59 in 1805, where it was solved three times over and solved very well, from three different standpoints.

[5] P. 55.

With the slow movement, Beethoven avoided problems. The *Adagio ma non troppo* of the Quartet in B♭ is the most elementary in plan among the quartets, the plan stemming directly from Haydn. Some details recall Haydn, too: the delaying action around the sixth degree (C) in the coda, and the excessively neat concluding gestures. Alternating with a *minore* of similar innocence, the main tune ambles with deliberate pace and with studied simplicity: a set of 4-bar phrases in the pattern *a a′ b a″*, with the first two phrases moving to V and I respectively, the next hanging on the dominant-7th chord, and *a″* making a little variation of *a′*. Rococo ornament occupies the center of interest in a movement of this kind, and the figurations in the variations at least sound interestingly brittle. All this may seem strangely uninvolved for Beethoven, but he was looking ahead to another *Adagio*—to the thoroughly complex harmonic essay *La Malinconia* prior to the Finale. For the rest, the present *Adagio*, simple or not, evinces immaculate workmanship, which is more than can be said for the opening movement of this quartet.

The *Scherzo*, another extremely skillful piece of music, depends on rhythmic effects of 3 × 2 as against 2 × 3 within the 6 eighth-notes to the bar in a moderate $\frac{3}{4}$ meter. It seems beyond coincidence that this unique study in triple-time ambiguity (hemiola) should come up in the one quartet of Op. 18 to feature another piece moving 6 to the bar—the $\frac{3}{8}$ Finale. Though the Finale moves appreciably faster (according to Beethoven's disturbing metronome marks), he must have welcomed echoes of this sort:

Example 43

Allegretto quasi Allegro.

In view of Beethoven's attention to harmonic investigations in Op. 18, Nos. 1–3, it is a striking fact that the first three movements of the present quartet contain among them scarcely a single outstanding harmonic effect. Exception may be made for the rich, Haydnesque C-major chord (major VI) that illuminates the end of the *Adagio;* but the first-movement development moves merely from V to vi and through a conventional circle of 5ths, and the *Scherzo* avoids modulation assiduously. It is as though the composer were saving his modulatory fire for the fourth movement, the second *Adagio* serving as slow introduction to the Finale. "This piece is to be played with the greatest delicacy," Beethoven goes out of his way to note on the score, and entitles the movement *La Malinconia.*

One thinks at once of the Heiligenstadt Testament of 1802, also of the half arrogant, half tortured letter to Amenda of July 1801, in which Beethoven finally allows himself to mention the deterioration of his hearing over the last few years. He was certainly no stranger to depression. Yet the mood of *La Malinconia* does not really seem to approach melancholy—not melancholy as we have learned to grasp it from the analogous slow introduction to the Finale of the Quartet in C♯ minor, the piercing melody in G♯ minor. *Il Misterioso* would seem a more apt description, or *Kleine harmonische Labyrinth.* (The very idea of titles for quartet movements is an intriguing one, and has not been elucidated by Riemann or other students of the period. *Les derniers soupirs*, after all, never turned up as an inscription on Beethoven's finished composition.) In any case, *La Malinconia* is the most unusual, the most original movement among the Op. 18 Quartets. The other quartet movements are not, most of them, really Haydnesque or Mozartian; but they could conceivably be predicted on the basis of the work of the earlier composers. Or—not to flatter ourselves too far—when in the actual case we set them against their predecessors, these other movements reveal a derivation that the mind can at least encompass, after the event. Of *La Malinconia* this can no longer be said, any more than it can be said of the *Eroica* Symphony or of the Great Fugue. The piece cuts drastically across the entire mass of Beethoven's early music, an arresting premonition of achievements to come.

For this reason, even if there were no other, the piece would deserve quotation and closer analysis than I have been according to the other movements of the Op. 18 Quartets. (And about time, the analytical-minded reader may grimly exclaim.) There is another sort of reason: without more or less detailed analysis, a piece of music of this density cannot really be reached. And one wants to reach it.

Example 44

The piece falls into two halves, the first of which (bars 1–20) is concerned with an upward chromatic shift from the B♭-major triad to the triad—minor or major—or 7th-chord on B♮. This involves the step F–F♯ between the 5ths of the triads, a step so sensitive that later its upward chromatic motion has to be continued, F♯ resolving ultimately to the G in bar 21: which will start the second half. The B-major triad could easily have been domesticated into the key of B♭ as the Neapolitan degree ♭II (B=C♭). But Beethoven takes care to do no such thing, presenting B minor instead as the most awesome of mysteries. This he arranges by means of a downward chromatic-scale passage in the bass (a favorite device; another famous example occurs in the introduction to the Quartet in C, Op. 59, No. 3), the cello sinking B♭–A–A♭–G–F♯ (bars 7–12). Up to now, the violin has been confined to the triad B♭–D–F, but under pressure from the last cello note, it turns with a great air of miracle to F♯.

Essentially, this note is maintained all through the rest of the first half—all through the fantastic eruption of alternating *forte* and *pianissimo* diminished-7th chords in bars 13–16, which sounds like some great earth-shaking revenge by the gods of diatonic harmony for the Promethean modulation of bar 12. Actually the first *forte* chord (bar 13), with G on top, points the route of resolution for F♯, the central disturbance. But at the moment this route is lost in the rising scale F♯–G–A–B–C; for in spite of the extraordinary dissociation in register, dynamics, harmony, and feeling, the *forte* and *pianissimo* bars are geared together melodically, moving up this scale between them. The dissociation in register splits the scale between the first and second violins, that is all, making a series of melodic 7ths and 9ths rather than plain upward steps—a Webernish conception, and by no means the last to be met with in the Beethoven quartets. The curious grace-note turns (*gruppetti*) which articulate the chords tend also to link them.

Nothing functional takes place in this passage. After it is over, the instruments simply regroup themselves around the same F♯ that started all the trouble (bar 17), the cello finally sinking to B (bar 18). But the succession of highly unstable diminished-7th chords—Beethoven loved to manipulate these chords, almost to the end of his life—has the effect of thoroughly flushing the bland opening texture, so that now almost anything can happen. In the second half of the piece, almost anything does.

In the first half, an antiphonal dynamic has been at work, one that bears a surprising resemblance to concerto writing. Bars 1–4 and 9–12 can be heard as "solo" statements, bars 5–8 and 17–20 as "tutti" answers, and bars 13–16 as a bar-by-bar exchange. Perhaps this textural model helps a little to rationalize the dissociation. Bars 5–8 sound a little obsequious, as is not infrequently the case in concertos when the orchestra is called on to answer a solo statement. True action must be reserved for the solo—and bars 9–12 certainly take action, what with that crucial shift from F to F♯. After the fracas of antiphonal diminished-7ths, in which the still voice of the "solo" seems to prevail, bars 17–20 again sound like an orchestral body, at once solicitous and slightly timid of a solo instrument, clearing the way for its next exploit.

The next exploit, in the second half of the piece, is a contrapuntal one. A sort of astonishing free *fugato* on a new pair of subjects is suffered to carry the harmony in the dominant direction over and over again—from E minor to B minor to F♯ and C♯ and so on, all the way up a perverse circle of 5ths and almost around to E minor again (see bar 37. Perverse, because natural rotation of the circle goes the other way, from E to A to D, etc.). This modulatory potential of fugue has occurred to every counterpoint student; Beethoven had fooled with something similar in a pair of "Preludes through all the Major Keys," written at Bonn (and not forgotten: ultimately he published them). In the magnificient half-fugal Finale of the Quartet in G, K. 387, Mozart had turned such chains of endless dominant modulations to aesthetic worth—inspiration, possibly, though certainly not a model, for the procedure in *La Malinconia*.

To hear merely an upward circle of 5ths in such cases would be too mechanical, though. Beethoven brakes the progress very subtly, first in order to bring out the melodic step F♯–G, and then in order to re-establish the tonic key B♭. The *first* quasi-fugal entry (violin 2, bar 21) drifts from the melodic note G—the 3rd of E minor—through B minor to F♯ minor. As accompaniment to the *second* fugal entry (viola, bar 23), the counter-subject (violin 1) strikes the high F♯ of prior fame, drawing it down to F𝄪—that is, to G: the same descending 7th that explodes between bars 12–13, and the same basic step that resolves the F♯ of bar 12 ultimately to the G of bar 21. Directly after the *third* fugal entry (violin 2, bar 25), the first violin forces an ingenious *stretto*—on the very same high F♯ (G♭) brought down to G♮ for the fourth time. Meanwhile the *fugato* subject expands from two bars to three in a rich lyric *crescendo*.

Under this G, in bar 28, the hypnotic harmonic pattern of the *fugato* breaks. The C triad, excellently grounded by the cello *sforzando* on its bottom note, has the retrospective sense of settling the quicksand harmony around F minor, which (as minor subdominant) is not so far from the tonic key B♭.

The dramatic alternation of *forte* and *piano* chords with grace-note turns is resumed, but now the alternation takes on the aspect of dramatic dialogue; the antiphonal members engage (bars 29–32). They are spurred into double time and focused into the same register, so that the rising chromatic-scale passage moves by plain steps, much more lucidly than before. Again the "solo" seems to prevail, this time not by means of sheer stillness, but by a second rich lyric outpouring of the *fugato* subject (expanded to four bars—compare bars 26–9). This gesture forecasts one out of the slow movement of Beethoven's Piano Concerto in G:

Example 45

Liszt proposed an inescapable program for the concerto, Orpheus taming the Furies in some post-Gluckian Inferno. The last "No" of the Furies, in the example above, finds its parallel in the newly rhythmicized cello figure of bars 33–5 of *La Malinconia.*

The bottom of the rising passage culminates in the step F♯–G, once again (viola, bars 32–3). At last this insistent step is associated with B♭, the tonic degree, high and strong in the first violin. The slow flywheel of the 5ths was checked, in bar 28, by an intimation of F minor. When the wheel stirs into motion again, the strongest point achieved, G minor (bar 33), is, like F minor, a close relative of the goal tonic. Further swings, to D and A, henceforth sound unstable, for thanks to the climactic violin note B♭ in bar 33, the low B♭ in bars 35–6 assumes more weight in the ear than the strange key of A minor it claims to be preparing as a Neapolitan.

From bar 37 on, a passage of rising chromatic chords articulated by grace-note turns (and now they sound like very ominous turns) appears for the third and last time, and most nakedly: all the complexities of dynamic or textural dissociation have melted away into an urgent unmistakable drive home. The concluding, rather theatrical half-cadence in the key of B♭ minor revolves around F and G♭, acting to exorcise the conflict of F and F♯ that had generated the essential action.

The big half-cadence reminds us—*La Malinconia* is after all a slow introduction to a fast movement, dimly modeled on the type invented for symphonies by Haydn and Mozart. What is to be introduced? As is often the case with Haydn, something ostensibly amusing and slight. Perhaps a rejection of melancholy.

The *Allegretto quasi allegro* (see p. 75) is a quiet, fast, pure, single-minded evocation of the *danza alla Tedesca,* the *Teutsche* of the Viennese ballrooms. Elegantly detailed, it reflects the impersonality of the ballroom, and yet at the same time, in a very strange way, seems more quintessentially Beethovenian than any of the earlier quartet finales. The frantic intensity of Op. 18, Nos. 1–3, the faceless bluster of No. 4, the glossy tour de force of No. 5—none of these qualities is wanted here, for such weight as the movement is to assume in the total form it gets from its juncture with *La Malinconia.* The dance shapes itself as a simple sonata structure without any development, almost a *perpetuum mobile*, with a minimum of contrast and with the running main theme never far from mind. *La Malinconia* had provided plenty of contrast, modulation, and motivic development. A jewel-like extension of the second subject in the "recapitulation" exhibits all the Mozartian polish and serenity of the Quartet in A. But as the "recapitulation" approaches its conclusion, the opening motif whirls into a note of disquiet—the first in the piece. Then a tonic $^6_4$ chord presages some kind of penultimate cadenza.

A concerto cadenza tends to recollect some earlier material, and what is to be recollected here is of course *La Malinconia*, or at least its first idea. (Its second idea, the *fugato*, had perhaps already been mirrored by the opening motif of the dance, with its upward 6th.) Originally, the awesome B minor which intruded upon the B♭ harmony was resolved in the most perverse way possible, *up* a circle of 5ths, but when in the present "cadenza" the B-minor triad materializes again, it resolves in just the opposite sense, *down* the circle. This makes light of the previous exploration. B minor and its F♯ are answered by a different diminished-7th chord, featuring not G but G♯, which softens into an E chord; a fragment of the dance returns in A minor; the *Adagio* shifts conventionally (with an almost audible sigh of relief) from A to D^6_5; the dance returns in G major, and slips through C minor and F^6_5 to the tonic key B♭. The wheel relaxes in the natural way B–E–A–D–G–C–F–B♭. The dance tune returns in B♭ and accumulates little canonic accompaniments—for Beethoven simply cannot leave counterpoint alone—prior to a Haydnesque slow-down and a brilliant *prestissimo* to conclude.

The remarks of Philip Radcliffe on the Quartet in B♭ are very much to the point.[6] The piece seems to gather strength as it goes along, movement by movement: an unusual dynamic, but one that Beethoven may very well have planned deliberately, in order to try for a new balance among movements in the classic cyclic form. If this was so, the blankness of the opening movement would constitute just as deliberate an element in the design as the richness of *La Malinconia*. The dynamic is oddly reminiscent of the later Quartet in B♭, Op. 130. Parallels are not to be drawn very closely between 1800 and 1825, of course, but Op. 130 in its own way also shows signs of disruption, and Op. 130 also proceeds with sharply

[6] Pp. 42–4.

diverse effects, movement by movement, up to the towering climax of the Great Fugue which formed the original finale.

In Op. 18, No. 6, too, the climactic statement is reserved for the Finale. Admittedly, the *Allegretto quasi allegro* is intrinsically a very slight piece of work, for all its sparkle; to mention one obvious index of the slightness, the texture amounts to little more than a solo for Schuppanzigh all the way through (as is also true of the Finale of the C-minor Quartet, in which however the texture seems much more meretricious). And *La Malinconia*, for all its quite astonishing technical prowess, is an emotional sphinx, dealing with pathos entirely from the outside, revealing an almost heartless preoccupation with its own harmonic meditations over those of the poor melancholic. Yet the aggregation of *Adagio* and *Allegro* sections (compare Op. 130!) seems somehow to carry the day; it is a case of the whole being larger than the sum of the parts. As Radcliffe suggests, possibly Beethoven set the Quartet in B♭ at the end of the publication because he considered it a fitting climax to his quartet project; and one could certainly see why. Although "there is a strange diversity between the movements, not only in merit but also in idiom" and the work as a whole does leave "a curiously mixed impression," the composite Finale stands out as the most arresting conception in the entire Op. 18 series.

· 5 ·

Beethoven was twenty-eight when he started work on the series, and thirty when he finished it. It is true that he developed as an artist more slowly than some of the other great composers, or rather, that he came to produce works of real consistency and authenticity only later in life. Think of Mozart's Quartet in G, K. 387, written at the age of twenty-six, or Schubert's Quartet in A minor, written at the age of twenty-seven.

It was almost a willful thing with Beethoven. In music composed by Mozart or Schubert in their twenties, and indeed in that of some lesser men, an artistic conception often seems to be realized perfectly in its own terms, even if these terms appear limited in the light of the composer's later work. But with early Beethoven this does not happen very much. In the first period, it is as though he himself were obsessed by the unconscious knowledge that he has not yet caught his stride. He will not let well enough alone; he is always thinking; style and idea rasp. What communicates itself almost palpably from his music is an enormously intelligent fascination with material and *métier*, a fascination far exceeding any instinct for provisional perfection.

He experienced no special difficulty in "finding himself," I should suppose, but he was not often satisfied to stay with what he found. He had no special difficulty with musical technique, far from it, but he was not often satisfied until he had tried it on some new problem which would have a way of making technique look inadequate. The final artistic results were interesting, explosive, and uneven—each of these things, probably, in an unusual degree.

Even in their own terms, then, the Op. 18 Quartets will be granted to be erratic works. There are bad spots within many of the movements; and within total compositions, some movements succeed as wholes a great deal better than others. It has been suggested that the first and second movements stand out in the F-major Quartet, the first and third in the G-major, the second and fourth in the A-major, the *La Malinconia* complex in the B♭-major, and the minuet (minus the trio) in the C-minor. The most consistent of the quartets is the first composed, D major, Op. 18, No. 3; within its decidely old-fashioned framework, it maintains balance and decorum more steadily than any of the others. Still, I think we should consider it a bloodless criticism that would prefer this quartet finally on this account. Once Beethoven had bitten into the apple of the F-major Quartet, the second composed, consistency was harder to achieve, but the problems posed and the gestures at solution became infinitely more mature and exciting.

Halfway through the composition of Op. 18, a process of disruption would appear to have set in—to generalize from signs such as experimentation with novel kinds of movements, modeling on other compositions, dipping back into older material, and falling back on some indifferent standards of work. Characteristically, Beethoven was beginning to question the very nature of the undertaking he was engaged in. With the piano sonata, he had been questioning for some time; and little more than two years are to pass before he is conceiving the *Eroica* Symphony. Or perhaps the fact is that at this point of the project his energy was beginning to flag. Six was an ambitious number to start off with in quartet writing—he might have rested easier with three, if easy resting had ever occured to Beethoven. When his interest did flare in these later quartets, it flared more imaginatively than ever, in ways that shed light ahead. Such is the case with the transparent, haunting minuet of the Quartet in A, and also with the ending of the Quartet in B♭—*La Malinconia* itself, and the whole conception of its juncture with the *alla Tedesca* Finale.

All in all, the best-realized movements are probably the dance and dancelike numbers. The two pieces just mentioned belong in this category, which can also admit the elegant F-major *alternativo* in the slow movement of the Quartet in G; and generally speaking, the minuets and scherzos (and some of the trios) are striking little successes, even though their sophisticated modesty can sometimes fall into self-effacement. But once again, it would seem bloodless to settle on a preference for movements which count in a sense as the least ambitious. The trouble is that elsewhere Op. 18 is all ambition. Ambition bristles especially in the numerous passages of formal counterpoint, which seem on the one hand to be looking for some tougher, more individual means of expression, and on the other hand to be chasing the shadow of Albrechtsberger and Haydn. Besides textbooks, Albrechtsberger wrote quantities of chamber music featuring all kinds of archaic learning, and Haydn never let anyone quite forget the fugal finales of his Op. 20 Quartets—in his later music, fugue tends to turn up at the most unexpected moments. Beethoven's determined contrapuntal exercising showed absolutely the right instinct, and of course it worked up excellent muscles for the future. At this point, however, it cannot be said to have been winning many races.

The formulation by Hadow—"In later life he touched deeper issues: he never wrote with a more complete mastery of his resources" [7]—conforms to Victorian wish, not to hard analytical fact. Beethoven was handling some resources admirably, but others—such as formal counterpoint—he was not, at least not always. And unfortunately for critics, a clear relationship does not hold between technical mastery and expressive result. Something is askew with expression all through the Op. 18 set, and the trouble cannot be linked in a simple way with technical success or failure. When the expression does not seem forced, it generally seems unfocused; and when it seems forced—to take the clearest case—either slipshod work may be involved, as in the Quartet in C minor, or exceedingly sophisticated work, as in the D-minor *Adagio affettuoso ed appassionato* of the Quartet in F. *La Malinconia* itself, the most impressive harmonic essay, plumbs melancholy in a curiously aloof and speculative way. The quality of intensity and intelligence in most of the fast movements seems to go with impersonality, and the athleticism with brittleness. Perhaps the little dances, asking least in expressive terms, overreach themselves the least.

In both technique and expression, Beethoven was more interested in following up dazzling new ideas than in polishing classic medallions.

[7] P. 8.

Haydn, it is known, did not much sympathize, and probably Mozart would not have sympathized either. The Op. 18 Quartets made excellent sense to Beethoven's own generation, however, and to the early nineteenth century.

Later times have come not so much to agree with Haydn as to lose interest, by and large; at present these works cannot be said to attract a great deal of attention from players, audiences, or critics. Nor are all commentators as concerned as Hadow, or as the present writer. Vincent d'Indy, for instance, who went through the Beethoven quartets as a matter of routine in his formidable curriculum at the Schola Cantorum, delivering commentaries and drawing diagrams for every one of them, found no need to talk about Op. 18 at all outside of the classroom. Covering Beethoven's chamber music for a lay publication, he restricted himself to "only those productions which really deserve to be regarded as masterpieces of Art," a limitation that resulted in a few words on Op. 18, No. 3, taken as an example of the first-period style, and charitable silence on the other five. This in a publication that was supposed to be a *Cyclopaedic Survey of Chamber Music!*

D'Indy is an exasperating critic: always half right. There are indeed no masterpieces among the Op. 18 pieces, and the listener who is restricted to a diet of masterpieces will be wanting to get on to the next course. *Non si pasce di cibo mortale chi si pasce di cibo celeste*, as the Statue says in *Don Giovanni.* Such a diet is doubtless all right for the amateur who has other things to do with his time, and selectively the professional too assumes such a regime, making secret pacts with himself not to bother with anything short of the "masterpieces" of certain composers best left unnamed. With certain listeners and certain other composers, though, there comes a point at which every musical gesture assumes interest and —more—a consuming fascination. If we care to know Beethoven (or Mozart, or Schubert), everything he does will reveal facets of a personality that concerns us even when he is not working at full consciousness or with final aesthetic success. It may not be revealed at once; and this is where the work of historical imagination comes in. It is needed to put Beethoven's living gestures into some kind of living context.

Hence the need to understand ambition as well as result, idea as well as limitation, "exterior context" as well as "interior context." These contexts complement—it is tempting to say, counteract—the force of another context, which affects our response to the Op. 18 Quartets most deeply and inevitably: the retrospective context of Beethoven's later music. The "Razumovsky" Quartets and the late quartets supply a standard not only of style and expression, but also of artistic consistency. With Beethoven, the comparison between early and late music can seem especially unkind, for reasons that have been touched on above; this fact, and the inevitability of the comparison, are already evidence of a sort of historical approach to Op. 18. The more responsibly this approach can be followed through—the more fully the context can be grasped—the more interest and value will be found to attach to these six quartets. Though to be sure, our taste for them can never be quite the same as the partaking of "masterpieces of Art." They will doubtless always remain a merely mortal, not a celestial, nourishment.

BOOK II

4

AFTER THE *EROICA*

Quartet in F Major, Op. 59, No. 1

A book on the Beethoven quartets is three books, through which certain kinds of continuity are bound to be tenuous at best. Consideration of the sixteen quartets sweeps the student somewhat roughly through almost the full span of Beethoven's creative activity. With ominous ease the quartets separate themselves into slots provided by the old categorization of Beethoven's work into "three periods": the six of Op. 18 in 1798–1800; the three "Razumovsky" Quartets, the "Harp" in E♭, and the *Quartetto serioso* in F minor in 1805–10; and then five more in 1824–6, the late quartets. No other genre—not the sonata or the symphony—illustrates Beethoven's entire creative range so fully. But the process remains illustration, lucky but more or less random illustration; real historical draughtsmanship is impossible within this framework. The taut line of development connecting the "three periods" and all the individual works is obviously not to be drawn in a study restricted to these or any other sixteen pieces. In themselves the quartets do not illuminate the veritable stylistic revolutions of Beethoven's career, and many important questions about this can only be sketched, anxiously, by way of preface, parenthesis, or postface.

This the reader will not at first regret; quite properly, his interest focuses on the individual works of art, not on the career. But the lack of a firm historical continuity makes itself felt immediately on turning from any one group of quartets to the next. To put the matter simply: whatever critical stance has been worked out for the early group seems at once inadequate for the later one. The later quartets seem to breathe in a different world; when the evolutionary charting is sketchy, the critic may find himself at sea. The response to art, furthermore, does not only involve a more or less purely aesthetic reaction to this, that, and the other isolated work. More or less intellectually, we assemble and order the works into an artist's total *œuvre;* this *œuvre* itself has a beauty, a "logic," and a wholeness comparable in some sense to those of the single work of art. Between the *œuvre* and the single work a dialectic of appreciation may be said to exist, whereby we can even take pleasure in a quite indifferent piece of music for what it reminds us of the structured integrity of an entire lifework. The sense of the whole depends on all the individual pieces, but it is also true that the sense of the individual piece is illuminated by the cumulative light of the totality. Something is missing when one work or a group of works is examined—however lovingly—apart from its natural matrix.

With no composer, perhaps, is the working of this dialectic so compelling as with Beethoven. On the one hand, there is the deep quality of consciousness, discipline, and purpose in the corpus as a developing whole. On the other hand, the individual works grow more and more individual, more breathtakingly unpredictable—yet controlled, almost predicted by the radical evolutionary curve of the corpus. I think we need have few misgivings about speaking of "three periods" and "revolution" with Beethoven, though the terms are obviously limited and even vulnerable. The term "revolution" should cause no trouble unless it assumes the implication of a clean cut with the past—an impossible implication, which our political experience of the word should warn against in any case. There is no other term to refer to an evolution suddenly accelerated to a dizzying pace, such as Beethoven went through in 1802 and 1803. The "three periods" or "three styles" correspond to an obvious, primitive fact in Beethoven's *œuvre*, too, though every time the phrases are used one longs to talk of more and more substyles or subperiods, and I take it we never lose sight of the elegant lines of steel binding all periods and all works together. It is sometimes said that the work of all artists falls into these same three periods, as though by natural law. If so, one can only conclude that the partition is sharper with Beethoven than with (for instance) Bach, Handel, Haydn, Mozart, Wagner, Brahms, Schoenberg, or Bartók. Not to speak of anyone's very early music, the *Eroica* Symphony seems to differ more profoundly from Beethoven's last quartets than Bach's Cöthen music does from his last Leipzig works, or *Das Rheingold* does from *Parsifal*. Of the great composers, perhaps only Verdi and

Stravinsky arrived at stylistic syntheses comparable in relative distinctness to Beethoven's third style—and they only at a very advanced age. Verdi, moreover, conspicuously lacks the smooth, lucid evolution of style and conception, work by work through the *œuvre*, that serves as counterpoise to stylistic revolutions.

In Beethoven's case, the revolutions marking the major style changes can be seen to have been precipitated by circumstances in his ill-managed emotional life. It seems beyond coincidence that the shattering move into the second period should come at exactly the same time as the shattering Heiligenstadt Testament of October 1802. Drafted as a letter to his brothers, this famous document reads less as a letter or a will than as a great unburdening cry of grief at his deafness and solitude—mingled with apology, self-justification, self-pity, pathos, pride, hints of suicide, and presentiments of death. Or the Testament may be read as an elaborate fantasy-threat directed at his brother Carl—very remarkably, Johann's name was never written in the spaces left open for it: this interpretation has been proposed by Drs. Editha and Richard Sterba, in their posthumous psychoanalytical study of the composer. That Beethoven was driven all his life by an irrational and inordinately violent possessiveness toward his brothers (or, later, towards Carl's son as surrogate) is the burden of their melancholy, skillful demonstration. The Sterbas view the Testament rather coolly as one more symptom of a lifetime obsession; the older view of it as the monument of some peak disturbance, some near-breakdown situation in 1802, still seems to me preferable. For the date is what seems so significant, given the facts of Beethoven's artistic activity. To this date, possibly, can be related a new awareness of himself as artist—if not as man—in a repeated side-reference: "It seemed to me impossible to leave the world until I had brought forth all that I felt was within me. . . . With joy I hasten to meet death—if it comes before I have had the chance to develop all my artistic capacities, it will still be coming too soon. . . ." [1] He had never spoken in quite this way before. In any case, the neurotic details are not much to the point. Other artists have suffered neurosis, breakdown, chronic depression, extreme illness, and destructive love affairs without experiencing the amazing artistic after-effects that such things seem to have produced in Beethoven.

The situation around 1802 in Beethoven's music can be reconstructed from the sketchbooks, if not quite fully, certainly much more so than the private details bearing on the Heiligenstadt Testament. As he wound up work on the early set of quartets, in 1800, Beethoven turned back to

[1] Thayer, p. 305.

the sonata, with the *Grande Sonate* in B♭, Op. 22. He devoted the next two years to this genre, by and large, along with work on the ballet *Prometheus*, the Second Symphony, and some other compositions. In half a dozen piano sonatas (Op. 26; Op. 27, Nos. 1 and 2; Op. 28; Op. 31, Nos. 1, 2, and 3) and in another half dozen for violin and piano (Op. 23; Op. 24; Op. 30, Nos. 1, 2, and 3), he rapidly pressed experiment and solution, bending the classicism of the 1790's into astonishing tensile spirals. But a marked change occurs soon after the Heiligenstadt Testament—or, for all we know, directly afterwards; that closely the sketches are not dated. His thoughts turned from sonatas to compositions of an ambition never before imagined: in particular the Third Symphony, the *Eroica*, during 1803, and the opera *Leonore* (renamed *Fidelio*) during 1804 and 1805. Again, it can be no coincidence that these two works are so strongly, so unusually shot through with extramusical ideas, and that the ideas should be ideas of heroism. Other works of 1803 and 1804 fall under the sway of these two, in mood and scope. Even the few sonatas are now heroic—the "Waldstein" and the *Appassionata*. With this set of works Beethoven made his revolution: not a sharp cut with the past, but an abrupt phase of evolution forced by psychological factors which necessarily remain obscure.

The key work is the symphony—a real "watershed" work, not only in terms of his own *œuvre*, but also in terms of our whole musical tradition considered as broadly as we please. There will be occasion to say something about this great work in the following pages. With his (to some people) embarrassingly simple but unerring sense of symbolism, Beethoven inscribed the piece to Napoleon, as is very well known, and then tore up the title page when he saw revolution betrayed. But he did not tear up the symphony, and now there was no more chance of turning back to the aesthetic of Viennese classicism than there was of returning to the *ancien régime*. Though efforts were made, even by this composer. After the *Eroica*, Beethoven's quartets like everything else he wrote breathe in a different world from that of the 1790's. Hearing the second-period quartets today, one breathes and listens differently than one does to Haydn, Mozart, and the Quartets of Op. 18.

In response to the difference, criticism has to bring in new techniques and methods of articulation, learn a new metabolism, and at the very least commit itself to a new intensity of attention. What has to emerge first of all is a fitting stance for this music in general. The F-major "Razumovsky" Quartet—greatest of the three in Op. 59, I should say, in spite of something unsettled in the sequence of the movements; certainly greatest in its superb opening *Allegro*—can serve, almost as well as the symphony, to introduce Beethoven's second period and whatever critical equipment may be brought to bear upon it.

· 2 ·

Beethoven's theme simulates a long lyric utterance, surging up four octaves, filling the entire quartet space. One is reminded—but only very

Example 46

dimly!—of the slender theme of the Quartet in B♭, Op. 18, No. 6. Rhythmically very square, the theme serves almost ostentatiously as an arsenal of well-defined motivic material: a fundamental rising-scale motif covering a 4th, an eighth-note motif, and a cadence motif on a firm anapaest rhythm. Everything sounds direct and crudely powerful, yet the real basis for power rests in a rather celebrated point of harmonic subtlety.

If Beethoven's idea was to bring his theme up from the depths, he was more or less bound to begin it in the cello, with no bass below. This was a plain invitation to fruitful ambiguities. Not only does the first phrase begin low, it also lays low, turning suspiciously around C, the dominant degree. The recurring C vaguely implies a harmonic root, biasing these first bars already in the dominant direction—a bias helped by the throbbing C on the top of the accompaniment, and tacitly allowed by the hollow accompaniment chord (there is only one) itself. Of course, the little phrase speaks so firmly that one can scarcely credit the harmonic indefiniteness with which it offers to tell its story—and in any case, two F's unofficially confirm the tonic stability. (Without them, the dominant would have the edge: try changing the F in bar 1 to a D, and the F in bar 3 to an A.) The total impression, if we have time to think, is less delicate than willful, less equivocal than forthright but askew.

The cello melody rises from C to F and then to a half-cadence on G, supporting a no-longer-ambiguous dominant $^4_3$ chord. This G in bar 8 develops as a key detail. The next phrases (in the violin) deploy themselves like a balancing lyric continuation of the original two; but the inflexible way in which they parrot the original motivic material jars just as much as the fact that a single harmony (the same V^4_3 on top of the same G) is sounding all through the 8-bar section. In spite of first appearances, then, Beethoven is dealing less with tunes here than with a great *crescendo* of preparation. The novelty comes in combining such a passage with thematic exposition, and in bringing it so explosively early in the piece.

The opening statement of the "Archduke" Trio, Op. 97—a later work —bears a certain superficial similarity to this one, in its rhythmic profile and in its general impetus toward melodic climax. But the comparison (which can be extended past the themes to the pieces as wholes, and even, indeed, to the periods during which the pieces were written) simply points up the radical nature of the quartet and the normality of the trio. The trio is what the quartet only pretends to be—genuinely lyric. Less dynamic and disruptive than the quartet, it was just the work to impress such composers as Schubert and Brahms.

In the quartet, clouded harmony in the first phrase has clarified into a dominant chord at the cadence of the second. The dominant chord holds fast for a full eight bars, its cadential quality turning into a very strong sense of anticipation. Then bars 17–18 add more sinew—a solid root for the dominant, and a strong 9th resolving up through D–E–F to the first stable tonic sonority in the composition. This makes for an arrival of the greatest force. Throughout these 18 bars, the feeling of preparation has grown in urgency as the melody thrusts up and up. And one sore spot stands out: the note G, which marked the first change of harmony. This

G, the second degree of the scale, rears itself out of F, then seems to get stuck and to beat away very determinedly before marching back.

As usual in the largest sonata movements, the main theme will return at the main hinges of the form. But in this piece the theme is transformed more deeply than ever before. After a broad close to the exposition, the theme seems to return verbatim, and in the tonic key too; the listener supposes that the formal repetition of the exposition is under way. However, the sixth bar of the theme moves up not to F but on the spur of the moment to G♭, a degree higher and infinitely more intense. We have been thrust into the development section, and the intensity of the shock, as much as the intensity of the chromatic note G♭ itself, suffices to stir a long series of developmental modulations pointing, as will appear, to D♭.

Later the sense of this G♭ is expounded, as well as its connection with D♭. During the first 12 bars of the recapitulation—during three out of the original four phrases—the theme follows its original path; the V^4_3 chord on G has started its pulsing. By bar 13, however, the rising sequences in the violin turn to the minor mode, whereupon the cello G sinks to G♭—which holds even more persistently for another *ten* bars, the violin threshing around the same G♭ in various other registers. In other words, G♭ is now heard as a warp of the original "sore" G. The tension grows quite intolerable. At last G♭ resolves to F, treated not yet as the tonic but as the third degree of D♭ major. It takes another 16-bar period before these flat regions can be forgotten, and the parallel step D♭–C can bring D♭ back again around toward the tonic F major.

So Protean a theme must in the coda be somehow contained. Beethoven takes one obvious course: he gives out the theme not as a slow *crescendo* but as a triumphant *fortissimo* from the start, not with a harmonic question mark but (at last) with full and frank harmonization underneath. (The passage, illustrated on p. 103, sharply contrasts F and G by juxtaposing their major triads.) This stabilizing version of the theme pares it down to two phrases, the sequel evaporating harmlessly up to the heights and down again. A few cadential periods later, the theme is suggested once more in a sort of inspired sublimation. Only three elements endure—elements which we now see to be of the very essence: the first motif (the other two are lost); the idea of a great sweeping ascent from the depths; and the "sore" note G, with its pulsation, desiring the tonic. The great ascent is revealed as the outcome of the modest rising-scale motif, and the G is "explained" downwards from A. While G beats violently again in the bass, the violin climbs a scale up to the

Example 47

highest note in the piece, three octaves above middle C. There it rests for five whole bars, seeming to dispose the G fathoms below to resolve, resume, and resolve again to an F that is finally a serene, unclouded tonic.

Those other motifs are not entirely lost, either. The violin in its descent recalls the eighth-note motif, and the concluding modal cadence contains a hint of the cadence motif.

These are extraordinary transformations of a theme that was already extraordinary enough in its plain statement. In their grandiose way, the transformations are perfectly in scale: the theme itself invites the catastrophe of the recapitulation, which in turn requires the huge double affirmation of the coda. Of course the full scope of Beethoven's conception reveals itself only in the light of all the rest of the movement. We should look back over it in some detail, starting (in the example on p. 93) at bar 19, the point at which the main theme arrives so forcefully at the first true tonic sonority.

The interesting fact about this arrival is that it is an artificial one. Or, more correctly, Beethoven seems to have wanted only the fact of arrival; he had no intention of doing anything with the F that is arrived at (the basic exposition, after all, was accomplished by this time). The next six bars prevaricate: in bar 20 a low C deliberately undercuts the harmony, and inconclusive diminished-7th chords build up to a cadence which in effect restates that of bars 17–19. Here a solid tonic passage commences—only to take on the air of a bridge starting up. So although a great deal seems to be happening, there is no really definitive statement, only a brilliant show of motivic energy. The prevaricating bars suggest the anapaest rhythm of the cadence motif. The bridge makes a bucolic extension of the eighth-note motif, running into canons on the first motif. These in turn sprout new, useful triplet figures.

The actual modulation to the second group is done just a little roughly—but significantly—by juxtaposing F- and G-major triads. Suddenly there is a very forceful new arrival, at G. The high melodic line E–F♯–G and the dominant-9th chord echo the prior arrival, D–E–F,

Example 48

which can now be heard as a stage towards the present one. F and G, the notes around which the long opening revolved, stand out as the cadential goals in the first large section of the movement.

But by this time serious action is to take place. A solo cello theme in G erupts out of the triplet figuration, relaxing rather majestically into C major and a lyric second theme (in whose cadence notes A–B–C we may hear a resonance of the two prior arrivals). The subsequent cadence figures bear a very individual stamp, and seem bent on exploring the total pitch firmament once again. The first of them uses entwining triplet *arpeggios* in all the instruments. The second (illustrated on p. 108) uses a series of cryptic half-note chords, irregular harmonically and very widely spaced; one thinks, oddly, of Webern. In sonata form, the section after the second theme was a traditional place for small harmonic clouds, but Beethoven is extremely bold (and, with his new touch in the recapitulation, even capricious). A third and final cadence idea picks up the light canons of the bridge, devising a new motif—a variation of the rising-scale motif in the rhythm of the eighth-note motif. This admirable combination does important service in the development, and reappears in the last passage of the coda.

One of Beethoven's most tremendous development sections is to follow; but as Tovey remarked, there is at first no sign of unusual scope or even of unusual imagination. The development starts with the main theme in the tonic (or is it *on* the dominant? a nice paradox at this point), its second phrase forced up to a dramatic new note, G♭. This sets up a modulating dialogue on the theme, whose accents, harmonies, and accompaniment figuration all prove to be grist for Beethoven's developmental mill. The eighth-note motif forms itself into a neat sequence; the harmonies proceed in standard fashion from I to IV to ii to vi; the Webernish half-note chords turn up, and also a strong dominant which the listener takes (correctly enough) as that preparing the home key. All this holds to a predictable scheme, but gradually unpredicted greater rhythms begin to assert themselves. The first violin extends the eight-note motif into a leisurely rhapsody, while the harmonies move away with sublime unconcern. After about 16 bars Beethoven settles in the key of D♭, a much more remote region than those touched earlier in the development (even though it was foreshadowed by the rupturing G♭ at the start). He is loath to leave; for another 16 bars he makes up warm, nostalgic versions of the last cadence theme in D♭, expanding it and rounding it lyrically. There is a sudden lurch, and an even grander landscape is revealed.

Contrapuntal episodes had haunted the development sections of the Op. 18 Quartets, but Beethoven had never before worked on a scale that allowed or demanded the massive formality achieved by counterpoint here. A giant double fugue unfolds, with a secondary subject grown out of the combination motif of the cadence theme, and with a principal subject that is to all intents and purposes new, in spite of the familiar anapaest rhythm. The entries of these subjects, at 5-bar intervals, sound stately, rather scholastic, and enormously deliberate for a sonata-form episode. There is enough time for three regular entries, plus two different *stretto* ones, before the second *stretto* turns extremely loud and dissonant, and grinds its way harshly up to a stop. This abrupt climax—it is on an inchoate diminished-7th chord—smashes the fugue, only to collapse numbly to a new strong dominant. After yet another lengthy diversion, the true dominant is sounded while the violin soars quietly up to the highest part of its range, to high B♭–B♮–C in solo whole-notes. The two arrivals in the opening period of the exposition flash back to the ear.

An arrival—but not yet at the main theme: at its prevaricating, chromatic, anapaestic sequel. And not yet at a firm tonic sound; the material is given initially over a I_6 chord, which is undercut as before by a loud C. Beethoven must have felt reluctant to dispel the harmonic ambiguities of his first theme any earlier than the coda. But of course he wanted a *forte* recapitulation; if the decision was to hold the lucid *forte* version of the main theme in reserve, it was a brainwave to use the prevaricating passage in its place at this juncture. The passage starts *forte*, continuing a little differently in view of a different and clearer goal: pre-establishment, in fact, of the hollow accompaniment harmony (A and C) of the coming theme:

Example 49

When the main theme arrives, it arrives *piano* again, so that it can make a *crescendo* again—the catastrophic *crescendo* with the G♭ that has already been discussed. The ambiguous note C is stressed further by means of repeated scales. If one still hears A trumpeting away on the cello, it will seem to sink to the G, thence to G♭, and finally—after the shattering new build-up—to an equivocal F.

Equivocal in that F is treated not as the tonic, but as the third degree of a temporary D♭ tonality—resuming the key of the main center of the development, and with it a great sense of range and exploration. Only after 65 bars of this recapitulation is a real tonic sonority heard, at the majestic entry of the lyric second theme. In honor of its new role, perhaps, Beethoven reorchestrated the second theme richly. Thereafter things move directly to the gigantic double affirmation which makes up the coda. Preoccupation with tonic stability here, to the exclusion of even so much as a gesture in any other direction, helps balance the extended digression to D♭ in the recapitulation. Rarely, in any case, did Beethoven end a composition with such serene breadth, such a perfect inertia.

Our account of the movement has been mainly descriptive, perhaps to the point of drabness. But there is so much to describe. As we have said, a study of the quartets alone does not trace Beethoven's development step by step; coming upon the first "Razumovsky" Quartet after the six of Op. 18 is like coming into a new artistic universe. It is like a first reading of Chapman's Homer, a first visit to Athens or Venice, a first kiss. The richness of detail, the originality and fertility of musical idea, the commanding coherence, the sheer smooth density and complexity of it all, are fairly breathtaking. Little wonder that in the 1800's quartet players who liked Op. 18 found Op. 59 a closed book. There had never been such a quartet before; and the piece remains breathtaking in any context.

Yet perhaps the primary impression is not so much of fecundity as of span, purposeful span. Already indicated by the opening theme itself, a sense of horizon grows on the listener with every large gesture of the piece. Contractions—for there are a few in the second portion of the exposition—only contribute to this sense as a foil to the pulse of the essential progress. The modulations which mark the stages of this progress are few and monolithic, and manage to give the piece such slow-swinging power, that by the time D♭ forces its way into the recapitulation we are not at all amazed (as well we might be) that it maintains itself so long and so successfully. Unusually large digressions have been placed within our experience—the unexpected warm detour to D♭ in the development, and the protracted cool explorations of the double fugue. In the coda, detail is stripped away to reveal the sure framework. Multiplicity without confusion, extension without vacuity, prolongation without delay, scope without either flaccidity or tedium: all this falls within the new range of Beethoven's second period.

Of all the compositions between Op. 18 and Op. 59, one in particular springs to mind in connection with the F-major Quartet: the *Eroica* Symphony itself. So much is remarkable about the symphony, in purely technical terms as well as in terms of "program" or extramusical impetus. But the most remarkable single fact about it is its span. It dwarfs every previous effort of the classic composers, and opens the door to

The Damnation of Faust, the *Ring*, and the Mahler symphonies, to say nothing of Beethoven's Ninth. Something of this scope is attempted in the F-major Quartet—though the quartet medium might seem to be the last place to try for it—and stands out as the commanding feature of the work. Only Beethoven would have forced open this door, and only Beethoven cared to pass through to conceptions such as that of the Quartet in B♭ of 1825 with the Great Fugue.

In quality, the *Eroica* Symphony is entirely different from the quartet; as different as the key of E♭ major, in Beethoven's ear, from the key of F. But technical parallels between the two works are quite close. At the heart of the conception of each opening movement lies the idea of a theme destined for earth-shaking reinterpretations—not so much in the development section, as in the recapitulation and coda. In both movements, the change in the recapitulation hinges on one "sore" note. In the quartet, an ostensibly bland G gets stuck and has to be bent violently to G♭. In the symphony, a far from bland—in fact, a distinctly mysterious—C♯ becomes D♭ at the recapitulation, causing luminous digressions in distant keys. The quartet theme and the symphony theme both lie in the bass region, accompanied above by a pulsation which refuses to budge (this is true in the symphony at least for the duration of the C♯). Then climactically in the coda, each theme is simplified, and coarsened, into a triumphant statement, up in the treble register. This is done differently in the symphony than in the quartet, by means of a fourfold fanfare. But the principle is much the same.

Great contortions in the recapitulation and coda go hand in hand with the singular aspect of the development sections in these works. Writing the *Eroica*, Beethoven experienced his vision of a gargantuan development, less a digression than a journey of exploration, proliferating into many distant episodes which bespeak personal energies over and beyond the prescriptions of the exposition proper. Not only do the developments of the *Eroica* and the Quartet in F run longer than the respective expositions—in itself an unusual circumstance—but the proportional lengths are almost identical, about 3:2 in each case. The development of the *Eroica* includes a fragmentary but very impressive double *fugato;* the double *fugato* in the quartet is larger, more formal and more central. In each case Beethoven mops up the *fugato* in the same curious way, by swirling it up into a passage of inchoate, angry noise. Here, certainly, the palm goes to the treatment in the symphony—the matchless stripping away of melody, harmony, and rhythm until only dissonant noise remains, a descent into the dark night of the heroic soul. By comparison, the diminished-7th chord in the quartet seems more than a little perfunctory.

For Beethoven, massive developments like these needed to incorporate some decidedly new material. In the quartet, as we saw, this is the main fugue subject. The fugue is central here. The new element in the symphony is the famous E-minor theme introduced after the inchoate crisis following the *fugato*. The symphony includes a number of effects of slow tonal diversion recalling the rhapsodic violin deflection from F major to D♭ early in the quartet development. Both works, finally, plan some special excruciation at the point of recapitulation—they had to, after the immensity of developmental action. The "wrong-beat" horn entry of the *Eroica* finds a parallel in the brilliant reversal of first-group material in the quartet recapitulation.

The analogy between the two first movements comes in scope and technique, not at all in mood. Lacking in the quartet is the sense of inner conflict that first drove Beethoven, it would seem, to his heroic vision. He was not doing a *quartetto eroico;* the piece rather resists programmatic imaginings. For all its powerful drives and sharp explosions and new revelations, the quartet breathes an abstract quality that sets it in a different emotional sphere from the symphony. Its drives and explosions and revelations do not seem to emerge in response to conflict; rather, they are working out certainties, investigating tonal properties. Massive control, even a certain commanding serenity marks this movement—symbolized, perhaps, by the double fugue in the development, with its new theme, its energetic level gestures, and its crowning position within the movement as a whole.

As for the quality of tonal investigation in the quartet movement, this hinges on a crux of two notes, F and G, the tonic and second degree of the F-major scale. One may hear, or construe, the step from F up to G as a kernel not only of the rising-scale motif, but also of the whole idea of ascent. This basic idea is expressed at the beginning, as the theme screens tonal space; at the end, as F and G extinguish themselves below the violin high C; and at many striking points between. F and G mark the first forceful arrivals in the exposition, capping the dramatic tension of the theme itself. G supports the quite long, majestic preparation for the second theme (the G-major triad, dominant of C). Indeed, the juncture of F-major and G-major triads becomes a familiar sound in this composition. (The triads arise, of course, as a deepening of the crux of the notes themselves—another instance of the harmonic extension of a melodic detail such as occurs prominently already in the earliest of the

Op. 18 Quartets.) F- and G-major sonorities make the abrupt modulation in the original bridge, and they sharply salt the triumphant harmonized version of the theme in the coda:

Example 50

The G-major triad alters the fourth degree of the F-major scale, B♭, to B♮, canceling the subdominant (IV). In fact, the coda and the recapitulation avoid subdominant sounds like the plague. Harmonies of the sixth degree are used instead: that long D♭ (♭VI) in the recapitulation, and the ultimate progression in the coda, using D minor (vi). The latter progression—it is illustrated on page 96—makes a curiously effective modal cadence; does not the piece as a whole tend towards a loose modality, Lydian in fact? It is a later F-major composition, the *Heiliger Dankgesang* of the Quartet in A minor, Op. 132, that will strike a self-conscious Lydian pose. But already this movement—by its avoidance of the subdominant, by its insistence on G with B♮ above it, by its concluding modal touch—cultivates the slightly ethercal, very distinctive harmonic flavor of the Lydian mode.

This fact may help explain why the next movement of the quartet, the *Allegretto vivace e sempre scherzando*, was set by the composer in the unprecedented key of B♭, the subdominant. And this *Scherzando* is an even more extraordinary movement than the opening *Allegro*. Unprecedented indeed.

· 3 ·

At the start, thematic material is presented in what Tovey would call "a vision of dry bones." The monotone rhythm that inspires the whole piece appears first as an antecedent phrase, answered—with a sharp, characteristic dissociation of register—by a consequent phrase which modulates:

Example 51

To compare this with the unaccompanied opening of the *Scherzo* (also in B♭) of the "Archduke" Trio is to see, once again, the extremity of Beethoven's intention in the present work, and to clarify the "normality" of the trio.

Later in the piece, the consequent phrase proves susceptible to radical melodic transformations:

Example 52

In the last rearrangement shown, the monotone merely serves as a preface. The original consequent (transformed) has become an antecedent, with new consequences.

Then the vision can be bodied forth in many different ways: in a very important *fortissimo* combination with canonic overtones—

Example 53

and in a recapitulation (in G♭ major) with wispy new countersubjects—

Example 54

and with one of those countersubjects in free inversion, and a free canon thrown in—

Example 55

Contrapuntal work is ostentatious, once again, just as in the first movement of the quartet and in every one of the Op. 18 series.

What seems to be central to this *Allegretto vivace e sempre scherzando* is not counterpoint in the ordinary sense, but the very process of bodying out. That sounds Beethovenian enough in spirit, though as a matter of fact he never elsewhere worked in just this way. A parallel may be thought to exist with the dynamic principle of the first movement of the quartet, which relies on the expansion of a theme in its repetitions and on the reinterpretation of one note within it. The *Eroica* first movement does something similar. But instead of the more typical sense of deepening or revelation in the thematic transformations, here on the contrary the effect is one of wonder and whimsy—Beethoven starts from something impossibly slight and carries it to implausible lengths, in bewildering diversity. There, a sense of cumulative growth, here of discontinuous transformation. The quality, in a word, is exactly appropriate to the sentiment named: *sempre scherzando.*

And if the fact of paradoxical bodying-out was central to Beethoven's conception, one can see why traditional sonata form—no less than the simple *A B A* "minuet and trio" scheme—proved inadequate to the intrinsic urge of his material. Sonata form is antithetical to the idea of paradoxical variation. At least in Beethoven's hands, sonata form worked out the given potential of themes, rather than displaying them in fascinating, novel, essentially additive guises. That was the sphere of the theme and variations, a much less dynamic musical form which a less sophisticated aesthetic had been able to encompass perfectly well. One thinks of the chaconnes and passacaglias of the Baroque era. Significantly enough, the closest parallel to the inner process of the present movement comes in Beethoven's so-called *Eroica* Variations, Op. 35, and in the work developed from them, the Finale of the *Eroica* Symphony.

So in the present instance Beethoven was driven to a thoroughly novel formal synthesis. Though the piece contains such obvious sonata-form elements as an exciting development section, it cannot without absurdity be pressed into a standard sonata mold—Vincent d'Indy and most other commentators to the contrary. The form—which is to say, the expressive shape—of this movement is *sui generis*, an imaginative combination of elements familiar in themselves from the dance forms and from the more highly organized sonata forms, but never associated in just this way. Sonata principles are in play, but the customary framework for these principles, "sonata form," is simply not present.

What is present—as a first level—is a ground-plan that was now interesting Beethoven in the Fourth Symphony and in the E-minor "Razumovsky" Quartet, a double Scherzo | Trio | Scherzo | Trio | Scherzo alternation. But the plan is raised to quite another level by tonal activity and by the corresponding inserted development section:

Scherzando I	Trio I →	Development	Scherzando II	Trio II →	Scherzando III
B♭	F minor	modulates	B♭—but rewritten with broad tonal digressions	Same as Trio I, transposed to B♭ minor	B♭, much abbreviated

What I wish to hear (with Riemann) as the "trio" behaves on the whole conventionally, beginning after a stop and ending after a formal cadence prior to the transition into the development section. It introduces a fairly sharp contrast of mode, tone, and material; it shapes itself as an elementary little ternary structure, with the second member repeated, and with only one odd bar to disturb the dancelike regularity of 4-bar phrases. At its second appearance, in B♭ minor, the "trio" barely changes.

The *scherzando* sections, on the other hand, are unique in construction and in rhetoric; they fall into nothing resembling a conventional dance form. Furthermore, they differ radically from one another, not so much in material as in harmonic action:

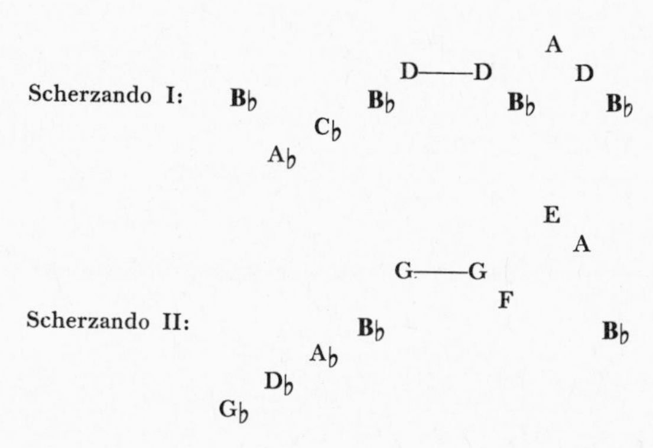

These diagrams are meant to chart the sequence of keys, from left to right, with bold-face type reserved for the clear tonic sections, which are the centrally important ones. Modulations happen so abruptly, even in *Scherzando* I, that in spite of really revolving around B♭, this section sounds unstable enough to encourage (indeed, to require) a development section later. It is the first and third bold-face B♭ areas that accommodate the mysteriously quiet "dry bones" versions of the thematic material, illustrated on page 104; in each place, the paradox of texture is compounded by paradoxical harmonic movement (B♭–A♭–C♭, then B♭–A–D). Both kinds of paradox are soon dispelled by the loud, triumphant, fully harmonized version of the theme, in the second and fourth B♭ areas. (The second B♭ area, near the beginning of the piece, does double service: as resolution of the paradox and as transition to the long contrasting D-minor section following.) The third and fourth B♭ areas act together as a loose *da capo*. The fourth one does not cadence, however, running instead to an expectant dominant and the stop which demarcates the "trio."

Scherzando II makes a wonderful free expansion of this tonal dynamic. Here the "dry bones" versions are always fleshed out with kaleidoscopic counterpoints, and the harmonic digressions are more serious than before—much more serious: G♭–D♭–A♭ in the first instance, and F–E–A in the second. These doubly paradoxical statements resolve to the same loud, fully harmonized tonic versions. But now the tonic has been reached in the first instance by a deeply subdominant route (I am reminded of the Finale of Schubert's C-major Symphony) and in the second, as though to balance, by way of the dominant.

Tonic centrality is kept in all three *scherzando* sections, then, though in *Scherzando* II Beethoven certainly seems to have stretched things as far as he dared. Much depends on recollection of the first time around and on the brute fact of *fortissimo* in the resolving B♭ places. Throughout, the tonal pattern is more dissociated (on the diagrams, more spread out vertically) than that of *Scherzando* I. All this runs contrary to sonata-form orthodoxy, of course, which would have the last statement of a large section harmonically *more* stable than the first, not less so, as here. A strong new dominant (the F) in a "recapitulation" would be particularly shocking. But once again, this is no sonata-form movement. Because after *Scherzando* II Beethoven intends to return at length to the tonic with "Trio" II, he can dare and profit from unorthodox tonal fragmentation.

Scherzando III, a concluding summary statement, brings the original theme in its original tonal position (but not in its original bare-bones texture). There is a reminiscence of the distant modulations of the development, dispelled once again by the theme fully harmonized (but no longer *fortissimo*):

Scherzando III: B♭ — A♭ — C♭ — reminiscence of development modulations — B♭

At this reminiscence, what serves to jog the memory is the progression F–F♯, for a hard juxtaposition of F and F♯ (G♭) had served both to begin the development and to end it. The first-movement development comes to mind, too. The present development, it should be said, works excitedly up the circle of 5ths—and introduces its own radical thematic transformations and bodyings-out.

One other technical feature should be mentioned, one that associates the movement with the opening *Allegro:* the conspicuous play of registers. There is even a parallel to the odd Webern-like place in the first movement:

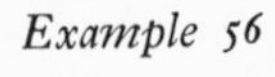
Example 56

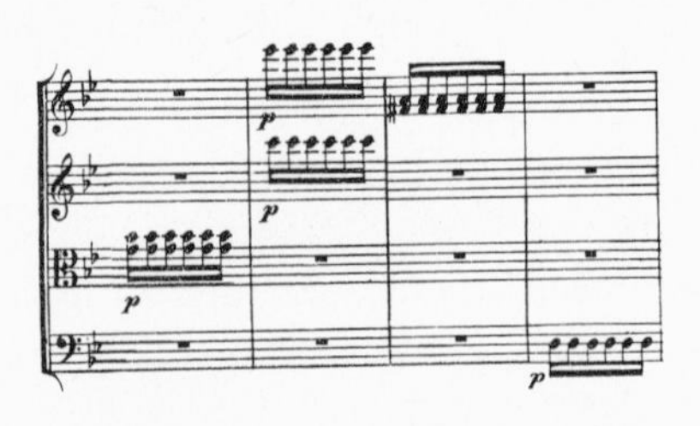

As can be seen in part (but only in part) from the various music examples above, the main theme itself tends to reappear with its octave registers freshly dissociated. The tension established by the first bars—the melodic consequent phrase octaves above the monotone antecedent—develops dizzily up to the amusing "sprung" gestures at the very end of the movement.

But these descriptions, once again, can give only a bloodless impression of this extraordinary piece of music. A. B. Marx dutifully counted (so Helm dutifully reports) ten shifting moods within it; that was his way of articulating something about its imaginative juxtapositions and its intense inflections of detail. By these qualities, he might have added, the movement forecasts Beethoven's third period in technique, if not in mood. Since fertility is at the heart of the conception, all the explosions, contortions, dartings, contrasts, and paradoxes are in a certain sense functional. This posed Beethoven an interesting formal problem, which he solved a great deal better than most analysts have been able to trace. Brilliant flexibility was needed in the form, too—and achieved, certainly; but on the other hand, the form had to hold all the manifold unpredictabilities in shape. So it is that the Scherzo | Trio | Scherzo | Trio | Scherzo alternation provides a certain humdrum stability offsetting all the adventure; and the adventure itself moves, after all, almost always to the same goal, the triumphant embodiment of the vision of dry bones in the home tonic B♭, *fortissimo*. Through it all, even somehow through the contrasting "trio," the original monotone rhythm broods or mutters or clangs: now subsidiary, now bodied out, now only a vestige, now—and ultimately—the bare loud resolving substance of the whole machine.

It is tempting to speak of this movement as an experimental one, if only because Beethoven never wrote anything else remotely like it. But that cannot be because of any lack of success in the "experiment"; the piece was never conceived as a study in some kind of *cul de sac;* the analogy of experimental method simply does not hold in art. Everything works—and "everything" includes incredible things. As an individual musical structure, this *Allegretto vivace e sempre scherzando* is one of the signal masterpieces of the second period, as much so as the opening *Allegro.*

· 4 ·

The *Scherzando* had defected to the subdominant, B♭; the main key of the quartet is restored by the third movement, *Adagio molto e mesto* in F minor. A full-scale slow movement in the minor mode is a rarity in Beethoven, especially past the first period. Besides the present quartet and the C-major "Razumovsky," the important examples occur in the

Eroica and Seventh Symphonies, the "Ghost" Trio and the D-major Cello Sonata, the Fourth Piano Concerto—a rather special case—and the Piano Sonatas in B♭ and A♭, Op. 106 and 110. Of all these, the present *Adagio molto e mesto* is doubtless the most profoundly tragic in intention, an essay in misery scarcely relieved by any response of sobriety or solace. The contrast with the ebullience of the first two movements is likely to catch the listener up very sharply.

In this respect the piece looks back to the *Adagio* of another F-major Quartet, Op. 18, No. 1, and it looks back in other respects too. For both movements, programmatic notes of pathetic import have been found scribbled against the sketches—a curious coincidence: with the early quartet, *Les derniers soupirs* of Romeo and Juliet, with the present one, *Einen Trauerweiden oder Akazien-Baum aufs Grab meines Bruders*, "A Weeping Willow or Acacia Tree over my Brother's Grave." The inspiration was as fictional in the one case as in the other, by the way: neither of Beethoven's brothers was dead when the quartet was written. (The Drs. Sterba have much to say about the composer's fraternal relationships.) In each case, one strongly suspects that an extramusical impetus must have stayed too close to the surface to permit the work of art to succeed as a free emotional artifact. Sentimentality was clouding Beethoven's vision; the technique is very impressive indeed, once again, but there is something overblown in the expression, something in the feeling that the technique does not properly support.

The actual sentiment naturally differs from that of Op. 18, No. 1. The rage, energy, and high tragedy of that *Adagio affettuoso ed ap-*

Example 57

passionato have turned into anguish, dejection, *mestizia* here. The mood is much richer, it must be said, and closer to the ceremonial grief writ large of the *Marcia funebre* in the *Eroica* Symphony, some of whose accents seem echoed here. Yet a certain objectivity and decorum makes the symphony seem both more genuinely touching and more sincere. The main theme of the *Adagio e mesto* is admirably calculated, with its hollow 5ths, its *appoggiaturas*, and its extreme compounded series of melodic dissonances. (The emphasis on the ♭VII degree, E♭, recalls the "trio" of the *Scherzando*, which had also figured in F minor; perhaps something Russian already informs these melodies, with their slight modal shading.) Calculation apart, however, the theme strives too greedily for gloom by means of insistent *appoggiaturas*, and it risks more than it prudently should through the weeping descant of its repetition. The gesture toward the relative major sounds a little glib; Beethoven makes it sound more so by repeating it at once with a decoration; and by adding a florid touch at the recapitulation, he will make it sound positively tawdry:

Example 58

Even the second subject of this movement must come in the minor mode, the dominant minor. The rich, very beautiful sequence emerging from it takes care to flush out many minor-mode sonorities; more of the traditional rhetoric of the minor mode is manipulated in the long series of cadences that follows. But these cadences harp on a note of despair ill sustained by the structure of the exposition as a whole. Once it occurs to the listener that one of them may be supererogatory, the entire emotional façade falls under suspicion. And the tempo, according to Beethoven's metronome mark, is set extremely slow.

A development section starts with a rather inexplicable turn to the major mode—which denatures the second subject when it now appears in this mode. After some modulations, a superb section ensues in which *pizzicato* cello *arpeggios* hold together fragmented, and agonized, canons on sections of the first theme. By the largest reckoning, the subsequent dominant preparation prior to the recapitulation lasts 17 bars—this in a movement whose entire exposition lasts only 45. The reckoning includes a striking digression to a new hymnlike tune perched in D♭ major, over and away from the dominant C. This frank *maggiore* balances the A♭ major which opened the development; perhaps both of them were needed to relieve the continual *minore* sonorities elsewhere in the piece. The note of consolation is unmistakable, yet once again excessive, fulsome, and essentially unearned.

Instead of an independent coda, this *Adagio* has another return of the desolate main theme (complete with its unpleasant florid touch, in octaves). For a last point of intensity, the violin brings the melody slowly down two octaves as the cello moves up and up to meet it; the converging lines almost meet, in a fine ultimate excruciation of D and D♭. At this point an emotional resolution is maneuvered which rings truer than the prayerful D♭ episode in the development. Gradually the violin shakes itself free of the texture and of the tragic obsession, and curls its way upward in a sort of fluttering cadenza. (One remembers the leisurely rhapsody of the violin in the development of the opening *Allegro*.) This transition—to the Finale—is perfectly gauged in psychological justness and in its larger rhythm. With a sense of almost physical release, the violin ascends to the very high C, three octaves above middle C, while the other instruments ground it airily by means of scales down to the low cello C. Then the violin too cascades down to a trill, still on C, waiting for the Finale.

"*Allegro. Thème russe*," Beethoven writes at the head of the new movement, with some satisfaction, it would seem, and with evident satisfaction the little Russian folk song turns up at once in the cello. According to rather imprecise tradition, the incorporation of Russian material

Example 59

in these quartets was the idea of Count Razumovsky, who was not only a Russian but the Russian Ambassador. The violin extends its trill unchecked; there is no further accompaniment. Perhaps the first thing we sense—besides relief after the mourning *Adagio*—is a curious external similarity to the theme of the first movement. A pulsing C on top of a hollow harmony, and a deep cello melody rising from the fifth degree to the tonic: Beethoven is making a subtle parallel with, or comment on, or parody of his opening *Allegro*.

The distinctions are egregious, of course, and they arise from the nature of the *thème russe*. The indefatigable Nottebohm found both this theme and the one used in the E-minor "Razumovsky" Quartet in a certainly contemporary folk song collection, one particular copy of which bears annotations in Beethoven's hand. The present song really belongs in D minor; originally dubbed *Molto andante* by its collector, it gains gusto from its emphasis on the "modal" ♭VII degree, C. The parallel with the two F-minor themes of the "trio" and the *Adagio*, with their E♭'s, is interesting, all the more so because Beethoven now refuses to take the song in its proper mode. Without having to change any notes, he wrests it into a cheery paradoxical F-major context by further emphasis of that very C. The initial D becomes an *appoggiatura* on to the dominant C, instead of a tonic, and later outlines of D minor in the tune are swept under the rug. Clear results of this odd procedure enliven the further progress of the movement.

An air of good-natured parody is present: for example, in the canons, which instantly start chiming away at the folk song, and, a little later, at the otherwise rather slight second subject. At the end of the piece, Beethoven plays various tricks on the *thème russe*, combining two of its phrases to make a comic double counterpoint, and then slowing it down to a pretentious *adagio*. This last transformation is not all for fun. Mock-expressive chromatic harmonies light up a not-so-secret A-major harmony (dominant of D minor) which is implicit in the tune but which had been avoided in the F-major interpretation previously.

The beginning of the song combines with bridge material, amusingly, in the development section, which modulates far before settling. It settles to a suspiciously long and vigorous D-minor plateau; this key would seem to make amends for the D minor that was short-changed within the *thème russe* itself. The way out is ingenious. Quietly things slip down from D minor to C minor, then to B♭—and in this key, the subdominant,

Example 60

the recapitulated folk song returns unexpectedly, its initial D now treated as a full-fledged subdominant. Altering one of the notes, Beethoven now wants us to hear the modal melody—which is really in D minor, which he has previously always pressed into F—as beginning in a third tonality, B♭. This reinterpretation bears a certain fantastic, lightly touched analogy to the reinterpretations of thematic material that are at the basis of the conception of the opening movement of the quartet.

Recapitulation by way of the subdominant certainly counts as an original effect, which Beethoven was to employ less wittily, and more expressively, in the first movement of the Sixth Symphony. (The symphony is in F, too.) Is the subdominant episode here an inverted reflection of the *avoidance* of the subdominant in the opening *Allegro?* or of the aberrant placement of the *Scherzando* in the subdominant key? The present recapitulation, in any case, makes no reference to the opening texture of the exposition, which so strikingly recalled the first movement —the solo cello with the violin C pulsing above it. That texture, one must therefore conclude, does not serve as an important functional thing in this movement, as it does in the other. Its role can only be understood as one of reminiscence or linkage.

There is another similar situation. The end of the exposition in the Finale employs the same cascade down from high C to the trill as was used to graft the Finale on to the *Adagio* (the notes in the violin correspond exactly, even though the notation differs and the speed is half as fast again, according to Beethoven's metronome marks). Since this detail too is omitted at the balancing place at the end of the recapitulation, presumably it too has to be understood principally as a link with the earlier movement.

In all this, we may come to feel some of the same exhilaration in the abstract investigation of tonal properties as informs the great opening *Allegro*. The last movement of the Quartet in F, besides being the only Beethoven movement to engage seriously with a Russian tune, ranks as one of the most elegant, spirited, and forthright of his finales—and the finale was always the touchy movement. That it strikes a tone wrongly scaled to the quartet as a whole, however, has been generally felt and expressed by the commentators in one way or another. The problem is a subtle one, because the Finale fits excellently with the *Adagio;* its slightly strained high spirits make a fine intellectual foil to those exaggerated tears, and the psychological transition is very wonderfully managed. But whereas the *Adagio*, sentimental or not, will pass as sheer relaxation after the two exhaustive early statements, the Finale leaves one wanting something more or at least something different—something heavier, I am afraid. There are some intrinsically less interesting movements that succeed better at the end of Beethoven pieces. The Finale of the Sixth Symphony is one. In the quartet, Beethoven was writing at the very top of his form, but his instinct for the larger coherence faltered.

In the light of this, the links mentioned above are especially interesting. The need for binding up the whole did not escape the composer. Already with the quartets of Op. 18, he was concerning himself with unification of the four-movement form; interrelationships of one kind or another are to be observed in all the early quartets. But in a way, the revolution of the *Eroica* Symphony seems to have marked a temporary setback to this development, or rather, a radical deepening of the terms of the problem, which was bound to delay its solution. The individual movements now grow so terrific that even Beethoven cannot always face them appropriately one to the next. Only the Ninth Symphony—not yet the Third—succeeds in assembling four titanic statements as a fully coherent whole, and then of course only by means of very special strategies. Among the quartets, it is the C♯ minor, Op. 131, of 1826 that achieves the deepest sense of total integration.

With the F-major Quartet, the *hubris* that conceived and executed the opening movement must have destined the difficulties to come. By a fantastic effort of energy Beethoven matched the opening movement by the *Scherzando;* then he seems to have felt driven to a lament as excessively mournful as the *Scherzando* is excessively brilliant. The suspicion of flatulence about this formidable *Adagio molto e mesto* suddenly suggests something unwieldy, and therefore inexpressive, about the sequence of the composition as a whole. The Finale can convincingly dispel the lament—in itself an emotional accomplishment of great power —but Beethoven really gave up the ambition to produce another statement on the scale dictated by the earlier three. Or did the very medium of the string quartet begin to appear insufficient to accommodate his grandiose vision, in spite of the *tour de force* of the opening *Allegro?* It is perhaps no accident that the next two finales, those of the E-minor and C-major "Razumovsky" Quartets, pointedly aspire to symphonic style and proportion.

Again the *Eroica* Symphony comes to haunt this discussion of the Quartet in F; for these are exactly the two main masterpieces of Beethoven, I think, that wrestle most seriously with the problem of the individuation of single movements. One feels after the first movement of the *Eroica* much as one feels after the first or second movement of the quartet—that so exhaustive an experience has been conveyed, and in so many facets, as to make any further communication superfluous. The *Marcia funebre* in the symphony carries off the impossible, but in both works the later movements are set awkwardly for the total impression. Mention has been made of the obvious technical parallels between the opening movements in the two compositions, and of a certain emotional kinship between their tragic *Adagios*. There are other parallels: for sheer overflowing variety of material and treatment, no compositions at this period can approach the first movement of the symphony and the *Allegretto vivace e sempre scherzando* of the quartet, though the two movements may have nothing else in common beyond their astonishing exuberance. Even the two finales are alike in setting themselves a delicate and uncommon task, the treatment of pre-existing material.

To say that the quartet occupies the same place within the genre as does the symphony within its genre is to say little, for after the Op. 18 Quartets anything written in 1805 would have had much the same effect. More than that: in various ways, the quartet seems to refer back to the *Eroica* Symphony itself, not merely in a general way to its revolutionary new sense of scope and freedom. Even though clear evidence from the sketchbooks is lacking, one would wish to think of the Quartet in F maturing in Beethoven's mind not long after the *Eroica*—the first towering peak, perhaps, this side of the watershed. It was inevitable that the Fourth Symphony and the next quartets should represent in some sense a retrenchment.

The image of what we take as our musical tradition is marked indelibly by the strengths and weaknesses of Beethoven's second period—or better, by its perfections and its excesses. The F-major "Razumovsky" Quartet stands with the *Eroica* at dead center of that image, magnificent embodiment of both.

5

THE "RAZUMOVSKY" QUARTETS

Quartet in E Minor, Op. 59, No. 2
Quartet in C Major, Op. 59, No. 3

After the *Eroica*, Beethoven's compositions become to a cardinal degree pointed individuals. Such a statement may seem distressingly untechnical, and hardly promising from the point of view of a developing criticism. But in the last analysis, it is a truism that ought not to be lost to view. If one were told to select one single metaphor for the *Eroica* Symphony, the "Emperor" Concerto, or a quartet from Op. 59, what would first come to mind—an organism, an action, an epic, a spiritual exercise, a demonstration, a train of emotion, an ordering of time? A mature Beethoven piece, I think I should be inclined to say, is a *person;* one meets and reacts to it with the same sort of particularity, intimacy, and concern as one does to another human being. The same cannot quite be said of Mozart's music, nor of Brahms's, nor certainly of Beethoven's earlier music. This personal quality goes some way to explain the stubborn universal impressiveness of the middle-period works, that *Humanität* which the German critics write about so feelingly. Beethoven seems to have struggled to project in art the quality of human contact that he saw himself cut off from by deafness and by the daemon of creation. That, for him personally, was perhaps the essence of the heroic vision.

The last "neutral" symphony was the Second, in D, which was composed over a relatively long period, from 1800 to 1802. D major was the traditional key for a vigorous symphony; Beethoven simply produced an especially good and a notably brainy example. *Mehr Sinfonie, als*

Beethoven, A. B. Marx might have said. But with the *Eroica*, the symphonies become such individuals—such "originals," in fact—that it is not surprising to see them sprout characterizing titles, descriptive subtitles, and even a Schiller poem with voices to declaim it. Had Fontenelle been there to ask "*Symphonie, que me veux-tu?*" the Ninth Symphony would have told him, for now the symphony is talking, talking back. With the piano sonatas, as usual, the revolution was adumbrated a little sooner, after the *Grande Sonate* in B♭, which was written together with the last of the Op. 18 Quartets. The "Moonlight" Sonata comes to mind at once; also at this time Beethoven published his first Bagatelles for piano, forerunners of the so-called "character piece" of Chopin, Schumann, Liszt, and the nineteeth-century salon musicians. Among the piano concertos, Beethoven's Third is still a genre piece; the Fourth and Fifth are people. Only Leonore and Florestan, or so we may consider, fail dumbly where instrumental pieces (and even their own Overtures) succeed better. Yet their failure is by no means certain, and in any case to be qualified in ways which it would take us far afield to analyze here.

Entstehungszeit: 1805–6 is about all the Beethoven specialists are able to tell about the time of composition of the "Razumovsky" Quartets. Though they are known to have been projected at the end of 1804, the autograph of the first was not written until May 1806. Work on them would have begun after the "Waldstein" and soon after the *Appassionata* Sonatas, in 1804, and must have been inextricably mixed with the final labors on *Fidelio* and on its subsequent revision (the first two performances of *Fidelio* came in November 1805 and March 1806). In the absence of contrary information, it is to be assumed that the three quartets were composed in their order of publication; next to nothing is known about Count Razumovsky's commission, except the story that he asked Beethoven to make use of Russian folk songs. During the same period the Fourth Piano Concerto was written. Add to these works the small Piano Sonata in F, Op. 54, and the not very small or agreeable Triple Concerto, not forgetting the three *Leonore* Overtures, and there emerges a series of at least nine major compositions for the three-year period after the *Eroica* Symphony of 1803. The Fourth Symphony followed the quartets directly. The Fifth mulled in Beethoven's head all through these years and did not settle out until some time later.

His conquest of the genres of musical composition is nearly complete: in no more than half a dozen years, symphony, sonata, concerto, opera, and quartet have yielded up a series of works of almost mythic celebrity and power. The three "Razumovsky" Quartets constitute a trio of sharply characterized, consciously differentiated individuals, beside whom the earlier quartets look, regrettably, like pasteboard. A big-boned creature, strong as iron, the Quartet in F breathes a certain athletic and intellectual self-confidence in its fast movements—and suffers an exaggerated contrast of grim tragedy in the middle. On the contrary, the Quartet in E minor, Op. 59, No. 2, struggles repeatedly with pathos all through its compressed, nervous fast movements, admitting in its middle an exaggerated contrast of rather grim serenity. The movements of the F-major Quartet grow so absorbed in their own processes as to leave the sequence of the entire work in doubt. But the E-minor Quartet is ready to check the full elaboration of the single movements in view of the integrity of the whole; there are deliberate simplicities in its layout, and as a result of this and other factors the piece holds together more stiffly than its brothers. The sentiment of the beginning is convincingly met at the end. The most decided overall dynamic is exhibited by the third quartet, the Quartet in C: a herald for the Fifth Symphony, it leads up to a Finale of great loudness and tub-thumping emphasis. And from the very first diminished-7th chord of its arcane slow Introduction, there is an air of conspicuous oddity about this composition—in its rambling cadenza of a first subject, in the runic folk-lament of its *Andante*, in its startlingly rococo *Menuetto: Grazioso*, and in its thoroughly unmanageable ending fugue.

If the C-major Quartet seems ready to go off the cliff at any minute, in this it only exaggerates a quality discernible in the others. None of them is a work at rest; all of them are explorers, and Beethoven may have been as amazed as anyone else to see where they were going. The symphony, it is usually said, dominated his progressing consciousness during the second period, as the piano sonata did in the first period, and the string quartet only late in the third. However, between the *Eroica* Symphony and the Fourth, quartets take over the leading role—"symphonized" quartets if you like, quartets of a scope beyond the experience and comprehension of Beethoven's contemporaries. Even the men in the Schuppanzigh Quartet laughed (nervously, perhaps) at passages in the F-major piece, and it was a complaint by their leader about this very composition that is supposed to have brought forth Beethoven's famous squelch: "Do you think I worry about your wretched fiddle when the spirit speaks to me?" Conservative composers such as Gyrowetz and the Abbé Stadler seem to have taken special offense at this music. Says Thayer: "Perhaps no work of Beethoven's met a more discouraging reception from musicians than these now famous Quartets." [1]

They were the first great works by Beethoven to have been lost on

[1] P. 409.

their essential audience. That is an ominous tribute to their temerity, and to their unprecedented individuality as well.

· 2 ·

The first movement of the Quartet in E minor, Op. 59, No. 2, stands almost alone in Beethoven's output for the wispiness of its thematic material. If the long opening melody of the Quartet in F soon reveals itself as a rich arsenal of motivic supply, the present movement creates an even more urgent sense of motivic promise without presenting any melodies at all. This is as true of the second group as of the first; Beethoven lays out the phraseology and manages the flow more subtly than ever before in the quartets, but he does not let his material coalesce very far beyond 2-bar melodic fragments. This quality—with much else—goes to paint the essential humor of the composition, a compound of brusqueness, tenseness, and hypersensitivity. The piece is more brusque than violent, more tense than angry, hypersensitive rather than actually in pain.

The quintessential note is struck by the very beginning, and also by the very end:

Example 61

As an alert, compressed, peremptory gesture, the first two bars beat even the Fifth Symphony. The moment of rest is marvelously evocative and typical. As for the last bars, they bring the broken-triad motif not in its habitual high-strung *pianissimo*, but for the first time *fortissimo*. Beethoven loved to reinterpret quiet themes loudly, as appears from many admirable passages in the F-major Quartet. But whereas each of those makes for a forceful culmination, this one is only a spasm, quenched as soon as it is allowed to flare, and with its raw nerve-endings—I refer to the insistent C–B steps—never entirely cauterized.

Indeed the movement as a whole is too nervous to engage in the massive expansion that is such a striking feature of the first movement of the F-major Quartet. It grows subtly in the small, that is to say, on the level of individual gestures and phrases, but much less in the large. The reinterpretations of the first theme—in the coda, the brief moment of emphasis just mentioned; at the recapitulation, the filling up of the evocative rests—seem merely interesting and efficient rather than revelatory. In spite of them, the recapitulation mirrors the exposition closely, and the beginning of the coda matches the beginning of the development section exactly. These two beginnings stand out conspicuously enough—explosively would be the better word; and Beethoven insists further on symmetry by expressly requiring repetition not only of the exposition but also of the entire development plus recapitulation. Now, the nineteenth century found little use for these traditional sonata-form repetitions, particularly the second of them. The F-major first movement is one of the earliest sonata-allegro movements from which both are dropped; the E-minor is one of the last in which both are retained. This seemingly mechanical difference reflects two divergent interpretations of sonata form, one of them more progressive, the other more symmetrical. Beethoven appreciated the difference already with the Op. 18 Quartets, and he seized upon it and refined it in the execution of these first two members of Op. 59.

It is certainly time these sonata-form repetitions began to be played as a regular thing in concert and recorded performances. Years ago, perhaps one worried about running a movement for a full eleven minutes, or perhaps one judged Beethoven's intention (which is quite plain: he went to the trouble of composing alternate transitions) absurd. From the modern repertory, however, players should have learned to suffer even more "absurd" intentions on the part of composers, sometimes to the very peril of their instruments, and even greater lengths. We have had Reger and Penderecki. If both repetitions in the E-minor movement were played, the compressed flow of ideas might sit in the ear less cryptically than it is apt to do in most current performances. The symmetry would have to be coped with; it could not be escaped. The size of the first movement might better balance, and so prepare, the very lengthy *Adagio*.

To see something of the subtlety of construction in the small, an extended extract is needed (see p. 122). As has been mentioned, Beethoven avoids forming his heady material into large melodic periods. The opening bar—a gauntlet, a metronome stroke, a primordial motif—outlines a 5th with enough sinew to stand by itself as an antecedent statement (a resource soon to be employed, in bar 19). But at present, what follows is heard not as a consequent but as an astonishing filling-out of the open-

Example 62

ing gesture. Melodically, the 5th is decorated with more substantial motivic materials—the broken-triad motif, and sixteenth-notes lunging at the upper neighbor, C, as though to anticipate the next sequential step. Harmonically, the bare progression i–V deepens to i–♭II–vii–V, encompassing the Neapolitan second degree, ♭II, in the boldest possible manner. This harmony will not be forgotten. Rhythmically, the two bars stretch to ten; the pair of 3-bar phrases with their evocative rests seems to need a final 4-bar dominant for stability, or at least four bars during which the dominant is searched out tentatively, in an almost declamatory fashion (bars 9–12). Finally the consequent phrase appears, from bar 13 on, another extended phrase touching ♭II again and swirling into a very emotional cadence.

The cadence is interrupted brusquely, in bar 19, for a sort of compressed repetition of bars 1–18. The two chords serve alone as antecedent, and to match this condensation, the consequent is also much shortened. It races up to the loudest and highest point so far, a *fortissimo* high F, the Neapolitan degree—harmonized, however, as the start of a rapid modulation. The new dominant and the second group follow almost immediately. As in other symmetrical sonata-form movements, such as the first movements of Op. 18, Nos. 5 and 6, a formal bridge passage is absent. Brusqueness of formal procedure goes along with brusqueness of material and of harmonic style.

The latter quality is of course provided right away by the sharp juxtaposition of the tonic and the Neapolitan (i and ♭II) between bars 4 and 6. Neapolitan harmony colors the rest of the movement, and indeed acts as a cementing force for the quartet as a whole. More than that, it forecasts other extremities of harmonic procedure, such as that in the highly explosive passage at the beginning of the development section. This place provides a perfect textbook illustration of Beethoven's expanding harmonic resources, and sounds as strange, rich, and tense as the textbooks promise. When the passage explodes symmetrically a second time to begin the coda, the very structure of the piece is felt to hinge upon the harmonic audacity.

It may be worth pausing for a moment over this matter. The following is a simplified amalgam of Tovey's well-known Tables of Key-Relationships:[2]

		II	*III*			*VI*	
THE DIRECT KEY RELATIONSHIPS:	from a major tonic: →	ii	iii	IV	V	vi	
	from a minor tonic: →	(♭II)	♭III	iv	v	♭VI	♭VII
		(♭*ii*)	♭*iii*			♭*vi*	♭*vii*

This differs from Tovey's original in treating the Neapolitan ♭II as an uneasy, half-time (and thus parenthetical) denizen of the minor mode. The arrows on the diagram mean to say that a major key is related "directly," which is to say most blandly, to five other keys only: ii, iii, IV, V, and vi (C major is related directly to D minor, E minor, F, G, and A

[2] *Beethoven*, pp. 12–13.

minor), and that a minor key is related directly only to ♭III, iv, v, ♭VI, and ♭VII (C minor is related directly to E♭, F minor, G minor, A♭, and B♭). A composer of Bach's era did not typically modulate much further than this, or employ passing harmonies reaching much further. But the classic composers, and pre-eminently Beethoven, expanded this scheme by the systematic mixing of the major and minor modes. This brought into range the italicized keys on the above diagram: via ii, iii, and vi, C major relates "indirectly" to II, III, and VI (to D major, E major, and A major—although Tovey warns of the ambiguity of the I–II relationship). What is more, the major tonic was also construed to relate "indirectly" to those keys which relate directly to the tonic minor. The arrows can crisscross.

The indirect relationships are the more extreme and the more dramatic; on these Beethoven capitalizes for the explosion that initiates the development of the present movement. With the help of the peremptory chords of bar 1, he knocks his way through the following series of indirectly related harmonies with the maximum dispatch:

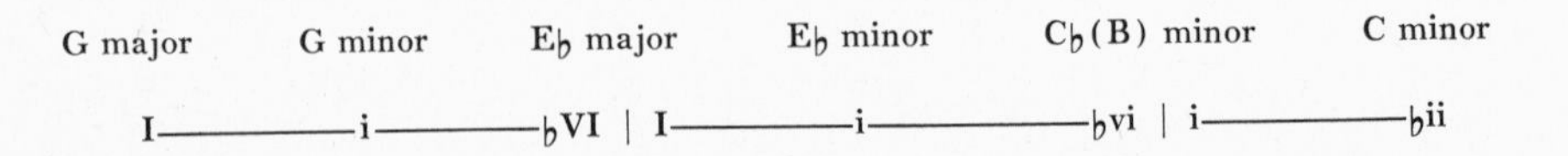

On page 126, the illustration of the beginning of the coda shows the parallel series:

(E major) E minor C major C minor A♭(G♯) minor A minor

(I)——i——♭VI | I——i——♭vi | i——♭ii

In this case, the modulations count as "passing modulations." On page 122, the original modulation to the second group can be seen already to play with similar intensities:

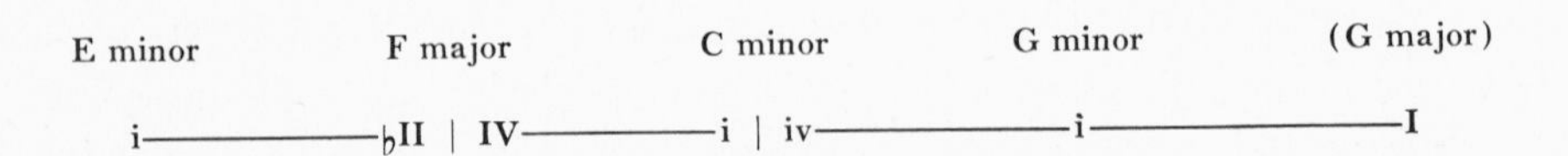

After its violent beginning, the development builds a good deal upon upward bass movement, mostly in semitone steps: B–C, A♭–B♭–B♮–C. This standard device for melodramatic excitement had not yet grown hackneyed in Beethoven's time. The quality of chromatic bass ascent gives this development quite another cast from that of the F-major Quartet, with its slow, almost somnolent excursions; the E-minor development is not only exciting, it is positively theatrical. Its conclusion erupts magnificently. After the upward harmonic crawling has destroyed all sense of key, strong measures are needed to restore the tonal equilibrium, and the piece settles in A minor, the subdominant, where Beethoven actually brings back great swaths of first-group material, little altered. (This sounds less stable than the account suggests, because the first-group material was never very stable in the first place.) By means of a repetition involving a pathetic *ritardando*, bars 19–25 of the original material are drawn out to 16 bars, working directly (as in bar 26) to a modulating sequence propelled by an off-beat trill. Whereas in the exposition the sequence moved down from F, now it vaults imperiously upward, by whole-tone steps in the violin and by semitones, again, in the bass:

B♭ C D E

B♭ B C C♯ D D♯ E

Here the sequence breaks into a unison of tremendous power, practically bursting with the trill idea. And allowing for octave transposition, the march is carried up one step further, to F♯, the true non-Neapolitan second degree which prepares the dominant. Curtly, after four more shattering bars, the tonic key and the recapitulation ensue.

This is all high drama. The evocative rests that aerate the first theme are filled by sixteenth-note figuration from the development, an imaginative addition which makes for continuity as well as for climax. After this, the recapitulation holds to the course of the exposition symmetrically, though by no means rigidly. The second group returns in the tonic major. It would have gone easily into the minor, but only at the risk of redundancy with characteristic minor-mode sonorities such as the Neapolitan.

The piece is perfectly definite in its actions, but its strength is strength through strain. Everything seems to contribute to the impression of tenseness. For instance, the mercurial second group incorporates an unnatural amount of highly expressive detailed inflection—unnatural on account of the tempo; the resulting quality is of emotionality self-consciously rushed, of sentiment constrained by the taut formal outlines. The one respite is gained in the coda, in a very beautiful momentary slow-down:

Example 63

This merges with the greatest skill into the most nervous motivic idea of all, a twitchy syncopation from the second group which here concentrates its attention on the step C–B. Over the violent dominant-9th chord, the piece practically bursts, once again. Indeed the step C–B, the upper parallel of the basic Neapolitan step F–E, has never been far distant. It is still echoing in the very last bars, while the first theme flares loudly (p. 120), after new Neapolitan cadences have promised to bring the piece to rest. As is often the case with Mozart, the first movement of this quartet ends just a little inconclusively, in order to link better to the subsequent statement.

One or two general remarks come to mind in connection with devices employed in this movement. As has often been remarked, in his early years Beethoven liked themes that move up sequentially from the tonic to some form of the second degree. Automatic intensity is the first obvious advantage accruing from such upward movement; soon other advantages occurred to him. Themes moving by sequence up to the conventional second degree (ii) are to be found in the First Symphony, the

Overture to *Prometheus*, the String Quintet, Op. 29, and the Quartet, Op. 59, No. 3—all in C major. The "Waldstein" Sonata (also in C) is an instructive deviant. The *Scherzo* of the Quartet in F, Op. 18, No. 1, is another example. Themes involving the much more suggestive Neapolitan second degree (♭II) are to be found in the F-minor *Appassionata* Sonata and in two quartets, this one and the F-minor *Quartetto serioso*, Op. 95.

It was a quartet, again, that proved to be the vehicle for Beethoven's definitive, most beautiful statement about Neapolitan relationships. By the time of the Quartet in C♯ minor, Op. 131, a theme in sequential chromatic steps must have seemed crude to Beethoven, though he still found a place for the bare juxtaposition of i and ♭II. In the C♯-minor Quartet this sound is reserved for the transition from the opening fugue into the second movement, and for the recapitulation of the second group within the Finale.

As for the trick of moving harmonies up the scale chromatically, that emerges directly from Neapolitan usages in the *Appassionata* Sonata and in other works of the time, even the *Eroica* Symphony. By the time of Op. 95, it seems no longer to interest Beethoven; he leaves it to Schubert, with whom it becomes an obsession, and to all later opera composers from Weber and Bellini up to the present day. In 1824 a critic who was grumbling at Schubert's endless upward-semitone modulations (in a setting of Schiller's *Gruppe aus dem Tartarus*) traced the device back to Rossini's *Tancredi*, which had been the rage of the Viennese season of 1816. But a particularly raw passage of this sort had occurred in *Fidelio*—the *succès d'estime* of 1814: the soldiers' appalled reaction to Pizarro at the conclusion of his first-act aria. Many more such passages had figured in the original version of the opera—for instance, in the beginning of the second and third *Leonore* Overtures—and were now cut out. The original version dates from ten years earlier, of course, at the time of Beethoven's first large-scale Neapolitan investigations, the *Appassionata* Sonata and the Quartet in E minor.

· 3 ·

"The *Adagio*, E major, in the second Razumovsky Quartet, occurred to him when contemplating the starry sky and thinking of the music of the spheres," wrote Carl Czerny, who knew Beethoven well after 1800.[3] For this "program" no substantiation exists in the composer's own hand,

[3] Thayer, pp. 408–9.

such as the remark about a brother's grave on the sketch for the *Adagio* of the F-major Quartet; all that Beethoven wrote on the score was a direction similar to that for *La Malinconia:* "This piece is to be played with great feeling." But Czerny is always credible, and the story seems to me instantly so. Infinite is not too grand a word for the contrast in mood that Beethoven planned here. In the most direct fashion possible, the *Adagio* transcends the tensions of the opening movement by a hushed, timeless ecstasy of contemplation—of the Pythagorean mysteries, if we are to take Czerny quite literally. Above the stars dwells the Father:

Brüder! über'm Sternenzelt
Muss ein lieber Vater wohnen.

Can Schumann have had this movement far back in his mind when he coined the slightly disingenuous phrase about "heavenly length"? Timelessness for Beethoven meant motionlessness; he quite rightly left a movement of this kind in the same key as its predecessor, albeit with a change of mode. Modulation, it seems to say, though the preoccupation of the previous movement, pales to nothingness in the light of the stars, like all the concerns of this earth. A purer contrast will shine without such worldly trappings.

Infinite and rather appalling, too, is Beethoven's confidence in the worshipful humility of his opening hymn. One hardly dares demur. Yet from another vantage point, themes of the same general type may be judged to succeed better in other works: in the slow movement of the Ninth Symphony, and in the *Heiliger Dankgesang* of the Quartet in A minor, Op. 132, whose Lydian accents are curiously suggested by the modal beginning of the present hymn. Actually the hymn only lasts eight bars; this movement falls into sonata form. Later movements of the same general character employ more static forms more effectively. A long second group ends with a typical cadence theme, puttering around IV and V of IV over the tonic pedal. The following passage, chosen more or less at random, illustrates the subtle motivic saturation of the second group by first-group material—also a characteristic of the opening

Example 64

movement, incidentally. Both main features of the hymn are here: a threefold sequence in long half-notes, and the single rhythmic contrast to it, a dotted-note rhythm. In one guise or another, the latter has echoed all through the many diverse phrases. The example also shows the gentle evolution of triplet scales, which now grow into a prolix cadential rhapsody.

The development seems rather conventional, and probably a flaw even within Beethoven's own frame of reference. It is not much helped by recollections of the previous movement, provided by the momentous intrusion of C's upon the B of the final dominant pedal. The recapitulation does one unconventional thing: it systematically extends the bridge and the second group, by three bars here, one bar in this phrase, and one bar in the other. Since each bar lasts for four seconds, no aspect of the movement contributes more hugely to the sense of never-ending amplitude or leisure than these seemingly slight extensions. After the cadence theme, there comes a $^{6}_{4}$ chord over which, almost like a cadenza, the hymn returns loudly with its accents and harmonies widely distorted.

Example 65

The strange intrusion of passion melts into the cadence theme. This is extended further yet, the triplet rhapsody drifting down to the bass for an enormously lengthy dying close. It is as close as Beethoven could come to nirvana.

He backs away from the vision gingerly, with an E-minor *Allegretto* movement of studied simplicity. Its delicate, half-pathetic melody is built out of a single halting rhythm; only three bars, prior to the final cadence, lack the obstinate one-bar rhythmic motif. The texture generally confines itself to plain accompaniment, the form to an uncomplicated binary arrangement, *a b a′ codetta*. Phrase *a* modulates in eight bars to ♭VII, D major; perhaps encouraged by this slightly deviant progression, the lapwing motions erupt twice in the *b* section to an unsuspected *fortissimo* and to harmonic regions which we recognize with a flash of understanding: the Neapolitan second degree, F, together with another violent dominant-9th chord stressing C over the root B. These direct and effective evocations of the opening movement are deepened by a new Neapolitan twist in the *a′* phrase, and by a dangling high C within the codetta.

At the trio, or as he calls it, the *Maggiore*, Beethoven pointedly writes "*Thème russe*," and the gentle listener had better beware. The 6-bar Russian folk song comes in a regular fugal exposition *a quattro*, joined to countersubjects in strict schoolbook triple counterpoint. A few bars hastily prepare a "counterexposition"—or what sounds in this context like a repetition of the first exposition in variation, the variation consisting of new countersubjects, this time free ones. After four fatuous entries just as before, things get louder and louder, and insane canons—still on the tonic—smash around for a while until the piece fritters itself away on a ludicrous compression of the Russian tune's cadence:

Example 66

This does not sound as though the composer inserted the Russian tune as an urbane compliment to his Russian patron, as Thayer thought conceivable. It sounds as though Count Razumovsky had been tactless enough to hand Beethoven the tune, and Beethoven is pile-driving it into the ground by way of revenge. To be certain the mayhem will not be missed, Beethoven has the minor-mode *Allegretto* repeated exactly, then the dead-pan *Maggiore* also exactly, and then makes a second exact repetition of the *Allegretto*. This may seem prolix; yet in the double repetition, the severe tonal limitation of the *Maggiore* sets off with especial clarity the Neapolitan digressions of the *Allegretto* itself. And in terms of absolute time, Beethoven is looking back not just to one exceedingly long movement but to two—unless the sonata-form repetitions in the opening *Allegro* were skipped. His metronome mark for the *Allegretto* is fast, 𝅗𝅥. = 69.

The Finale, a *Presto*, is also kept simple, foregoing the intellectuality and the wit, to say nothing of the finesse, of the Finale of the F-major "Razumovsky" Quartet. Like the Finale of the C-major "Razumovsky," this one is rather symphonic in conception; sometimes one can almost hear the triangle, bass drum, and piccolo of the Turkish Band assisting at some more ferocious *Entführung* or *Ruins of Athens*. Beethoven works toward a sort of externalized strenuousness that is one of his typical solutions to the problem of final resolution of the cyclic form. To this end, iambic and anapaestic rhythms drive the movement single-mindedly, and a long ternary tune is concentrated on in rondo fashion. The tune runs very rapidly and for the most part lightly, but with cranky *fp*'s stressing its irregular phraseology.

The first movement of the quartet is recalled directly, once again by means of harmonic details. The rondo tune has gained a certain notoriety for its stubborn squatting on C (VI) for two-thirds of its first phrase, even though the tonic key is of course E minor. Schoenberg

Example 67

remarked rather bitterly that the tune might as well be heard in C major making cadences on iii, and that the piece dramatizes the ambiguities latent in the classic tonal system. However this may be, when the bass C budges, it will certainly be noticed. It moves of course to B, marking out more coarsely than ever the step C–B which was stressed in all the other movements. This bass step comes four times within the tune as a whole—which includes very little else of harmonic consequence.

A codetta at the end of the tune rants a little; perhaps it had to, in order to counteract the heavy off-key beginning. A second subject led into by a brisk transition still holds to the minor mode (v) and indeed features a Neapolitan progression. When this second subject returns toward the end of the movement, it carries with it a new phrase singling out the Neapolitan beyond any shadow of doubt as the center of Beethoven's interest. The returns of the rondo tune itself are achieved by a long series of motivic grunts reminiscent of the return of the *Allegretto* after the *Maggiore* (p. 130). This travesty of a Haydn retransition takes

Example 68

itself so earnestly that we scarcely laugh with or at Haydn, or even with or at Beethoven. It is always C that is prepared—not the tonic E minor, but the off-tonic harmony on which the theme mulishly begins. Time and again this harmony rails and struts and jiggles before settling to B a little vaingloriously.

A development section—for this is a sonata-rondo—uses a formal double-counterpoint idea and then a distant transformation of the tune on a B♭ duly sinking to A. Besides being almost the only passage in the whole movement to depart from the minor mode, this also provides the one touch of sensitive whimsy in a deliberately coarse-cut work. The coda rants a good deal more, if not so licentiously as the Finale of the C-major "Razumovsky" Quartet. Beethoven restlessly invents all kinds of interesting cadence phrases, including some fresh Neapolitan ones. There is much chromatic violence in this coda, reflecting the more functional harmonic extremities of the opening *Allegro* of the quartet.

In Beethoven's minor-mode compositions, the sequence of feeling

Example 69

traced by the cyclic form is often basically the same. With all due qualifications, the E-minor Quartet, the F-minor, Op. 95, and the A-minor, Op. 132, go through a similar psychological journey: one way or another, each of them whittles away at the emotional complexity of its opening statement. Most directly this is done by the finale—in the E-minor Quartet, by obsessive rhythmic drive, constant minor-mode sonorities, and heavy repetitions of a rondo tune which is in itself sufficiently repetitious. The brusqueness of the first movement has been shaded to something more on the order of simple vehemence, the tenseness to athleticism, the hypersensitivity to overstimulation.

All this makes a satisfactory enough response to the sequence of the early movements—the nervous opening *Allegro*, the mystic *Adagio*, and the *Allegretto* which starts out so harmlessly and then turns so savagely on its Russian tune. In itself something of a monster, this Finale is scaled to the job at hand, in a way that one cannot quite feel about the intrinsically more agreeable Finale of the F-major "Razumovsky" Quartet. In retrospect, the middle movements can be seen to have been kept very level, in terms of harmony and rhythm, as though strategies were required to smooth down the complexity of the first. All four movements stay in E (minor and major), even the trio, and all of them stress the Neapolitan relationship F–E and its upper parallel C–B. This makes for a heavy unity of effect, and even runs the risk of monotony, but runs it safely, I think. Coherence of the total cyclic experience was manifestly one of Beethoven's aims, and he achieved it more integrally here than in most other compositions of the period.

A distinct echo of the Finale of the E-minor Quartet comes up in the Finale of the C♯-minor, Op. 131; without wishing to make too much of the parallel, I should all the same call it closer than that between any other two Beethoven quartet movements. The Quartet in C♯ minor is the very work in which Beethoven brought movements of the cyclic composition to their highest degree of integration. If that were the only aim, or if it were to be considered the paramount aim, the Quartet in E minor would probably count as the best of the "Razumovsky" set. Something in the way of consciousness, however, has been sacrificed to the inner coherence. Can it be a coincidence that the next quartet takes a sharply different tack, playing with disturbance and even dissociation? In later quartets Beethoven found himself coming back to questions raised by the E-minor, a process that does not occur with the others of the "Razumovsky" set. There was a need to test and answer the questions again, from newly achieved levels of technique and emotional awareness.

· 4 ·

While the first quartet of Op. 59 expends its major energies on the first two movements, and the second achieves a viable balance, if a rather stiff one, the third quartet tilts sharply in the opposite direction. After a less substantial beginning than that of either of its companions, the Quartet in C drives toward an overpowering finale. The relative weight of the movements is probably the simplest fact regulating the personalities of the three quartets and setting them off sharply from one another.

The C-major Quartet is generally the most fluid. It lacks a grandiose *Adagio* of timeless tragedy or of timeless serenity holding up action in the middle. Here the slow movement—*Andante* qualified *con moto quasi allegretto*—moves restlessly through an unusual series of vicissitudes; the *Andante* occupies the intellectual center of gravity of the quartet. It overshadows the first *Allegro*, which on the other end is also shaded by an opening slow introduction creating an excessively nebulous piece of mystification. From this the *Allegro* never quite recovers, and its disturbing accents may be said to haunt the quartet as a whole.

Now, traditionally, a sonata-form slow introduction will begin on or near the tonic key and then work its way to an extended dominant, generally after appreciable harmonic digressions. Some such formula covers even so extreme a case as *La Malinconia* in the Quartet in B♭, Op. 18, No. 6, where the digressions extend to mystification. *La Malin-*

conia has many points of contact with the present piece. But the Quartet in C begins in limbo—with immediate digression carried to the point of outright confusion. A small but critical change of principle; Beethoven had adumbrated it in the *Leonore* Overtures—also in C—but he never found occasion to apply it again. The listener is left completely in a fog at the start of the quartet for many bars, an effect that is carefully compounded by melodic and rhythmic vaguenesses to go along with the harmonic obfuscation.

Like other Beethoven slow introductions in C, such as those of the *Pathétique* and the last Piano Sonata, Op. 111, this one can be approached as a case history of that most shifty of harmonic resources, the diminished-7th chord. In a movement that creaks forward in a faceless *pianissimo*, a series of four of these chords demarcates the sometimes clear, sometimes shadowy main accents. The second part of Example 70 shows the main accents and the four chords, with their embellishing *appoggiaturas* indicated by small notes.

Example 70

Included are all the three diminished-7th forms that exist, involving the complete set of twelve notes in the chromatic scale (in bars 1–2, F♯ A C E♭; in bars 8–9, A♭ B D F; in bars 14–15, E G B♭ D♭). The notes of chord no. 2 are restated and regrouped as chord no. 4, which actually stretches all through bars 18–28, first with D in the bass, then with B. So all in all, this particular form of diminished-7th is displayed in three out of its four possible inversions, with A♭, D, and B in the bass successively. (Beethoven manages to complete the spectrum by slipping in the fourth inversion, with F in the bass, as a passing harmony in bar 13.) Of the three diminished-7ths, this one manifestly assumes most importance for the present purpose—which, it develops, is resolution via the step A♭–G to the dominant of C. As we have been informed, but will not actually hear for a long time, C major is to be the central tonality.

The schematic aspect of Beethoven's mind should never be discounted; very likely he had some kind of half-abstract investigation going here, as he did in Op. 111, where the three different diminished-7ths follow one another in lucid sequence both in the introduction and within the miniscule development section later. But schematic plans of this sort in Beethoven are involved with some aesthetic end that is not merely schematic. In the present case, obscurity is the end, lifting gradually as the passage proceeds. As the cello rolls gloomily and aimlessly down an arcane series of harmonies, and the violin inches up and away from the rest of the instruments, Beethoven displays a very ingenious, indeed a slightly fantastic means to clarify the harmonic situation.

It seems to hinge on the fact that while embellishments to the diminished-7th chords may sound very excruciating, in actual fact they limit the ambiguity of these chords. The unembellished chord no. 1 (bar 1–2) is utterly vague because capable of resolution to any one of eight triads (A minor seems suggested by the sequel). But the *appoggiatura* C in chord no. 2 (bars 8–9) pulls in only a few directions, particularly toward A or C; so that when Beethoven deflects the harmony to E♭ instead, he does so with the air of pulling off a magic trick that is soon to be exposed. Chord no. 3 (bars 14–15) is embellished by an *appoggiatura* F resolving to E in the bass, after which the D♭ within the chord resolves to C (bar 16). F–E and D♭–C spell out F minor positively, albeit F minor envisaged less as a tonal center than as supertonic of the prestidigital key of E♭.

The violin pulls higher yet, and the cello lower yet, to the last of the diminished-7ths—the last, the most enigmatic in detail, and yet harmonically the clearest of all. The piercing viola F♯ (bar 18) draws the harmony away from F minor, which in any case lacked proper subdominant grounding. Then the resolving steps occur a 5th higher than just previously: C–B in the first violin and eventually (bars 28–29) A♭–G in the viola. These steps spell out C; around this note the violin and cello slowly circle each other, as is indicated on the diagram on page 135 (bars 19–22). There can be little doubt that the diminished-7th chord is now behaving like a dominant of C, prepared suitably enough by some hints of F minor (iv) and E♭ (♭III). A♭ sinks to G—and as the *Allegro* touches ground briefly at C major before springing into its cadenza flight, the brisk new motif sounds very much like an inversion of all the slow resolving steps of the introduction.

From the cloud there emerges a tenuous fleeting cadenza of a first theme for violin, punctuated as though by recitative chords. The phrases flow so freely that they do not even make regular sequences; a 5-bar phrase is answered by six bars:

Example 71

At later appearances, the flight sometimes takes even longer to settle. To be sure, a steady upward progression through the octave underlies the rhapsody, beginning with Beethoven's favorite thematic sequence from the tonic to the second degree:

Bar	29	30	34	35	40	41	42	43
	E	F	F	G	A	B♭	B♮	C
	I		ii		ii		V	I

The sound of the second degree (marked *forte* here: bars 34–5) is destined to echo later in the quartet, just as the Neapolitan second degree did in the E-minor Quartet. And the upward step itself becomes a pervasive neat motif for the first movement, occuring in the bridge, second group, development, retransition, and coda. The culmination of the upward march through the octave resembles a passage from the F-major Quartet illustrated on page 93, the two passages functioning similarly, as major arrivals at the first strong tonic sonority in each composition. Yet for various reasons, the arrival makes a much less portentous effect here, and when finally arrived at, the tonic is handled vigorously but lightly.

Soon a real concerto sound thins the texture:

Example 72

The weave is transparent all through the graceful bridge passage and the second group, which seems to eschew serious contrast. Schuppanzigh the first violin is not the only one who is given something "grateful" to dig into; alternately the three other instruments assume a *concertante* role, culminating in a very flashy threefold trill—an unmistakable concerto fingerprint. All of Beethoven's mature concertos—the last three for piano, the Triple Concerto, the Violin Concerto, and the *Romances* for violin and orchestra—were conceived within a year or two of the "Razumovsky" Quartets.

The strangely subdued development section first makes a half-hearted attempt to press the opening violin rhapsody into motivic shape. By hasty steps the harmony ascends from E♭ to E minor to F—only to find itself at the subdominant, where the long bridge passage from the exposition is duplicated closely (instead of 18 bars moving from C to G, 15 bars move from F to C). A passage of dominant preparation, built canonically from the opening motif, stands out as the most imaginative and strongest part of the development, and indeed as the one passage of appreciable tension in the whole *Allegro*. The slow introduction is recalled by the dissonant harmonic progressions here, and not only in a general way; but now the disturbing sense of mystery is relieved by plenty of motivic, contrapuntal, and harmonic clues. The build-up is formidable and fantastic, suddenly tremendous.

Instead of a great climax at the point of return, Beethoven proposes

Example 73

an elegant relaxation. The tonic is delayed, the chromaticism dies hard, and there is a warmth and grace to the new figuration assumed by the violin rhapsody which seems to make light of the serious business of dominant preparation. Even the opening motif has mellowed. Everything now is to be played *piano* or *pianissimo.*

This urbane recapitulation takes a good deal of well-disciplined variation and revision; for instance, the bridge can now be safely curtailed. The only real surprise, however, comes at the abrupt conclusion:

Example 74

A moment of uncertainty, then a sharp change in mood, a testy contradiction of the smooth, high-spirited flow that preceded it (the patent motivic derivation notwithstanding). Even more than in the E-minor Quartet, the first movement here ends inconclusively, as though to anticipate the contrast of the following *Andante.*

This procedure recalls Mozart; and of course, any C-major quartet with a mystery-making slow introduction would have brought the same association to the mind of Beethoven and his contemporaries as it brings to ours: Mozart's so-called "Dissonance" Quartet in C, K. 465, the last of the set of six dedicated to Haydn. Theodor Helm actually observed a near-quotation from the first movement of K. 465 in Beethoven's first movement—both passages coming from the bridge sections! The symmetrical, restrained treatment of sonata form rather resembles the practice of the earlier composer, for the coda is hardly a coda in Beethoven's sense of a "terminal development," the recapitulation makes no grand assertions, and even the development proceeds quietly, in the main. Mozartian, too, is the high polish of surface detail, and especially a certain sophisticated virtuosity of workmanship, a stylishness that is as marked here as it is rare in other compositions of these particular years. Not much is to be learned by placing the present movement next to another notable *œuvre d'hommage*, the Quartet in A, Op. 18, No. 5, of half a dozen years back. Periodically Beethoven seems to have felt a need to refine his technique and achieve once again, from each new vantage point, the relaxed brilliance that Mozart had encompassed better than any other composer. There is another "Mozartian" essay among the late quartets of 1825–6, the Quartet in F, Op. 135.

Op. 59 assumes quite another vantage point than Op. 18, as Gerald Abraham remarks in his brief but sensitive account in the "Musical Pilgrim" booklet. The insistent permeation of the whole movement by the opening motif marks the difference:

> It is the all-pervading use of this tiniest possible motive that gives this movement its real life, its real unity, and finally stamps it as the work of the mature Beethoven. Everywhere it stabs through the fabric of the rather conservative harmony; it makes crevices, inserts itself into them, and widens them. If Beethoven had actually wanted to paint a symbolic musical picture of rococo pattern-music disintegrating through the workings of his new motive-technique and his new dynamic style, he could not have done so more graphically.[4]

Did Beethoven actually want anything of the kind? Most probably not; but in the third movement of the quartet, the *Menuetto: Grazioso*, some such intention must have been lurking not far beyond the threshold of his consciousness.

The complex, restless *Andante con moto quasi allegretto* has come in between. One problem was to modulate the feeling from the *Andante* to the emphatic half-fugue Beethoven planned for the Finale. This he accomplished in an extremely interesting way, by a kind of refined parody of the classic style—a reinterpretation or surrogate, not at all a travesty, of a dis-

[4] P. 46.

tant musical idiom. He wrote a minuet instead of a scherzo, and a minuet of the most studied rococo symmetry and blankness. The first strain makes 8 bars out of a 4-bar phrase repeated, closing naïvely in the tonic. The second strain inserts 4 bars entirely on the dominant before a repetition of the opening 8 in gentle variation. The one point of interest is an 8-bar codetta. *No* modulation occurs until the trio.

One would have to look far in Mozart's mature music before finding anything as elementary as this. Beethoven's early works, on the other hand, afford plenty of similar examples, some of them in fairly recent sonatas (Op. 22; 30, No. 2; 31, No. 3; and 54). These minuets are sometimes marked *grazioso*, like the quartet movement; the term crops up again in Beethoven's very last minuet, the concluding number of the "Diabelli" Variations, which are also in C major. (Between Op. 59 and the Variations, in 1823, he wrote only one real minuet, the one in the Eighth Symphony.) For Beethoven, the word *grazioso* would seem to have had a special connotation of old lace, as it were—of a past not so very far removed in actual years, but in spirit further from this particular composer than the age of Bach or even the age of Palestrina. His evocation is neither sentimental nor sardonic, but dreamlike, abstracted in all senses of the word, almost affectionate. What is it that Beethoven sees in this rococo vision, behind the curiously insubstantial syncopated harmonies, the limpid ornament, the passionless melodic cliché?

And so to say that there is no interest in this minuet beyond certain details of the codetta is not quite to do justice to one's feeling for it. There *should* be no further interest; but the whole process has its own powerful fascination and its own special unnamable aura. To be sure, one responds with the benefit of superior knowledge: the "Diabelli" Variations, after endless vicissitudes, transmogrifies a low contemporary waltz into a minuet parody which practically evaporates in its own delicacy. The same quality informs this minuet—though not the trio that comes with it. As compared with the somewhat Mozartian opening movement, the classic style is reflected in quite another way: not as a real image, let us say, but as a virtual image, in a mirror that is dark-glassed yet crystal-clear. This reflection is closer to something we may sense already in the Quartet in G, Op. 18, No. 2, and closer still to various magic pieces from Beethoven's third period.

Leading to the Finale, an 18-bar transition fashioned out of motifs of the minuet bears a resemblance to the slow introduction at the beginning of the quartet. The passage seems to me perfunctory (as does also the trio that comes with the minuet). For convenience, the main theme of the Finale

Example 75

is cited here not in its original form, but together with the half-note countersubject that appears later, at the recapitulation. The main fugue subject—for that is what it is—flaunts not only a sequence, which is standard in fugue writing, but actually two internal free repetitions, which is certainly not standard. Beethoven's lifelong model of fugue was *The Well-tempered Clavier*, which he had learned to admire from his teacher at Bonn, Christian Gottlob Neefe, a third-generation student of Bach, and which he was still copying down in absent-minded extracts on sketch-sheets for the last sonatas. Hardly one of the forty-eight fugue subjects of *The Well-tempered Clavier* includes internal repetition. Despite its very great speed, Beethoven's theme has a rare flatulence about it which spreads inevitably to the rest of the movement.

But although we—I—may not much approve of the movement, there is no denying its self-consistency. The repetitions within the subject spawn an unusual number of direct phrase-repetitions later in the piece, culminating in a real "Rossini *crescendo*" working through an identical 2-bar pattern eight times in succession. Few movements in Beethoven, certainly none at all in the quartets, stretch their material so unscrupulously. Furthermore, the two repetitions within the subject work to a purpose, stressing features wanted for the total structure. The first of these is the prominent second degree, the sound of D minor in the context of C; this is underlined by the chromatic inflection of the countersubject in the recapitulation (cited above), becomes a tireless concomitant of the concluding cadences, including the one in the "Rossini *crescendo*," and promotes the following rude intrusion in the coda:

Example 76

The second feature, stepwise ascent up the scale to the high tonic, also recurs most strongly (though not exclusively) in the coda, where for instance the violin twice sweeps up the scale from middle C to the C three octaves higher. It may be remarked further that the double chiming of the circle of 5ths in the first bars of the subject (vi–ii–V–I) seems to be writ large in the penultimate *fortissimo* of the development. The prolixity of the fugue subject was obviously no accident or simple miscalculation on the composer's part.

The reader will not have failed to notice, and the listener should not fail to hear, that the two features grossly stressed by the subject and by the rest of the movement are ones that characterize—less grossly—the opening movement of the quartet. Like the finales of the other two "Razumovsky" Quartets, the present Finale makes pointed reference to the earlier movement. Even the cadential three-octave climb of the violin parallels the cadential spurt at the end of the first movement (compare Ex. 76, above, with Ex. 74, p. 139. In fact, before the fugal answer appears at the very beginning of the Finale, the 10-bar viola solo might be heard to echo the texture of the main subject of the first movement—the rhapsodic unaccompanied violin flight.) Beethoven treats frank tonic sonority skittishly all through the fugal exposition, which begins reasonably enough on the dominant, but which refuses to answer with the tonic degree, and then brings two more subject entries on the dominant. The fourth entry extends the 10-bar subject to 16 bars leading at last to a strong tonic arrival:

Example 77

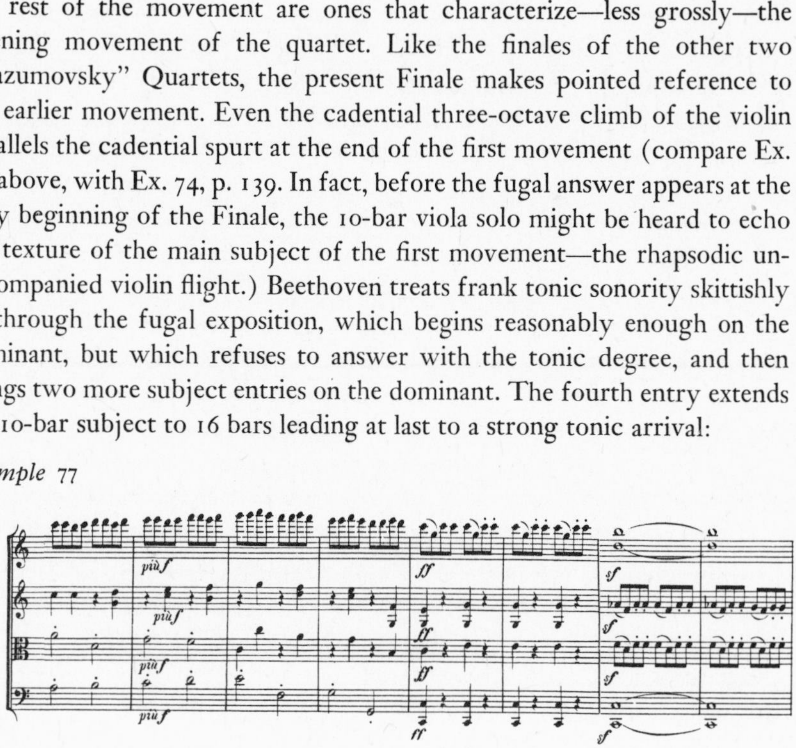

This clarion call recalls the fanfare marking the first strong tonic arrival in the first movement (p. 137). Both passages even move momentarily to the characteristic second degree.

With this arrival, fugal action stops; an abridged sonata-form movement emerges from these beginnings, the abridgment consisting in ellipsis of the final cadences customary to a second group. A lengthy development section makes no reference to traditional fugal devices. Instead it works over the subject in successive fragmentation, and makes the clarion call modulate up the scale magnificently. The last few bars of the subject are expanded into an 8-bar rising scale seized upon as a solo by each of the four instruments in turn, while the others pad away behind the soloist for all the world like a Verdi orchestra. A scandalous comment, this, on the academic pretensions of the beginning.

The recapitulation brings the same irregular fugal entries *a quattro* as in the exposition, only with the new half-note countersubject superimposed. The effect is more obsessive than particularly forceful or imaginative. A perfectly enormous coda makes loud cadences and repeats itself endlessly, a garish but nonetheless formidable display of might.

It is hard to understand the anxiety that some commentators seem to have felt about the fugal credentials of this Finale. Obviously it does not belong in the late Beethovenian category of genuine fugal movements, the series initiated by the Piano and Cello Sonatas, Op. 101 and 102, and crowned by the Great Fugue of the Quartet in B♭. Obviously it does belong in another, clearly recognizable, early category: sonata-form movements with a first group (or part of a first group) made up of a fugal exposition designed to recapitulate with the addition of a new countersubject. Such pieces figure in the Sonata in F, Op. 10, No. 2, the First Symphony, and the Quartet in C minor, Op. 18, No. 4; less stiltedly, the second movement of the Ninth Symphony will revive the same principle. Mozart, in the first of the quartets dedicated to Haydn, the G-major, K. 387, had concocted his own marvelous sonata-form-fugue amalgam, as a sort of response to the famous strict fugues of Haydn's Op. 20. Beethoven's early scheme is closer to Mozart's notion than to Haydn's, but does not seem to trace its ancestry directly to the work of either earlier composer.

The commentators have called this Finale symphonic. Certainly its barnstorming fury—or its commanding ebullient power, if you prefer—looks ahead to the Fifth Symphony, another composition in C that makes the most shattering of overstatements in its concluding pages. These are the accents of the hero turned demagogue; Beethoven, who had torn up a title page in 1804, remained unable to meet the Napoleonism latent in his own work for quite a few more years. That he should have tried for a note of ostentatious triumph in the string quartet medium is remarkable but, as was remarked in connection with the F-major "Razumovsky" Quartet, far from uncharacteristic. Besides symphonic overtones, rather surprising *concertante* ones resonate in the first movement of the C-major Quartet, and also in the minuet, the trio, and the Finale. The coda of the Finale has a decided operatic swing, reminiscent of the joyous hectoring *strettas* at the end of many Beethoven overtures. All this seems to add up to a willful effort to break the proper bounds of quartet writing, to transcend the intimate medium used so elegantly in the three earlier movements. Whether piled-up repetitions and noise and up-the-scale ascents will accomplish any such release, may be doubted. In spite of Beethoven's effort, the memory of the *Andante* in A minor remains to haunt the memory after all the endless Finale cadences have been stilled.

· 5 ·

This *Andante* is an astonishingly impressive piece and quite unlike anything else Beethoven ever wrote; in this double respect—though probably in no other—it can claim kinship of a sort with the great *scherzando* movement of the F-major "Razumovsky" Quartet. The very genre seems strange, and the mood of restless brooding not only singular but also uncharacteristic of the man, somehow—and enormously convincing anyhow. Someone has guessed that Beethoven was trying for something "Russian" here, as a complement to the frank *thèmes russes* of the other two quartets. The guess makes every kind of sense. Beethoven is known to have had an interest in folklore, like everyone else at the time; probably he entertained some vague image of perennial bleakness as the Russian national humor, and, more specifically, of "harmonic minor" sounds as characteristic of Slavic modes. Within the theme itself, the aberrant melodic use of the augmented 2nd G♯–F between the sharp seventh degree (G♯) and the minor sixth (F) might as well have sounded Russian, to early nineteenth-century ears, as Turkish or Bulgarian or Jewish. Viennese, in any case, it very definitely is not.

The overall mood comes first of all from the highly unified rhythmic treatment. Similar rocking $\frac{6}{8}$ figures appear in practically every one of the two-hundred-odd bars, often with cello *pizzicato* notes marking out the strong beats. (The cello commences with a series of eight evenly-spaced

Example 78

pizzicato low E's, an excellently glum *ostinato* effect.) The steady flow has caused Daniel Gregory Mason among others to speak uneasily (or not) of rhythmic monotony. Admittedly, it is most unusual for a Beethoven composition. So is the amount of on-the-spot repetition, as appears from the large set of extracts reproduced in Example 78. Typically, it will be seen, a 2-bar cell is involved in a threefold repetition, with the third appearance compressed or otherwise altered so as to run into something else. Like the Finale of the quartet, the slow movement contains a good deal of

fat. Perhaps even more than the unvarying flow, this feature contributes to the commanding sense of obsession, and at the same time could certainly be said to court monotony.

However, if the piece is paced as Beethoven directed, as *Andante con moto quasi allegretto*, the problem of holding the listener's attention does not become serious. This is because the evenness is offset by a restlessness most unusual for a lyric movement, a specifically harmonic restlessness all the more striking because the previous movement admits so few harmonic surprises, once the slow introduction has found its way safely to C major. Beethoven was working for an unlikely amalgam here: harmonic instability, suggesting disturbance and passion, and rhythmic and repetitive sameness, suggesting on the contrary dull obsession.

The minor sixth degree F leads the way, in its melodic and harmonic ramifications. The long tune leans toward F at the start of its second strain. Directly after its rather Brahmsian codetta (the second excerpt on pp. 146–7), a bridgelike passage begins emotionally with F minor—and what is more, with F minor intensified by Neapolitan details (the third excerpt). This highly charged conjunction of A minor and F minor (i and ♭vi) illustrates again the use of indirect key-relationships, discussed in connection with the E-minor Quartet. A somewhat feeble second subject on C closes with a cadential passage over C harping on *its* minor sixth degree, A♭ (the fifth and sixth excerpts). A sort of development section moves toward the original F minor, and thence far down the circle of 5ths and even farther up again. Each stage occupies between 2 and 6 bars, a relatively level state of affairs by ordinary development standards:

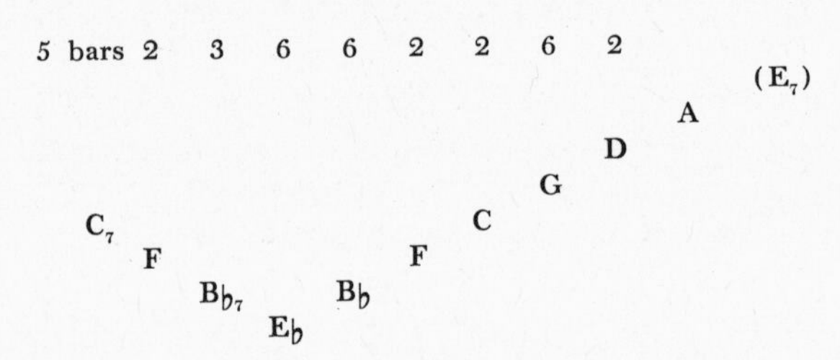

All these temporary key-centers use the minor mode (except of course for the C_7 and the B♭7); the only real major-mode relief in the whole piece comes with the second subject at its three appearances. The diagram is intended to clarify the schematic nature of this development ground plan. The central key E♭ stands in the tritone relationship—or rather, non-relationship—to the tonic A minor, that is to say, as remote as possible.

When the key of A turns up, at the end of this solemn swing of 5ths, it makes no especially strong effect, though the resumption of the cello *pizzicato* does suggest that a recapitulation is at hand. A really dramatic return to the tonic key is being held in reserve for a slightly later point in the piece. At present a much-repeated half-cadence (the last excerpt) ushers in the second theme—and rather surreptitiously; closing, as before, with a cadential passage over A harping on F (♭VI). As though suddenly sick of this nagging note, Beethoven throws it the reins and lets it hiccup the rhythm and shy right back to E♭, where the second subject moves as though freed into an unexpectedly ethereal register. E♭ is the most remote, destructive tonal region for a digression from the basic key of A. But Beethoven insists on it sweetly, and then takes the occasion to write a superb return passage in preparation for the tonic, a broad and mysterious expansion of the descending *pizzicato* cello scale within the opening tune.

This now makes the major dramatic resolution—to the ominous *pizzicato* E's, twelve of them this time, reinforced by piercing held E's in the higher instruments. There is a new bleakness to the theme as it returns entire—complete with repetitions!—to form a weighty end pillar for the edifice. By way of coda, the F-minor gestures of the original bridgelike passage are actually brought up again, but are rationalized away directly. The *pizzicato* scale works itself out numbly under the concluding pedal, beating around the tonic and dominant, and touching once again the note F that plays so large a role in the over-all structure.

"*Wie altertümlich naiv das ist, wie urmenschlich!*" exclaimed Theodor Helm in 1873, citing at the same time A. B. Marx's original characterization of the movement as "*seltsam fremd*." The ostensible contradiction here may be worth pursuing a little way. The "unusual strangeness" of the piece is strangeness from the point of view of the classic Viennese style; this naturally fascinated Marx, who grew up during the last flowering of that style, and fascinates anyone immersed in Beethoven's *œuvre* as a whole. Beethoven relished the stylistic contrast and put it in the sharpest possible relief—for the *Andante* sits between the unusually Mozartian *Allegro* and the unusually rococo *Menuetto: Grazioso*. At the same time, it is hardly thinkable that a listener happily oblivious to the classic purities will find himself in the least estranged by this music. On the contrary, perhaps no other movement in the Beethoven quartets calls up so instant a response of aesthetic recognition. In listening to it, one responds less to the person Beethoven, his era, or his artistic code than to something universal and timeless, even something subartistic.

And the path to this quality, it seems clear enough, was the typical one of Beethoven's time. Whether "Russian" or not, the movement makes its own individual reference to the *Volkston* that Herder and Goethe had learned to admire, the early romantic image of blind harpers chanting ancient bardic lays. Something of this image is invoked by the brooding repetitions, the "harmonic minor" progressions, and the cello *pizzicato* which seems now to strum, now to toll, now to carp like a muted gong. Even Schubert, the arch-Viennese, caught this chthonic tone here and there in his songs and ballads, and even in his other music; Beethoven's *Andante* stands as a dim model behind Schubert's first major instrumental work, the Quartet in A minor of 1822. But the melancholy of Schubert's opening is more refined, more balanced, weaker, less disturbed, less disturbing—in a word, less "strange." What Beethoven plumbs in his slow movement is exactly the mystery of the primitive, the *urmenschlich*, as Helm put it. This is the well in which each menacing, half-articulate cello stroke seems to find its deeper resonance.

Doubtless the frequent stressing of F in this movement can be taken as an apology for the augmented-2nd assault on F within the original tune. Things are much less clear with the E♭ episode in the "recapitulation," which certainly fills no standard formal prescription. In fact, classification of this *Andante* as a movement in sonata form makes little sense, even though it incorporates a section rather like—yet curiously unlike—a development section, and even though it manages what sounds like a "second theme" with passable sonata-form normality. For, on the other hand, the "first theme" extends itself into a leisurely rounded tune with subdominant inclinations, and even sports a lengthy 6-bar codetta over a tonic pedal—which is as undramatic an arrangement as could have been devised. The heavy *da capo* of the tune suggests *A B A* arch form, not the two-part balance that is basic to classic sonata form. Throughout, the very steady motion and the hypnotic on-the-spot repetitions negate the characteristic sense of rhythmic flux associated with the sonata dynamic, even in slow movements. And what is that protracted tritone E♭ doing *after* the substantial tonic return? To speak of such a movement as a sonata form with irregularities is like calling a dog irregular when it grows long whiskers, washes its face, and miaows.

A forecast of the harmonic anomalies of this movement—I do not speak of an explanation of them, or a justification—can perhaps be traced in the slow introduction at the very beginning of the quartet. In the course of its shadowy stalking of the tonic key C, the introduction briefly suggests A minor, E♭ major, and F minor; A minor, C, E♭, and the major and minor forms of F are also the keys of the *Andante*. Prominent E♭'s and A's can be detected in the other movements, too. But although Beethoven probably had some unifying idea in mind here, it does not appear to me seriously effective. As at a number of points in this quartet and in the "Razumovsky" series at large, the idea is not completely realized in aesthetic terms. Technique and expression are still not always quite securely bound together; and small wonder, considering how technique and expression were each bounding into unexplored territory.

· 6 ·

After the *Eroica,* one is tempted to say, it was inevitable for Beethoven's quartets to have grown to formidable proportions, taken a new look at their life's ambition, and stormed the threshold of the symphony. A new world was being explored, and if the string quartet was going to find a place in it at all, it had to smash the fragile, decorous boundaries set by the classic image of chamber music. In the wake of the style revolution of the *Eroica* Symphony, *Fidelio,* and the *Appassionata* Sonata, a new "symphonized" quartet necessarily had to come into being.

Yet all we are saying, when we speak of "necessity" and "inevitability," is that after the event the historical sequence makes excellent logic. The quartet could also have got lost in the shuffle of the great style change, as did the violin sonata, comparatively speaking, and the oratorio, and the wind ensemble of the 1790's. The first thing to appreciate is the imaginative leap whereby the quartet was made to seem even available, at this juncture of Beethoven's career. Something in the genre clearly held his interest: something in the texture, or the tradition, or the expressive possibilities inherent in the intimate confrontation of equal members. Perhaps something had been suggested to him by the quartets of Op. 18, half a dozen years before, though it would require some special pleading to maintain this on the evidence of those works alone. Perhaps it was simply a vision, an aspiration.

If so, it was one that instantly proved itself. The expressive range that Beethoven found available to him as he composed the second- and later the third-period quartets seems actually broader and more deeply radical than that of the contemporary symphony, sonata, or anything else. (The point is worth making; if it did not hold, a book of this sort would probably not come into existence. This vision, and this realization, made the string quartet for Beethoven a major genre, as it has been for only one or two other composers—Haydn and Bartók.) To think back over the dozen separate movements of Op. 59 is to be struck by the boldness of the expressive imagination at work. The exaggerated lament of the F-minor *Adagio molto e mesto,* the stellar quiet of the E-major hymn, the wonderfully brilliant *Allegretto vivace e sempre scherzando* of the F-major Quartet, the parody minuet of the C-major—Beethoven is manipulating unheard-of extremes with an enthusiasm that is infectious or awesome, or both. The three sharply differentiated opening movements stamp their character inevitably on the three quartets as totalities. The C-major Quartet, for example, after suffering at the start from a bizzare piece of slow obfuscation, turns out to be in every way the most dissociated of the three individuals. There is the trancelike minuet, and there is the A-minor *Andante con moto quasi allegretto*—the true exotic among Beethoven's major utterances, and as such a little warped as well as more than a little fascinating. The consuming fugal Finale was faced with a very serious, almost frantic task of reintegration.

The dizziest stylistic contrast of all is that between fugue and folk song—between the C-major Finale and the first-movement development of the F-major on the one extreme, and Count Razumovsky's little Russian tunes on the other. This is especially striking in view of Beethoven's whole history with the quartet as a genre. The same dualism is already hinted at in the Op. 18 Quartets, with their strong contrapuntal bias and with the novel *allemande* Finale in the last of them, the Quartet in B♭, Op. 18, No. 6. Much more strongly, the country dance and the Great Fugue grip the consciousness as a guiding polarity for the last quartets of 1825–6.

"After," in the sense of "in pursuit of" or "in imitation of"—in this sense too the "Razumovsky" Quartets are after the *Eroica*. One thing that interested Beethoven was to see how far the quartet could adopt the symphonic ideal, though certainly he understood the paradox inherent in the whole undertaking. The symphonic ideal builds from the special powers of the symphony orchestra, obviously. Four instruments cannot do the work of forty, and the thrill of witnessing their heroic pretense at it is—while perfectly real—less serious than the satisfaction of seeing them realize their own very considerable potentialities. The finales of the last two "Razumovsky" Quartets, with their mock orchestral sweep, strike an inflated posture only too characteristic of Beethoven's symphonies and overtures of the second period. It is not very surprising to read of Habeneck playing the C-major Finale with full orchestra. (François-Antoine Habeneck was the conductor of the Paris Conservatory Concerts after 1828, and Beethoven's first champion in Paris. The second was Berlioz.)

Beethoven was overplaying the paradox. For a time he stopped writing quartets, and when he returned to the genre he no longer cared to cultivate symphonic vehemence. When he wanted something apocalyptic, as in the Great Fugue, he got it out of contrapuntal friction. The Great Fugue has been played with orchestra, too, but the composer's own transcription was for the eminently abstract medium of piano, four hands.

Texture is not the only problem in the "Razumovsky" Quartets. Beethoven's overuse of sonata form betrays the symphonic urge once again, for this form feels most at home in the symphony first movement, especially as Beethoven was handling it now. The impetus appears most clearly in the first movement of the F-major Quartet, with its direct stylistic evocation of the *Eroica* Symphony. To be sure, the role of sonata form in the quartet pieces can be overstated, as was done by Vincent d'Indy. Hearing the *Allegretto vivace e sempre scherzando* of the F-major Quartet or the *Andante* of the C-major as though they followed a real sonata plan distorts something fundamental in the way they actually move. Yet the pieces are unquestionably saturated with the *spirit* of sonata form; at this brief period of Beethoven's career, it truly obsessed him—how brief will appear in the sequel. D'Indy noted that an actual majority of the quartet movements surrender themselves to sonata tendencies: every one of the opening movements, slow movements, and finales, and even one of the scherzos. (The surrender was not unconditional, that is all—a not unimportant reservation.) This universal saturation may have led to magnificent results in the unique *scherzando* movement, but it acted to stifle lyricism in the slow movements. For the C-major Finale, it provided a backdrop that is merely demagogic.

A moment ago the reader was asked to look back over the dozen separate movements of Op. 59. The proposal was not altogether a didactic one. Something about the movements invites separate consideration, as much as consideration within the quartets as total works of art. In other words, another problem, that of cyclic unity, did not rest fully under the composer's control; some of the movements had grown too large and self-absorbed and selfish to yield to his efforts at binding up the totality. To these efforts, the greatest interest attaches in view of his later experience with the genre, but sometimes they fall short of immediate instinctive conviction. A case has just been mentioned, that of the presumptive parallels between the introduction and the *Andante* of the C-major Quartet. The finale turned into a special problem, right away in the F-major Quartet; in this work the first movements achieve so much that the conclusion is really beggared. Beethoven had to start retrenching a little, scaling the first movements down from the heroic proportions suggested by the *Eroica*, and struggling to adjust some kind of viable balance among the movements as a set. This took real effort, for the pieces are more than a little heavy on their feet.

The quartets may outdo other contemporary Beethoven compositions in expressive range, then; as totalities they may not hold together so well. There is after all a likely connection between these two facts. Preeminently the "Razumovsky" Quartets are explorers, experimenters—this last term is one that has to be handled gingerly, but it may serve to indicate the sense in which the vision sometimes outstrips sure achievement. At a number of points in the course of these works, technique seems speculatively to force or to test expression. In their own day they puzzled and even repelled listeners, and unless we see why, we are not likely to appreciate the real gain in quartets composed by Beethoven three or four years later. The gain was in smoothness, agility, balance, total power.

For with the exception of that famous problem child, the Quartet in B♭, Op. 130, the quartets after the "Razumovsky" set do not bring up the same aesthetic questions. The exploration becomes, as it were, more professional, the goal more precise, the course more resilient and sure. And nothing is lost in the way of excitement, freshness, or wonder, if perhaps one scruple of a reservation can be made for a further essay in retrenchment, the Quartet in E♭ of 1809. The fact is that exploration was typical of the man to the last working year of his life; no other composer has ever kept constantly moving and looking with such astonishing results. "Art demands of us that we shall not stand still" was his quiet statement to Karl Holz in 1826. The "Razumovsky" Quartets are flawed simply by a slightly hectic infusion of Beethoven's characteristic vital energy. After the *Eroica*, in the great rush of revelation of what was crying out to be done with notes, we could hardly expect it to have been otherwise. We would hardly want it otherwise.

6

THE QUARTETS OF 1809–10

Quartet in E♭ Major, Op. 74 ("The Harp")
Quartet in F Minor, Op. 95

Beethoven was at the confident peak of his activity; during the first decade of the 1800's the flow of music from his pen is awe-inspiring. This flow was hardly diminished by the revolution of 1802–3 which produced the *Eroica* Symphony, even though now each new project raised much greater imaginative and technical issues. As was mentioned in the previous chapter, more than nine important compositions stem from the three-year period stretching from the *Eroica* to the "Razumovsky" Quartets, the fair copy of which was begun in May 1806. In the next three years, Beethoven completed at least another nine major works. Between 1806 and 1809 there came three more symphonies, the Fourth, Fifth, and Sixth ("Pastoral"); three concertos, the Fourth and Fifth ("Emperor") for piano, and the Violin Concerto; three less familiar chamber-music pieces, the Cello Sonata in A, Op. 69, and the pair of Trios, Op. 70; as well as the Mass in C, the *Coriolan* Overture, and various smaller compositions.

This era of superb, surpassing fecundity—the second period proper, or the heart of the second period—tapered to an end in the years 1809 and 1810. As Thayer remarked, "the close of 1809 terminated a decade (1800–1809) during which—if quality be considered, as well as number, variety, extent and originality—Beethoven's works offer a more splendid exhibition of intellectual power than those of any composer produced within a like term of years; and New Year, 1809, began another (1810–19), which, compared with the preceding, exhibits an astonishing decrease in the composer's productiveness." [1] The details and the causes of this hiatus in Beethoven's output are not directly to the purpose here, for the decade 1810–19 is, after the very beginning, empty of quartets. It is interesting, however, that at the turning point, in 1809–10, quartets occupied his main attention once again. After the "Emperor" Concerto was finished early in 1809, a quartet—the Quartet in E♭, Op. 74—stands as the main work of a year that otherwise yielded the rather slender Piano Sonatas in F♯, G, and E♭ (*Les Adieux*), and not much else of moment. In 1810, although much time was spent on the incidental music for *Egmont* and on sketches for the "Archduke" Trio, the one substantial production was the Quartet in F minor, Op. 95.

The Quartets in E♭ and F minor were written about a year apart, then: an appreciable span of time, by Beethoven's earlier standards. But on this occasion, nothing of first importance appears to have occupied him in between. There would seem to be every reason to consider the two quartets together, in the same way that we naturally group together the six Quartets, Op. 18, or the three of Op. 59. Indeed, the two share certain technical proclivities—in the attitude toward sonata form, for example, and toward the key sequence of movements—and both exhibit a poise and control that mark a decided advance over the earlier period (or subperiod). Nonetheless, between the two there is a cleavage in aesthetic stance unlike anything that differentiates the "Razumovsky" Quartets from one another. The E♭ Quartet is an open, unproblematic, lucid work of consolidation, like some others written at this time. The F-minor Quartet is an involved, impassioned, highly idiosyncratic piece, problematic in every one of its movements, advanced in a hundred ways. One work looks backward, perhaps, the other forward. Or to put it better, one work looks outward, the other inward. It would be hard to imagine any composer grouping these antipodes together as a single opus.

The contradictory aspect of the quartets of 1809–10 is curious, and even seems to be reflected in Beethoven's treatment of the dedications and dissemination of the two pieces. One is inclined to suspect some circumspection on the composer's part, perhaps in response to the tepid reception given to the "Razumovsky" Quartets. These had been published early in 1808, and Beethoven was not one to ignore the fact that they were less understood or admired than any other important music he had written. In 1808 he may have privately made up his mind to take the next opportunity to write, have played, and publish a quartet that would be pre-eminently "available" to his essential public. That, in any case, is what he produced within eighteen months in the E♭ Quartet.

[1] P. 483.

On the contrary, the F-minor Quartet—"*Quartetto serioso*," Beethoven called it, very remarkably—takes its point of departure not in availability but in introspection. This for Beethoven was expressed in terms of complex technical problems, some of them stubbornly picked up again from the "Razumovsky" series, others posed anew. With this work, the quartet becomes for the first time Beethoven's private workshop. For an unusually long period of time he withheld the piece from publication and even from performance—one would like to say, exactly on account of its problematic and personal nature. Actually, in these years he would appear to have grown stand-offish about publication in general. Departing from his earlier practice of issuing new works promptly within a year or two of their completion, he now held on to this quartet for six years, the "Archduke" Trio for five years, and the Violin Sonata in G and the Seventh and Eighth Symphonies for four, before releasing them all together, in 1816. That was a real orgy of publication, after many lean years.

Beethoven did not even have a commission for the F-minor Quartet. He dedicated it to his very close—perhaps his closest—friend Nikolaus Zmeskall von Domanovecz. The E♭ Quartet, however, was inscribed as though pointedly to Prince Lobkowitz, dedicatee of Beethoven's first quartets, the ever-popular, always "available" Op. 18. Lobkowitz had recently banded together with Prince Kinsky and the Archduke Rudolph to become one of Beethoven's most official patrons. In response to the composer's interest in a *Kapellmeister*'s position at Cassel, an interest which they must have seen to be disingenuous, the three princes offered him an annuity from their own purses if only he would remain in Vienna. That was no onerous condition. In view of past and current performance, they had every reason to expect an ample bounty of music in the coming years; "they were bitterly disappointed," Thayer remarks. But it is hard to suppose that Prince Lobkowitz had any complaints about the first fruit of the new arrangement, the Quartet in E♭, when it was played at his palace soon after completion.

1809 was an important year, in terms of exterior event. The annuity from the princes was a major victory; Beethoven was elated. His immediate response was to plan marriage, however, and the subsequent rejection of his proposal to (presumably) Therese Malfatti appears to have hit him extremely hard. During this crisis, Zmeskall may have proved an especially true friend. In May 1809, Vienna suffered its second invasion by the French (the first invasion had helped to spoil the premiere of *Fidelio*); this time the occupation lasted five months, and was enlivened by a two-day siege of shelling. Thayer repeats the well-known story about Beethoven sheltering his ears with pillows in his brother Carl's cellar, and remarks on the general disruption of life and harassment under foreign rule, inflation, and the rest. Beethoven could not take his habitual long summer holiday; what was perhaps worse, most of his friends and patrons had left the city—and one could not repeatedly divert oneself by writing *Les Adieux* sonatas. More to the point, Nottebohm claimed to read in a sketchbook of 1809 evidence of Beethoven's inability to settle down to work on major projects:

> The appearance of the following pages bears witness to the fact that Beethoven lacked the composure and inner peace for the continuation of his usual activity and the execution of larger compositions. Except for work on a sonata movement, which, to judge from the number and character of the sketches, came rapidly to its final form, these pages reveal no continuous larger sketches. Rather they are filled in part with drafts left undeveloped, in part with theoretical examples and exercises, and in part with notations of various kinds. The period in which this blocking of compositional activity can be remarked may be ascribed to the middle two or three months of the year.[2]

Give or take a few months, this sounds very much like the Quartet in E♭: a rather marvelous piece written at a time when the composer could not fully concentrate.

· 2 ·

The slow introduction that opens the Quartet in E♭ grows mainly from a single motif, a sort of "*Muss es sein?*" or (better) "*Möchte es sein?*" which is presently to be answered—*forte* and *allegro*—in the affirmative. The motif always concludes tentatively, and it leans strongly toward the subdominant, but for 17 bars of *poco adagio* the piece seems to take pains not to modulate properly to the subdominant key or to any other. Modulation, it will appear, is no prominent feature in any of the movements of this quartet. The final phrase of the introduction, though starting with a dramatic minor-subdominant chord, does not modulate either, but slides upward to the dominant through a series of deep harmonic obfuscations. Mystery-making after an initial clear tonic was traditional in slow introductions, and Beethoven was following tradition here—more closely at least than in the introduction of the C-major "Razumovsky" Quartet. He

2 *Beethoveniana*, II, 263–4.

Example 79

made material for his obfuscation by picking out the two middle notes of the main motif and multiplying them into a rising chromatic sequence; the phrase as a whole sounds like an astonishing protraction of the motif. The chromatic step returns modestly at one point in the ensuing *Allegro*, within the bridge.

The *Allegro* is touched off by an *arpeggio* motif which resembles the introduction motif just closely enough in melodic and rhythmic profile to suggest its affirmation or resolution. After this bright antecedent, a peaceful consequent phrase touches the subdominant over a tonic pedal (bars 28–31). This harmonic arrangement calls to mind a Mozartian habit heeded by Beethoven in his very first quartet, Op. 18, No. 3, in D; at present it recalls to the ear the subdominant inclinations of the *Poco adagio* which has just been heard. A brisk antecedent moving from tonic to dominant, and a lyric consequent over a pedal—this corresponds in basic plan to the first theme of the E-minor "Razumovsky" Quartet. But there everything was tense, irregular, passionate, here everything is gracious, balanced, untroubled, even a little glossy. One might say something similar about the introduction of the present quartet by contrast with the cryptic introduction of the C-major "Razumovsky." Unlike any of the quartets of Op. 59, this Quartet in E♭ is ostentatiously at peace with itself. The sense of supreme and easy technical control strikes the listener forcibly.

Calm extends to the formal plotting of the first movement too, very noticeably so. The recapitulation involves no serious functional changes from the exposition, and the few modifications that do occur seem to proceed out of a kind of relaxed improvisation, imaginative froth thrown up almost without calculation by the superb technical machine. A passage such as this burgeoning of the cadence of the original theme—

Example 80

lacks the momentousness of the reinterpretations of prior material in the F-major "Razumovsky" Quartet, or for that matter in any of the first three numbers of Op. 18. One cannot feel that the change was "necessary" for the total formal coherence; it feels more like a rich spontaneous gesture, of a kind that is rather new, I believe, in Beethoven's music of this period. Certainly the preceding quartets were too high-strung to allow much of it. The quality looks forward to another Quartet in E♭, the Op. 127, whose first movement features an almost continuous process of dreamlike variation.

A further instance of calm or simplicity of structure comes with the development section. Concise and facile, the second group of the exposition has concluded with a sharply rhythmicized figure in the new key of B♭ (V), stressing D, the third degree of B♭. On this D the harmony pivots, the development opening abruptly with the main theme in G major (III), so that the brisk *arpeggio* goes up from G to B to D (the same D). During 10 bars of the development, only a single modulation takes place, as for once Beethoven allows the subdominant urge of his material to ease the tonality around from G to C. But no further. When the consequent phrase appears a second time, it stays in C for a full 8 bars; whereupon this key is celebrated for 14 additional bars, with very strenuous orchestral sounds and with repeated cadential phrases slicing the melody away into smaller and smaller fragments. Then things quiet down of themselves and the harmony moves directly back to E♭, over a long, highly colored 16-bar period. Fourteen bars of the simplest dominant preparation, still impressively scored, lead to the recapitulation.

Now the interesting fact about all these figures is the great length of the development, and at the same time its relative vacuity. It lasts 62 bars, by the clock 20 per cent longer than the exposition, yet it encompasses less real action than any opening sonata-allegro that Beethoven had written up to that point. Not altogether unfairly, this development could be described as a single great C-major statement led into by two routine modulations and led out of by a single monolithic swing back to the tonic E♭. Such a section differs in principle from the development of the *Eroica* Symphony or the F-major "Razumovsky" Quartet. In a sense, it operates by a diametrically opposed principle. In those movements the middle section consists of unstable, uncertain explorations, the instability achieved chiefly by means of modulation. In this movement the middle section amounts to an impressive nonmodulating plateau. To stretch a point, there is here a rather startling suggestion of static *da capo* construction.

Perhaps the opening movement of the Sixth Symphony, with its pastoral purple patches, first started Beethoven thinking along these lines. But the present development section limits itself more severely than that of the Symphony, and the development of the first movement of the Quartet in F minor, Op. 95, carries this kind of limitation further yet, though in an utterly different spirit.

What is obviously the most striking special feature of this movement, its unusual emphasis on instrumental devices of several kinds, should probably be thought of as compensation for the modulatory reticence and the studied simplicity of form. The *pizzicato* passages, the brilliant first-violin passage work, and the rich coloristic mood effects make their formidable contribution to the over-all temper. And the way Beethoven blends them into the quartet texture—where they do not really belong—bears witness again to technical control, to a compositional virtuosity matching the purely instrumental virtuosity. *Pizzicato* comes up right away in the bridge of the exposition; one by one, the four instruments pluck away busily at the *arpeggio* in the main theme. (This passage and its more sensational derivatives earned the quartet its nickname "The Harp"—for no very commanding reason, we may think today, with the Bartók quartets twanging in our ears. But at that time probably no quartet had ever employed *pizzicato* so brashly.) The impressive 14-bar dominant preparation for the recapitulation has the *pizzicato arpeggios* swept up through three octaves and accelerated from quarter-notes to triplets, from triplets to eighth-notes, and from eighth-notes to *arco* triplet-eighths. Doubtless this made a thrilling sound in 1809. Some instrumental effects dim with habitude, though; the passage does not seem so strong today.

More successful, at least in my opinion, are the extended fireworks at the start of the coda, which provides a surprisingly broad, slow-moving, and strong peroration for the piece as a whole. Although the first-violin part looks like a concerto, with its cross-the-string figuration in sixteenth-notes, there is no disparity of effect. And most successful of all is the very last idea, resuming the *pizzicato arpeggios* in contrary motion:

Example 81

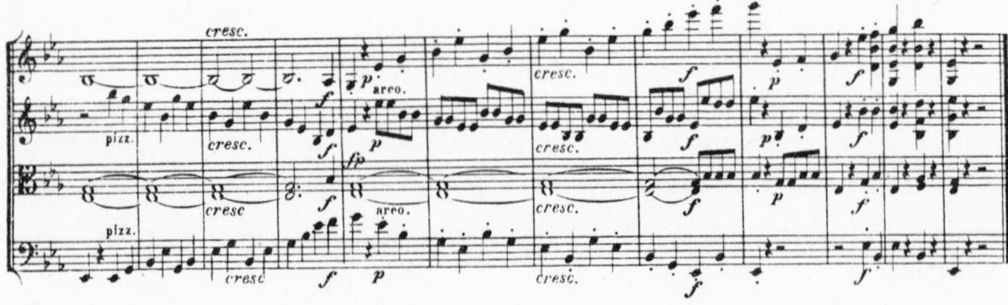

The musical stream is distilled down to its simplest basis in the E♭ triad; there is a flash of whimsy here, and a sense of intellectual show-off, and above all an unintellectual feeling of inspired spontaneous play. Something a little similar ends the first and last movements of the Eighth Symphony, which Thayer (but only Thayer) believed to have been sketched at the same time as the quartet. This instance of thematic "liquidation" is the most genial touch in a genial movement—an unusually brilliant yet unostentatious piece, taut yet in essence serene, intellectual yet unproblematic in its musical thought, raising no major new issues.

The slow movement falls for once into the subdominant key, A♭, the traditional place for it, but also a place that accords well with the inclinations of the first movement. This *Adagio ma non troppo* is a lovely piece of music, relaxed, almost slack by comparison with the serious slow movements of earlier quartets. It banks almost entirely on its opening melody, and this melody makes no effort to generate anything like a sonata dynamic, as usually happened before. It simply appears three times in increasingly rich versions (which can be classed as light variations), with episodes between. By keeping the two episodes tentative in organization, and by leaning them both in the subdominant direction, Beethoven minimizes contrast with the main tune. Even the motivic work tends to minimize contrast: the first period of the melody, scored rather poignantly high, revolves around the third degree (C) and the step that stresses it, D♭–C; then this descending step recurs insidiously—often intensified by two or more quick notes—as a motif or motivic element in both episodes. The step D♭–C (IV–III) also forecasts the tendency of the episodes to modulate to the subdominant.

That Beethoven in his earliest years revealed little gift for melody pure and simple is an old criticism. I do not see that any revisionism is called for, so long as one appreciates his impressive development in this matter. The superb lyric achievements of the last period came only after years of experience: after continual external tinkerings with melodic lines, which can be discerned in sketches for slow movements, and after continual internal testings of feeling, which can only be hypostasized, but which must have been as rigorous as the technical apprenticeship. For technique alone does not seem to suffice to explain the process of development. In this process, the melody of this *Adagio* occupies an important place; it is certainly one of Beethoven's best lyric ideas to date. Tender, and yet at the same time slightly remote in emotional quality, it manages to avoid anything weighty or pretentious, slow as it may go. The force of this remark may appear by comparison with Florestan's aria in *Fidelio* or the *Andante con moto* of the Fifth Symphony—to pick examples not entirely at random.

Once the main melody has come to a slightly drawn-out, peaceful full close, the first episode begins directly with what promises to be a contrasting tune in the tonic minor—as though in apposition to the main melody; one thinks of those Haydn slow movements built on the naïve alternation of major and minor sections. But the pathetic accents of the new tune are not given a chance to take hold. After a normal 4-bar phrase, the lyricism cedes to solemn, rather abstract dramatic gestures pulling the music along to a tentative close (in C♭) and then to a second stab at the episode tune in the minor subdominant, D♭ minor. A single 4-bar phrase is still all that will crystallize; the new 4-bar consequent that emerges serves as a transition rather than as a genuine lyric member. It settles into lengthy—indeed diffuse—dominant preparations for the return of the decorated main melody.

As for the second episode, it starts with a cursory turn to the major subdominant and forms an innocently soulful 8-bar period modulating to its own dominant (i.e., from D♭ to A♭). The period is duly repeated, with touching new comments from the first violin (fascinating, as well as touching: they make a sort of free canon). Instead of rounding out this lyric beginning, Beethoven appears to lose interest; having reached A♭, he takes the opportunity to commence his main melody again, in the minor mode. (Probably more than one listener has thought of Schubert's *Das Wirtshaus* here.) This potential minor-mode variation has the effect of a very curiously placed false start, for after only one phrase, new dramatic gestures interrupt and hurry into the entrance of the entire melody, in the major mode, for its third and last appearance. So there is not much to get one's teeth into except for the main melody, which grows more gorgeous in each successive manifestation. Both the delicate ornamentation of the melodic line and the involved figuration below it are progressively elaborated. Some of the opulent sonorities resemble points in the slow variation movements of the late quartets.

The gigantically calm coda is perhaps the most admirable part of this whole calm movement. Instead of resolving, the main melody halts for a moment on its last dominant chord—which is run directly into the minor tune of the first episode. This sounds less like a statement in apposition, then, and more like a recollection or something insubstantial. The familiar 4-bar *minore* phrase gets no further than before, and thematic fragments in light counterpoint attenuate themselves pensively. The important step D♭–C echoes in a repeated series of slow dying closes. Things are becoming very ethereal; but the low cadential V-of-V and V chords, eight bars before the end, restore a sense of involvement. In a movement that has self-consciously eschewed strong dominant harmonies, these chords sound wonderfully warm.

After so quiescent a slow movement, an intense scherzo is definitely in order. The piece (which Beethoven does not mark *Scherzo*, only *Presto*) is evidently a benign twin of the famous third movement of the Fifth Symphony; but what counts as benign in relation to the symphony still sounds violent enough within the framework of this quartet. Among features that show kinship with the symphony are (of course) the notorious driving rhythm; the key of C minor—which Beethoven never took lightly; the jocose, noisy contrapuntal trio; the *da capo* of the *Presto* in a deepening *pianissimo;* and the grandiose deceptive cadence at the end, running into A♭ (♭VI) and a long passage of transition to the Finale:

Example 82

Since this piece of mystification is leading not to triumphant C major—as in the symphony—but to cheerful E♭, things will proceed differently, and Beethoven actually contrived a repetition of the deceptive cadence one step higher, on the Neapolitan degree, D♭. The "availability" of this passage to Schubert is manifest in his first impressive quartet, the unfinished *Quartettsatz* in C minor of 1821, as well as in his last quartet, Op. 161, in G major.

The *Presto* goes fast and furious, in a well-behaved sort of way; nothing here will raise Prince Lobkowitz's eyebrows. It manages a bold sequence through the Neapolitan degree (D♭) without losing its grip on formal checks and balances in the correct classic spirit. The trio, which behaves less well, Beethoven originally marked *Più presto quasi prestissimo*, as well as *fortissimo* throughout, but it is interesting to see him in effect change his mind about the former direction when he comes to supply metronome marks for the quartet a few years later. He sets identical marks for both *Presto* and trio, 𝅗𝅥. = 100 and 𝅝. = 100; he might then just as well have used this notation:

Example 83

—a notation which takes one cue from Beethoven's own dotted-whole-note indication, and another from his rubric "*Si ha s'immaginar la battuta di* $\frac{6}{8}$" (in later years he might have written simply "*tempo di due battute*").

The initial odd-footed phrase in gauche double counterpoint is illustrated above. When, immediately, this phrase is to be repeated, it gathers extra voices and becomes a parody textbook exercise in third- and fourth-species counterpoint, nine bars long. There follows a pair of derivative phrases, modulating. Then the initial phrase rounds out the form by roaring through its material in contrapuntal inversion—a belly-laugh at all pedants, and a belly-laugh at the composer himself.

For during the difficult months of the French occupation, he was occupying himself with the compilation of counterpoint exercises for his patron-pupil the Archduke Rudolph. Copybook models for this trio would have been running around in his head—doubtless to Beethoven's own disgust. But in any case, formal counterpoint in a quartet was practically a tradition with him by this time, a point of honor, an automatic response. In this piece, as in the E-minor "Razumovsky" Quartet, the obligatory contrapuntal display comes as a raucous major-mode trio. Beethoven repeats the *Presto* literally and the trio literally a second time and then the *Presto* once again, as though to be sure nobody misses the schoolboy naughtiness of it all (but the effect, as in the Fifth Symphony, is a good deal better than that). Only after the third time round for the *Presto,* when it is progressively hushed, does the long transition which so impressed Schubert usher in what must surely be some particularly formidable concluding statement.

But not at all. What ensues is a particularly refined and economical variation movement on a slight, elegant *allegretto* theme. This is as conspicuously light a finale as could have been conceived.

The tune has two main points of interest: the quaint syncopated harmonic rhythm and the piquant modulation scheme, the first half closing on a G-major triad (III) and the second half pausing on a D-major triad (VII) before returning to the tonic key E♭. The six variations, all in tempo and in time, hew closely to the theme and range themselves in an almost childlike order. Odd variations (Nos. 1, 3, and 5) are each marked *sempre forte* and concentrate on figuration, whereas even variations (Nos. 2, 4, and 6) are each marked *sempre dolce e piano* and concentrate on lyric expansion and small harmonic subtleties. Each of the variations, like the theme (but more so), harps on a single kind of rhythmic motion. Taking an idea from the cadences of the original theme, Variation No. 1 joins various canonic eighth-note patterns to simulate continuous eighth-note motion. Variation No. 2, a warm, smooth viola solo, moves in continuous triplet-eighths. No. 3 speeds up to continuous sixteenth-notes. No. 4 slows down to continuous quarters. No. 5 uses a syncopated motif involving sixteenths. No. 6 combines continuous eighth-notes and triplet-eighths simultaneously. It is all lucid in the extreme.

In the three quiet, lyric-harmonic variations, the central cadence can be deliciously altered. The note G, it is demonstrated, may seem at first to act as V of vi in the key of E♭, but it may also act as iii, in Variation No. 4, or simply as the third degree of the E♭ triad, in Variation No. 6. Here Beethoven boils the whole tune down harmonically to the scheme Tonic | Nontonic | Tonic; and with a quiet show of mastery, he chose

Example 84

for the "nontonic" sonority a completely unexpected one, a rich Brahmsian ♭VII (D♭) in place of VII (D) as before. This simplifying or liquidating variation recalls in a way the coda of the opening movement of the quartet, which reduces everything to a buoyant, spiritual play of E♭ *arpeggios.*

A coda commences with fragments of the melody of Variation No. 6, in which I seem to hear the elegant folk-accents of *An die ferne Geliebte*

Example 85

echoing or fore-echoing across the years. An amusing repeated cadence pattern resumes that D♭, again in the bass, with small regard for grammatical orthodoxy, after which a series of accelerating half-variations leads to a rather sudden quiet ending. But the suddenness points out the sly disposition of the final tonic chord with G on top!

In his *Cobbett's Cyclopaedia* article, Vincent d'Indy brushed aside this movement as one that "adds no element of novelty." In point of fact, suave, half-humorous, nicely balanced variation movements that build from *allegretto* tunes and feature slightly remote modulations *are* new in Beethoven's works at this time. These characteristics are missing in earlier sets of variations, such as that of the Quartet in A, Op. 18, No. 5, and in later ones, such as those of the last quartets. Other examples at the present period occur in the Violin Sonata in G, Op. 96, the Piano Fantasy, Op. 77, and the Piano Variations, Op. 76 (on the tune that later became the Turkish March in *The Ruins of Athens*).

D'Indy was just not interested in this sort of novelty, that is all. He sensed what is obvious enough: that the radical fresh areas of experience which Beethoven has led the listener to anticipate, in one composition after another, are left aside here. This holds for the quartet as a whole, a work of consolidation rather than of exploration, a work which though by no means content to repeat something that has been done before, is content to move within an expressive framework laid down by its predecessors. I have suggested that some retrenchment may have been called for after the disruptive tendencies in the "Razumovsky" Quartets, and also that the stance may have been partly "political" on the part of the composer, and that it may have been partly forced on him by the difficult conditions of 1809. To put it another way, in J. W. N. Sullivan's famous formulation, the Quartet in E♭ cannot be said to contribute seriously to Beethoven's "spiritual development." For Sullivan,

> The transition from the fourth to the fifth symphony is not the transition from one "mood" to another, both equally valid and representative; it is the transition from one level of experience and realization to another; one might say that the transition is vertical, not horizontal. And the third and fifth symphonies are more important than the fourth in the history of Beethoven because it was the deepest things in him that conditioned his development. The greater importance the world has always attributed to the third, fifth, seventh and ninth symphonies compared with the fourth, sixth and eighth, is not because of any purely musical superiority they possess, but because everyone is more or less clearly aware that greater issues are involved, that something more important for mankind is being expressed.[3]

The Quartet in E♭ is not one to raise deep questions and great issues—that is what D'Indy saw. Liberation from the necessity to raise and meet them, indeed, helps give the piece its special *élan*, as does also a sense of quiet exhilaration in artistic processes circumscribed and carried through with elegance and tact and perfect accuracy. These qualities, which are hardly to be dissociated from the fact of technical control, do rather definitely represent an element of novelty in Beethoven's bank of expressive resource.

· 3 ·

His next major piece of work, the Quartet in F minor, ultimately published as Op. 95, differs from all this so radically that one almost imagines

[3] Pp. 155–6.

him setting himself some sort of spiritual exercise. (Better that picture, anyhow, than the one about the "Immortal Beloved.") Instead of a classicizing work whose one faintly troubling tendency may be in the direction of facility, this is first and foremost a problematic work which thrusts in the direction of eccentricity and self-absorption. But Beethoven at his most quirky is Beethoven possessed. In this quartet, as in none of the others so far, he evokes that almost tangible sense of the artist assaulting a daemon of his own fancying; and unless our response is to call the whole illusion into question, we are likely to admire (or worship, if we are Sullivan) the process of assault, conquest, assertion, or becoming that the illusion permits. Not only does the quartet belong safely on Sullivan's major axis, it probably counts as Beethoven's most perfectly coordinated axis composition to date, and by any reckoning his least prolix.

The F-minor Quartet is not a pretty piece, but it is terribly strong —and perhaps rather terrible. One does not hear it with the joy and the *Mitgefühl* that the E♭ Quartet should evoke; the piece stands aloof, preoccupied with its radical private war on every fibre of rhetoric and feeling that Beethoven knew or could invent. Everything unessential falls victim, leaving a residue of extreme concentration, in dangerously high tension. But strength, not strain, is the commanding impression; the listener is confronted with expressive authority as secure as that of the E♭ Quartet. Once again, this authority is not to be dissociated from consummate technical control, a quality that comes out clearly, I believe, if the composition is considered together with the E-minor "Razumovsky" Quartet. That Beethoven was dissatisfied with the E-minor Quartet I should not dare to say, but certainly in the first movement of the F-minor he addressed himself all over again to expressive and technical problems broached there: to pain and violence and the raging alternation of feelings, to the minor mode and the Neapolitan step and the rationalization of rhythmic discontinuities. What was often merely brusque and hypersensitive in the earlier composition has become entirely forceful here. The F-minor Quartet is a nugget statement of the world of the E-minor.

If the opening period of the earlier work was original, complex, and even eccentric in construction and expression, these qualities are pushed to some kind of limit here (see p. 170). As in the E-minor Quartet, the initial outburst is cut off by a rest, and then answered by a sharply contrasted new idea. Also as in the E-minor Quartet, the first theme theatrically offers to repeat itself up a step on the Neapolitan degree, G♭. But we have experienced that sort of thing before; the violins suppress the cello with a 12-bar lyric passage contradicting the

Example 86

explosions of the start in a quite remarkable way. Turning pathetically back toward the tonic key, this passage dwells upon the semitone C–D♭, upper reflection of the original Neapolitan step F–G♭. Repeatedly D♭ sinks down to C, in bars 6–10, 11–13, 14, and 14–15. What is this leisure doing in the drastic, shotgun atmosphere of the opening 5-bar statement?

In the F-minor Quartet, individual notes and individual note-relationships are forced into the consciousness more strongly, perhaps, than in any previous composition by Beethoven. This is partly a consequence of the extreme sense of compression. We have seen Beethoven working to convince us of the significance of certain notes—with G and G♭ in the first movement of the F-major "Razumovsky" Quartet, for instance—and we have admired the massive draughtsmanship by which such points were made. Here the same sort of thing is accomplished in a single stroke, with a violence unknown to the earlier music. There is an urgency to every "sore" note that sticks out of the fabric, and with this new responsibility, a new opportunity for expressive manipulation. The Neapolitan step is of course unshakably planted, and the tritone C–G♭ between bars 5 and 6 haunts the ear for the rest of the work. (I hear it echoing already in the descending D♭–G between bars 9 and 10.) So does the step D♭–C which has emerged as the principal substance of the lyric interruption. Then, as the opening figure is resumed, compressed, erupted, and evaporated into the second group, the progression F–G♭–G♮ (bars 18–20) stabs a wound that will somehow have to be healed in the sequel.

In the E-minor Quartet, the modulation to the second group was done abruptly enough, with scarcely any buffer. Here the switch almost alarms; three or four bars suffice. The shuddering inflection in bar 23 seems to legitimize the move to D♭, the second key, which in any case has been anticipated by the harping D♭–C of that lyric passage. The second group itself is just as curt: a rocking figure several times repeated (10 bars) running into an extraordinary cadence (9 bars) settling into a little tonic *ostinato* (4 bars); then the cadence, even more intense, and the *ostinato* are both repeated.

All through the Quartet in F minor one senses Beethoven's impatience (or fury) with conventional bridge and cadential passages of every kind—the more or less neutral padding material of the classic style. In the "Razumovsky" Quartets he labored to individuate such passages. In the E♭ Quartet he enjoyed stylizing them. Now he will simply do without them. The particular radical ellipsis of the F-minor Quartet may never be needed again, but through it Beethoven gained a new resource of expressive immediacy which is drawn on in all the later music.

As for that extraordinary cadence, its contributions include sheer ferocity; extreme dissonance as preface to extreme relief and swift resolution; and a recollection of the first group. The opening gesture of the movement is recalled by the *fortissimo* unison scale followed by the long rest, and the lyric passage that interrupted those gestures is recalled by

Example 87

the poignant answer here with its semitones. Even more important, the progression again involves an upward semitone step to the Neapolitan degree, I–♭II (D♭–D♮, or strictly speaking D♭–E♭♭; this is in the new key of D♭ major). Eight bars earlier, the cadence had come on the upper reflection of this step, A♭–A♮ (A♭–B♭♭). Since the passage counts as the most memorable in the whole exposition, its handling in the recapitulation faced Beethoven with a problem and a rare opportunity. The solution is analyzed by Tovey:

> The development is a short process of Mozartean straightforwardness and Beethovenish violence, and it leads punctually to a recapitulation in which the first group is represented merely by the moment at which it executed the transition [i.e., bars 18 ff.—see p. 170]; and here it has the audacity to execute the original transition to the original complementary key (♭VI). After four bars in this key, the second group quietly swings round to the tonic major; but now comes the evidence of Beethoven's imagination at its highest power. Only two other masters could have been trusted to see the right thing here—viz. Schubert and Brahms. Anybody else would have exactly transcribed the fierce outbreaks upon ♭II; but the colour value of ♭II has gone. It is hardly distinguishable from ♭VI. Beethoven substitutes the ordinary supertonic [♮ii, G minor], and does not even sophisticate it by making it major. The glare of common daylight is the one thing that can inspire terror at this juncture.[4]

[4] *Beethoven*, p. 107.

This brilliant stroke occurred to Beethoven at the last moment. Nottebohm gives a very late sketch of the recapitulation which simply moves to ♭II, like the exposition. The ordinary supertonic, it should be added, serves as an iron resolution to the Neapolitan sounds earlier, a resolution upward: F–G♭-G♮, from I to ♭II to ♮ii. Such upward resolution is carried further yet in the Finale of the quartet.

What Tovey calls a "short process of Mozartean straightforwardness and Beethovenish violence" is indeed a single "process," a single arc of 22 bars without preface, postface, or any real interior seams. That in itself is remarkable—though how characteristic and how right for this particular piece!—but not as remarkable as the harmonic situation. For the entire passage hovers around the tonic key, which is ambushed at the beginning and glimmers through all the admirable fracas of diminished 7ths, 9ths, and enhanced dominants. The dotted-rhythm motif of bars 3–5, though introduced nowhere else in the movement, does find a role here, perhaps on account of its naturally stormy quality; the whole 22-bar section wants to sound like the storm in the Sixth Symphony (which is also in F minor), with its echoes of operatic *temporali* back and forth from Gluck to Rossini and on. Lightning strokes, rainy hushes, soughing branches, roars of thunder—all are maneuvered with much verve and with instrumental virtuosity worthy of the "Harp" Quartet. Characteristic intervals batter the ear: F–G♭–G♮, D♭–C, and finally a splendid crux of D♭ and E♮—

Example 88

before the composer plunges into a harshly truncated recapitulation of the first group.

The whole formal scheme is as ingenious as it is original. For the sake of over-all compression, an abrupt modulation was wanted in the exposition; so the new key—not even a very close one, by the way—was suggested ahead of time by an unusual lyric passage right in the first group. Meanwhile, the very placement of this lyric passage adds to the general mood of discontinuity. Then in the recapitulation, for greater brusqueness, amputate that lyric passage entirely; there is no new key to prepare. When Beethoven anyhow "has the audacity to execute the original transition to the original complementary key," this will have a novel feeling of instability about it. Which in turn can be very beautifully dispelled by the subsequent inevitable swing back to the tonic (within the second theme, at the third repetition of its rocking figure). Since the exposition and the recapitulation include such vivid harmonic contortions as those of the opening bars and of the repeated second-group cadence, the middle section—one rather hesitates to call it a "development"—can forgo modulation and achieve its violence simply by means of dynamic and orchestral storm-effects. Here perhaps lies the fundamental difference in conception between the treatment of the Neapolitan step in the F-minor Quartet and in the E-minor. The earlier piece works out the tensions of the step in a large, complex development section. The later piece handles them tersely, almost aphoristically, within the exposition and the recapitulation. The difference reflects a swing in Beethoven's practice that will become more and more pronounced in his later music, a swing away from traditional development procedures toward more flexible and more gnomic expression.

In reparation for the truncated recapitulation, a coda is required lasting almost exactly as long as the "development," after starting with

Example 89

a very similar ambush. D♭ is recalled, and also the opening motif, more brazenly than ever before. In the final liquidation, the cello flings out the same crux of D♭ and E♮ that had emerged at the end of the "development." This now sounds like a skeleton of the opening bars: F–E♭–D♭–C–D♮–E♮–F reduced to D♭–C and E♮–F. The cello D♭–C, in particular, on the bottom of the C string, seems to crystallize all the semitone obsession of the piece—the Neapolitan steps, the harping lyric passage of the exposition, and the poignant conclusion of the second-group cadence.

It also provides a fantastic promontory from which the second movement can be experienced. For it seems to me that the famous unaccompanied cello scale which introduces the *Allegretto ma non troppo* takes at least half of its tension from its relation to this liquidating D♭–C in the cello. D♭ at the end of the first movement is answered by D♮ at the beginning of the second; only after several halting *portamento* notes does D–C♯ explain itself as a simple scale in the new (and far from simple) key of D major. This makes for an excruciating discontinuity, of course, and arguing from a discontinuity may seem like arguing from a vacuum. However the excruciation is far from unprepared. The opening movement bristled with semitone relations, the step D♭–D♮ occurring at its most memorable juncture, the second-group cadence in the exposition. And does not the cello now gingerly line out the very sonority that Tovey describes as climactic in the first movement, the supertonic G triad—sophisticated, now, into the major mode?

In any case, the confrontation between D major and F minor stands as the most extreme between movements in any Beethoven work, bar

Example 90

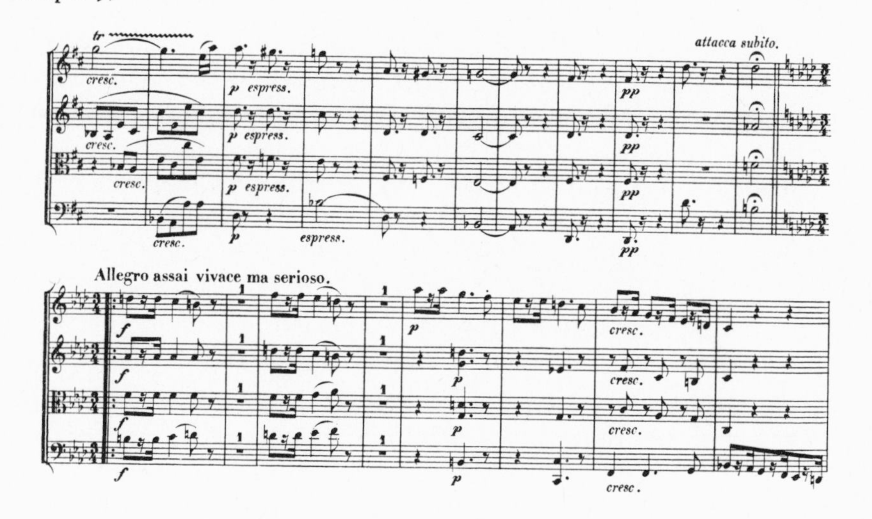

none. The second key of the first movement already represented an enhanced dominant, D♭ (♭VI) in place of C (v). D♮ in the second movement represents an enhancement of the enhancement. Furthermore, this D-major *Allegretto ma non troppo* keeps importing B♭, its own minor sixth degree—the same enhanced dominant relationship (♭VI) that is made so much of earlier. As a result, the joint between the second movement and the third can hang on the progression D–B♭–B♮, which is parallel to F–D♭–D♮ between the first and second. In both situations the cello leads the way. These joints can only be sustained in the light of various violences in the early movement, as described, and strong measures later, too. The very fact that they are sustained contributes centrally to the expressive sense of the work as a totality—to its strength, its poise, and its hermetic virtuosity.

A lyric slow movement poised—one might even say, racked—in this way is obviously not designed to register any sort of consolatory relaxation. When Beethoven wants that, he may as well leave the slow movement in the key of the first movement, as he does with the Quartet in E minor. But at this point the F-minor Quartet parts company for good with the E-minor: in place of a grandiose, mystic, somewhat sentimental turn away from the preoccupations of the start, here the prior disturbance is continued and actually enhanced. It is not often that an extended lyric statement in the classic style attains a level of psychological intensity as high as that of the opening movement. The most obvious technical index of this is the continuing chromaticism—in itself an unusual feature for a slow movement, particularly for one ostensibly in the major mode. This *Allegretto ma non troppo* has a subtlety and a deep sense of involvement that are even rarer. It does not represent a resting place or a point of reflection but a newly intense stage on the journey that was initiated by the outburst at the very beginning of the quartet.

After the introductory cello scale, an emotional, fluid melody emerges. It comes to a formal full close; a fugue is developed; the melody returns with a greatly spun-out coda. This would amount to the familiar *A B A* dynamic if not for the fact that the fugue ruptures hugely in the middle, so that the piece is experienced as a sort of retrograde *A B* | *B A* arc, hinging on a crisis of expressive intensity. Indeed the hinge acts as a climax for the quartet as a whole.

In orthodox fashion, the fugue begins with one instrument following

Example 91

another at fairly regular 4- and 5-bar intervals. A marvelously melancholy subject winds downward through ambiguous chromatic steps, with a countersubject mirroring and thus intensifying the chromaticism. A chromatic subject in D brings to mind Book II of *The Well-tempered Clavier*, and this may also have occurred to Beethoven; but for Beethoven a chromatic fugue subject was pretty well committed to modulatory vicissitudes well beyond Bach's expressive range. Only a fugue so committed, of course, could serve his purpose at the present juncture.

Already at the fourth (first-violin) entry, illustrated above, the charged chromatic lines are causing problems in terms of the harmonic underpinning. The Neapolitan harmony suggested by the end of the subject (i.e., the B♭ of bar 51) works its way back into the prior bar; then a dark piercing tritone figure (second violin) obtrudes enough to repeat itself in triple counterpoint, the figure thrown up to the top of the churning harmonies (bars 51–2, 53–4). *Strettos* begin to crack the fugue apart. Things happen very fast, until in bars 57–9 the outer instruments strike a catastrophic new tritone (G–D♭) in place of the original 4th-leap of the subject. The tritone *incipit* cannot continue. Instead the violin singles out the lamenting chromatic essence of the subject, the descending semitone motif of its first full bar.

This makes for a climax of passion rarely matched by Beethoven himself (bars 60 ff.). The effect is helped by a sudden stoppage of the involuted harmonic rhythm, on a strong low E♭ (a note scarcely anticipated; some sort of weak diminished harmony was in line for bar 60, a fact that seems to be acknowledged retrospectively by the cello F♭ in bar 62). The E♭ harmony resolves pathetically to a very distant tonic, A♭. This is a tritone away from the point at which the fugue began, D.

The rupture has to be healed from the outside—by the opening cello scale, moving enharmonically through incredible, unfathomable tonal spaces. The cello is treading on razor blades, and the upper instruments are whispering through their teeth memories of the semitone lament, which, indeed, seems to be frozen into the cello line itself. The semitone step B♭–A, finally, hollowed almost to nothing in bars 77–8, marks the tenuous return of D major. The fugue tries again.

At this point the fugue subject seems to want to get along; witness the new hasty countersubject. Perhaps it no longer dares explore the chromaticism of its fourth bar, which had proved so disruptive. Entries now stumble in at 3-bar intervals, a compression which masks the well-calculated lowering of intensity on other grounds. The harmony will not attempt to digress any further: it comes simply to the dominant, and the subject takes on fresh blunt energy by submitting to inversion (a standard fugal resource used in a rather unusual way). Imitations press more closely; the new countersubject coalesces; rich tritone figures emerge again, only to be fobbed off around a circle of 5ths in preparation for a very strong, leisurely return. The passion of the previous climax is recalled, but it is passion resolved and encompassed.

This return involves the entire opening melody, complete with the cello scale, reduced from its original *mezza voce* to *sotto voce*. But after the melody there is yet another breath-taking reminiscence of the crisis that halted the fugue. The final cadences of the melody are interrupted by the fugue subject (or rather, gently combined with it, for the first violin continues very elegantly with its cadence line). Free *strettos* starting

G–D, A–D, and D–D are topped by a high tritone A–E♭, and as before this tritone *incipit* collapses into a lamenting semitone step, B♭–A. Supported by another unanticipated low bass note, an open-string C, this step has just the flavor of the prior D♭–C over the bass E♭. But when E♭ moved to F♭, that was a feint. Here, when C moves to C♯, the harmonic aberration is guided directly back.

Example 92

All this may seem to imply that the original *allegretto* melody, the *A* of the *A B* | *B A* structure, is overshadowed by the fugue (*B*). That cannot be, of course; the movement lives on the mysterious balance of the two. Beethoven thought enough of the melody to build an exceptionally long, serene coda out of repetitions of its cadential figures. Yet there can be no doubt that the lyric flow was restrained with the brooding fugue in mind, and the coda bolstered by way of compensation. The melody itself, after a heavy surge towards the minor subdominant in the first phrase, hangs largely around the dominant. Sensitive—indeed hypersensitive—inflections around B♭, A, and B♮ take the place of modulation or even of other incidental harmonies. (Perhaps that is the price for venturing so frankly on an early strong subdominant. Perhaps the cello scale, twisting the other way, was needed to keep us on an even keel.) In short, this not quite a "melody" in the self-contained sense that melodies figure in slow movements of the E♭ Quartet or the C-major "Razumovsky." The *Empfindsamkeit* (almost debilitation) and unrest (almost uncertainty) and curious muted pathos that mark this melody apart from any other in Beethoven are as much a matter of over-all construction as of the highly refined sense of scoring and nuance.

Next to this, even the glum fugue subject sounds almost craggy and predictable. That it bears distinct analogies with the start of the melody was observed (and exaggerated) by Hugo Riemann. The point surely lies in the way Beethoven coaxes from the fugue the same lamenting semitone (B♭–A) that is of primary importance in the melody too. The last fragment quoted (the recollection of the fugue after the return of the melody, before the coda) aggregates and reconciles the two. They cleave together, we now understand, as an inseparable dyad. The many repeated B♭'s within the superb long coda cement this impression, as well as preparing for the new link forward to the next movement.

If the reader has been prepared to follow me in regarding the first movement of this quartet as a fresh attack on problems broached in the E-minor "Razumovsky" Quartet, he may also see this second movement as an actualization of the slow movement of the C-major "Razumovsky." Beethoven cautiously accelerates the tempo by one notch, from *Andante con moto quasi allegretto* to *Allegretto ma non troppo*, and he lightens the relentless *minore* of the earlier piece to the deeply shadowed major mode here. All the same, he is dealing with a basically similar vision of restless lyricism. Both pieces have a particularly complex notion of the stance appropriate to a slow movement. The role of the cello is curiously parallel, as is the use of tritone relationships at the points of greatest contrast; the very striking chromatic passages away from the A♭ climax in this work, and away from the E♭ eruption in the other, closely resemble each other in harmony and texture. The F-minor slow movement is the finer, because less "strange" and forced, less gaunt, and less obsessive. And because the composer is no longer harboring any compulsion about sonata-form procedures in his slow lyric utterances.

At all events, the disturbed accents of this *Allegretto* or of the "Razumovsky" *quasi allegretto* seem finally laid to rest. They no longer haunt Beethoven in the quartets or in other music. Slow movements now become increasingly serene: the path indicated not by the C-major "Razumovsky" Quartet but, however broadly, by the E-minor.

The third movement of the Quartet in F minor is as surprising as its predecessors, though for an opposite reason: not for its complexities but for its simplicities. Essentially it ranks in the familiar category of Beethoven's driving scherzos, which generally set out to strike a gross contrast with their slow movements. Here the contrast sounds like a real denial, in view of the link between the movements through the diminished-7th chord on B. The rhythmic idea itself, especially as aerated by rests at its first appearance, is likely to recall the motif of bars 3–5 of the first movement. The link and the first few bars have been quoted on page 175.

The main section of the piece is ostentatiously dry and square—dry on account of the gritty writing in 3rds, which can slip into real double counterpoint at the 10th or as easily into hollow unisons; square because its brief, single span of 40 bars is made up of five 8-bar phrases of two 4-bar phrases each, balancing rigidly left and right. The whole effect is rather constipated. We must not call the movement a scherzo, because Beethoven specifically marks it *Allegro assai vivace ma serioso*, so perhaps we may call it a march—a serious, three-legged, tough little quick-march. The *Alla marcia, assai vivace* of the Quartet in A minor, Op. 132, will move at about the same rate.

The contrasting trio is neither dry nor square nor even fully organized. A sort of *schwärmerisch* chorale in block chords never gets past its initial phrase; between repetitions of the same phrase, the simple violin figuration keeps going in a curious club-footed fashion. The whole interest here is in the harmonic treatment. The march, after the diminished-7th link from the previous movement, fell directly back from the dominant key to the central tonic F minor, which it hammered loudly and stiffly for its remaining 24 bars. It did not have the time (or the inclination) to modulate. The trio does not have the wit to modulate; it simply finds itself in certain extremely distant keys: first in G♭, the Neapolitan degree which started all the fury in the first place, and then in D major, the excruciating plateau of the slow movement. This amounts to a kind of irresponsible summary—*ma serioso!*—of harmonic regions achieved with great expressive labor earlier in the piece. After a strange passage in B minor, F minor returns by way of the same diminished-7th chord on B.

Crotchety, succinct, asthmatic—the march runs through its motions again, and then the trio and march are brought around another time, but in contracted versions. The second trio starts the chorale first directly in D (a very pointed reference to the crux of F minor and D) and then safely at last in C. For the third march, the 24 *forte* bars suffice, played *più allegro*. The compression begins to border on the grotesque.

As though to dispel any such suspicion, Beethoven introduces the Finale with a moment of decided relaxation: eight bars of *Larghetto espressivo* before the advent of the *Allegretto agitato*. Technically, these bars may be considered to liquidate the obsessive dotted rhythms of the march, and certainly they contribute to the general coloring by piling up D♭ on top of C, with B♮ thrown in for good measure. However, their main role would seem to be to modulate the feeling into something more familiar and available, after the fine eccentricity of the march and trio. They reproduce the standard heavy accents of high lament which Beethoven had sounded in (for example) the F-minor *Adagio molto e mesto* of the first "Razumovsky" Quartet. This tone would have been too obvious for the slow movement of the present work, and even now it maintains itself for no longer than two short phrases. In emotional terms, this suffices to prepare a movement designed to bring the quartet a modicum of normality in shape and sentiment.

Not that the construction of the *Allegretto agitato* fits any textbook prescription; it makes its own combination of sonata and rondo features. But though the transitions may still be as brusque and passionate as ever, and though the recapitulation may happen before one quite notices, the dynamic is always immediately comprehensible. One is not always being confronted by those searing harmonic intrusions and rhythmic juxtapositions which give the earlier movements their sense of the problematic. Details of counterpoint and figuration, particularly at the recurrences of the taunt main theme, are marvelously varied, resulting in an almost Wagnerian overload of rich inflection; yet these details sound like no more than decorations of the always more or less predictable swing of the rondo repetitions. In consequence, this movement avoids the harshness that had shadowed earlier parts of the quartet. In particular, its pathos is simpler and more direct than that of the opening *Allegro*.

Some distinctly stormlike effects are heard, as in the first movement, but the first movement includes nothing so innocent as the second subject here. A somewhat half-hearted development runs into a false recapitulation in the subdominant—as also happens in a later finale that resembles this one in a number of ways, the Finale of the Quartet in A minor, Op. 132. Everything is exceptionally laconic, and the *agitato* humor (in one sketch Beethoven glossed it with the nonexistent word *languente*) is excellently projected. Less garrulous than the Finale of the E-minor "Razumovsky" Quartet, the Finale of the F-minor also blusters less. This movement, this quartet as a whole, is not going to end in the oblivion of sheer raging exhaustion.

Beethoven's concluding touch reopens unexplored expressive vistas. Grandiose D♭'s have slowed down the coda to a strange halt on a *tierce de Picardie*, that is to say, a major-mode tonic, scored low in the strings and marked *ppp*. For the first time in its life the piece seems positively to mark time. Then, as though something silently snapped, a very fast *alla breve* section emerges in the major mode, a fantastic evocation of an *opera buffa* finale in which all the agitation and pathos and tautness and violence of the quartet seem to fly up and be lost like dust in the sunlight. Through the speedy repeating cadential figures, a single chromatic motif isolates itself: F♯–G–G♯–A, a reflection of the F–G♭–G♮ of the opening movement, and at the same time a way of resolving it into the clear major 3rd, F and A. There are evanescent contrapuntal touches—as evanescent as "*Questo è il fin di chi fa mal*" in the final scene of *Don Giovanni.* Everything is effortless and amusing and trite; the texture glistens; it is all over in a second or two (like everything else in this compressed quartet). A perfectly astonishing conclusion.

Also thoroughly problematic, like so much else about the Quartet in F minor. Was Beethoven "serious" in calling a piece with such an ending "*Quartetto serioso*"*?* The seriousness seems kicked in the rear—delicately kicked, but kicked all the same. Vincent d'Indy, who congenitally grew tight-lipped as Beethoven grew playful, was prepared to dismiss the whole passage as one "without interest or utility of any sort." It is hard to argue with a joke except by saying that you don't want to hear one. Yet there is a genuine idea about how to end a piece of music here, in spite of something uncertain reflected in the joke and in the lack—or at best tenuousness—of relation between the ending passage and the rest of the composition. The germ of the idea is even traceable in the last page of the Quartet in E♭, Op. 74.

Perhaps Beethoven did not exactly see how to end the Quartet in F minor, or to put it better, did not exactly "feel" how to end it. He had perhaps never engaged so directly with the darker emotional forces. He was perhaps himself overwhelmed. But in 1810 he had reached a stage of compositional virtuosity—the point has been made in connection with both the E♭ and F-minor Quartets—that allowed him to gloss over doubts with great ease and with a certain impressive show of *sang-froid.* The suspicion is strengthened by what seems clearly to be a much deeper success with a similar problem later, in the Quartet in A minor, of 1825. Beethoven had a habit of returning to half-solved problems. Through their finales, in fact, the two minor-mode quartets of the second period can be related directly to the two minor-mode quartets of the third: the E-minor "Razumovsky" Quartet to the C♯-minor, and the F-minor to the A-minor.

To glance ahead, for a moment: the Finale of the A-minor, after resuming the pathos of the first movement of the composition in a dynamic analogous to that of the F-minor Quartet, concludes with an analogous *volte-face* to the major mode, *Presto.* Again the first impression is of lightness and play, as though a great weight of involvement has been lifted. But the shadows are not quite forgotten, and the contrast in mood, though again staggering, is not so puzzling because (among other reasons) the new major-mode material is led in to by a definite thematic passage. The concluding section itself is longer and more self-sufficient; Beethoven can afford really to look at it. In this ending, the prior pathos seems genuinely—"seriously"—encompassed. The play seems genuinely earned or achieved.

One more Beethoven piece belongs in this discussion: the Overture to *Egmont*, which was written at just the same time as the F-minor Quartet, and which also resolves its basic tonality of F minor by means of a new concluding section in the major mode. The process is rare enough with Beethoven to make it certain that the parallel with the quartet was interesting him. One has the distinct impression of an inversion of means, as though the composer had seized upon a single technical idea to see how opposite emotional effects could be wrung out of it. For in place of the evanescent play of the quartet, the F-major "Symphony of Victory" at the end of the Overture strikes a loud and violent (and indeed rather blatant) note of triumph. This much was directly inspired by Goethe. Yet by comparison with the late quartet, both earlier compositions may be seen together as thrusting aside their prior action a little too hastily—in the one case humorously, vehemently in the other. Only in the A-minor Quartet did Beethoven achieve a really integral sense of dissolution. And in quite a different spirit, he realized something analogous at the end of one of the major-mode compositions of the same period: the Quartet in E♭, Op. 127.

· 4 ·

In the opinion of the present writer, and not his alone, certainly, the Quartet in F minor stands at the highest summit of Beethoven's artistic achievement up to the end of the second period. I trust the judgment is not unduly influenced by the seemingly proleptic tendencies of this composition, tendencies which have struck all the commentators with varying degrees of force. The matter of the finales is only one of many ways in which the quartet seems to look forward over the relatively lean years of the next decade, and to store techniques, attitudes, and actual ideas for the composition of the late quartets in 1825–6.

For example, the very impressive fugal section of the *Allegretto ma non troppo* brings to mind almost inevitably Beethoven's well-known preoccupation with fugue in the last period, which played itself out in the Great Fugue and in the opening movement of the Quartet in C♯ minor. As a matter of fact, the smooth, chromatic, expressive *fugato* of the early quartet comes as close in feeling as any other Beethoven fugal extract to the C♯-minor work; ordinarily his fugues are not "expressive" but violent, and the contrapuntal texture is not sinuous but gritty—as in the contrapuntally inclined march of the Quartet in F minor. The march, in turn, can look like a first manifestation of ideas developed in another movement from the late quartets: the *Scherzando vivace* of the Quartet in E♭, Op. 127. That larger movement bears a number of points of contact with the march, though it also leads a life of its own over and beyond that of the earlier composition.

In more general terms, the Quartet in F minor seems to foreshadow aspects of the technique of the late quartets in its dominant qualities of conciseness, directness, and instant confrontation of contrast. But in the later works, even when contrast is forced very hard, the effect may not be so abrupt—as is true of the Finale of the A-minor Quartet by comparison with the F-minor.

Both the E♭ and the F-minor Quartets handle sonata form much more coolly than the earlier pieces. They pay little attention to sonata procedures in any of their movements save the first, and even there the development sections have become surprisingly simple—in the E♭, little more than a lengthy tonal plateau, and in the F-minor, a single stormy process hovering around the tonic key. Beethoven was moving away from the "heroic" type of development section, the development on the *Eroica* model. Here too the quartets of 1809–10 anticipate the later ones, which develop all kinds of astonishing new alternatives to the traditional exposition, development, recapitulation scheme, without at all abandoning the underlying principles of sonata form.

Another matter is the tendency to interrelate and link movements of the cyclic work. With Beethoven, as has been seen in one composition after another, this was accomplished largely by harmonic means. And the quartets of 1809–10 carry this tendency forward more subtly and more securely than the "Razumovsky" series. That the Quartet in E♭ employs as many as three different keys for its four movements (E♭, A♭, C minor, E♭) is already indicative; previously Beethoven had used three keys in only one sonatalike work—the recently composed Piano Trio in E♭, Op. 70, No. 2, using exactly the same three!—but in such later works as the Quartets in B♭ and C♯ minor, he will find a need for four keys and six, respectively. With the E♭ Quartet, he must have attached importance to the fact that the plateau-key of the first-movement development, C, is the very one that recurs so surprisingly in the *Scherzo*. Relationships among the movements extend further. To cite one: C–D♭ is a prominent step in the *Adagio* and D♭ is its main subsidiary key; the *Scherzo* moves dramatically through D♭ too; and the Finale makes its most arresting harmonic point by the insertion of D♭ into the otherwise bland E♭ tonality.

Things work even more interestingly, or in any case more intensely, with the Quartet in F minor. The first movement throws D♭ and D♮ against F minor; the second movement can therefore maintain itself in the extraordinary key (for this context) of D major. The solo cello scale at the beginning of this movement accepts the situation, in some awe, and so stresses it. Then the parallel degrees B♭ and B♮ color the D major of this second movement, and it is by way of a diminished-7th chord on B♮ that the end of it links back to F minor. In F minor again, the march takes care to strike one resounding G♭ Neapolitan chord, sufficiently reminiscent of the opening movement, with its arresting Neapolitan steps. The trio reiterates not only G♭ but also the D major of the second movement. Semitone articulation continues to be important in the Finale, from the brief *Larghetto espressivo* introduction through the *Allegretto agitato* up to and including the major-mode conclusion, *Allegro, molto leggieramente*. The new motif F♯–G–G♯–A dimisses and dissolves all the convoluted B♮'s and D♭'s, as everything resolves up into lucid major 3rds.

The significance of these technical details, it should be said, is not uncontroversial; even so, one is reminded of how much more confidently technicalities can be talked about than their aesthetic results, which are what finally matter. That the two are connected feels very sure; greater intimacy among the movements makes the total experience more continuously self-aware, and seems to raise the level of insight to a special plane. A certain kind of discipline implied in the concept of an ordered totality reflects back on the individual movements, too. Even considered separately, their new flexibility makes for a new sensitivity of response, and their remarkable directness of expression seems to preclude sentimentality, bombast, or any sort of overextension of feeling. Thus in the first movement, although the pain and the spleen will cow the listener sooner than charm him, he will as likely submit to the integrity of the experience contained there as to the sheer ferocity of the action. The emotional current is altogether too intense to be turned off with the next movement, the superb *Allegretto ma non troppo*, which deepens the sense of disturbance and tempers it with a very equivocal sweetness. Toward the end of the work, as often happens with cyclic compositions in the minor mode, the complex experience of the beginning is resumed and simplified. If here less seems to be lost than usual, that is partly because the last two movements seem almost to set about analyzing aspects of the first: the march filtering out its quirkiness and anger, the Finale concentrating all its agitation and pathos. And then the delightful, astonishing, problematic major-mode conclusion, with its curious glance ahead to Op. 127 and Op. 132.

Forward-looking stylistic tendencies, too, can be talked about much more confidently than the qualities of individual works of art—and to do so is a considerable temptation at this particular point in a book on the Beethoven quartets, when attention is about to turn to the last period. Reviewing the last works of the second period, the Quartets in E♭ and F minor of 1809–10, we can formulate the contrast between them in terms of one of them looking backward, the other forward. But to consider one looking outward, the other inward, is closer to the aesthetic point. The Quartet in E♭ seems public and available, an open book by contrast with the surrounding quartets, an essay in sophisticated—if temporary—retrenchment. Perhaps it occupies the true turning point among the Beethoven quartets. At the turning point of a pendulum, the momentum is temporarily zero. The Quartet in F minor, written only a year later, is Beethoven's most self-absorbed and uncompromising and fraught with energy, the energy turned squarely in on itself.

A quartet is not a spiritual diary, but some quartets much more than others appear to take substance from a deep inner process of introspection and emotional synthesis. It is the penetration and (I believe) the hitherto unmatched directness of the inward look that establishes the particular greatness of the Quartet in F minor. It would be pleasant to think that in entitling it *Quartetto serioso*, Beethoven was referring to its unmatched seriousness in insight. That quality too points to the future. It is, in fact, ultimately the chief signpost to the third period.

BOOK III

7

VOICE

A book on the Beethoven quartets is three books, we have said, through which certain kinds of continuity are bound to be tenuous at best. From the Op. 18 Quartets of 1798–1800 to the second-period quartets, and then to the late quartets written fourteen and more years afterwards, it stands to reason that there can be no real effort at historical draughtsmanship, in spite of signposts, retrospective gestures, and all the apparatus of historical formulation. With ten *opera* out of more than a hundred and thirty—of course they are not all equally important—there can be no idea of covering the evolution of style and concept. Simply in their own terms, the three groups of compositions embody different sorts of emotional penetration on the part of the composer; they demand correspondingly different commitments on the part of the listener. The critic who is sensitive to these differences will find himself reacting by automatic reflex in one way to the quartets of Op. 18, in another way to Op. 59, and in another to Op. 131. So if the reflex is not resisted, as I certainly think it should not be, the three groups of quartets will in some respects elicit rather different approaches. This the reader will see reflected even in a mechanical aspect of organization in the present chapter, among others.

Furthermore, with each group of pieces there will be a difference in the amount and quality of attention on which the critic may fairly expect to draw. This third book must be the longest and most intense for the rather simple reason that the music of Beethoven's third period is the most admired and the most thought about. For several generations, the late music has been gaining in interest, sympathy, prestige, and circulation what the earlier music has actually been losing to revisionist taste.

Critics have closed ranks about this music, performers now play it and program it without any special alarms, and the common listener (to adapt a term from Virginia Woolf) has found a special place for it in his essential musical experience.

The situation after Beethoven's death was very different, of course. That his last compositions were not accepted has always been known, but the extent and duration of the rejection has been made clear only recently in *Beethoven: Naissance et Renaissance des Derniers Quattuors* by Ivan Mahaim. After digging into concert records from all over Europe, Mahaim brings forward fascinating statistics about the circulation of the five late quartets and the Great Fugue. For example, in the twenty-five-year period after Beethoven's death, Vienna—that great musical center—can boast a grand total of no more than *seven* public performances of any of these works. In a fifty-year period, up to 1875, records of performances in nearly a hundred towns from St. Petersburg to Boston extend only slightly above the one thousand figure. Inexplicably enough, it was the Quartet in F, Op. 135, that was the most unpopular. As for Mahaim's favorite piece, the Great Fugue, that appears to have waited twenty-seven years for its second public airing, and only fourteen such hearings can be traced in all the time up to 1875. In view of this scarcity of performances, special interest and special respect attaches to Wagner's famous tribute to the Quartet in C♯ minor in 1870, and also to the analytical essays on the quartets by Theodor Helm, which were published as a book in 1885 after appearing serially as early as the 1870's. The Great Fugue was a tightly closed book to this author, as Mahaim does not fail to observe,-but in the appreciation of the other late quartets Helm must count as a pioneer.

The history of musical taste affords few more striking phenomena than the subsequent change of attitude toward this body of music. To try to analyze all the causes for the change and gauge its larger significance would take us far afield. This much is clear, however: it has to do with the main line of musical evolution into the twentieth century, and new ways of comprehending new music have helped to illuminate the third style. Various trends of modern music can be seen to be prefigured by technical aspects of the third style; for Stravinsky, the Great Fugue is "this absolutely contemporary piece of music that will be contemporary forever. . . . It is pure interval music, this fugue, and I love it beyond any other."[1] At the same time, the twentieth-century consciousness has been able to respond very directly to something in the expressive content of the

[1] *Dialogues and a Diary*, p. 24.

late quartets—something overreaching and pure and characteristically indefinable. "In the last string quartets spiritual experiences are communicated of which it is very difficult to mention even the elements," wrote that aggressively common listener J. W. N. Sullivan. "And yet it is just this music that most moves us and impresses us as containing the profoundest and most valuable experiences that any artist has yet conveyed . . . experiences that we recognize both as fundamental and as in advance of anything we have hitherto known. With such art we make contact, for a moment, with

> The prophetic soul of the wide world
> Dreaming on things to come.

It is to this kind of art that Beethoven's greatest music belongs and it is, perhaps, the greatest in that kind." [2]

In spite of this new well of sympathy, it cannot be said that the really discerning, full-textured study has been written about Beethoven's third period. One cannot draw on a generally accepted account of the style and the rhetoric, as one can with the earlier music. Sympathy and prestige are all very well, but articulation is another matter; the challenge to technical analysis is very great, and the challenge to emotional confrontation appreciably greater. None of the writers on Beethoven has failed to recognize the centrality of the problem, however, and none has failed to say something about it. While the art required for their weaving may still be lacking, the main strands of the last style have probably been isolated. We can return to card them in the chapters to follow.

Motivic work, for example, grows more momentous, as Beethoven makes his thematic material ever more terse and pregnant. Walter Riezler speaks of "a refinement and sensitiveness in the part-writing, and a feeling for the depth and significance of the smallest detail, such as is to be found in none of his earlier works." [3] Like so much else—like the quality of intense introspection that goes along with it—this seems to have been forecast by the Quartet in F minor of 1810. Simultaneously, the power of the form grips the listener more acutely than ever before, both within the individual movements, and among movements linked together in the most imaginative ways. Concern for part-writing is reflected in a growing preoccupation with formal counterpoint, the main monuments of which —fugue, canon, chorale—abound in the last compositions. In the area of harmony, new ideas develop about modulation, cadence structure, and

[2] Pp. 227–8, 250–1.
[3] P. 219.

sometimes even tonality itself, when Beethoven experiments with the old church modes. There is an attendant sense of spiritualization, which has struck all commentators without eliciting from them very much in the way of verbal articulation. Principally, perhaps, it is the whole matter of musical contrast which is treated most radically, and which as a result opens up whole new unexpected areas of consciousness. Since formal principles such as that of sonata form depend first of all upon contrast, these principles too now yield patterns of unprecedented flexibility and expressive force.

Now, with some justice, the various features enumerated here might be considered to be inward, subtle, technical, and even esoteric. If every impulse of the last style tended in this one direction, there might be a basis for the formidable barrier that the late works used to be said to present—do they still present?—to the common listener. But an equally strong "public" impulse accompanies the "private" one: a striking new directness of emotional appeal, a determination to touch common mankind as nakedly as possible. Never in the past had Beethoven reached so urgently for immediacy. There is something very moving about the spectacle of this composer, having reached heights of subtlety in the pure manipulation of tonal materials, battering at the communications barrier with every weapon of his knowledge.

The great exemplar of this drive is the Ninth Symphony, of course, the major composition just prior to the last quartets and the one under whose shadow they were initially conceived. (The present chapter might have been christened prettily "After the Ninth.") As Wagner never tired of driving home, the Ninth Symphony brings to the orchestra words, poetry, and the human voice, in an effort to make instrumental music more articulate. The voices sing about man-to-man fellowship, and they are not delicate about exploiting the naïve *élan* of a military rally and the naïve awe of a churchly rite in order to force their point. At the heart of the undertaking stands that famous (or perhaps one should say, notorious) finale tune—half folklike, blinding in its demagogic innocence, torn from the womb of recitative without a shred of accompaniment clothing. Even before the Finale, a note of immediate popularity in the melody of earlier movements of the Ninth Symphony can hardly be mistaken. It is the very clasp of Beethoven's hand.

To many musicians and critics of a certain modern intellectual temper, this impulse of Beethoven's last period has proved more than a little embarrassing. We live in the valley of the Ninth Symphony—that we cannot help—but we would probably breathe easier if the mountain were hidden by a perpetual cloud, by a critical smog of our own manufacture. Yet I am certain that the unique richness of the last period derives exactly from the duality of introspection and solicitation, the inward-outward, public-private aspect of the art. There is a range and an ambition here not matched in *Threni* or *The Art of Fugue*, in *Parsifal* or *Falstaff*—nor in Beethoven's Quartet in F minor, which by comparison can seem one-sided on account of its self-absorption.

Unique, of course, but not wholly unprecedented, even if the duality is rarely apparent in the last works of the other great masters. The clear precedent is Joseph Haydn, with his hymnlike slow movements and folklike rondo tunes, his mystic tone in the last church music, and his growing conviction about the "universal language" of music and a heritage of humanity to carry with it. A generation ahead of the Ninth Symphony, Haydn's last symphony, in the same key, the "London" Symphony, No. 104, has a finale theme of a just vaguely similar studied naïveté. Whether Beethoven felt any kinship in this matter with his old and little-appreciated master, is hard to say; his first recorded kind word about Haydn was muttered on his deathbed; but however this may be, the historical climate contributed to his own idea. So did Beethoven's personal situation. The deafness—after 1816, virtually complete—that drove him inward on his own resources drove him on the rebound to repeated outer assaults upon personal sympathy; a process with both pathetic aspects and also, in his dealings with friends and relatives, with nearly tragic ones.

A string quartet is not so exhibitionistic a creature as a choral symphony (though Beethoven did want to make his last quartet discuss its playful decisions in public). Nonetheless, the five quartets and the Great Fugue which occupied the end of Beethoven's composing life, after the Ninth Symphony, are drenched in evocations of the human voice. These evocations mean to sing or to speak instantly to the heart, like the songs imagined by Beethoven's poet at the climax of *An die ferne Geliebte:*

> *was mir aus der vollen Brust*
> *ohne Kunstgepräng' erklungen,*
> *nur der Sehnsucht sich bewusst . . .*

In the last period, the illusion of art concealing art, of communication "without the adornments of Art," is among Beethoven's very particular studies. One is carried away, astonished, and ravished by the sheer songfulness of the last quartets—by recitative and aria, lied, hymn, country dance, theme and variations, lyricism in all its manifestations. The first of the series of late quartets, the Quartet in E♭, Op. 127, is of all Beethoven's works his crowning monument to lyricism.

· 2 ·

Let us preface an examination of this quartet with some other evidences of the new vocal impulse.

Probably the most eloquent witness is the famous *Adagio* movement inscribed "*Cavatina*" in the Quartet in B♭, Op. 130. This title means an opera song of modest scope and, over the years, of varying characteristics. The term is used freely by Rossini; Weber had used it for Agathe's smaller soliloquy in *Der Freischütz;* and Mozart might well have used it for Tamino's air *Dies Bildnis ist bezaubernd schön* in *The Magic Flute.* The first violin takes the role of the singer, while the other instruments play the orchestra—a division of forces so pat that a mezzo-soprano or a baritone with a good high G (and a good sob) could sing the violin part without a single grace-note's alteration. One would have to search the repertory hard to find another quartet, symphony, or sonata movement of which this could be literally maintained. The *Cavatina* assumes a thoroughly operatic stance. Vocality is more than evoked. It is practically transcribed.

Operatic, too, is the shape of the principal melody, a long, loose ternary song occasionally disturbed by declamatory pressures. Beethoven had not written many opera songs; one does not have to look far to find a direct structural model for the *Cavatina.* The *Andante* of Florestan's aria in *Fidelio* is built just like it, only out of shorter members. In both songs, Phrase A closes on the tonic, but its repetition deflects under declamatory pressure to a slightly remote cadence; an expressive Phrase B traces sequences of no great weight, and a repeated Phrase C begins and ends on the tonic and establishes an earnest climax. The elegant orchestral echoes and repetitions, as Florestan catches his breath at the end of his phrases, could likewise have served the *Cavatina* as model for the action of the lower instruments.

They also borrow something from the woodwind echoes in the *Adagio* of the Ninth Symphony, upon whose hymnlike tone the *Cavatina* enlarges in its own more intimate fashion. In principle, each phrase or phraselet of the hymn is echoed by the accompanying instruments, or else commented on by means of the important motif of bar 1. (On p. 197 Phrase A is illustrated in the form it assumes in the *da capo;* from bar 49 on, the melodic line corresponds exactly, the accompaniment very nearly so.) The repetition of Phrase A is disturbed by recitative urges—a model

Example 93

for them can be found in *Abscheulicher! wo eilst du hin?* or, if you prefer, in the instrumental recitatives of the Ninth—leading to a *cupo voce* cadence in C minor. Then in Phrase B sentiment and texture become more intimate. One almost hears a Mozartian clarinet and bassoon, in sorrowful dialogue upon the motif, leading the singer by the hand and then passionately breaking out of the circle-of-5ths sequence to provide a 5-bar phrase and a rhetorical climax. "*Was würde ich?*" Tamino, in *his* cavatina, asks rhetorically at this point. The climax, with its characteristic descending 6th, retraces that of bars 5–6 (or 53–4). The repeated Phrase C resumes the hymnlike tone and texture of Phrase A; the close of the long melody is heavy and prayerful.

The following *beklemmt* section (bars 41–9) makes a second serious contrast in texture, and modulates more seriously, to C♭ (♭VI). While the accompaniment begins to throb in triplets—which reminded Riemann of the *Arioso dolente* ("*Ermattet, klagend*") of the Sonata in A♭, Op. 110, and might also have reminded him of a place in the Sonata in C, Op. 111—the melodic line becomes not merely broken, as in the two sonatas, but stammeringly out of joint with the accompaniment. It is an extraordinary effect, and one that hits straight in the guts, though to my mind Beethoven and his commentators too have been winded by it to the point of accepting some pretty crass melodic and harmonic constructions here. (Crass, in spite of the very interesting fact that a sort of variation of the principal tune is taking place.) In any case, a prime fact of the matter is how the *beklemmt* section is terminated. It shows every sign of easing into a full-scale *B* section—only to be cut off almost at once by a dark gesture resonating hugely with associations. The cello F♭–E♭ of bars 47–8 recalls the C-minor cadence of Phrase A, and the violin in bar 47, dilating on a 6th, recalls the many descending 6ths earlier in the song (notably a climatic drop from G to B♮ in Phrase C). Most radically of all, these bars all but duplicate a progression from the previous *Andante con moto* movement, and an extremely prominent progression at that:

Example 94

Closer confrontation of the various movements of a work is another crucial feature of the last quartets, to which we shall return. At the moment, the point of all the associations is to magnify the drama of the interruption.

Then the placement of the *da capo* of the principal melody in the key of E♭, in spite of the implication of A♭ in bars 47–8, acts to justify the drama. Phrase A returns quietly and yet with a remarkable fervor, an aura much helped by subtle action in the second violin—contradicting the previous C♭ tonality with C♮ and carrying the repeated step G–A♭ up to B♭–C.

The amplitude of Phrases A and C makes everything else in the piece sound taut. The emotions touched on in the *beklemmt* section, someone has said, are so intimate that it hardly seems right to be allowed to witness them; but we witness so briefly that all Beethoven needs to balance the form is an integral return of the 8-bar Phrase A plus a new conclusion lasting only 9 bars longer. Cascading echoes and repetitions, this conclusion carries the climactic surge from B♭ to F (bars 53–4) up to G (bars 57–9, echoed in the cello). All through the song the note G—the third degree—assumes cardinal importance. The opening motif flowers gracefully in 10ths and 6ths among the various instruments, through the various registers (bars 58, 59, 61, 62).

As for the violin's final exclamation, closing on G, that owes something to another vocal tradition, not the aria so much as the lied. Beethoven had a facile little habit of ending lieder with feminine cadences on motto words—"*nur dein!*" in *Andenken*, "*O Hoffnung!*" in *An die Hoffnung*, and "*Adelaide!*" in the song named for that lady. The effect is more of a tender, calculated confidence than of any sort of constructive pillar, more sentimental than epigrammatic. In the *Cavatina*, the sentiment recalled is apparently that of bars 45–6, ending the *beklemmt* section.

In one of the conversations with Robert Craft, Stravinsky judges the *Cavatina*, together with half a dozen other movements from the late quartets, to be "pedestrian." Even with the maximum exercise of charity and sophistry, it is hard to grasp the force of the adjective in reference to the play of technique in the *Cavatina*. The sentiment of the piece may not suit Stravinsky, or us, but "pedestrian" we cannot call it without discounting Beethoven's own conversation with Karl Holz, second violinist of the Schuppanzigh Quartet, when he said "that the *Cavatina* was composed in the very tears of misery, and that never had one of his own pieces moved him so deeply, and that merely to relive it in his feelings always cost him a tear." The sketches which record the compositional process are extremely copious. It is a reasonable guess that this quite extravagant comment stuck in Holz's memory because it corresponded with his own feelings in the matter, and those of audiences to whom he had played this particular movement. Beethoven's wish, in transcribing for quartet an unwritten opera song, must have been to make the most immediate kind of emotional overture. In the eyes of his essential public, then or now, I do not think it can be said that he failed.

· 3 ·

The urge for direct communication found an obvious outlet in the use of recitative, "a kind of Prose in Musick," as William Congreve defined it, "a more tuneable speaking." That is to say, the outlet was obvious in vocal compositions. In instrumental ones, the lengths to which Beethoven was prepared to go in adapting the vocal style testifies to the overpowering strength of his need for immediacy of address.

In the late years, the first instance comes in the Sonata in A♭ of 1821, and the most celebrated in the passage beginning the Finale of the Ninth Symphony, where the cellos and basses reject a parade of themes and then finally elect one, all in wordless recitative. (We know that this is what they are doing from the words added by a baritone when he appropriates this music later: "O friends, not these sounds; let us rather strike up something more seemly, more joyful.") Also most remarkable in concept is the *Dona nobis pacem* of the *Missa solemnis*, which bends the liturgical words into a recitative for contralto (*ängstlich*), tenor, and soprano beseeching peace against stormy battle symphonies sounding in the orchestra.

The first of the late quartets, the highly lyrical Quartet in E♭, does not contain any wordless recitatives, unless one counts the strange interruption that shakes up the third movement, the *Scherzando vivace*. In the Quartet in C♯ minor, Op. 131, numerous touches of recitative—edging into a rhapsodic or cadenzalike style—help make the wonderful transitions in and out of the A-major *Allegretto* Theme and Variations, and also in and out of the G♯-minor *Adagio* (which sounds, by the way, as though in another context it might have grown into another *Cavatina*). Each of the three other quartets shows the influence of the Ninth Symphony at the beginning of its finale. The original finale of the Quartet in B♭, the Great Fugue, opens with an *Overtura* rattling through a parade of all the thematic shapes to be utilized in the piece. The Finale of the Quartet in A minor, Op. 132, is led into by an almost hysterical violin recitative, with tremolo and all the trimmings—the rawest that Beethoven ever conceived. The Quartet in F, Op. 135, precedes its Finale with a regular slow introduction adopting all the rhetorical tricks of a solemn *recitativo accompagnato*.

In this instance parody, or rather self-parody, is definitely to be suspected. As is very well known, Beethoven wrote words for the instrumental recitative here: "*Muss es sein?*" and later "*Es muss sein!*" The impulse to give his quartets voice was certainly carrying him to extremes. It must be admitted, though, that these rubrics have been more effective in starting silly metaphysical speculations than in clarifying just exactly what it was he wanted to communicate.

· 4 ·

A very distinct genre of popular lyricism sprouts insistently in the dance movements—none of them is an actual scherzo—of the last quartets. At once native and naïve, it takes its point of departure in quite another area from the operatic world of *cavatina* and accompanied recitative.

The neatest example is the *Presto* of the Quartet in C♯ minor, the "trio" section of which can be sketched in its entirety as a simple one-line

Example 95

paradigm. This amounts to little more than a string of tiny self-contained melodic strains, more or less songlike cells with an almost absurdly popular ring. Beethoven marks them *piacevole*—"agreeable, pleasant." None of the little phrases requires more than two different note-lengths; their harmony tends to collapse into drones or *unisoni;* their shape hews rigidly to the simplest of all 8-bar patterns, comprising two very similar 4-bar halves with a tonic cadence typically even after the first half. I shall refer to phrases of this sort as "doublets." What is evoked here is not the opera house, but the village green or else the nursery. We are to respond to these childlike strains as unguardedly as children to nursery rhymes, we are to be swept away by the *Volkston* of the half-dainty, half-clownish country dance. In the "Pastoral" Symphony, the *lustiges Zusammensein der Landleute* had provided a merry occasion for a medley of such dances.

Spiritualized dance parodies had often occupied Beethoven's imagination, probably under the dim impetus of Haydn, once again. The relatively disembodied texture of the string quartet suited the impetus well. Already in Op. 18, a little *contredanse* parody scurries through the slow movement of the Quartet in G, and a *danza alla Tedesca* alternates with *La Malinconia* in the oddly prophetic Finale of the Quartet in B♭. In the "Razumovsky" Quartets, there are the movements based on Russian tunes, and the eloquent, ethereal transformation of the *Menuetto: Grazioso* of Op. 59, No. 3—in mood, perhaps the clearest prophet of the late quartets. In one instance Beethoven actually quotes from pre-existing, non-Russian dance tunes. Two phrases in the trio of the Quartet in A minor (Nos. 2 and 3 in the example below) reproduce trivial *allemande* ideas tossed off in the early Vienna days, when Beethoven wrote dances for the balls at the Redoutensaal.[4] Naturally, the reproduction is not literal; the evocation achieves a wonderful dreamlike quality by means of the subtle rhythmic dissociations and also by means of the formless medley of the sequence of dance fragments.

For doublet phrases are primitive as formal building blocks. If a composer insists on coaxing them to generate fully rounded tunes, as Beethoven does with the finale tune of the Ninth Symphony, the outcome must have the effect of studied naïveté. One can play them over again and leave it at that, as he does with the *andante* tune in the slow movement of the Ninth. Or one can treat them to ornamental variations, as in the Piano Fantasy, Op. 77. Or one can simply string them in a row, as in the trio of the Quartet in C♯ minor which is outlined in example 95. The resulting construction (or nonconstruction) throws all the weight on the slender, flitting snatches of song—which is doubtless where Beethoven wanted it. The ear can hardly organize the random melodic array into larger periods, at least not without running an appreciable risk of pedantry. This construction I am referring to as "medley."

Nothing could be more inconceivable for Beethoven in the early years. It arose now, presumably, in response to his impatience with the rigid binary prototype for the structure of trios in minuets or scherzos. Writing the Quartet in A minor, he even tried "medleys" in other movements besides the trio of the second movement, as we shall see. The latter instance is the most whimsical of all. The jigsaw puzzle is too involved to allow it to be sketched in its entirety as a line-diagram, but here are its constituent cells:

Example 96

[4] *Werke*, Ser. 25, p. 368, and *Supplemente zur Gesamtausgabe*, VIII, 37 (also 18).

The extra bars at the beginning of No. 1, which seem to tune their peasant fiddle around the inevitable drone, scarcely disturb the doublet feeling.

Another batch of doublets—they crop up everywhere in the late music—is shown below. The first four do in fact proceed to round them-

Example 97

selves into naïve ternary tunes. Nos. 8 and 9 play parallel roles in their respective finales, as secondary themes in the tonic key, prior to the first modulation. (At first the C♯-minor tune may seem to jar emotionally in this company, but perhaps after all there is a drop of rustic in its bile.) Nos. 7 and 8 operate within the opening and closing movements of the Quartet in E♭, Op. 127. In recapitulation, both of them flower into ornamental variation:

Example 98

Ornamental variation, as has been said, is one of the natural means by which doublet phrases can extend themselves.

The interesting thing is to see this happening in an opening movement, which necessarily sets the character for the entire work. An opening movement built out of an innocent doublet phrase designed to return in ornamental variation promises a very different mood than that struck by typical compositions of Beethoven's second period. The promise holds for the Quartet in E♭ as a whole.

· 5 ·

Beethoven had composed a quartet in the key of E♭ once before, the "Harp" Quartet, Op. 74, in 1809, and one ostensible similarity between the two first movements is worth mentioning. The composite theme of Op. 127 can be thought of as a more "extreme" version of the theme-type employed in Op. 74, namely, an antecedent-consequent idea passing from force to gentleness. There a brisk tonic-to-dominant *arpeggio*, isolated by an evocative pause, was answered by a lyric "doublet phrase" biased to the subdominant (see p. 159). Here a resonant fanfare, marked *Maestoso*, slowly builds up the E♭ tonic triad to the dominant B♭ and beyond to a rhetorical pause on C. This melts into a lyric doublet (*Allegro*) circling down four times from C harmonized as the subdominant or as the closely related chord ii_6.

Subsequently, in Op. 74, the brisk antecedent *arpeggio* serves to open the development, drifting from G around to C, which turns out to be the one important key of the section. Likewise in Op. 127, the antecedent *Maestoso* returns to start the development in G, drifting round to C, which is again—and more organically—the strong development key. The *Maestoso* even returns once more within the development in such a way as to stress this key.

At this point any parallel ceases, abruptly, for the *Maestoso* never appears again, neither to introduce its consequent in the recapitulation, nor anywhere in the coda. It falls victim to the single-minded lyric ambition of the movement as a whole. In Op. 74 the consequent phrase seems to complement the antecedent, according to the best classic principles of checks and balances; together they form a neat symmetrical pair whose intrinsic contrast fructifies the movement up to its final gesture. In Op. 127 the consequent seems rather to escape out of, articulate, and supersede the antecedent, which therefore can and does wither away. The rhetoric is after all quite different. This movement lives not on contrast but on the inherent beauty of the consequent doublet phrase.

No quartet fast movement in Beethoven moves so lyrically as this one. Among the quartets its gentle utterance occupies a special place analogous to that occupied by the opening of the Sonata in A, Op. 101, among the sonatas. "*Mit innigster Empfindung*," he writes on the earlier composition, "*teneramente*," "*sempre piano e dolce*" on the present one. The phrase structure of the exposition seems unbelievably simple, hardly conducive to dramatic tensions:

FIRST GROUP:	antecedent (*Maestoso*)	6 bars	
	consequent (*Allegro*)	|: 8 :|	(|: 2 × 4 bars :|—"doublet")
	forte	10	
BRIDGE:		8	(4 + 4 in sequence)
SECOND GROUP (iii):	second theme	|: 8 :|	
	1st cadential phrase	8	(3 × 2 + 2)
	2nd cadential phrase	8	(2 × 4)

Only the *forte* passage following the first theme (it perhaps recalls a parallel place in Op. 74) involves any rhythmic sophistication on the level of the phrase; everything else tends to fall into repeating 4- or 8-bar patterns. We might almost be listening to a garland of folksongs.

Yet in spite of its almost voluptuous tenderness, the basic doublet phrase of the first theme is inherently contrapuntal, more so than any earlier quartet theme. It combines three important elements: the melody itself, a *cantus firmus* in unobtrusive parallel motion (cello), and a murmuring syncopated voice (viola):

Example 99

This skeletal species counterpoint will clarify itself as the work proceeds. At first the phrase is repeated in a loosely knit variation (bar 15 ff.) involving an aborted gesture at imitation, a fresh *appoggiatura*, and a sequential melisma in the cello. Action of this kind becomes very characteristic of the piece and contributes greatly to its particular loveliness, its unique sense of efflorescence. One of the spontaneous variations that are applied to the doublet in the recapitulation has already been illustrated (p. 203). New details, often of a light contrapuntal nature, decorate the first theme at every one of its repetitions, and the same is true for the second theme.

Indeed, a process of continuous free variation seems to supplant traditional developmental energy in this movement, in interest at least, even perhaps in function. Certainly the development section proper is undercut. It begins forcefully, with a return of the *Maestoso* spread out over four octaves of G, melting as before into the lyric consequent phrase. But instead of modulating or fragmenting, the latter molds itself into long lyric periods, more ample than before on account of an inversion stretching upward (bars 85–9, etc.), and much more emotional on account of a cadential detail reminiscent of the second theme (bars 96, 112). The new lyric periods are absolutely plain in harmony: 16 bars in G major followed with the least possible fuss by 16 or more in C. Here a thoroughly novel quality of flatness is achieved by the use of canons, and essentially strict ones, at the unison or octave (canons between violin 1, 2, and viola, bars 98, 102, 104; between viola and cello, 97, 99; between violin 1, 2, and cello, 112, 113, 115; between cello and viola, 112, 114). Work of this sort probes the contrapuntal potential of the theme in a timeless aspect without touching on possibilities for dramatic movement. This very impressive passage —but it does not appear to have impressed many commentators—is one of Beethoven's most extraordinary conceptions for a development section, comparable only to the first-movement development in the Quartet in B♭, Op. 130.

And dramatic modulations do not really interest the composer in the 50 bars remaining for his development section, any more than in the first 42. C minor feints at the key of A♭ and shakes with some conventional modulatory bluster, but the *Maestoso* fanfare that emerges remains on C (in which direction it had pointed at its very first appearance, at the start of the movement). C is already heard as a dominant of F, forecasting a second lax swing around the circle of 5ths (G–C, C–F). Thereafter new blusters and a new nod to A♭ return simply enough to dominant-9th chords built on the same C.

What all this is preparing is not the anticipated tonic key E♭, but the

Example 100

first note of the doublet, C, and its first harmony, the F-minor triad, ii_6 of E♭. The intention is to recapitulate the consequent phrase alone, without its antecedent; and almost absent-mindedly the *Maestoso* drops out of the quartet once and for all, never to be heard of again (though possibly it will be heard echoing behind certain phrases of later movements). The paradoxical idea of preparing not the actual key of a theme but the off-tonic sonority on which the theme happens to begin, Beethoven had learned from Haydn and employed in several earlier quartets: in the first movement of Op. 18, No. 3, and most spectacularly in the Finale of Op. 59, No. 2. The direct precedent for the present situation, however, comes not in quartets but in piano sonatas. There are two Sonatas in E♭, Op. 31, No. 3, and Op. 81a, *Les Adieux*, which have first-movement themes starting on ii_6 or its close relatives ii^{6}_{5} or IV_6 and which recapitulate them by means of secondary dominants.

Whatever Beethoven had in mind with the sonatas, with the present composition he seems certainly to have meant to soften the recapitulation. The feeling is altogether different from the emphatic, forceful, or triumphant recapitulations in most of the previous quartet first movements. The doublet slips in obscurely, with an effect neither of enhanced strength nor of Haydnesque wit, but simply of a paradoxical new lease on life and staying-power. As its phrases repeat themselves in gorgeous variation (p. 203), the sense of the return is perhaps left in doubt; some sort of developmental action could still be going on. However the recapitulation unfolds quite symmetrically—which is to say lyrically. There is a new modification to the last of the cadential phrases:

Example 101

The expressive semitone inflection in bars 234 and 239, absent from the exposition, seems to trace back to a poignant detail of the second theme. In turn, the semitone allows Beethoven to move very beautifully toward the subdominant, again, in order to start the coda.

This coda consists of a sweetly obsessive series of repetitions of a newly touching and newly repetitive version of the doublet (bars 249–56) together with recollections of the inverted version of the development and of the original form. Seven times the song circles its way down from ii or IV or ii_6 to the tonic, while the *cantus firmus* isolates itself and migrates now above, now below the melody. The whole effect approaches that of an inexact, ruminative, and inexpressibly tender round. The fourth-species syncopations, introduced at the very start, remain a quietly insistent but constantly varied feature. They allow a piercing detail near the very end (bars 278, 280):

Example 102

This movement is a burgeoning, not a dramatic statement. It soon shakes free of the strong, benign, inchoate *Maestoso* that launched it initially and concentrates on the intimate *aveu* of its contrapuntal doublet. Of this Beethoven never tires. He caresses it endlessly, melting and shuffling the melody itself, urging the syncopations back and forth, exploring fresh regions and registers with touches that are always familiar and never quite the same. The composite theme itself provides the single impressive element of contrast, but contrast is abandoned with the *Maestoso* halfway through the piece. The second theme, far from contrasting with the first, adopts its gait and mien and also a suspicious number of its melodic details. Even its key, G minor (iii)—a minor key!—seems chosen to contrast as little as possible. No less lyric than the first theme, the second sits over a static pedal G which scarcely budges all through the transparent cadential phrases; when the second theme recapitulates in the tonic major, certain original minor-mode inflections are preserved, so that the change of mode makes surprisingly little difference. Strong contrasting articulation is avoided at the point of recapitulation also, as has been mentioned. From the development, what remains in the memory is the section of canons, with its timeless, almost mystic quality.

Sensibility, not structure, is the heart of this piece. Obviously form as such is not the major expressive element. Yet the art required to mold unobtrusive form that will support the repetitive leisure of such a piece is very considerable, as many nineteenth-century composers (or their listeners) learned to their sorrow. The expressive climax of the development comes with the lyric phrases at the beginning and the canonic meditation, for the blustering passages go nowhere and develop nothing significantly. Beethoven must have thought them necessary to set off the recapitulating theme in an unexpected fresh softness. As the fragile little recapitulation might hardly have sufficed to discharge all that curiously dissociated violence, the repetitions of the coda are required or justified. There is about the structure of the movement an ease and instinctive mastery that hides itself, yet frees the lyricism that the composer wished most to develop.

· 6 ·

The melody that generates the second movement of the Quartet in E♭, *Adagio ma non troppo e molto cantabile*, is a famous miracle of beauty. "Were some malignant power to permit us to retain but a single page of Beethoven," wrote Daniel Gregory Mason, as usual a little stiff-necked, a little moving, "this page, which gave him such endless trouble in the writing, might well be the one we should cherish for our solace and delight." [5] Mason was refering to the extensive sketches for the melody, which so struck Nottebohm that for once he printed a whole set rather than just a sample. (The suspicion is that Beethoven's best music was the most laboriously sketched, and the most laboriously sketched the most spontaneous-sounding.) In addition to sketches, a sort of early draft for the melody may perhaps be recognized in Leonore's aria *Komm, Hoffnung* in *Fidelio* (see p. 213). However this may be, its natural vocal quality has never been in doubt. Three months after Beethoven's death, it was sliced off the front of the *Adagio* and published as a song upon that occasion: *Beethoven's Heimgang*, with words beginning "*Es wand sein Geist sich von des Staubes Randen los.*"

What one cherishes is its calm directness, its sense of freedom, its simplicity and its economy. The form is spare, the harmony plain. Everything devolves upon the melodic line ranging through the great span of an octave and a half—the opening upbeat 4th capped by an entire 6th; the soaring octave leaps in the first strain; the new 6th in the second strain, flowing all the way up from the subdominant D♭ to a high B♭; and the beautiful gapped octave—like catching one's breath—down to the delicate cadence. Think of the impressive A♭ melody of the *Andante* in the earlier E♭ Quartet, Op. 74. By comparison with Op. 127, it is a lyric prisoner.

[5] P. 174.

Example 103

The quite unusual luxuriance of the movement as a whole is already forecast within the melody, simple as it is in outline. Half-improvisatory contrapuntal graces are accumulated by almost every segment of it, especially when the cello repeats the two strains originally played by the violin. The free variation technique of the opening movement of the quartet is recalled in such details as the disembodied descant of bars 7–10, the opulent fattening of the melody by the second violin in bars 15–16, and a whole series of imitations or half-imitations of the opening upbeat 4th (cello, bar 3; viola, bar 7; violin, bars 15–16). Even the harmony changes a little in the repetitions of the strains. In bar 17 the important subdominant climax shines because in bar 13 it was shadowed.

After the repetition of the last strain, there are yet two and a half bars of highly articulated concluding material to come—this melody is in no hurry to proceed. Bar 18 provides an echo for the gapped-octave fall of the violin. Bar 19 (after first suggesting a further echo) makes a rich chromatic close. Bar 20 adds a halting 3-note cadence-figure. Each of these three ideas—the echo, the chromatic close, the 3-note cadence—plays its role later in the movement.

Listening to the melody, we have scarcely been worrying our heads about the likely continuations. When a very ornate but essentially regular variation of it ensues, however, it may occasion some surprise, for the melody had certainly not advertised itself as a peg to support a variation chain. The repeated structure of the melody is normal, but variation themes do not normally indulge themselves in leisurely threefold cadences, nor do they at once start gathering to themselves pregnant yet (it would seem) carefully unorganized decorations, as this melody has done so beautifully. Even the opening ground for the peg has been softened, by two bars of preliminary dominant. Not surprisingly, then, with such a beginning, the present variation movement turns out to be a much more organic conception than that of the traditional classic variation model.

All Beethoven's late variation movements, with one exception, move so far from the classic model as to leave it almost unrecognizable (and sometimes unrecognized). We can leave the song of Op. 127 suspended in the air for a moment to consider *la grande variation*, as Vincent d'Indy aptly called it, in general terms.

In point of fact, the use of variation form for slow movements of sonata works is not common in the early years. (Light *allegretto* variation movements, as in the Finale of the Quartet in E♭, Op. 74, pose their own distinct problem.) The stumbling effort of the Quartet in A, Op. 18, No. 5, was ventured only under Mozart's banner. The second period affords few important examples: the *Appassionata* Sonata, the Violin Concerto, the Fifth Symphony, and the "Archduke" Trio. The first three of these rank (to my mind) among Beethoven's least satisfactory slow movements at a time when, indeed, he was not conspicuously happy with slow movements in general. The dramatic thrust of the sonata style kept getting in the way of lyricism, as the "Razumovsky" Quartets show.

But in the third period, Beethoven is even placing slow variation movements as finales; the new interest in song automatically awoke a new interest in variation. This became a technical preoccupation second only to fugue. His last great work for piano, the *Thirty-Three Variations on a Waltz by Diabelli*, and the *Lento assai* of his last quartet, F major, Op. 135, might be characterized as a compendium and as a microcosm, respectively, of the art of variation. In the C-minor Sonata, Op. 111, and in the slow movements of the Ninth Symphony and the A-minor Quartet, he proceeds on the traditional plan of gradually increasing embroidery of the theme. However, in each case he combines this simple variation principle with larger structural considerations—with other themes in other keys, or at least with important modulatory digressions. This happens also in the *Adagio* of the Quartet in E♭, Op. 127. Only the *Andante ma non troppo e molto cantabile* of the Quartet in C♯ minor, Op. 131, fails to make some such effect with its cluster of variations—for reasons that hopefully will appear later, when the composition is considered as a whole.

The contrast in method is instructive, especially in view of the close resemblance of the variation themes:

Example 104

Everything is a little more sharply etched—a little less purely lyric—in the theme of Op. 131: the dialogue between two instruments closer, the motivic work more obvious, the harmonic changes more frequent, the inflections more chromatic. What is so similar is the essential melodic outline and the harmonic scheme, and especially the treatment of the octave ambitus.

The *Andante* of Op. 131 does not depend on architecture but on the series of brilliant, astonishing revelations in the individual variations. Beethoven had practiced this sort of thing in the "Diabelli" set. Most of the variations change time-signature and tempo (what they do *not* change is the tonality), a sure sign that variety is of the essence. Variation 1 holds motivically to the theme and keeps the original time and tempo, but ornaments it in a mood of endless free burgeoning characteristic also of several later variations. Variation 2 turns the theme into a country dance, and Variation 3 turns it into a highly abstract canon. Variation 4 slows and elaborates the theme, and then Variation 5 speeds it up and strips it down —each about as far as Beethoven felt was practical, no doubt. Variation 6, slowed to *Adagio ma non troppo e semplice*, makes a climax of weight in a sublime, hymnlike mood very characteristic of Beethoven's late slow movements. A fragmentary seventh variation initiates a ruminative yet strangely tense coda during which the first strain is tried repeatedly in its original unvaried form, in the keys of C, A, and F.

These harmonic digressions in the coda are not functional, and they do not disturb the sense of the variations as an iridescent chain, with the heaviest link at the hymn-variation, Variation 6. I do not see a very pressing necessity in the sequence of the links here, any more than in the classic Mozartian model, with its obligatory *Adagio* variation one from the end. The formal principle of Op. 131 is more purely lyric than that of Op. 127 —even though the theme itself in Op. 131 may be less purely lyric. For in Op. 127 the six variations and coda are formed, not like a chain with seven links and a plummet, but like a symmetrical *A B A* design with a very significant cap in the coda. The theme and Variations 1 and 2 together constitute the first element. Variation 3 constitutes the second. Variations 4, 5, and 6 as a unit complete the design. The essential articulation is harmonic, but Variation 4 emphasizes the three-part arc by means of thematic recapitulation to go along with the tonal return.

As for that essential harmonic articulation, Beethoven recaptures it in an extraordinary fashion, in a few bars of terse revelation within the coda.

Example 105

These harmonic digressions *are* functional; by relating the tonic key of A♭ to E major by way of C♯ (D♭) minor, they pull together the three key-areas of the movement as a whole. The theme and the first two variations stay in A♭. Variation 3, the *B* section, moves with a spasm to E major (F♭,

♭VI), a key which creates the highly charged sense of an enhanced dominant, as is usually the case with the minor sixth degree. Variation 4 returns just as abruptly to A♭, with Variation 5 balancing the digression to E by stressing the deep minor subdominant (iv, C♯ or D♭ minor), and Variation 6 resuming the tonic.

(One can hark back to the original melody for a scent of these harmonies. Possibly its most striking melodic progression, in bars 3–4, links the tonic to the sixth degree of the scale—albeit the major scale, not the minor. The climactic harmony, in bar 17, is the subdominant, albeit the major subdominant—but the minor subdominant gleams in the chromatic close of bar 19, which counts as the most colorful harmonic progression.

(The retrospective revelation of the coda was imitated directly by Schubert at the end of the *Adagio* of his String Quintet in C. It is nicely emblematic of the difference between the two composers that Schubert's gesture should be more colorful in detail but simpler in function, reflecting only one prior harmonic area, not two.)

The first variation in Op. 127, as has been said, is thoroughly complex in detail—the most complex Beethoven ever wrote—although it follows the phrase structure of the theme strictly enough. All the variations in this movement seem to cleave a little to their predecessors; here the opening texture resumes the opulent parallel 6ths which ornamented strain 2 of the original melody in its repetition. The 6ths melt into dense, flexible imitations on motifs derived a little energetically from each fragment of the melody in turn, and destined to expand each harmonic detail into a tiny moment of intensity. The invention is too spontaneous to allow close parallelism between the strains and their repetitions; everything burgeons as freely as the variations to the doublet phrase in the first movement of the quartet. The lush, vibrant texture dries up only at the very last bar, as the 3-note cadence-figure follows the echo and the chromatic close. This serves to prepare the more highly strung variation to follow.

Still in A♭, Variation 2 changes to duple time and slightly accelerates the tempo: *Neue Kraft fühlend*, as Beethoven expresses a not dissimilar transition on another occasion. Here he tries out a distinctive light *obbligato* style used a number of times in the late quartets—in the contrasting section of the *Heiliger Dankgesang* of Op. 132, in the *Andante con moto* of Op. 130, and in certain variations of Op. 131. What is typically involved is some kind of fast-dancing dialogue, with crisp syncopations and trills, lucid harmonies, a deceptively popular swing in the bass, and much air—small rests separating fugitive motifs making much play with *staccato*. Beethoven likes to write these passages very "black," that is, in sixteenth-, thirty-second-, and sixty-fourth-notes. There exists a letter (analyzed by Heinrich Schenker and Oswald Jonas) in which the composer discusses a refined point of technique in this variation.

The climactic subdominant harmony from bar 17 of the theme now obtrudes angrily as a minor subdominant, preparing another touch of minor subdominant (C♯ minor) at the very end—which can twist abruptly to E major for the crucial Variation 3. The echo, the cadential close, and the 3-note cadence-figure are all smoothed together by the florid figuration.

That the central contrasting key-area should be led into not by a proper modulation but by a spasm, and that it should be left in just the same way (see below), is entirely typical of Beethoven's methods in the last period. Not to speak of the Great Fugue, similar dissociated strokes isolate the *B* sections of the slow movements of the Ninth Symphony and the Quartet in A minor. These are cases close to home; each of them "non-modulates" to a form of the sixth degree, as here, and each of them creates its own variety of that insistent religious experience which also inspires the *Cavatina* of the B♭ Quartet and the climactic *Adagio* variation of the C♯-minor. Indeed, Variation 3 is a hymn-variation of the melody, slowed to *Adagio molto espressivo* and simplified into *alla breve* time. Sustained by quiescent chords, the elemental melody picks out only certain chief notes of the original theme, a procedure quite opposite to the busy ornamenting of the early variations. The decided tone of prayer makes a spiritual crown for the movement, and for that matter, for the quartet as a whole.

E major makes one think back to the mystical E-major hymn in the second "Razumovsky" Quartet, and also—as Philip Radcliffe observes—to the slow variation-finale of the Sonata in E, Op. 109, whose half-cadence resonates so curiously in a harshly scored augmented-6th chord here. This chord clarifies itself into plain ♭VI of E (as though to remind us that E major arose in the first place as ♭VI of A♭) and marks a displaced variation of the cadential echo (bar 74, last beat) before falling into an alarmingly Brahmsian version of the chromatic close (bar 75):

Example 106

In this variation the 3-note cadence-figure is passed over.

Almost with a sense of relief, Variation 4 drifts back to the original mood—back to Tempo I and A♭ major, with figuration first resembling that of Variation 1, but sprouting into new riches of trills and slow-sweeping *arpeggios*. Presently the melody is restored almost verbatim, in the same pair of dialoguing instruments that had it originally; this accentuates the strong sense of return in the *A B A* structure. By eliminating subdominant harmonies from the second strain, Beethoven makes the melody sound all the more emphatic in its return, and circumspectly keeps the sequel fresh. After the chromatic close, a brief extension of the 3-note cadence-figure leads innocently to the subdominant and to Variation 5.

Perhaps this wonderful passage does not altogether earn the name of variation; if you wish, call it an episode in the subdominant with strong thematic connections. Of its 13 bars, the theme is followed only by the first 4, a bare gentle canon tracing the characteristic melodic 6th and ending on the characteristic half-cadence. Thereafter Beethoven falls, abstracted, into a meditation upon the subdominant note D♭ (C♯) and upon its minor triad—the note itself spread out as a sonorous four-octave pedal, the triad wound around in sequential double counterpoint (derived from the chromatic close that had first glowed with C♯ minor, many variations ago). Beethoven is celebrating the subdominant climax of the original melody, in bar 17. This becomes clear as almost tentatively things slip back on the track with a recollection of the end of the melody (bars 17–18):

Example 107

From D♭ (C♯) the line moves not up the major scale to high B♭, but up the minor scale to B♭♭ (A). The cadential echo is heard one extra time, in the cello, as though to confirm the return to the major mode as the rich trills break in once again; but the chromatic close and the 3-note cadence-figure are saved for Variation 6.

The last and simplest and shortest variation glides over the melody in continuous flowing sixteenth-notes. It sounds similar to the second variation in the *Adagio* of the Ninth Symphony, and just as serene. Were the powers so malign as to permit us to retain of Beethoven but a single bar, we might take this last variation of the chromatic close:

Example 108

Again the subdominant is avoided, to save its darkening color for the terse coda which retells the whole harmonic story of the movement. The main material of this coda is that which is due after the chromatic close: the 3-note cadence-figure. This was bypassed in Variations 3 and 5, but now comes into its cadential own (see Example 105, p. 214).

The treatment of the three cadential ideas is only one aspect of the superb shaping of this piece. Besides being the most sensuously beautiful movement Beethoven ever wrote, it is one of his masterpieces of expressive form and without much doubt his most sophisticated structure in a slow movement. The rudimentary *A B A* arc is articulated as subtly as a great cathedral articulates its basic cruciform plan (the simile is Tovey's): the first member freely embroidering the theme, the central member reducing it to a mystic vision in a remote tonality, and the final member restoring the theme to its original aspect—more or less, in spite of the placid decoration of the last variation. In spite of the subdominant meditation of the penultimate one, Variation 5, Variations 4–6 sound together as a unit, moving as they do in the same tempo and with figuration that is not identical but not very variable either. Speaking purely (if one can) of architectural eloquence, this movement goes deeper and further than other slow movements of the last period. In terms of structure, the Ninth Symphony seems bulging by comparison, Op. 130 merely happy and correct, Op. 132 austere, Op. 131 permissive. Only the *Lento assai* of the last quartet, the Quartet in F, Op. 135, inscrutably the simplest of all, is built so perfectly and so eloquently.

· 7 ·

Variations, in the Quartets in E♭ and C♯ minor, allowed Beethoven to work up to a luxuriance unparalleled in his earlier music. That was one obvious path for lyricism to travel—the sometimes primrose path to Richard Strauss. In the Quartet in F, the same technique allowed him to attain an unparalleled quietude, simplicity, and (one might even say at first) sobriety. This small variation movement does not seek extraordinary frontiers for its theme; it looks steadily in on the theme and seeks its purest essence. Instead of unity in variety, the effect is simply of unity—the unity of a circle, not that of a crystal, a leaf, or a cathedral. To characterize the piece as a microcosm of the art of variation, then, is to think of microcosm in a very particular way.

The innovation of this set of variations is its thorough-going lyricism; it sings all the way through. Beethoven marked it *cantante e tranquillo*, "singing . . ." where the weaker conventional term would have been *cantabile*, "singable" or "songlike." Embroidery, decoration, and ornamentation are simply not in the picture, and far from investigating imaginative transformations of the theme, the composer now seems reluctant to disguise it. Variation 1, which starts at bar 13, flows directly out of the initial thematic statement, like a melodic continuation. The violin eases

Example 109

its way up to the high octave in the same note values, tempo, dynamic, etc., adding some chromatic inflections but deserting none of the important notes of the original tune. Variation 2, *Più lento* and a little *beklemmt*, strikes the one appreciable note of contrast—something less than tranquil, yet carefully muted in its distress or menace. Variation 3 restores the theme to all intents and purposes literally, achieving such novelty as it wants by means of a trancelike free canon above. (This accords excellently with the small cadential echoes at the end of the theme.) The last variation, Variation 4, changes the figuration, but not the tempo and really not the mood. The exquisite and exquisitely singable violin arabesques seem once again to carry the impulse of the previous variation—that is to say, of the theme mirrored in canon—up to its natural lyric fulfillment.

So solid is the lyric continuity between the theme and Variation 1, and between Variations 3 and 4, that various critics either have overlooked the construction of the piece as a set of variations or else refuse to recognize it. They speak merely of a threefold *A B A* pattern—which of course exists, superimposed upon the fivefold pattern; both are essential to Beethoven's idea. His intention to force the *A B A* feeling is obvious, but the four variations are equally obvious, lucid, and strict. (The contrasting *Più lento* section can "count" as the standard *minore* variation—Variation 2—just as well as a middle *B* section.) To miss or to minimize the recurrent pattern of the thematic matrix is to miss something fundamental, because the recurrence contributes to the fundamentally static, contemplative quality of the movement as a whole.

People may have been put off by the brevity of the theme, but the fact is that its 10 bars succeed in conveying much of the character of Beethoven's typical variation themes, with their full 16 bars and their repeated strains. There is a touch of repetition at the beginning (bars 3–6: p. 219), and there is plenty of sequential pressure up to the melodic climax. But the theme forgoes modulation; and like every other detail of the technique, this seems calculated to build that fundamental hovering, almost mystic quality. Even the brief cadential echoes work in this direction. They were borrowed rather exactly from Op. 127, but whereas in that work they settle a long, eventful melody, here they harp on a curiously premature conclusion. No modulatory excursions outside the regular variation scheme, such as mark the superimposed *A B A* pattern in Op. 127, disturb the static effect. There is not even a modulatory feint in a coda, as in Op. 131. There is no coda.

The variations of Op. 127 and Op. 131 treat subdominant harmony with great subtlety. In Op. 135 the subdominant is almost entirely absent—a circumstance that suggests a startling parallel with an even more ostentatiously mystical movement, the Lydian *Heiliger Dankgesang* of Op. 132. The theme of Op. 135 uses no subdominant triads up to a pair of plagal cadences in the last two bars, and even this detail is excised from some variations. It is restored, quietly, to illuminate two bars at the end of the piece which serve in lieu of coda. The sense of this studied reticence with so standard a harmonic resource as the subdominant is very hard to specify, and it is not much easier to characterize the feeling when the plagal cadences are finally restored. One can speak of security and grace, perhaps, of lightness, and of an incredible transparency.

These feelings have been growing all through the final variation, with its limpid violin figuration, which sounds so pliant and which is in fact so perfectly rigid in technical manufacture. There is nothing quite like it in Beethoven, this combination of severity and ineffable tenderness, this tearless clarity of vision, an emotion self-absorbed yet entirely open. Though passion and even warmth have long since been distilled out of the song, its tranquillity belongs very much in the world. In fact this variation seems to me to modulate the feeling decisively away from the mysticism that earlier was enveloping the work. It is not a voice enlarging or exhorting, it is a voice stating; an unimaginably beautiful speaking voice, perhaps, rather than a song; but unmistakably a human voice.

For Stravinsky this movement is another "pedestrian" one. In a more romantic age, Theodor Helm could rhapsodize in a contrary vein: "Never in his wanderings through the gulfs and labyrinths of the human soul had Beethoven sung anything more noble and inward than this Adagio [sic!] of his last Quartet—outwardly so small, consisting of but 54 bars, but inwardly so deeply significant." [6] Without much favoring this language, I rather agree with Helm's superlative. In the *Lento assai* of the Quartet in F, Beethoven seems to touch a true note of sublimity missing from the other hymnlike slow movements of the last years; even the hymn-variations of Op. 127 and Op. 131 emanate a slightly sententious tone which can bring to mind those earnest religious maxims that he liked to jot down or set in frames. In Op. 135 there is no suspicion of straining for solemnity, as in the *Cavatina* of Op. 130, or straining for asceticism, as in the *Heiliger Dankgesang* of Op. 132. The piece is neither operatic nor churchy, nor excessively humble either: it may *look* plain, but the sonority is so calculated that the term "sobriety" hardly seems to do justice to the fullness of the effect. The game with the subdominant has something to do with this fullness. Beethoven's own characterization is just: "*cantante e tranquillo*," which he wrote on the final score, after trying "*süsser Ruhegesang oder Friedensgesang*" in a sketchbook.

For a certain generation of musicians and listeners, this movement will stir memories of Arturo Toscanini, who used to perform and broadcast it at the beginning of orchestra concerts along with the second movement

[6] P. 310.

of Op. 135. The impression is unforgettable, and while such memories remain, one can never be sure about the freshness of one's critical response. From the puristic point of view, Toscanini's action was sufficiently horrifying; it falsified Beethoven's texture, and ignored the progress of feeling between movements of the cyclic work—a powerful development in the late music, which forms the burden of the remaining chapters of this study. All the same, the idea of magnifying the song in such a way as to project it to the *Millionen*—that corresponds to something very deep in Beethoven's own conception, whatever it destroys in the manifestation. One wonders how puristic he himself might have felt inclined to be about it.

For in essence—to resume the burden of the present chapter—the vocal impulse represents a grandiose impulse toward directness of communication. Elemental song in the form of the country dance, the folk song, and the nursery song, and sophisticated song in the form of the aria, lied, recitative, and hymn, all converge in the major effort for immediacy of contact. The gradual development of Beethoven's lyric sensibility, from the gauche beginnings of Op. 18 to the superb flights of the last period, is too large a matter for treatment here; say only that the process proved as laborious and as valuable to him (and can prove as inspiring to us) as his development of harmony, motivic work, fugue, and so on. Yet I think one misses the point if one views this progress purely or even mainly in technical terms. All the developments were forging language; the development of song was forging language straight for the "common listener." This was, after all, Beethoven's most significant response to the Romantic stirrings of the 1820's, a response that did not fail to impress the nineteenth century. If perhaps the impression has dimmed for later, revisionist generations, something has been dimmed of Beethoven's essential voice.

8

CONTRAST

Quartet in E♭ Major, Op. 127
Quartet in A Minor, Op. 132

In the last years of his life Beethoven had become a very great celebrity; information about him is much more plentiful than in the earlier years. Not to speak of accounts and descriptions and conversations (recorded in Conversation Books) and correspondence, more than a dozen sketch-books are preserved containing material for the last quartets of 1824–6.[1] The history of these quartets, outlined very briefly, is as follows.

Early in 1822 Beethoven mentioned in a letter that he was working on a string quartet—for the first time, presumably, in a dozen years, since the Quartet in F minor of 1810. And late in 1822 he was treated to a loquacious, flattering request for "*un, deux, ou trois nouveaux quattuors*" from a Prince Galitzin in St. Petersburg. It is strange how large a role was played by Russian noblemen—Lobkowitz, Razumovsky, and now Galitzin—in the story of Beethoven's quartets. Beethoven very gladly accepted the fifty ducats, and in the next couple of years he is speaking of his quartet plans to all sorts of people: to Charles Neate of London, who was interested in a commission on behalf of the Royal Philharmonic Society, to the publishers Peters and Schott, to friends, and to celebrity-seeking visitors. However, in these years he was fully occupied, not to say preoccupied, with the *Missa solemnis* and the Ninth Symphony, two works which cost him more trouble than almost any others in his whole career. It was necessary not only to compose them but also to promote and sell them, and this was an exhausting process, especially as Beethoven

[1] See pp. 383–4.

went about it. Meanwhile his old friend Ignaz Schuppanzigh of the Schuppanzigh Quartet returned to Vienna—from a long stay in Russia, where he had been helping to spread Beethoven's reputation. Beethoven began to see a great deal of the new second violinist, Karl Holz; quartets assumed a larger and larger place in his thoughts. In 1824, not without urgent promptings from Prince Galitzin, he got to work seriously on the commission.

The first quartet, E♭-major, Op. 127, appears to have occupied him from May 1824 to February 1825—a rather long period. It was rushed off to St. Petersburg, and was at once performed in Vienna by the Schuppanzigh Quartet. About this performance, unpleasant intrigues developed, which were reconstructed in a detailed study by Alfred Ebert. Though the premiere was a failure, the piece soon became one of Beethoven's most gratifying successes.

The second quartet, A-minor, Op. 132, was finished in July 1825, after more than a month's delay caused by illness, the most serious that the composer had experienced, at least in recent years. Beethoven had the piece played publicly in November—again to great acclaim—before sending it to the prince, who had a right to be annoyed on this account. Like all the music after Op. 127, the Quartet in A minor was published posthumously. The opus numbering implies erroneously that the piece postdates two quartets composed subsequently. It ought to have been numbered Op. 128; confusion arose because Beethoven's directions were vague, because more than one publisher was involved, and because the particular publisher of Op. 132 held things up with a view to issuing it as part of a complete Beethoven series.

The third quartet, B♭-major, Op. 130, is often said to have been worked on simultaneously with the A-minor. This is not quite true; the sketches show that although the two works were thought about simultaneously, the essential work on Op. 130 ran from August to November—a rather short period, indeed a very short period, considering that there are six movements and that one of them is the Great Fugue. The commission was now fulfilled, but Beethoven went on to compose two more quartets, the C♯-minor—already begun—and the F-major. He had been promising quartets to different publishers, and Op. 127 had made a good impression; no doubt this provided a sufficient outer goad to continue writing quartets, even though grandiose plans for operas, oratorios, and symphonies were in the wind, and there were those who urged him to set his sights higher than mere chamber music. But an inner feeling must have been goading him, too: a sense of disquiet, of unfinished business, about the Quartet in B♭. This seems indicated by remarkable happenings a little later. In March 1826, when this quartet received its first performance, most listeners felt that the great fugal Finale was a mistake—and on some level at least (we shall return to this question) the composer came to agree with them. He withdrew the Finale and arranged to publish it as a separate work, as a *Grosse Fuge* for string quartet and simultaneously in an arrangement for piano, four hands (Op. 133 and 134 respectively).

Meanwhile he was working on the Quartet in C♯ minor, Op. 131, completed in July 1826, about a year later than the A-minor. The last of the quartets, F-major, Op. 135, was finished in October. Only then (or to be quite precise, between September and November) did Beethoven return to the Quartet in B♭ and compose its substitute finale. It was to be his last completed work. He fell ill again in December, lingered through four operations, and died in March 1827.

The five quartets and the Great Fugue were composed in a single span, then, over two and a half years during which no other projects were carried forward. In a rather curious way the situation parallels that surrounding the composition of the six Quartets, Op. 18, in 1798–1800. Schuppanzigh is present on both occasions. The use of appreciably older material can be fairly suspected in the case of the C-minor Quartet, Op. 18, No. 4, and in that of the E♭, Op. 127. Each group of quartets contains a work in B♭ betraying clear signs of disruption—quite literally so with Op. 130. The same work by Mozart, the Quartet in A, K. 464, evidently interested Beethoven in 1798 and again in 1825. After the Quartet in F, there are indications that for the time being he was through with the genre. In the total lifework, the late quartets form a closed, as well as a closing, episode.

There is a persistent conception or misconception about the late quartets which derives some small support from the chronology of composition, and which turns up in one form or another in almost all the literature. This is the view of the three middle quartets (in A minor, B♭, and C♯ minor) as a specially unified group. For the fact is that one thematic configuration, stated most simply at the beginning of the A-minor Quartet as G♯–A–F–E, occurs prominently in all three. The configuration dominates the Great Fugue; and it follows that critics who make the most of this view of the late quartets tend also to be partisans of the Great Fugue, which they prefer as the finale of the Quartet in B♭ over the piece later substituted for it.

The thematic parallels among the quartets are quite unmistakable. The question is what to make of them (the familiar crux of analysis and criticism—what aesthetic sense to make out of observed or "analyzed" fact). Is there an interrelationship among the three works on an actual level of aesthetic response? This seems to me the very heart of the matter, but it is not something that most writers on the late quartets treat at all squarely. In fact it is very hard to penetrate behind the language of Marion Scott ("Their contents are so glorious, so inter-related and metaphysical, that one might almost think Beethoven regarded them as an ABC [*i.e.*, A minor, B♭, C♯ minor] of the world to come. . . ."),[2] or Ivan Mahaim ("The climate of the Great Fugue ties these three quartets to one another, placing them as though under the same firmament. . . ."),[3] or Paul Bekker, who in 1911 was the first to bring the matter up ("The A minor, B flat major and C sharp minor quartets thus form a triptych, differing markedly from the preceding E flat major quartet and the succeeding F major. . . .").[4] The word "triptych," with its *echt* Wagnerian flavor, provides a clue to what all this cloudy writing really means. These quartets, Bekker and all those who follow him are saying, are to be experienced on some level as a continuity; the aesthetic sense of any one of them depends not solely on itself but on the others. This is clearly proclaimed by the most extreme of these critics, who indeed will not content himself with a mere triptych theory, Deryck Cooke: "What I hope to show is that the set of five constitutes a self-contained unity, a single continuous act of creation, in which Beethoven persistently developed certain implications of two basic pitch-patterns."[5] And it is exactly this notion of a "self-contained unity"—take it in fives or in threes—that seems to me anachronistic and dangerously mistaken.

It may be helpful—it is always helpful—to consider the three middle quartets in conjunction, for purposes of analysis. But equally illuminating parallels can be drawn among other groups of quartets, or among the entire set.

There are, to begin with, similarities of over-all plan between the first two quartets, the E♭ and the A-minor, similarities which commentators fascinated by bonds among the middle three have missed. Both works bank more heavily on their slow movements than any other of the quartets, earlier or later. This is a matter of the relative weight of all the

[2] P. 266.
[3] P. 309.
[4] Pp. 327–8.
[5] P. 32.

movements, of course, but even in absolute terms the *Adagio* of the E♭ Quartet stands out as the most monumental of Beethoven's variation movements, and the fifteen-minute *Heiliger Dankgesang* of the A-minor occupies a quite special place in his output. The slightly later quartets begin to use more than one slow movement—with the result that the individual slow movements become less weighty. Even the large variation movement in the Quartet in C♯ minor is not an *Adagio* but an *Andante ma non troppo e molto cantabile.*

Another parallel between the first two quartets concerns dance-derived movements. Each features dance movements of considerable extent and density and contrapuntal elaboration (a clear enough holdover from the fugal *Scherzo* of the Ninth Symphony, which just precedes the quartets in time of composition). Again, when later quartets multiply the number of dance movements, they cut down on the individual pieces, typically turning them into ethereal little folk-parodies.

Perhaps most striking of all is the way in which the Quartets in E♭ and A minor end. Beethoven employs a very distinctive scheme which, as it were, *dissolves* the finale into a concluding section treating previous material in a spiritualized, very loose "variation." Foreshadowed in the Quartet in F minor of 1810, this particular arrangement seems to be unique to the quartet as a genre. The concluding section makes a sharp break with the finale proper, which, in compensation, is kept notably short on internal contrast of one kind or another. By the employment of this type of finale, the Quartets in E♭ and A minor are linked together in terms of their fundamental sequence of feeling—this in spite of basic characters as remote as the two keys themselves. In the other quartets, resolution is handled differently, indeed more normally.

However, neither consideration of the first two quartets nor consideration of the middle three will do to give an adequate sense of what was evidently Beethoven's major technical concern at this period: nothing less than the whole matter of musical contrast. This is so fundamental that at first its significance or novelty may be hard to grasp. Certainly he had been deeply interested in the principle of contrast at every stage of his career. But at the present stage he would appear to have begun an exhaustive reconsideration of the problem from the ground up, with a particular eye to extremes, both positive and negative. Thus in every one of the late quartets, from Op. 127 in E♭ to Op. 135 in F, one can detect a very striking tendency to minimize contrast within certain of the movements. This occurs to an extent in the two finales just mentioned. In the opening movement of Op. 127, as we have seen, contrast is minimized within the framework of a first-movement sonata form—a paradoxical endeavor. In Op. 132, 130, and 131, contrast is minimized within the dance and trio. In the *Lento* of Op. 135 the same thing is done within the variation form. Another famous interest of the third period is directly related to this general impetus, the interest in fugue; this will occupy us in a later chapter.

And already in Op. 127 one can trace in certain movements exactly the opposite or complementary tendency: a tendency to maximize contrast. This may provide a key to the understanding of a sometimes misunderstood piece, the *Scherzando vivace* of the Quartet in E♭. The same idea is employed for more powerful expressive ends in the first movement of the Quartet in A minor, and is carried to the point of diminishing returns—or so it will be suggested—in the first movement of the Quartet in B♭.

Contrast will prove to be a convenient avenue of study to the late quartets, particularly to the Quartet in A minor. But perhaps it is not superfluous to remind ourselves that ultimately, and most seriously, our interest is presumably not in stylistic features and techniques any more than it is in groups of quartets—in pairs or "triptychs." We should be attending to each separate work of art in its own private intensity. The dangerous end-result of Bekker's view is seen in the remark of Walter Riezler—otherwise an extremely sensitive critic—that "it may certainly be said that these last Quartets no longer have the individuality that from the very beginning was so typical of Beethoven's works." The phenomenon, he says, is hardly expressible in words:

> What however does not appear so clearly and impressively is the individuality of the work as a whole. The three Quartets of Op. 59, though all written in one year, are as distinct from each other as three sharply defined personalities. It is true that there is a clear line of demarcation between these three late Quartets, in as much as each work in itself is perfectly balanced, the sequence of movements assures to it a certain "wholeness," and, particularly, the first and last movements respectively "begin" and "end" the works in the truest sense of the words. But there are threads that cross these lines of demarcation and connect one Quartet with another. . . .[6]

Individuality, integrity, coherence—these are hard conceptions to distinguish, and in my view the Quartets in E♭, A minor, and C♯ minor are Beethoven's greatest works because each creates a more profound and

[6] Pp. 234–5.

individual impression of coherence than he or anyone else had achieved before. Contrasts—within movements or between movements—may be more extraordinary than ever, but the really extraordinary thing is how inevitably the expanding range of sentiment is subsumed into a total integrity.

As for the "threads" crossing lines of demarcation, their meaning seems to me no greater than that of parallels that can be drawn among Beethoven's compositions at any period. Such parallels have been drawn very many times in the course of this study; as didactic aids they help focus on the individual qualities of the works under consideration. But in themselves the "threads" contribute nothing to the aesthetic weave. Granted also that the "style of the late quartets" has a certain synoptic beauty of its own, and that an appreciation of this is even necessary as a context for response to the individual members. So it is with the "Razumovsky" Quartets and the neighboring compositions of 1803–6. But once again, this is a different and (crucially) a more abstract matter than the direct aesthetic experience of particular works of art. It is not enough to allow the late quartets "a certain 'wholeness' "; each of them provides us with a separate paradigm for wholeness. What truer criterion could be found for individuality in works of art is hard to know.

· 2 ·

Whether the first suggestions for the Quartet in E♭ really came to Beethoven as early as 1822, and whether any of those early ideas remain in the piece as we now know it, is not ascertained. But it would make very good sense. 1822 was the year of his last piano sonatas, and it is these works, more than the intervening *Missa solemnis* and Ninth Symphony, which develop the lyric impulse that comes to fruition in the first of the late quartets. In discussing the first movement of the Quartet in E♭ (on p. 205), mention was made of the Sonata in A, Op. 101, with its intimate, songlike opening movement. Lyricism also inspires the Sonatas in E and A♭, Op. 109 and 110, from 1821. Another outcome of the lyric impulse was the forging of the theme and variations into a superb instrument for slow movements of large works. The Sonatas in E and C minor, Op. 109 and 111, contain the most elaborate variations prior to the *Adagio* of the E♭ Quartet, which has been analyzed on pages 210–18. Transference of the idea of variation from the piano sonata to the string quartet follows naturally enough, especially if the Quartet in E♭ can be thought of as originating in 1822.

Song, not drama, grounds the tender first movement of this quartet, and song, however superbly and strongly molded, inspires the theme and variations of the *Adagio*. Somewhere the later movements had to find a place for another quality—for something tougher, more intellectual, and more disruptive. As Beethoven planned the total sequence of feeling, the Finale was to return to the relaxed simplicity of the opening, leaving only the *Scherzo* to introduce the essential note of contrast. Indeed the *Scherzando vivace* is one of Beethoven's most explosive pieces, bursting with energy and malice, crackling with dry intelligence. To make the dance movement the center of tension in a cyclic work was in any case unusual, though something of the sort had been accomplished in the earlier E♭ Quartet, Op. 74.

Internal high contrast, I think one can say without forcing the case, is the clue to the quality of this movement in itself, as well as to its admirably calculated role within the quartet as a whole. Having recently conceived the second movement of the Ninth Symphony, Beethoven was in the right frame of mind for an unusually involved *Scherzo;* from the Ninth Symphony, too, he carried over the idea of fugue for a start. After a prefatory *pizzicato* fanfare—there are no timpani in a string quartet!—a fugal exposition stamps out a shaky path: subject in the

Example 110

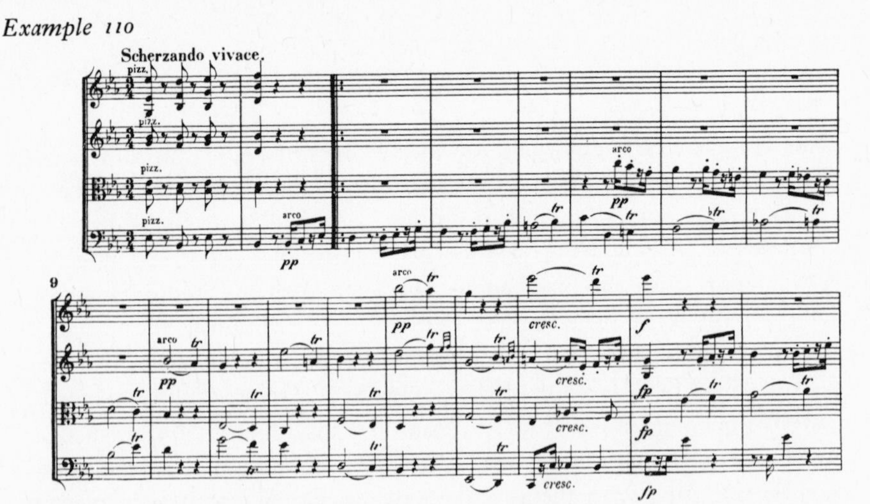

dominant (cello), answer by inversion (viola), a humorous 6-bar echo episode, subject in the tonic (first violin), answer by inversion (second violin). And thereafter, fugality and counterpoint cease abruptly, and begin, and cease, and begin again. Much more pointedly than in the Ninth Symphony, the issue here seems to be not the fact of fugue, but the tension between contrapuntal material and the noncontrapuntal surroundings in which it is placed. This provides an ideal matrix for the play of contrasts.

The basic material smells of the schoolroom: a stiff, musty piece of ostentatious two-part counterpoint recalling, at first glance, something out of the Great Fugue or the third movement (*Allegro assai e vivace, ma serioso*) of the Quartet in F minor, Op. 95. The latter serves as a distant but true model for the present *Scherzando;* its counterpoint is just as rigid, if more *serioso,* and it opens in the same distinctive fashion with dominant and tonic phrases. In Op. 127, some of the rigidity results from the fact that everything about the first 15 bars works to stress the third beat of the bar; so that when in bar 16 the second beat is struck chromatically in preparation for the tonic entries, there is a particularly dirty bump. Accompanying these entries, a loose new countersubject continues to strike away at the second beat, a sharp contrasting detail carrying through into the homophonic section marked—in the language of the Ninth Symphony—*ritmo di tre battute:*

Example 111

which is not musty at all. The *A* section of the *Scherzo* closes promptly and in good order on the dominant. In the repeat, the *pizzicato* fanfare of bars 1–2 is skipped; nor is it ever heard of again.

The *B* section piles contrast upon contrast, pressing dangerously and deliberately toward the breaking point. A gesture of unprecedented strength begins it: a *fortissimo* unison sweeping up almost four octaves, a compression of the total rhythm of the subject. What the unison leads to is an idea of unprecedented weakness: a miniature dancelike phrase for the first violin which cheapens the subject (or rather the inversion) into a 2-bar sequence. This is made even more grotesque by fussy accompaniment *arpeggios* in the cello and by continuing little squawks on the second beat. But contrapuntal habits die hard. The dance-phrase instantly inverts itself and starts deploying its elements through the various instruments; and by the time it also doubles itself in 3rds and accompanies itself by its own inversion, the counterpoint is assuming a kind of nightmare seriousness. A fleeting but quite distinct suggestion of more majestic movement—

Example 112

is knocked down by a second loud upward-sweeping unison. (This happens to be a precise compression of the main subject in the minor mode, with some of its most unexpected notes accentuated.)

In this whole series of madly contrasted ideas, none lasts more than a few bars. It is perhaps hardly surprising that the piece cracks up at this point. A fragmentary, hushed, grinning $\frac{2}{4}$ *Allegro* free-associates its way in, and by the time we get over the shock we have perhaps been made to see how rigid the rhythm had been becoming. The interruption has a heavy gestural quality, something like recitative. Though it sounds shocking, it does not sound quite wild because the whole atmosphere has been getting surreal, because tenuous melodic connections obtain with the previous unison—

Example 113

and because tonally speaking everything is reined in hard. The prior dissociated action had been taking place in a tonal field more restless than anything else in the entire quartet: the original unison deviated to C minor, and then the harmony jerked its way up from C–F to D♭–G♭ to D–G. But now a circle-of-5ths sequence rolls back from the second unison, starting on D, to G minor (the $\frac{2}{4}$ interruption) to C minor (the same interruption a second time) to C_7 to F minor to $B♭_7$ (very briefly) and thence to a return of the initial fugal exposition in the tonic E♭.

As compared with the one at the beginning, this second fugal exposition is much less shaky, admitting no deviation from the tonic and no episode. In compensation, its four regular entries accumulate new accompaniment or countersubject material of increasing density and brilliance. A drawling coda seems designed to set up a concluding witticism which plays on the second beat once again.

The rhythmic figure of the witticism accelerates neatly into the trio. Two main ideas, one in the minor mode and the other alternating in the major, rush through a series of keys that seem to make no particular expressive point:

|: i–VII :|: VII–v–III–i–V :|

One is reminded of the rambling trio of the Quartet in F minor or of the dance-tune "medleys" in the quartets to come; but the present *minore* has less intrinsic character—very little, in fact, except as a gross foil to the overstimulated *Scherzando* itself. This is duly repeated, and the trio begins whirling away for a second time until suddenly checked by a rest, after 8 bars, as though someone had misread the directions. Much the same thing happens in the Ninth Symphony. Beethoven compounds the joke about the second beat in this sardonic close:

Example 114

And then the Finale: one of Beethoven's sweetest and simplest-sounding, as well as one of the most perfectly conceived and executed. The folk-like tone is so magical and true, so lively and calm, that one feels solemn to talk about subtleties of construction, long-term harmonic relationships, goals and contrast—all that. But folk accents can sound banal just as easily as enchanting. What sets and assures the tone is the way the musical elements are put together.

Beethoven was getting less and less inclined to start a movement directly with its main thematic material. The opening 4-bar phrase here, beginning squarely off key, serves as a preface to the theme, not as a theme—which makes Theodor Helm's comparison of these bars with the opening of Mozart's Quartet in E♭, K. 428, essentially trivial. (Both passages do run through nine of the twelve chromatic notes without repetition, a process which in the classic style makes for some disturbance; but whereas Mozart's effect is tense, Beethoven's is comic.) The more meaningful analogy would be with the opening of the Finale of the *Eroica* Symphony, though the present preface seems to look forward to the rest of the movement in a far more integral way.

Thus the prefatory lunge toward G proves to be the main spur of harmonic contrast in a movement which otherwise can afford to stay very quiet in this respect. Twice at important junctures a strong G breaks in on the E♭ harmony—though the preface as such recurs only once; it drops out unobtrusively before the piece is half over, like the *Maestoso* antecedent in the first movement of the quartet, like the *pizzicato* fanfare in the third. Rhythmically, the half-note A♭ on the second beat (bar 1) establishes a pattern for the main theme itself (which also has A♭'s on the second beat) as well as for one element of the second group, later. After rearing up to the step G–A♭ (in bar 1), the preface collapses by degrees, making little scrambling echoes of G–A♭ by means of several other upward steps. The same step G–A♭ grounds the first bars of the main theme; G–A♮ seems all the more piquant thereafter, in bar 7. The same step G–A♭ is perhaps heard supervising the climactic step B♭–C in bar 8.

Oddly prepared, the main theme itself is decidedly odd, in spite of its homely swing. A♮ in bar 7 grates because it contradicts the stolid A♭'s of bars 1, 5, and 6, because it blunders into a tritone with E♭ at the beginning of bar 7, and because its modulatory ploy is so thoroughly cold-shouldered. There is something odd about the large rhythm, too. Though the phrase falls into a regular 8-bar module, inside it feels lopsided, with its fourth bar (bar 8) somehow out of place. Are we quite sure how many A♭ bars and how many A♮'s are required? The third movement of the "Pastoral" Symphony comes to mind, with its village bassoonist who has trouble counting his cadences. The second half of the tune ambles just a little loosely; a less prolix, less droll arrangement might have been as follows:

Example 115

Later, indeed, Beethoven actually does remove one of the A♭ bars; at present, terse propulsion is certainly not wanted. The ambiguity of phrase construction rubs quietly against the folklike innocence of the tone. And some subtlety of construction is welcome to offset great plainness everywhere else.

No ambiguity clouds the immediate sequel, for example, a guileless "doublet" tune which becomes a faithful pendant of the main tune. This doublet was quoted on page 203, one of a set of examples to show how heavily Beethoven relied on the note of popular lyricism in the last quartets. In the Finale of Op. 127, one soon gets the feeling of a "medley" of folklike phrases, a feeling that is experienced even more clearly with certain dance movements and trios in slightly later quartets. After the first theme, the tunes are square and ingenuous, jogging along in all-but-continuous quarter-notes. These tunes follow one another amiably with next to no transitional material.

On page 205, in the course of a discussion of the first movement, a diagram showed the extreme regularity and simplicity of phrasing in its exposition. A parallel diagram on page 236 will show a parallel situation in the exposition of the Finale (italics being used for phrases which in the recapitulation are simply excised). Transitional material scarcely exists; one can hardly speak of a "bridge," for Beethoven merely breaks the first four bars off the main theme—a paradoxical break—and runs them successively through the four instruments: a pair of statements in the tonic, and then, without any modulatory interlude, a pair in the dominant. (This will work, on account of the modulatory itch of the original A♮.) A 2-bar extension, and we are quite ready for a new folklike doublet in the new key.

For sheer effervescence it would be hard to match this garland of themes in Beethoven's earlier music, though their quality is captured

FIRST GROUP:	*Preface*	*4 bars*
	main theme	|: 8 :|
	secondary theme	|: 8 :| (|: 2 × 4 bars :|—"doublet")
	main theme	*4 cello*
		+ 4 viola
	in V:	*+ 4 second violin*
		+ 4 first violin
		2
SECOND GROUP:	third theme	8 (2 × 4 bars—"doublet")
		+ 4 (variation of second half of doublet)
	fourth theme	6 + |: 4 :|
	cadential phrases	4
	to I:	6
		6

again and even heightened in the Finale of the Quartet in F, Op. 135. *Bonhommie rustique*, Romain Rolland called it. What is so striking is the combination of an evocation of cloddishness, on the one hand, and the most utterly refined treatment of melodic and harmonic detail, on the other. Perhaps the combination, so stated, seems classical enough. But it does not seem Haydnesque any more—the detail is altogether too elegant. Nor Mozartian—the connotation is too earthy and plain.

At the close of the exposition, after the fourth of the tunes has made an extra-heavy cadence in the dominant, light cadential phrases turn back to the tonic and begin to concentrate on the backward step A♭–G. Thus prepared, the preface booms in again on G. A tonic return seems to be just around the corner. However, we are denied the full sense of security that a rondo would provide, in favor of a very playful development section heading toward C minor (which is of course the direction implied by the G of the preface). Beethoven amuses himself by making frivolous combinations of the first theme and the third, by running away with the eighth-note figure of the first theme, and by somersaulting around a warm and thoroughly contrapuntal circle-of-5ths sequence. This leads smilingly but rather swiftly to the key of A♭. Here, in the subdominant, the main theme returns very high in the viola, and following it the secondary doublet theme complete with all its repetitions.

Commentators have tended to brush off the formal plan of this movement as lucid and obvious. Certainly nothing about it is likely to strike any listener as abstruse. All the same, the enormous subdominant return

—32 bars, encompassing the main theme and the subsidiary theme—must be the most obstinate "false reprise" in the whole classic repertory. Doubtless the lengthy emphasis on A♭ can be heard as outcome of the G of the preface when it returned to open the development—the large relationship G–A♭ expanding the step G–A♭ within the preface. After 32 bars, at all events, a brilliant transition (almost the only one in the piece) climbs up very ethereally to E♭; the modulation is grounded by G–A♭–G high in the cello.

In the tonic key, E♭, the full recapitulation takes place, beginning with the same 32 bars, which are (wisely) now handled with some variation. Rhythmic compression would still be out of the question. The first theme merely concentrates on canonic decorations and new harmonies, and takes more time to solidify its harmonic underpinnings. The subsidiary theme is treated as shown on page 204, among other ways.

At the close of the recapitulation, cadential phrases settle around the note G, just as they did at the close of the exposition. This time the preface does not ensue. The tonality lightens miraculously, and yet securely for the moment, into C major, as the tempo softens into $\frac{6}{8}$ time. Rustling, dizzying scale figures in triplet-sixteenths begin to blur all the edges. Beethoven evaporates the first phrase of the main theme into a 3-bar phrase, by following bars 5, 7, and 8 of the original but dropping the redundant second A♭ bar:

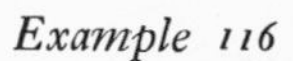
Example 116

Velvet-gloved, this phrase swings powerfully from instrument to instrument, from the key of C major (where G moves once again to A♭) to A♭ to E to E♭, again without any real modulations in between. At last, after seeming not to notice, the composer accepts the awkward modulatory energy of the original A♮ and whirls the tune through incredible, forbidden regions. This is sheer dream:

Example 117

or so at least Walther must have thought when he used such harmonies in narrating his dream to Hans Sachs (relationships based on the augmented triad are unusual in Beethoven). Home in E♭—there is a 10-bar tonic pedal—the phrase begins to reiterate the upward step B♭–C of bar 8, which appears in the repeating cadential phrases. The scoring grows very exquisite, the sonority very full. Bars 9–12 of the original tune are swept into the stream, their bluntness like everything else melted into the eddying $\frac{6}{8}$ flow. A flash of major and minor sonorities around B♭ and C, a further crystallization of the theme, and the piece is suddenly silent:

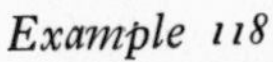

Example 118

It is the clownish A♮ that emerges as the final irreducible essence.

· 3 ·

Hugo Riemann's *Meisterführer* through the Beethoven string quartets is not a very satisfactory work by present-day standards. And Riemann was never more quirky than in his discussion of the present quartet. The main themes of the three later movements, he was convinced, derive from the opening *Maestoso* in the first. He claimed to show in detail how the *A* section of the *Scherzando vivace* counts as Variation 6 of the *Adagio* tune; he confidently called for "*einigem gutem Willen der Hörer*" to support analysis of the *B* section in an analogous way; the trio he styled Variation 7. "*Il faut le vouloir, pour le voir,*" Romain Rolland remarked.

Exactly so: there was a real and a right incentive—a real *vouloir*—behind Riemann's fantasy. One can laugh at the *particular* analysis while at the same time sympathizing with the *general* compulsion to account for the extraordinary sense of coherence created by the sequence of movements in Beethoven's greatest compositions. Perhaps it is no accident that Riemann's wildest effort along these lines should be applied to just this piece—to the first of the late quartets, works in which this sense is more overpowering than ever before. One looks compulsively for the "objective correlative"—for thematic bonds, tonal interrelationships, *Urlinien*, rhythmic matrices, psychological sequences. Riemann was not the last, nor even the least intelligent, to engage in such an effort.

Lyricism—it has been said many times—is at the heart of this quartet, inspiring the intimate *aveu* of the opening movement, the popular swing of the Finale, and the great stream of melody in the *Adagio* variations. Probably the inspiration had to do with the late piano sonatas of 1821–2, but the outcome had to be different. The difference lay in the fact that quartets had a commitment to monumentality which sonatas never assumed. Much the same point, it may be recalled, was made about the quartets of Op. 18; as compared to the very adept and flexible sonatas of the 1790's, quartets in Beethoven's early view had to be more substantial and more formal—even stiffer, as it came out at first. This tacit assumption about the proprieties of the genres remained. A piano sonata might aspire to the scope of a symphony, but if lyricism was the order of the day, it could also enjoy the luxury of intimacy. A small quartet, on the other hand, was as unthinkable as a small symphony.

Nonetheless, the Quartet in E♭ starts out on the scale of a lyric piano sonata. By chamber-music standards, the first movement is delicate and retiring, and by any standards at all for sonata form, it minimizes dramatic contrast to a remarkable extent. One single fact can stand as an emblem of this quality: the almost complete absence of dominant articulation. The second group comes in the mediant, iii, the development stays in III, IV, and VI; and even the dominant preparation for the recapitulation sets up a different dominant—B♭ hardly figures in the piece at all. As the traditional carrier of emphasis and high potential, and as the automatic device for excitement in a sonata movement, the dominant was exactly what the present composition wanted to renounce. (Beethoven will shortly attempt the opposite *tour de force*, namely, writing without subdominants.) In place of the dominant (B♭), the sixth degree (C) assumes special importance. C is the note from which the much-varied consequent phrase unwinds, the peak note of the initial *Maestoso* and the root note of the final one, the chief key of the development section.

On the whole, this section avoids "developing," dwelling instead upon fresh lyric periods and mystical canonic meditations. Much more than development, a process of free variation provides the ongoing energy in this movement. In its many reappearances, the main theme is almost smothered by rich decorations. Problematic in this movement, as I apprehend it, are those sections that are the most traditionally "developmental": the blustery, highly motivic transitions between the canonic periods and the C-major *Maestoso*, and between the *Maestoso* and the recapitulation. They introduce a curious amalgam of impersonality and pain, a quality which jars in context and finds no response later in the quartet (the *Scherzando* is merely spooky). One can admit the necessity for something more energetic at this juncture in the movement, and admire the linear impulse, the large dimensions, and so on, without feeling sure that Beethoven has hit upon the right mood and the right material.

Nothing in the coda picks up this quality again, and the following movement provides instead expansion of the lyric thought. There is expansion in the essential melodic span, in the characteristic phraseology, in tonal ambitus, in texture, and with all this an expansion—a great deepening—of range of feeling. If (as I believe) one hears this *Adagio ma non troppo e molto cantabile* constantly in reference to the first movement, only a small part of the reason can be anything as mechanical as Riemann's thematic relations. Likewise, only a part of the sense of cohesion stems from linkage provided by the two bars of introduction (see p. 211), though clearly Beethoven's increasing concern with the moments of continuity between movements reflects a growing concern for the intimate facing of the movements in question. The *Adagio* opens with a tentative spelling-out of the dominant-7th chord of A♭, its root (E♭) picking up the tonic of the movement whose cadence has just been sounding. So the introductory bars quietly encourage us to think of A♭—the key of the new movement—as a transitory function of the original E♭, that is, to hear the second movement as a function of the first. Even the first downbeat of the tune, which calls for the new tonic A♭, is handled for just a moment with a nostalgic E♭ chord.

Besides the consummate lyric art of this *Adagio* and its quite extreme luxuriance of texture, the strength of its structure should be emphasized. No other Beethoven slow movement, I would judge, quite matches it in this respect. It is a structure based less on contrast than on similarity, emanating from variations on a single theme, the last of which ends up by resembling the theme rather closely in a number of ways. In the middle, serenity deepens to prayer, and luxuriance deepens to intensity.

The hymn-variation in E major serves as a spiritual climax for the whole quartet. The architecture is eloquent and weighty—another "expansion" upon the delicate formal outlines of the first movement. No lyric piano sonata—prior to Schubert, a couple of years later—had tried for this kind of scope.

It is the *Scherzando vivace* that supplies the intellectual, mordant note, the note of contrast. Even a note of parody: the cryptic introductory *pizzicato* fanfare seems to make light of the *pizzicatos* introduced at the very end of the *Adagio* variations. (*Qua* introduction, the fanfare softens the jar of A♭ to B♭ between the movements. It never recurs; it never needs to recur.) Then while the countersubject makes light of the distinctive off-beat trills of Variation 4, the subject itself mimics the rhythm and line of the dark half-variation in the subdominant, Variation 5. Mockery would be a way to characterize the purely linear relationship between the *Scherzando* subject and the first great lyric sweep of the *Adagio* tune. The latter moves directly up the scale from E♭ to high F, from low 5th to high 6th (p. 211); this range, as Riemann saw, equals that of the *Maestoso* of the first movement (the 9th B♭–C), and that of the main theme of the Finale (B♭–C). What points all this up, I take it, is the emphatic treatment of the very same range by the *Scherzando* subject and answer—cranking all the way up the hill and down again as though the notes B♭ and C contained the whole world of music between them. But in fact the slightly crazed imagination of this piece finds infinitely more to occupy itself with, even a kind of fast nonsense in its trio. Not only does the *Scherzando vivace* form an excessive contrast with the rest of the quartet, in itself it is excessively contrasty—as witness that $\frac{2}{4}$ *Allegro* interruption. The impressive consistency of effect in the preceding *Adagio* is radically countered.

And the rustic Finale again renounces contrast and drama. Beethoven, who seems in early years to have experienced considerable uneasiness about how to end a cyclic work, here solves the problem with the utmost simplicity. One could argue that in this movement, once again, the dominant B♭ is overshadowed, either by the subdominant A♭, seat of the big false recapitulation, or by the sixth degree C, which is strongly indicated by the preface figure and favored both by the development section and the dissolving section at the very end. But the tonal dynamic is very quiet, much too quiet to disturb the dancelike regularity of these pleasant tunes. If they move to the dominant for a second group, they do so with no more sense of mission than a medley of *contredanses* turning up in one new key after another.

The folk dances suddenly become dreamed or disembodied, the clay on the dancers' shoes whitened into some kind of glittering dust. The exquisitely calculated journey leads to a castle in the clouds, a fantasy world; but many magic casements open from it onto the real world. The main theme, of course, remains, in a spiritual transformation. The "non-modulations" from C to A♭ to E to E♭ recall a striking feature of the large structure of the *Adagio*, in which the first sudden key-change—if the reader will thumb back to page 216—is from A♭ to E, after which the E-major hymn-variation broods upon C, and its final note E slips into E♭. Thereafter, in the Finale, cadences stress the step B♭–C, issuing from bar 8 of the main theme: a playful echo of the first movement, and indeed an echo of all the melodic and harmonic sixth degrees that quietly, or less quietly, have illuminated the various movements. Yet in the very last bars, as we have seen, A♮ rather than C remains as the final irreducible essence. Not that A♮ cannot be interpreted as a tendency-note that plays in, via B♭, to C.

· 4 ·

The world of play and the world of song are not lost to Beethoven's later compositions; nothing is ever lost. But in turning from the Quartet in E♭ to the Quartet in A minor, Op. 132, the listener could hardly be blamed if he imagined himself witness to some great reaction, some act of revulsion against the very sources of the lyric vision. In sentiment these two adjacent quartets differ as categorically as other well-known twins: the Fifth and Sixth Symphonies, or the earlier Quartet in E♭, Op. 74, and the *Quartetto serioso* in F minor. One would like to discern something purposeful here: not a manic-depressive swing, but a sharp eye for the extreme expressive limits of technical explorations. Will the technique invert?

Like the *Scherzando vivace* of the E♭ Quartet, but with far more serious intentions, the first movement of the A-minor works to maximize and control contrasts of the greatest intensity. The next composition, too, the Quartet in B♭, will pursue this idea. The technique is diametrically opposed to that of the corresponding first movement of the E♭ Quartet, and in character the two movements could hardly stand farther apart: as far apart as song and suffering. No other piece by Beethoven carries a sense of suffering so close to the skin and treats the experience so deeply and so objectively, at least to my apprehension. One can speak of objectivity, I think, because for once Beethoven seems to be dealing with pain itself, rather than with attitudes or responses to pain. Defiance (even bluster) seems to be at issue in the Fifth Symphony and other C-minor works, such as the Quartet, Op. 18, No. 4; excess nervous energy, in the E-minor Quartet, Op. 59, No. 2; rage, in the F-minor Quartet, Op. 95. In these earlier works, accordingly, conflict is subjected to some kind of positive treatment. The essential action of these works evolves out of the resolution or the attempted resolution of musical contrasts.

The first movement of the Quartet in A minor, however, is concerned not with action but with passion. Contrast is not rationalized but endured; more than any other experience, frustration sets the mood. Conflict is seen simply as the condition of suffering rather than as a challenge that is likely to be taken up. Control involves comprehension and introspection rather than resolution in any ordinary sense.

In the service of such an expressive vision, the play of extreme contrasts found its most serious application. Or have it the other way around: the play of extreme contrasts gave Beethoven the technical means to control such a vision. (To say that he is dealing with pain is not to imply that he was writing musical autobiography—setting down his own feelings on any particular, or ideal, occasion. It is not even necessary to identify him with the grateful "convalescent" named in the inscription to the third movement, though I do not see what to make of that particular text unless we allow that Beethoven was, as he supposed, on some level inventing, imitating, manipulating, referring to or dealing with feeling.) Technique and expression are inextricably bound together, and the attempt to talk about them separately—which may or may not have been provisionally useful in the case of the Op. 18 Quartets—can only muddle the issue here. I scarcely know a piece of music that catches the feelings so tightly; though talking about this is harder, always, than analyzing details of musical contrast.

Of these—for example—the most sensational must be the place where the development section of the first movement ruptures, an analogue to the place in the E♭ *Scherzando vivace* where the $\frac{2}{4}$ *Allegro* breaks in (compare the first bars on p. 246 with p. 232). The case is one of pure absurdity: the material itself, the canonic texture with its skinny octaves, the sudden straight-laced diatonicism—not to speak of the pause which introduces the passage—all constitute a contradiction of everything experienced thus far. If the movement does not smash entirely, that is only because from the start contrast has been pressed to the brink.

Contrast defines the main theme itself on the most basic gestural level. Every time the theme or even a 2-bar segment of it comes—and

Example 119

this movement is ridden by its main theme—there is another confrontation between the *cantus firmus* in whole notes and the marchlike melody attached to it as an unshakable double counterpoint. One is blank and inexorable, the other high-strung, emotional, articulate, and endlessly variable; Beethoven plays them off perfectly one against the other. But in fact everything on the first page twitches with contrast. Even within the impassive *Assai sostenuto*, the F in bar 8 tears grossly, after the series of five diminished-7th chords heard previously. The violin *arpeggio* in bar 9—prolonging that F—is like a scream; the premature tonic chord in bar 10 is like a hand clapped over the mouth. The insecurity of the main *allegro* theme itself, forecast by this hysterical greeting, expresses itself principally in the matter of texture and register; the whole movement is astonishingly "advanced" in this respect. Just when the theme appears to be catching hold, with a vigorous quarter-note figure which will grow more and more important (bar 20), an *adagio* bar cuts off the flow, only to be cut off in turn by a second screaming *arpeggio*. A new statement of the theme (bar 23) is newly wrenched in texture and register, as the melody finds its way from violin 2 to viola to cello to violin 1. The modulation to the second group is initiated by an extremely abrupt fanfare on B♭.

The entire first group has suffered a nervous crisis of indecision. The one thing it is sure about is its vocabulary of chromaticism, its web of semitones echoing back and forth from the *cantus firmus* to the marchlike counterpoint itself. (The modulation is spurred chromatically, too: B♭ sounds in reference to A.) The introductory *Assai sostenuto* strikes an evident note of mystery; at the same time, it seems anxious to lay out the chromatic tone materials for the piece in a painstakingly schematic way. In point of fact, the famous motif G♯–A–F–E is presented in something a little like an orthodox fugal exposition (bars 1–2, subject in i; 3–4, subject and inversion simultaneously on V; 5–6, inversion in i; 7–8, subject and inversion on V). Beethoven is charting not only the motivic channels for the piece, but also its tonal field: A and E, with clearly marked by-paths into F and C.

It is toward F that the original modulating B♭ is guided. But the dominant preparation interrupts itself briefly to accommodate a spasmodic canonic theme in—of all places—the subdominant, D minor. The second theme (in F) asserts another drastic contrast: in this atmosphere of excruciation, it has the *sang-froid* to open with a couple of beats of vamping accompaniment, as though a slack Italian aria were appropriate to the occasion. Magically, the innocent and very lovely tune that emerges *is* appropriate—a fact "explained" only very minimally indeed by certain details recalling the main theme (the sixteenth-note, the *appoggiatura*). After the second theme, various cadential figures flow quietly and freely. For the first time the piece relaxes from the controlling dynamic of fits and starts.

The movement has been following the course of a sonata exposition quite clearly. It even comes to a self-conscious full stop on F, though, to be sure, this stop also manages to reintroduce the characteristic tone of insecurity. A development section starts up reasonably enough with a few bars of whole-notes—a punctuation, that is to say, in the tempo and with the material of the *Assai sostenuto*—modulating to G minor for sequences derived from the main theme (see p. 280). It soon appears, however, that both the development and the recapitulation are going to be handled in an entirely novel way.

This can be taken as another sign of the disaffection with traditional sonata procedures which informs all of Beethoven's late work. More to the point, it can be felt as a true response to the particular exposition at hand. For whereas the traditional development section exaggerates contrasts, introduces new ones, and surmounts them all, the exposition of the A-minor Quartet has hardly left room for exaggeration and has exposed conflicts that may be too disturbing ever to be surmounted. Something quite different has to be attempted, and Beethoven is prepared to risk a

Example 120

sort of psychological low-point. A curiously unimpressive and fitful passage ensues, more a deflection from the problems of the exposition than an engagement with them. Feelings of indecision and pain are muted into frustration and futility. There is no strong progress and no clear outcome.

Here a key role is played by the "absurd" interruption mentioned previously. With a single nihilistic gesture, it is able to trivialize the whole first surge of the development and nullify its move from F to G to C minor. (The surge, it should be said, works for emphasis by means of rising sequences and a cadence built on the vigorous quarter-note figure first heard in bar 20.) Something even stranger defeats the next parallel surge, which heads rapidly toward E minor (bars 99–102). At least the quarter-note cadence now gets a decisive answer, in the form of a loud statement of the orginal 4-note *sostenuto* motif. But this serves only to prolong, not to resolve the cadence; nothing is proposed; there is a real failure of nerve. As if hypnotized, the *sostenuto* motif repeats itself and flags, as the marchlike counterpoint works grievingly to support it. All that can happen is another *arpeggio* scream from the violin and—still in E minor, bars 119 ff.—a terribly premature return of material from bar 9 and onwards.

What we are embarked upon is nothing less than a large section running in principle through the entire exposition (complete with the introductory *Assai sostenuto*) but moving from E minor to C rather than from A minor to F, as originally. From the point of view of classic form, of course, the tonal situation here is as aberrant as the nature of the development section itself. To refer to the passage as the "E-minor Recapitulation" is to stretch terminology hard, for the basic idea of a sonata recapitulation is not only (or even principally) to repeat all the original material, but to repeat and rationalize it all in the tonic key. In Op. 132, this latter function of "recapitulating" is separated off and reserved for a next section, the "A-minor Recapitulation," which touches on all the important themes yet another time, now at last in the tonic key. This is an entirely novel *ad hoc* solution to the problem of coherence in the sonata style.

If the reader will care to place the 16 bars following bar 103 (p. 246) next to the first 8 bars of the movement (p. 244), some of the parallelism and some of the peculiarity of the "E-minor Recapitulation" will become apparent. The bars are half as long, the tempo is about twice as fast. In the same time-span, the 4-bar *cantus firmus* appears three times in different registers (cello, high cello, violin), the original fourth statement being replaced by a 4-bar pedal B (merging into the quarter-note motif: a new detail). The main theme itself (bars 121 ff.) acquires emotional new decorations, which perhaps recall similar decorations in the first movement of the Quartet in E♭. Other modifications work more functionally, to undermine slightly the aberrant E-minor tonality. Thus the statements of the *cantus firmus* now do *not* form themselves as a quasi-fugal exposition pointing in the direction of the dominant. E minor is already too "dominant" in reference to the basic key of the piece. The canonic bridge theme, which had moved oddly to the subdominant, now explains itself: in the E-minor recapitulation it appears handily in A minor, anchoring the tonality to that central key. As a help, the prior passage is rewritten with rather strong new pedals and canons stressing D minor. Coming directly after E minor, this D minor (subdominant of A minor) warns definitely of the ultimate destination, even though the second group is drawn out even a little longer than before.

The destination once reached—after the self-conscious full stop has come on C, by analogy with the previous stop on F, and has again been undercut—Beethoven luxuriates in it for the 72 bars remaining to the movement. There is scarcely a gesture away from A minor now. "Luxuriate" gives the wrong impression, though, for the "A-minor Recapitulation" does not carry suggestions of relaxation, but rather of obsession, increased intensity, and pathos—and it will have been with just these qualities in view that the whole strategy of a double or divided recapitulation was chosen.

In a way, the A-minor recapitulation is the most brilliant thing in the whole movement. Just the three chief themes are exposed, divested of all their connective tissue and yet intensified by means of piercing new details. Doubly self-conscious, they make no pretense of confronting one another properly, and they offer no excuse for the failure of energy. Their inability to modulate away from A minor has much to do with the sense of pathos and obsession. Yet even at the very start, the long-delayed return to the tonic sounds—incredibly—less like resolving than like suffering, less awaited than feared, less stable than helpless:

Example 121

The main theme gradually asserts itself, urgently trying to move sequentially up and out, but it cannot even maintain its old B♭ fanfare; the violin sticks on B♮ while the quarter-note figure beats away in utter frustration below. The canonic bridge theme develops one futile extra bar—and cannot modulate (modulation had been its *raison d'être*). The second theme comes in the major mode, A major. With what fantastic care Beethoven introduces the C♯!—

Example 122

The original anacrusis of three eighth-notes (A B C♯) dissolves into the vamping triplets, and vitalizes them. What is heartbreaking here is the certainty that this vision cannot last, and that we are to be made to hear the last bar lapse back to the minor mode. Thereafter, new variations of the main theme build a peroration speaking of new trials and new despair. The vigorous quarter-note figure makes a curt final cadence in 2-bar phrases: no very determined conclusion.

The movement leaves an unforgettable aftertaste. Principally it is the bittersweet flavor of the main theme, the omnipresent marchlike counterpoint etched against its grave invariable *cantus firmus*. The inherent conflict has been seized, but it has not been settled; its world of frustration is left for the later movements of the quartet to copė with. In addition, the memory of the lyric second theme lingers, a simple 8-bar span heard only three times and never developed. Of the manifold contrasts in the piece, that "absurd" interruption in the development may be the most sensational, but the second theme is certainly the most haunting and the most moving. As presented in the "A-minor Recapitulation," in its baldest form, it presages other bald block contrasts to be heard within the quartet as a whole: between the first movement and the second, and between the Lydian *Heiliger Dankgesang* of the slow movement and its alternating section of new strength, *Neue Kraft fühlend*.

The second theme of the A-minor Quartet, then, may be said to echo or encompass the commanding lyricism of the E♭ Quartet. It is an ironic echo, turned toward pathos; song has been, as it were, inverted.

Of the five movements of the Quartet in A minor, the second and fourth are experienced in a curious and unique way as subsidiary. They are way stations on the total journey, *intermezzi* in the total action, points of stasis in the total experience. The last movement will rather explicitly pick up the unfinished business of the first, after the central slow movement has presented what is probably Beethoven's most extraordinary vision. That he himself saw it in this light seems indicated by his care in sealing off its strange F-Lydian modality from the A-minor world by means of the two dance movements in A major: the leisurely *Allegro ma non tanto* on one side, and the momentary *Alla marcia, assai vivace* on the other.

Thus the quartet fills both of the traditional alternative positions for the minuet or other dance movement, the position between the first movement and the slow movement—see Beethoven's Quartets, Op. 18, No. 5, and 59, No. 1—and that between the slow movement and the finale. It is perhaps tempting, but certainly misleading, to go on and speak of "symmetry" in the over-all structure: misleading not only because of inherent problems in the concept as applied to an art that exists in time, but also because of such cardinal nonsymmetrical features as the trio in the second movement, the crucial recitative linking the fourth to the fifth, and in the Finale, the concluding pages of resolution to the major mode.

The main section of the second movement is an exhaustive and highly refined contrapuntal study, though perhaps at first it sounds like nothing of the kind. Of its 119 bars, plus full-scale repeats, every one involves an unequivocal reference to the basic 2-bar cell in double counterpoint of bars 5–6:

Example 123

The basic idea contains three distinct motivic elements: that of bar 5 in violin 1; that of bar 6 in violin 1 with or without its upbeat eighth-notes; and the upward quarter-notes with which the piece commences. In such a conception, naturally, conventional sonata drama finds no place, and the contrast with the first movement of the quartet is complete and almost malicious. This *Allegro ma non tanto* is low-keyed, abstract, level, cool, monochromatic, meticulous, amusing—everything that the other movement is not.

An exhaustive contrapuntal study—but not really an exhausting one, as some listeners have been known to feel, and say, and write. Working within well-defined limitations, Beethoven achieved a range of variety that counteracts the thematic single-mindedness with brilliance to spare. Tovey said that fugue can be talked about only by analyzing every bar, and here too only minute scrutiny will reveal all the facets of this superbly polished piece of musical jewelry. We shall have to restrict ourselves to one or two details: for instance, the way in which the second of the motivic elements —the eighth-note figure of bar 6—finds its way from the first beat of the bar to the second. This shift emerges as an important new feature of the return, the second *a* of the *a b a* form:

Example 124

The introduction of the off-beat motif as a droll echo, in bars 76–8, has been foreshadowed by the four-eighth-note figure of bars 71–5—another detail appearing for the first time in this return. Beethoven is pleased enough by the off-beat idea to extend the return passage by two whole 4-bar phrases whose main purpose seems to be to repeat the echoes; and he is amused enough by it to bring it up again at the final cadence of the codetta:

Example 125

The sixfold repetition of the first motivic element, always from E, is a sufficiently tickling idea; the off-beat motif in bar 118 is a delicious addition; but perhaps the smartest little touch of all is the textbook harmony of bar 119.

(The same sort of play with motifs shifted to the second beat enlivens the cadence of the *Scherzando vivace* of the Quartet in E♭ [p. 233]. These two dance movements, as was remarked at the beginning of this chapter, are Beethoven's most extended and contrapuntally his most elaborate; as adjacent compositions, they betray a number of similarities in technique. Yet once again the feeling is of an expressive inversion of means. One piece serves as the active center of its quartet, the other as a distinct resting point. One piece is dry and flat, the other contrasty.)

The work is not short, and needs to modulate—to F and C, keys which also figured in the opening movement. However, the quality of key-contrast differs in these movements as radically as everything else. In the second movement, tonal tension seems no more stirring than in a fugue by Bach. Even the trio comes in the tonic key, without so much as a change of mode—a rare arrangement in Beethoven's works to date, but one that will be employed regularly in the three last quartets.

The tunes and doublets thrown together for this magical medley of a trio were cited on page 203. The trio works with off-beat accents too, but in a quite different way, with the effect of spiritualizing tawdry *allemande* clichés into a strangely insubstantial distillate of popular lyricism. This innocent tone and the sophistication of the main section stand at opposite extremes of some sort of spectrum, and it is not surprising to find the trio harmonically very quiet. A lumbering bear-dance phrase switches momentarily into $\frac{4}{4}$ time: an echo of the "absurd" interruption of the opening movement. The texture closes in warmly. After the dance runs its course—one is tempted to say, after the disembodied band recedes into the distance—the *Allegro ma non tanto* returns verbatim, quite unruffled. For once there is no full or token return of the trio. Perhaps that reflects an essential lack of engagement between the parts.

One final note on the *Allegro ma non tanto:* a model for it can be found in Mozart's Quartet in A, K. 464:

Example 126

This was the piece that Beethoven had studied twenty-five years earlier, in connection with his other Quartet in A, the Quartet in A major, Op. 18, No. 5. Mozart's minuet—also a second movement—begins similarly with a low unison motif moving up a 2nd, designed to be joined with a more mobile descending figure (bars 9–12). Then the double counterpoint formed in this manner becomes the mainspring of the action, if not the sole spring, as in Op. 132. Mozartian—no, Beethoven's composition is not quite that; but one cannot help feeling that if Mozart had still been living (aged 69), he would have found it to his taste, more so than most of Beethoven's other music. Its grace, workmanship, and something about its humor—so purely professional and strange and inward—would surely have struck a responsive note.

· 5 ·

Contrast—the third movement of the Quartet in A minor forces contrast more profoundly than any previous piece of music. Not that such a statement lends itself to nice statistic proofs; we are not furnished with any meter or scale to quantify musical contrast. But there are certain superlatives that Beethoven invites or rather demands. Like the Great Fugue, this movement is utterly radical in conception, a fantastic vision—devastating, *unerhört*.

Stravinsky calls the Great Fugue an "absolutely contemporary piece of music that will be contemporary forever," a characterization that could apply as well to the *Heiliger Dankgesang eines Genesenen an die Gottheit, in der lydischen Tonart* ("Holy Song of Thanks to the Godhead from a Convalescent, in the Lydian Mode"). The Lydian hymn proper opens the movement and forms the pillars of its *A B A B A* structure. "Contemporary" in that the piece makes up its own new language—in spite of the fact that the Lydian mode was an archaism, and a sufficiently remarkable one. But of course no one had ever used the Lydian mode in this way. To accommodate it, Beethoven imagined a unique harmonic, rhythmic, dynamic, and textural order. This self-contained, hermetic world is twice confronted with the ordinary world of the *B* section, which Beethoven marked *Neue Kraft fühlend*. The two do not mix, they do not understand one another, and it is only by a sort of miracle that they do not wipe each other out or simply collapse. This is one measure of the seriousness of the musical contrast.

As for the archaism, that must have seemed as radical at the time as any of Stravinsky's neoclassic essays. But in spirit Beethoven's gesture was Romantic, not neoclassic. Just as his obsession with folk song in the 1820's owes something to Rousseau and his natural man, so Beethoven's experiments with the church modes in those years—the Dorian *Incarnatus* of the *Missa solemnis*, the passage for *Brüder, über'm Sternenzelt* in the Ninth Symphony, and the present Lydian movement—owe something to the vogue for medieval Catholicism expressed by Romantic poets like Brentano and Novalis. Schubert was setting Novalis as early as 1819, and Padre Baini's panegyric biography of Palestrina, the "Saviour of Church music," was to come out in 1828. The Lydian hymn summons up some infinitely remote liturgy, a ritual music of romance that tenuously looks ahead to *Parsifal* and the Fauré Requiem. Already in Beethoven's lifetime, pious archaeology was beginning to enshrine the great a-cappella school of church music. The *Heiliger Dankgesang* seems to anticipate the nineteenth-century Palestrina revival in the way that *Pulcinella* anticipated the current Vivaldi fashion.

As astonishing as any of this is the programmatic conception, which is set forth so much more explicitly here than in the tentative or tacit programs attached to not a few earlier slow movements (*les derniers soupirs . . . Eine Trauerweide oder Akazienbaum* . . . the "starry heavens"). As is well known, the impetus came out of Beethoven's own experience of illness in April 1825. The Lydian mode gave him a rarefied atmosphere for his hymn of thanks, whispered by a convalescent who has just, and barely, passed a supreme crisis. He still seems to be under oxygen. But the hymn is twice interrupted by a thrilling vision of new strength (*Neue Kraft fühlend*), strength which has not been attained, and which perhaps never will be attained. The determination to include this concrete reference within the convalescent prayer recalls another famous bald gesture of Beethoven's last years: the *Dona nobis pacem* of the *Missa solemnis*, which incorporates a concrete depiction of the warfare against which peace must be sought.

In the opening statement of the *Heiliger Dankgesang*, contrast is minimized to an almost unbelievable degree. Use of an old church mode re-

Example 127

duces harmonic tension automatically; and once Beethoven had settled on the Lydian, he held to it scrupulously, using just the diatonic notes—the white notes on the piano—with never a sharp or flat to ruffle them. In the harmony, he restricted himself to triads, one single functional 7th-chord (G_7), and a Spartan ration of nonfunctional dissonance. The five phrases of the very simple hymn tune are all kept the same length (4 bars); the phrases all make the same little *crescendo;* every one of the notes is of the same value (half-note). The harmonization goes note-against-note in the four instruments except for occasional quarter-notes at cadences. Also, the contrapuntal preface and interludes between phrases all last the same length of time (2 bars); they too move exclusively in a single note value (quarter-note). Between them they make do with only two different canonic motifs—different in melody, though identical in rhythm and analogous in general contour. All the imitations come at the space of a half-note. All but one come at the interval of the unison or octave. These are some of the statistics behind the monumental flatness of this opening hymn, its celebrated mystic aura. There is a primordial quality here that recalls, in a way, the hushed unison folk tune for Schiller at the end of the Ninth Symphony.

(While he was ill, Beethoven scribbled off this preposterous canon for his doctor:

Example 128

Liszt could hardly have thought of a more Mephistophelian travesty of the *Heiliger Dankgesang*.)

The mystic aura is furthered by the unnaturally slow tempo and the scoring or, rather, by what seems to be an unnaturally slow tempo on account of the scoring. The image is orchestral: forty strings could sustain the hymn at this speed with comfort, but four can bear it only with a sense of strain, tenuousness, and a certain gaucherie. This Beethoven certainly wanted, as the contrast with the superbly idiomatic instrumental sound of the *B* section implies clearly enough. Again one thinks of the Great Fugue, another work in which the instruments are made to outdo themselves, and in which their unhappy striving is incorporated into the essential aesthetic.

It is between the hymn proper and the *B* section—*Andante, Neue Kraft fühlend*, D major, $\frac{3}{8}$—that contrast is so profoundly forced. In one massive contradiction, all the asceticisms of scale, melody, harmony, rhythm, and texture disappear. The style resumes that of Variation 2 in the slow movement of the E♭ Quartet (which is also an *Andante*): a delicate, brilliant gridwork of wide-spanning *obbligato* counterpoint sparkling with trills and rests and little syncopations, *spiccato* runs and active, sprung bass lines. In harmony, the vague untonal mysteries of the hymn give way to lucid, even simple-minded tonal progressions freely indulging the two common chords denied to the Lydian mode, the subdominant and the dominant-7th. The organization is lyric; Beethoven had rarely written such beautiful lyric phrases. Yet the effect of contrast goes deeper than any listing of the details can suggest. It has to do with the total quality of the form, something about the *set* of the contrasting sections: something almost preternaturally aloof and timeless.

Perhaps this can be put in relief by considering another composition of the same period, the *Adagio molto e cantabile* of the Ninth Symphony. The structural diagram looks similar: *A B A B A* . . . an alternation of contrasting tunes—a duple-time *Adagio* (B♭) and a triple-time *Andante* in third-related keys (G, D)—which belong, very roughly, to the same classes. The great difference lies in the relation between the tunes, which in turn involves a difference in the motivation for their alternation. In the symphony, the motivation is external; the modulation that spurs it comes as an arbitrary surprise. So when later versions of the first tune lead not to D but instead to G and E♭ and D♭, these different goals give the movement its real centers of energy. The quartet, on the other hand, lacks such energy, for the modulation is internally motivated and never changes. When it is time for the second *B* section, Beethoven impassively repeats the identical move. For some extraordinary reason, the single modulation seems profoundly at rest. Instead of surprise or revelation, the alternation here makes for relief and inevitability.

As for the internal motivation, that comes out of harmonic anomalies of the Lydian mode, which will require a moment's explanation. Since this mode contains the anomalous raised fourth degree, B♮, it lacks a true subdominant chord, and therefore it pushes hard toward the dominant key, C. Once Beethoven allows this fatal push to take place—already in the second hymn-phrase—a cadence in the tonic key becomes an impossibility. The necessary balance of a subdominant chord is simply unavailable, as the penultimate phrase of the hymn discovers. So the final phrase takes the only way out, retracing its steps and opting boldly for modulation, a deflection to another key center. The move to the A-major triad sounds "right" for a number of reasons, no doubt, A minor and A major having been the keys of the preceding movements, and A being the peak note of the initial imitative motif, in the preface to the hymn. It is also a fact that Palestrinian orthodoxy, as hardened in the textbooks, prescribes A as the cadence for the Lydian mode on F. The old familiar smell of classroom counterpoint emanates from this movement, as from so many others in the quartets from Op. 18 on; half-forgotten rules and legends are animated anew. A standard exercise of Albrechtsberger's contrapuntal curriculum, the "chorale fugue," half emerges in the concluding *A* section.

That a modulation from F to D via A can stabilize the hymn—that a modulation can stabilize—is perhaps the supreme paradox of this movement. Perhaps the paradox rationalizes the drastic contrast between the worlds of the *Heiliger Dankgesang* and the *Neue Kraft*. After the first appearance of the latter section, the harmony moves swiftly and stilly back to the Lydian F for a decorated version (or light variation) of the hymn. The various musical elements begin to get a little dissociated; contrast very gradually begins to intrude. The tune itself returns verbatim, in pristine, even, *cantus-firmus* notes floating up and away from the other instruments. Below it, the quarter-notes of the original background are slightly agitated into eighths and dotted quarters, twining and making all sorts of peaceful, unbelievable dissonances. Yet they are tracing the exact counterpoint of the original statement, and the original harmony, beat by beat—that unearthly harmony which, as Philip Radcliffe observes, "is sufficiently plain for the dominant sevenths, when they appear, to have an effect of peculiar tenderness and for the inversions of the common chord to sound remarkably rich." [7] Thereafter, the very same move to the A-major triad leading to a very light variation—hardly a variation—of the *Neue Kraft* in D. The hymn seems to resume. But how can the piece end?

Beethoven certainly could not bring back the hymn verbatim a third time, for a tonic cadence is impossible. He had to bring either more or less. He chose to bring less: in point of fact, no more than the first hymn-phrase—carefully stopping short of the second, which had modulated to the dominant. The final pillar of the *A B A B A* structure, then, is not another statement or variation of the hymn but a "liquidation," in the form of a lengthy treatment of the single phrase F | F E D E | F G F. In accordance with this limitation, only the first of the imitative fragments (the preface) survives, for newly extended developments. Its contour is related to that of the hymn-phrase, at the cadence: C A | G C—*F* | *G F*.

To look more closely at this final pillar of the *A B A B A* structure: what is heard first is a newly supple version of the contrapuntal preface, with its characteristic leap up from C to A brought even more beautifully into relief. If a second decorated version of *A* were indeed intended, with the elements a little more dissociated than before, this would be just the way to begin it. But the eccentric emphasis on the important cadential G's in the viola and cello (bars 170 and 171) amounts to an explicit canonic reading of the preface, forecasting severe contrapuntal action to come. The hymn tune enters as expected, only to be cut short indecisively and guided through the various registers by piercing, sober imitations. For the hymn (or whatever is left of it) is no longer harmonized by block chords. The texture has become entirely dissociated and fluid, and the preface-

[7] P. 117.

Example 129

motif for the first time interpenetrates with the hymn, forming a strict double counterpoint exposed fugally along with the shortened hymn-fragment: F | F E D E . . . in violin 2, answered at the 5th in the viola, at the octave in the cello, at the 5th in violin 1, and then at the 2nd in violin 2 (a *stretto* which is not carried through). A cadence pauses very solemnly on D minor—one would almost say piously, with that hollow 5th. Perhaps this means to encourage a final echo of the D-major *B* section. A first course of inquiry has been terminated.

A second course begins by turning quietly back to F—there is no "modulation"—in order to restate the original canon on the preface-motif, with its eccentric cadence G–F (violin and viola, bar 184, and perhaps carried through to the soaring violin G of bar 185–6). Bar 186 even suggests that the same fugal exposition is going to follow. This time, however, more of the hymn-phrase ensues—all of it, in fact: F | F E D E | F G F low in the cello, answered four octaves higher in the violin (bar 187, last note) and then at the 5th in the cello, *stretto* (bar 188). As the counter-subject dissolves into rich rhythmic agitation, this *stretto* stirs up an astonishing great climax. That four-octave span suddenly grows precarious; dissonance is as brutal as anything in the Great Fugue; the sheer volume generated terrifies, in light of the profound quietism previously. The violin trumpets the end of the hymn-phrase (. . . F G F) in two stages, *F* G F | *G* A G, leaving the cadential *F* as the real topic of the remaining bars. The step G–F cascades down and imitates itself in a passage of deep relaxation, ending in another very solemn cadence, this one on C.

Once again Beethoven turns quietly back to F, in order to initiate a third course of inquiry. The preface-motif sounds again in its original position, but now free of any canonic involutions. The hymn-phrase is reduced to only two notes, F and E, its second and third (which also echo the descending steps of the prior passage of *decrescendo*). The severity and passion and power are spent; F E is imitated up through four octaves, slowly and, as it would seem, endlessly until a fifth octave adds more of the phrase (F E D E | F) with a sort of muted shudder of finality. The movement concludes—or rather ceases—very simply with high A falling to the tonic. This seems to make a last reference to the leap up to A in the preface-motif, and to the A that had modulated away to the section of *Neue Kraft*.

This is one of Beethoven's superb pages. The gradual dissociation of the hymn in its three manifestations from an archaic, awesome chorale prelude into a granitic contrapuntal study of a single phrase—this is heard as a process of increasing spiritualization but also as one of enrichment, a confrontation of inherent complexities. The vision is not, in the end, at all a mystic one. There are commentators who discern deathlike transcendence in this passage, but I do not know what they can be hearing at the tremendous climax in the middle. Beside this strength the *Neue Kraft* pales. In what I have called a three-course inquiry into the first phrase of the hymn, Beethoven molds it and mirrors it with the primary end, surely, of stressing its linearity over any harmonic implications. (And if that was his idea of "medieval" music, he was not far wrong.) Canon and fugue establish a tonal field in which the two modulations—first to D, then even to C—can fade into unimportance by comparison with the purely linear energy of the notes themselves: in the three courses, the cool return to F

(1) F | F E D E·

(2) F | F E D E | F G F

G F (*etc.*)

(3) F E (D . . .)

F E D E | F

at the start of each course presages the acceptance of F as the ultimate high cadence. The "impossible" Lydian cadence is perfectly accomplished.

· 6 ·

The way out of this remote vision, Beethoven seems to have felt, was through another kind of remoteness. One thing we can be quite sure of, when the next music starts: this brisk business is not yet the Finale. It turns out to be a miniscule dance movement with the dimensions of a bagatelle; Beethoven had recently been writing such pieces for piano. If the trio of the second movement suggests a spiritualized country dance, so this *Alla marcia, assai vivace* suggests a parallel vision—a dandified march

Example 130

out of a Salzburg serenade or a stylish *opera buffa.* Yet the dotted rhythms stir a memory of the main theme of the opening movement. The perfectly jeweled phrases—8 bars to the dominant repeated, 16 bars to the tonic repeated—cannot be quite as innocent as they pretend.

The last cadence cedes (*attacca subito*) to an ambush, an annihilation, a sudden bleeding, palpitating cry in recitative for the first violin. *O Freunde, nicht diese Töne! sondern lasst uns Unangenehmere anstimmen* . . . the gesture is a real inversion of the Ninth Symphony (and the coming Finale theme, Nottebohm discovered, was born among sketches for the Ninth). Perhaps, then, the secret function of the march is to provide something from which the recitative and the Finale can recoil, like the dissonant racket that opens the symphony Finale. As in the symphony, if not quite so directly, the recitative dilates upon previous movements. The move to F immediately recalls the *Heiliger Dankgesgang,* in spite of the conspicuous B♭'s. The background motif (bars 25–6 and 31) echoes not only the cadence of the march but another cadence, too, that of the exposition and the "E-minor Recapitulation" of the first movement (see p. 249). The three-octave violin *arpeggio* prolonging F recalls the scream of the first movement; the descending step in bars 31, 37, 38, and 39 recalls the main theme; bars 44–6 reintroduce a crucified form of the motif G♯–A–F–E. Even more important, perhaps, the rhythmic flux reinstates for the first time in four movements the convulsions of the opening page. In 22 bars the recitative runs from *Più allegro* to *ritardando, in tempo, ritardando, immer geschwinder, Presto,* and *Poco Adagio.*

And there is no getting away from the sheer blatancy of this recitative. It is no dignified Gluckish thing—it sounds more like "rescue opera" or early Wagner; and coming right after the elegantly barbered little march—but by this time we are presumably habituated to such effects of contrast in the A-minor Quartet. The gesture has proved too coarse for some listeners; Thomas Mann speaks of "the naked human voice" and has his fictional composer parody the passage in a meretricious violin concerto. But the gesture cannot be dissociated from Beethoven's conception, which seems more openly "programmatic" here than anywhere else in the string quartets. What he wanted was a violent short-circuit to the world of pain that was opened up in the first movement and turned away from in the interim. Be thankful that he did not think of enlarging his quartet with a dramatic soprano to shout his directions across (a step that remained for Schoenberg).

What a recitative is supposed to precede is an aria; what Beethoven offers is at least a magnificently vocal melody which will dominate its rondo Finale to an exceptional extent. (It opens with two bars of vamping accompaniment, recalling the second theme of the first movement.) The noble middle cadence on the seventh degree, G—this recalls the *Allegretto* movement of the E-minor "Razumovsky" Quartet—makes the second half of the melody sound all the more admirably concise when it holds itself to a single 8-bar phrase. Melodic pressure is constantly upward, something that rather effectively frustrates the rondo episodes; all they seem able to do is develop the descending cadential bar of the melody—and their wispiness is increased by off-beat accents disturbing the $\frac{3}{4}$ meter. In the sense that the rondo theme shuts off any independent material of strength between its appearances, this movement too may be said to minimize contrast, up to the concluding section in the major mode. The result is an obsessive, distressed quality considerably simpler than that of the first movement, which remains very vividly in the ear as an emotional standard. The calculated lowering of the level of expressive insight has been anticipated by the recitative.

The world of the first movement is the world of A minor and of strong chromatic inflection. Mainly it is the step F–E which the Finale salvages from the *cantus-firmus* motif of the opening. F–E stands out in a dozen obvious ways in this *Allegro appassionato*, in ways that perhaps do not need to be detailed. The piece hews to the lines of a sonata rondo, with the anomaly of a pathetic gesture at a subdominant recapitulation before an unequivocal return in the tonic key. Here some fine new details of register and accompaniment figuration appear without disturbing the splendid hard lines of the melody itself.

At the end of the recapitulation, a curious *fugato* creeps in when we are not quite noticing. Regular entries of subject and answer in F major (cello, violin 2, and violin 1) are complicated by a mock *stretto* in the

Example 131

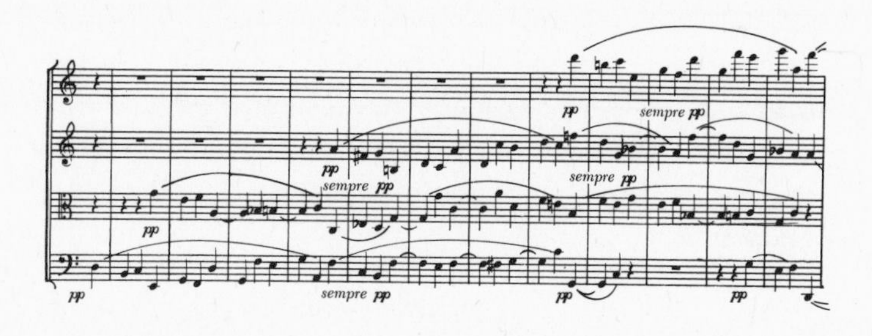

viola. The end of the last entry etches out F–E as accompaniment first to frantic motivic stirrings and then to a last statement of the rondo melody:

Example 132

There is a terrible forced quality to the melody as it appears in this fast version. *Allegro appassionato* becomes *Presto*, *presto frenetico*—the cello straining up to its highest register, the middle instruments beating away in dumb motifless eighth-notes, and the dynamics changed to *forte* with *sforzandi* in each bar (previously the melody had been marked *espressivo* and had never even reached a *forte*). This is another of those points of impending breakdown that harrow so many Beethoven compositions. Joined by the violin, the cello rears up to its climactic note, the penultimate high E of the melody—and freezes, as a phantasmagoric turn to A major blends into a concluding section which is perhaps the most amazing thing in this whole amazing quartet. E waits for 100 bars until its resolution takes place in the very last bar of the piece.

In this concluding A-major section, the great sense of release is tempered by a sense of recollection: of the trio to the second movement, the spiritualized country dance. The themes themselves are not very similar, but the key and meter are, and so is the phrase construction, which is to say the quality of the rhetoric. Disparate, naïve melodic fragments are thrown together in a dazzling "medley" of the kind Beethoven played with in various dances in the last quartets, notably in this one. The passage reduces itself to a collection of separate, self-contained, repeated ideas all squarely in A:

|: 8 :| 2 |: 4 :|: 4 :|: 4 :| 16

Then the whole passage is run through again (save only for the repeat of the 8-bar phrase)—a 50-bar block-repetition changed only in instrumentation and secondary details. The little ideas themselves make no obvious reference to the thematic material of the movement—the fourth of them, madly, quotes a place out of Mozart's A-major Quartet—until the last one, the 16-bar phrase (bar 336, then later varied as bar 385). F♮ has not been forgotten. It rubs itself away in this penultimate ploy:

Example 133

In technical terms, this cadential detail almost duplicates one illustrated on page 238, from the analogous point in the Quartet in E♭. Once again the major and minor forms of the sixth degree alternate over a tonic pedal; and the sixth degree, it will be recalled, has played a central role all through these quartets, in one form or another—C in the E♭ Quartet, F in the A-minor. Yet in spirit the two passages are poles apart. They epitomize, in fact, something felt rather generally in comparing the two compositions: the sense of an expressive inversion of technical means. In the E♭ Quartet, the passage is still looking ahead, even though it is the last event in the piece—a last new suggestive idea appended to the burgeoning Finale, a last tribute to the spontaneity that grounds the conception of the quartet as a whole. The parallel passage in the A-minor Quartet looks back, a last memorial to the minor-mode sonorities of the obsessive Finale, which has ceded only superficially to lightness and gaiety in the concluding *Presto* section. The expressive contrast is between song and suffering, between play and pain.

This language may appear to suggest a conception of the quartet in terms of an extramusical program. I have in mind no series of events or pictures, whether autobiographical or not, but the musical image of an underlying psychological progress that is generalized and essentially inchoate. Such an image appears in one great composition after another in Beethoven's *œuvre*. (The distinction seems to me valid and important, in terms of critical theory; but in any case, in this matter of extramusical "meanings" lack of purity may be less damaging to the critic than lack of imagination. Tannhäuser was sinful to submit to temptation, certainly, but Parsifal was rather lumpish not to respond to temptation at all.) The sense of a particular psychological sequence is what gives the late quartets their particular individual intensities—in spite of technical threads crossing from one to the other. And among the late quartets, the personality of the A-minor, because most agonized, is probably the most distinct of all.

One can hardly attend to the first movement, I think, without submitting in some way to an impression of suffering and frustration. Material, gesture, vocabulary, and form all contribute to this impression. The second movement turns from this root experience to a private world that is as perfect as it is surreal. The transition is really the most mysterious in the whole quartet—by comparison the *Heiliger Dankgesang* sounds positively earthy. Just as in the E♭ Quartet, Beethoven here invests his highly elaborated dance movement with a very particular shock-value. As a result, in any case, the *Heiliger Dankgesang* need not trouble itself dispelling the disturbances of the opening; it can concentrate on its own vision. The spiritual engagement grows more and more intense, as the hymn itself confronts the *Neue Kraft* section and finally concentrates on a fugal treatment of a single phrase, making that incredible climax and that incredible Lydian cadence. Then this mood is shrugged off by the *Alla marcia*, in a suspiciously off-hand way. Inevitably, and very soon, the scream of the recitative restores the passion of the opening more grossly, emphatically, and obsessively than before.

For the finale to return more grossly to the feeling of the opening movement is a standard dynamic for compositions in the minor mode, which Beethoven had followed (with all due allowances for differences) in all his minor-mode quartets: C minor, Op. 18, No. 4; E minor, Op. 59, No. 2; and F minor, Op. 95. In the last, something else was added: a first attempt at the "dissolving" conclusion used more securely now in the E♭ and A-minor compositions. In the early quartet, it may be that the emotional sequence evaporates a little too carelessly. In the A-minor Quartet, the concluding A-major *Presto* emerges so directly and so painfully out of the A-minor *Allegro appassionato* that the root experience stays firmly in mind. Despite an impression of liberation, even of play, the *Presto* is informed by a consciousness or encompassment both of the abstracted second movement with the country dances and also of the outer movements with their characteristic note of pain—this through the miniscule cadential phrase with its F♮. That fragile detail bears an astonishing weight of association, back through all the F–E steps of the Finale to the *Assai sostenuto*, and even back to all the F-major sections which occur prominently in almost all of the movements.

"I won't bother you with the rest of the quartet," says one of the characters in Aldous Huxley's *Point Counter Point*, "It's lovely. But the *Heiliger Dankgesang* is the crucial part." That is a poor way to look at a Beethoven quartet; what matters is not any single "crucial part" but the total sequence of feeling. And thereby hangs a cautionary tale; for when Spandrell is persuaded that after all the *Heiliger Dankgesang* does not constitute the real living proof of God, the soul, and goodness, but rather a turning away from reality, he gives up on life and walks deliberately into an assassination trap. When he is found, the needle is still scratching away at the end of the record (that would have been, in 1928, the first available electrical recording—the Lener Quartet). But it was Huxley, not Beethoven, who stopped after the third movement. Transcendence was not Beethoven's solution, not in the second or third movements or in the *Presto* conclusion.

On an intellectual level, one feels a compulsion to argue for the integrity of the Quartet in A minor. The contrasts within its movements and sections are on the face of it so wild that some effect of disparity might surely be anticipated. But in point of fact, and Spandrell perhaps to the contrary, the work has scarcely ever failed to impress listeners or critics as a convincing unity. Beethoven's unique achievement here was the creation of a psychological progress perhaps more arresting than in any other work—for Romain Rolland, the A-minor Quartet was "*l'œuvre la plus ardue peut-être et la plus profonde de Beethoven*"—which is nonetheless put together out of contrasts that can fairly be called dizzying. Only one other piece deals so extremely in contrast, the next composition, the Quartet in B♭.

I have discussed the Quartets in E♭ and A minor as a pair in the hope that something emerges from such technical parallels as the "dissolving" conclusions, the very weighty slow movements, and the contrapuntal emphasis in the dance movements. But by slightly shifting perspective, another sort of pair can be seen in the Quartets in A minor and B♭: these are Beethoven's two most radical and extreme compositions. They press contrast most recklessly, and it is no accident that they come up with the most mysterious emotional images. These two quartets have excited the twentieth-century consciousness most deeply of all. Next to them, the E♭ Quartet on the one hand and the C♯-minor and the F-major on the other seem collected and normal—even, possibly, tame.

Both perspectives have their value. And in the sequel, I shall group the B♭ Quartet, not together with the A-minor, but with the C♯-minor, as a second major-minor pair representing a climactic statement of characteristic opposite drives in Beethoven's artistic activity. These may be called drives toward dissociation and integration. For in the B♭ Quartet, the play of contrast leads to dissociation, as does not happen in the A-minor; and in the C♯-minor, Beethoven went even further than in the A-minor to create a sense of surpassing unity to the psychological sequence. This is not to say that it is necessarily a greater work than the A-minor. It is to say that already within the space of a single year, Beethoven is plunging ahead to all kinds of radical new explorations.

The new pair has one obvious feature in common, the use of fugue. This no longer extends simply to the inclusion of big but loose *fugato* passages within certain movements, such as the *Scherzando vivace* of Op. 127 and the *Heiliger Dankgesang* of Op. 132, but to the casting of entire movements. One quartet opens with a full-sized fugue; the other ends with a thoroughly oversized one, a fugue of unprecedented extent and ambition. The novelty is striking enough to warrant some special consideration. Especially so, when one of the movements in question, the Great Fugue, stands out as the most problematic single work in Beethoven's output—the most seriously or vitally problematic work, doubtless, in the entire literature of music.

9

FUGUE

The Great Fugue, Op. 133

Sketching the first movement of the Quartet in A minor, Beethoven paused to wonder how the *cantus-firmus* theme would look as a fugue subject:

Example 134

Some time later, as Nottebohm pointed out, he jotted down the subject in just this form for a second time, now with a view to pursuing it.[1] It led, of course, to the composition of the Great Fugue, the Finale of his third quartet for Prince Galitzin.

It is a temptation to relive the moment of creation in that original sketch page, to bear vicarious witness to the dawning idea in the composer's consciousness—the basic idea destined to germinate into some unique, uniquely destined work of art. Romain Rolland was so tempted; for him, the Great Fugue was the very germ of the Quartet in B♭, and—carefully assuring himself that the sketch in question was no later insertion—he found support for this insight in what he took to be the moment of genesis of the Great Fugue. To be sure, the next sketches for it occur during later movements of the Quartet in B♭, not at the beginning; if the fugue had grounded the conception of the quartet, it should have been the first movement to have been sketched. But then, why should the original doodle have been in B♭ rather than in A?

Perhaps the fugue subject did inspire the quartet at that moment—it does not much matter, for the sense that the Great Fugue dominates and

[1] *Beethoveniana*, II, 550.

justifies the quartet must manifest itself out of the completed work itself, not out of the composer's putative founding idea. More likely, the fugue subject was a swift, compulsive little investigation in the abstract. Or it could have been conceived for quartet without any thought yet of its context—a floating notion, like the *Alla danza Tedesca* movement which was sketched in various keys before coming to rest in the Quartet in B♭. What is known is that in these years fugue sketches came very naturally to Beethoven's pen. During the third period, fugue was the crop that he cultivated most eagerly and harvested most stubbornly. He rarely missed an opportunity to fertilize the ground.

The metaphor is admittedly a little invidious; and in fact the field was not overly fertile. This appears from the fugue sketches at large, which even by comparison with Beethoven's other sketches seem exceedingly labored. Over and over again the same ground is turned and harrowed, with new tools or the same ones, with an almost pathetic peasant patience. But the point, once again, as in the matter of the genesis of the Quartet in B♭, lies not in the background work but in the completed works of art. A composer does his best to make a virtue out of necessity, and sometimes Beethoven seems to flaunt his toil; strain is a real aesthetic factor—though I should never say the decisive factor—in certain of his most impressive fugues. And as long as this situation continued, fugue not unnaturally continued to be a primary technical preoccupation, resulting in one extraordinary movement after another within almost all the compositions of the third period.

The late fugues are not likely to be forgotten by anyone who has listened to them seriously, but it may still be worth emphasizing how many and how diverse they are. Some sixteen important works date from the decade preceding work on the late quartets. Three of these—the song cycle *An die ferne Geliebte* and the two sets of bagatelles—would scarcely take kindly to fugal intrusions, but of the remaining thirteen, as many as nine contain fugues that could be said to range from merely prominent to sensational. The sonata, once again, proved most suitable to the working out of new stylistic urges, and the years 1814–22 were devoted largely to two sonatas for cello and piano and six for piano alone. The first two of the series lack fugues, but fugue bursts out full-fledged in the Finale of the Cello Sonata in D, Op. 102, No. 2, in 1815. In 1816, the Piano Sonata in A, Op. 101, includes a hundred bars of fugue as the development section of its Finale. In 1817, Beethoven wrote a small fugue for string quintet, published as Op. 137, and sketched at others. In 1818, he delivered himself of the earth-shaking, encyclopedic fugal Finale of the *Hammerklavier* Sonata in B♭, Op. 106.

All of these are serious, vexed, pebbly, learned fugues; and for the moment Beethoven seems satisfied—not with the whole fugal idea, but at least with fugues of this character. When he returns to the general problem three years later, he does so from a somewhat different standpoint. The Overture *Zur Weihe des Hauses* of 1821, his first major orchestral work for seven years, finds him experimenting with a bland ceremonial fugue idealizing beyond anyone's imagination a traditional contrapuntal cliché. The Finale of the Piano Sonata in A♭, Op. 110, gives him his first occasion to write a lyric fugue, with a subject conspicuously mild and lacking in rough edges, and with a powerfully expressive (as well as powerful) climax. In the two other sonatas of 1821–2, Op. 109 and 111, the fugue-writing daemon rests.

But during 1822–3, Beethoven is welcoming the more or less traditional invitations to fugue offered him by the genres he attacked next—the piano variations, the Mass, and the symphony. In piano variations, fugue was traditional at least with this composer; like the *Eroica* Variations of twenty years before, the "Diabelli" Variations features a large fugue as its penultimate event—and in addition fits an ingenious lyric *Fughetta* variation into the mold of Diabelli's waltz. The Ninth Symphony has a *fugato* in the first movement, a theme in fugal exposition for the second movement, and among the episodes of the Finale two respectable double fugues, a joyous one for chorus and a stormy one for orchestra. With the *Missa solemnis*, composed in the period 1819–23, Beethoven gladly obeyed the conventional decree for fugal conclusions to the *Gloria* and *Credo*. His setting of *In gloria Dei Patris* is a very effective piece in the same genre as *Zur Weihe des Hauses*, and his *Et vitam venturi* is a masterpiece. The Mass also accommodates comfortably divers small *fugati* for voices, plus one that follows no convention whatsoever: the vigorous section for instruments evoking the storm and stress against which, in the *Dona nobis pacem*, peace is entreated.

So the appearance of fugal writing in the first two quartets for Prince Galitzin—in the *Scherzando vivace* of Op. 127 and in the climactic strophe of the *Heiliger Dankgesang* of Op. 132—was predictable enough, even without taking into account the contrapuntal itch that Beethoven had exercised in the quartet medium from the very start. We can look back to the quartet study-fugues of 1795, the *fugati* and double-counterpoint themes in Op. 18, the hectoring fugue in the third "Razumovsky" Quartet and the chromatic fugue in the slow movement of Op. 95, the raucous contrapuntal trios in the second "Razumovsky" and the "Harp." In the next two quartets, fugues figure centrally. The Great Fugue plays once again the role of finale—but what a finale! Very curiously, it resumes the key of the marathon *Hammerklavier* Finale and of the *Et vitam venturi*, B♭ major, as though returning obsessively to unfinished business. Then the fugue of the Quartet in C♯ minor takes the place of the first movement, assuming an altogether different responsibility, posing a new set of conditions. Indeed this is a fugue of a new kind, which Beethoven had scarcely considered before. The exploration would have continued, one feels sure, whether in quartets or in other music, if Beethoven had lived on.

· 2 ·

What did Beethoven want with fugue—with this "*Anachronismus*," as his dreary, devoted famulus Schindler was to write of the Great Fugue, "which belongs properly to those dark ages when the art of tonal combination was still determined by mathematical calculation"?

Here certainly is one of the classic questions about the third period. Doubtless the answer will continue to elude us; but we can be pretty certain first of all that it has nothing to do with antiquarian investigations. Not for ten years of Beethoven's life—not for ten minutes, probably. Secondly, we can and we must be certain to get behind the mystique about his transcendental struggle with technique, that dialectic between genius and material so dear to the Romantic Beethoven image. Thomas Mann has put it unforgettably, early in *Doctor Faustus*, when young Adrian Leverkühn and Serenus Zeitblom are bewitched by tales of Beethoven tearing the *Missa solemnis* fugues out of the recalcitrant ether:

> Kretschmar [this was the young German-American organist-composer] told us a frightful story, impressing upon our minds an unforgettable and awful picture of the sacred trials of this struggle and the person of the afflicted artist. It was in high summer of the year 1819. . . . The deaf man sang, he yelled and stamped above the Credo—it was so moving and terrifying that the blood froze in their veins as they listened. But as in their great concern they were about to retreat, the door was jerked open and Beethoven stood there—in what guise? The very most frightful! With clothing dishevelled, his features so distorted as to strike terror to the beholders; the eyes dazed, absent, listening, all at once; he had stared at them, they got the impression that he had come out of a life-and-death struggle with all the opposing hosts of counterpoint.[2]

[2] Pp. 57–8 (cf. Hamburger, pp. 171–2).

Schindler originated this tale; this was his view of the business. It may be that on bad days composing felt that way to Beethoven. But for us to view it that way is, once again, to confuse the genesis of the work of art with the work of art itself. The heroic struggle for personal mastery—that is biography; what matters is the aesthetic mastery manifest in the finished work of art. Now it may very well be that in pieces like the *Hammerklavier* Finale and the Great Fugue, Beethoven conveys, among other things, the very sense of his power struggle. But this aesthetic effect in itself is a partial thing. Sonata form must have been mastered after many heroic struggles, too, and so were the variation, the dance, and much else—in order to yield fresh instruments of musical expression. Until we start asking what the power struggle was really for, we have not yet begun to address the real question.

Beethoven was looking for alternatives to sonata form; that is easy enough to see. The years of his interest in fugue are also years of de-emphasis of the symphonic ideal established in the second period, the image of the *Eroica* Symphony and the "Razumovsky" Quartets. As he now shied away a little from sonata form, treated it more and more freely, and deflected it ironically to lyrical ends, fugue still offered him a fresh means to attain vehemence—but vehemence without the drama inherent in the classic style. The softening of traditional form has already been observed in the opening movements of the Quartets in E♭ and A minor. The Quartet in B♭ carries the process further, and the Quartet in C♯ minor takes the final radical step, replacing the sonata-form first movement by a fugue.

Prior to 1826, however, Beethoven valued fugue principally as a way of getting at the old problem of the finale. This problem, too, we have seen him attack in the quartets ever since Op. 18. In the C-major "Razumovsky" Quartet, he had actually attempted an amalgam of fugue and sonata form—prematurely, as it must seem. His dissatisfaction with ordinary first-movement form must have extended to the sonata-rondo arrangements which were used more than anything else for finales by Haydn, Mozart, and Beethoven himself. These forms leaven the dramatic style of the sonata with straightforward returns of a single idea, the rondo tune. Fugue, too, involves straightforward repetitions of a single idea. A fugue subject is at once more pliable and interesting than a rondo tune, easier to bring in frequently and easier to vary. And fugue eschews high contrasts, high relief, modulatory development, and all the other tired characteristics of the sonata style.

Beethoven's prettiest problem lay in the opposite and seemingly irreconcilable habits of fugue and sonata in the matter of tonality in the large. In the latter style, change of key is a dramatic, fully responsible act. In the former, it is a matter of placid routine. The fugue composer is able to drift innocently in a tonal field that has hardly any potential—or to use a quintessential simile of Tovey's, the fugue composer is able to slide on and off the tonic key as gently as the White Knight in Alice slides on and off his horse. Consequently, fugue allowed Beethoven to flirt with textures that were unusually flat from the harmonic point of view, something he now liked to do even in nonfugal compositions. To progress from one such plateau to the next, he sometimes strips gears with an almost Stravinskian effect—the Great Fugue, Stravinsky's favorite Beethoven piece, is full of such abrupt jolts. Otherwise Beethoven worked to blend in progressions and passages that are more in the sonata style. Sometimes these sound incongruous enough, though in the C♯-minor Fugue, which is harmonically Beethoven's most accomplished, I am not aware that anyone has found them so.

Characteristically, fugal rhythm is unruffled, sonata rhythm nervous and contrasty. So fugue also allowed Beethoven to indulge his penchant for *perpetuum mobile*, which otherwise had played itself out in the dance-form and scherzo derivatives. This he does very noisily in the B♭ and A♭ sections of the Great Fugue, quietly in the G♭ section and in the Finale of the Sonata in A♭, Op. 110.

Most fundamentally, of course, "the two cultures of music" (in August Halm's phrase) differ in the way themes are handled. Fugue examines a single theme, examines it in a host of ways—by every means short of reflection through essential contrast, the method of sonata. So the re-examination of the problem of musical contrast which seems to have occupied Beethoven so deeply in the late years found itself centering upon a familiar, indeed an ancient musical tradition. Contrast of a certain kind could be minimized by the relentless exhaustion of a single taut musical idea promised by the underlying principle of fugue.

Generations of musicians had established the various lines of inquiry: extensive fugue anthologies had been put together by many composers, pre-eminent among them Bach, and the proven resources had been codified by many pedants, eminent among them Beethoven's own teacher of the early Vienna days, Johann Georg Albrechtsberger. All this Beethoven happily absorbed. The majority of his fugal essays are ostentatiously "learned," submitting their material to great batteries of the traditional fugal devices.

Now in order to grasp his own individual kink in all this, it may be helpful to think of the resources of fugue in two categories: *resources of contrapuntal combination* (use of countersubjects, invertible counterpoint, *stretto*, pedals, and in the larger sense, fragmentation of the subject for purposes of episodic development), and *resources of thematic modification* (augmentation, diminution, inversion, *cancrizans*, syncopation, and some other rare ingenuities). In the latter category might be included the use of tonal answer and also change of the mode of the subject—an important resource from the expressive point of view, however simply it comes into play when the subject is moved from the tonic to certain other degrees. In principle, the devices of thematic modification treat the subject in a rigid manner. Free variation of the subject is a possibility, but one that is treated very gingerly by eighteenth-century composers and theorists.

Beethoven never hung back from devices of contrapuntal combination; all the same, I believe his fugues can be shown to center more and more upon resources of thematic modification. And in this area he was campaigning in the advance guard. Such, at least, is the lesson of his final efforts, the Great Fugue and the Fugue of the Quartet in C♯ minor. The main interest of the Great Fugue is thematic transformation, sometimes pursued at the expense of an interest in fugue and an interest in counterpoint itself. Transformation counts as a dramatic kind of free variation; the subjects of the Great Fugue never suffer rigid modifications in the traditional manner. The C♯-minor Fugue gets its artistic capital out of *reharmonizing* the subject, reharmonizing it *de novo*, without reference to contrapuntal combinations; this also counts as a type of free variation, a modern type with no substantial tradition. More impressively than any other fugue, furthermore, this one exploits a "device" which Bach barely knew but which Beethoven knew very well: the projection of the subject into the form. To make certain aspects of a theme resonate in the very structure of the total piece was something that Beethoven had done with sonata themes and also with earlier fugues—the "Razumovsky" Finale, whose supertonic from the subject returns at gross junctures of the piece; the fugue of the Op. 95 slow movement, which modulates according to the chromatic prescription of its subject; the Great Fugue itself, whose most titanic modulation picks up the modulation implied within the subject. In the C♯-minor Fugue, the subdominant inclination of the subject and the Neapolitan response determine not only the consummate emotional shape of the movement itself, but also that of the C♯-minor Quartet as a whole.

The underlying principle of fugue is to examine a single subject. It seems deeply right for Beethoven to have added to the traditional stock of tools a new one which he had developed elsewhere for the probing of thematic possibilities. Thematic transformation, too, the great preoccupation of the later nineteenth century, was very much in the air in 1825. Schubert's *Wanderer Fantasy* had been published, though it is not recorded that Beethoven saw it. Berlioz's *Symphonie fantastique* was only three years away.

· 3 ·

Indeed, for Philip Radcliffe, Beethoven's Great Fugue "is best understood if regarded, not as a highly eccentric fugue, but as a kind of symphonic poem consisting of several contrasted but thematically related sections and containing a certain amount of fugal writing." [3] But there is another point of view about this eminently problematic work. It is pithily expressed in the title of an informative article by Warren Kirkendale, "The 'Great Fugue,' Op. 133: Beethoven's 'Art of Fugue,' " and Kirkendale is able to support his view by drawing into consideration not only Bach's *Art of Fugue*, but even the treatise on composition by Beethoven's old teacher, Albrechtsberger. In a passage known to Beethoven, the theorist lists a large number of fugal "*Zierlichkeiten und Künste*" (including one of his own invention) with the cautionary note that seldom can all of them be fitted into a single composition. Beethoven took this as a challenge, according to Kirkendale's view; he resolved to write the fugue with all the known devices. "Without the suggestion of a great theoretical compendium the 'giant movement,' the *Great Fugue* would never have been written. . . . The *Great Fugue* was his *Art of Fugue*, his summary of the various fugal techniques. . . ." [4]

Admittedly, that sounds rather like Beethoven. In earlier fugues he had exploited all the "resources of contrapuntal combination," even *cancrizans* (retrograde writing) in the *Hammerklavier* Finale. But he had never explored the limits of variation to which a fugue subject is susceptible, still less constructed a related series of fugues on one skeletal subject transformed, that is, on one subject pressed into different versions each with a different emotional connotation. For this Albrechtsberger may have provided the theoretical recipe, but Bach, in *The Art of Fugue*, offered the practical, artistic model. Beethoven would have seen the syncopated and "gapped" versions of Bach's inverted subject:

[3] P. 138.
[4] P. 24.

Example 135

and he could have taken them as inspiration for the curious B♭ version of his own subject, to go along with the bookish sanction of Albrechtsberger's own prize *Zierlichkeit*. Over and above details, however, the whole grandiose conception of *The Art of Fugue* must surely have caught Beethoven's fancy, as later it was to catch Busoni's. What more likely than his resolve to match Bach's great exemplary anthology in a single fugue that he would actually call "*grosse*," when it shook free of its quartet and demanded its own rights as a separate opus?

Yet I am not sure that this may not be getting hold of the problem at the wrong end. Did Beethoven set out to write an "art of fugue," and then find that the way to get size and intensity was to write movements using various transformations of one central subject? Or did he set out to investigate the possibilities of thematic transformation, and then find that the one vaguely useful model for such work was Bach's *Art of Fugue*, the one vaguely useful textbook Albrechtsberger? The question is more than a quibble; on its answer depends, for instance, our judgment as to whether Beethoven's essential impetus was radical or archaizing. And if thematic transformation, not contrapuntal encyclopedism, is concluded to be the first source of compositional energy here, that conclusion may help rationalize some of the problematic aspects of the work at hand.

It may help rationalize the quite remarkable first event in the piece, the section Beethoven is pleased to miscall "*Overtura*." This section hurls all the thematic versions at the listener's head like a handful of rocks. (Probably he is too stunned to notice that they range around the circle of 5ths from G to C to F to B♭, thus forecasting the main harmonic motive force of the entire fugue.) In a shattering four-octave *unisono*, the lumbering version of the A♭ Fugue accelerates into its violent trill; then comes the simple dancelike version in $\frac{6}{8}$ time; then the self-abnegating version that will provide the G♭ *fugato* with its *cantus firmus;* then the strange "gapped" version that is presently—and very abruptly—to be revealed as the countersubject in the B♭ Fugue. Between each two of them, a cryptic *fermata*. So this *Overtura* is nothing like an overture to an opera or an introduction to a quartet—to the Quartet in E♭, Op. 74, for instance, or to the Quartet in B♭ itself. It behaves less like a book's introduction than like a table of contents. It looks like a mnemonic sheet out of a sketchbook, a random series of jottings for a "functional analysis." A parallel exists with another gigantic finale, that of the Ninth Symphony—in spite of all the extremely interesting differences: the symphony throws out themes which are known because they have already been played, whereas the quartet obscurely catalogues unknown material; the symphony talks over the themes in recitative, whereas the quartet rattles through them in a show of maximum contrast. One primary fact is being set forth here: the paradox that four themes, utterly incongruous in feeling, can be made out of the same note-set.

This seems to matter enough to Beethoven for him to insist on it at the end of the composition, or very near the end. The four versions are

Example 136

better organized now, all of them being held to the tonic key, with the lumbering version (now the third in order) reaching up to a new melodic climax on high G. The first two versions break off harshly at A♭, doubtless in memory of the prominent A♭ key-area earlier in the composition. (The countersubject in the *Meno mosso e moderato* fragment is quietly rewritten here to provide an extra A♭.) But Beethoven is still stressing the paradox. The themes have all been pulled together—fantastically different as they can still be heard to be. They have provided material for an extraordinary, coherent structure—grotesque as they still sound in bare juxtaposition.

After the *Overtura*, the various sections or movements which make up the Great Fugue do not in fact probe fugue to the limits of contrapuntal artifice, as Kirkendale's view would seem to require. The aesthetic effect that goes with probing of this sort differs from that occasioned by rhythmic drive and high dissonance level, or by ingenious thematic relationships among sections. After the *Overtura*, a well-disciplined Double Fugue in B♭ uses one version of the basic theme as countersubject. Later an excellently undisciplined Fugue in A♭ treats another version of the theme. On the other hand, an intervening lyric section in G♭, using a third version, cannot be considered a fugue at all; all that happens, after a peculiar *fugato* exposition, is an 8-bar sequence and a closing entry over a tonic pedal. Then there is a fourth version of the basic theme sustaining a simple, almost comic dancelike passage which is scarcely developed contrapuntally, but which does repeat itself insistently and does recapitulate as a powerful vise for the total structure. In a lengthy concluding section, other versions of the basic theme are thrown out teasingly, then abandoned. The thematic transformations, in other words, range stylistically beyond the bounds of fugue and even beyond the bounds of counterpoint.

Moreover, the actual Fugues in B♭ and A♭, considered as individual structures, can hardly be said to make so very much out of the purely contrapuntal resources of the genre. This does not make them bad fugues or bad pieces of music; it just means that their character is not entirely or principally a matter of contrapuntal elaboration (but of rhythmic drive, which is in spirit similar enough in both of them). In the B♭ Fugue, the main "device" after the double counterpoint of the exposition is—thematic transformation. Two compressed versions of the subject-pair are introduced, neither of which is at all so simple a matter as a standard diminution. Since these compressed versions work by themselves, not together with the original subject-pair, interest centers on their integrity as transformations, not on their contrapuntal potential. Even the A♭ Fugue, which would be the one section Beethoven could have meant to describe as *recherchée*, impresses less through its fugal development than through the extraordinary burgeoning invention of its material. At the end of the A♭ Fugue, thematic versions from earlier in the composition return to make a climactic recapitulation. But the way this is managed does not seem calculated to reconcile all the manifestations of the basic theme; it has the effect, once again, of stressing their paradoxical co-existence in the same universe.

Material to be transformed needs certain qualities and can dispense with others. The basic theme itself needed to be a little paradoxical—a little conspicuously strange, perhaps, lest it lose its character in the transformations and lest it play itself out too soon. (That was the probable trouble with the *Hammerklavier* Finale.) On the other hand, Beethoven did not need to make his basic theme strictly invertible or capable of *stretto*, and did not mind when its fragments turned out to work better as stiff *cantus-firmus* fragments than as flexible contrapuntal members. In his conception, contrapuntal elaboration was really secondary.

Of course, the basic theme had already enacted a sort of transformation, as Romain Rolland's sketch page shows so graphically. Behind its eight notes lies the famous grouping of four which nagged at Beethoven all through the last years. Originally, and most baldly, the notes occurred as a *cantus firmus* at the very start of the Quartet in A minor; then—as Nottebohm hinted, and as Paul Bekker insisted, and as Deryck Cooke has blown up into a rigorous general theory—these four notes underpin many themes in the last quartets. It is a familiar figuration: 7–1–6–5, tonic, dominant, and the two affective semitones which, in the minor mode, naturally support the tonic-dominant 5th. It had been used as a thematic outline by every composer in two hundred years, and notably for fugue subjects. The development *fugato* of Beethoven's last Piano Sonata, Op. 111, exemplifies the class perfectly, and so does the nonfugal first movement of the Quartet in A minor.

Entering on the development of the A-minor Quartet, however, Beethoven stumbled upon a new potentiality of the set, when it is hoisted up a semitone:

Example 137

The harmonic instability—moving up from F major to G minor, from temporary tonic to supertonic—was most appropriate at that juncture, but strange and thoroughly unfamiliar when this transposition of the set was used as a fugue subject. The set no longer settles around the tonic-dominant 5th (1–5); it levitates unstably around the supertonic-submediant 5th (2–6). The tense chromaticism, and the sense of striving always upward to the supertonic and beyond, are crucial determinants of the mood of the Great Fugue:

Example 138

Although the simple form shown in line 3 of this paradigm actually occurs at one point (see p. 289), the four notes in this position will not complete or even outline a real fugue subject. Beethoven pushes his way up the scale again, doubling the number of notes (and the tenseness) in a free, and therefore always slightly strange, sequence which vaults up from supertonic to high octave as conclusion.

Such is the theme to be transformed; but after transformation, its shape is not even preserved within the individual ostensibly homogeneous sections. Past their initial expositions, the various subject-versions are quite likely to find their rhythms and pitches altered a little. Already the *Overtura* throws out variant note-arrangements; Beethoven is working less with fixed pitches than with the general shape of the theme—a semitone up somewhere around the tonic, followed by a large leap of one sort or another. In the "regular" four-part exposition shown on page 285, the basic theme actually assumes four slightly different forms. (The variants cannot all be explained away as errors in the print or in the printer's copy, though some errors certainly occurred, as appears from a comparison of the Great Fugue with Beethoven's piano arrangement.)

Here too is a state of affairs that can seem unclear, or even desultory, as long as the Great Fugue is regarded principally as a synoptic essay in fugal composition, a "great theoretical compendium." But if thematic transformation is the main driving force, the free thematic treatment makes a certain sense. Not to push the term "transformation" too far, one can still say that even in sections on one particular version—one individual transformation—of the basic theme, Beethoven is ready to modify that version further than any textbook would ever recommend. "*Tantôt libre, tantôt recherchée*," he wrote on the top of the Great Fugue, putting into motion much mystical speculation about Freedom and Necessity, *das Ich und das Walten*, and so forth. He might better have written *Plutôt libre que recherchée*. Freedom better supports the guiding compositional idea.

· 4 ·

As the Great Fugue proceeds, its sections grapple with the basic theme in principle more and more closely; this is an important fact for the over-all sense of the work. The *Overtura* throws out a bewildering series of versions of the basic theme, but the Double Fugue in B♭, which follows directly as the first major section or movement, has as its main subject another theme, rhythmically very vigorous but melodically less individual. It was well observed by Sidney Grew that "this is a theme cramped

Example 139

into the interval of the diminished fifth (D to A♭), rebellious of its confinement, and almost desperate in its effort to escape into the open—which it contrives to do after the great full close in D minor." [5] Normally, though not invariably, a "gapped" version of the basic theme accompanies it as a strongly conflicting countersubject.

Pitches are treated loosely, but from the beginning the rhythm of this countersubject stands out strikingly, and all the more so in the sub-

[5] P. 146.

sequent syncopated transformations. These harsh staggering accents slashing across the galvanic driving rhythm of the main subject constitute the chief topic of the B♭ Fugue—and for good measure Beethoven throws in two additional rhythmic figures, subsidiary but well marked for a time. Given this amount of purely motor material, it is perhaps no wonder that the B♭ Fugue skirts modulation for the most part, and that it uses only a modest array of contrapuntal devices relative to its considerable length.

The exposition through the four instruments is essentially orthodox, not to say stiff—and loud; Beethoven directs an unrelieved *fortissimo* all the way through, and grimly marks *ff* or *f* or *sf* on every note of the countersubject at every one of its many appearances. The novel notation —tied eighth-notes for quarters—conveys the grasping urgency of the theme so well that Beethoven kept it even in his piano version of the Great Fugue. Laconic exposition is the business of the first pages of the B♭ Fugue. Yet Beethoven does seem to have wished to demarcate them as a subsection rather sharply from the rest; the fifth entry, in the tonic, already sounds climactic, on account of the new homogeneous (indeed, almost anticontrapuntal) texture, the placement of the subjects in the prominent outer instruments, and new chromatic inflections, which are accentuated in the strangely expressive cadential surge up to E♭. So emphatic a subdominant cadence is calculated to pull the listener up short, especially this close to the beginning of a composition.

A second subsection starts with a new exposition of three entries under a new cover of continuous triplets (which do not make a really new countersubject, but only rhythmic figuration to counteract the incessant twitching). The third entry is actually a distorted answer in C minor (ii), distorted in the direction of A♭, an important degree in this composition. Then Beethoven latches on to the *very end* of the answer —its one point of distinction from the subject—as motivic material for a short episode surging up to F. The motif is marked with a bracket on the musical example above. Three more entries strive furiously for climax: the first (in F) by doubling the subject in 3rds, a favorite Beethovenian means for emphasis; the second (still in F) by jumping the gun in *stretto;* and the third by swerving heavily to D minor, the first and only serious modulation in the entire B♭ Fugue.

At this entry, as though petrified by the very prospect of modulation, the piece seems to be in danger of cracking under the tension of its own rhythmic fury. This tendency can be observed in more than one *fugato* of Beethoven's middle period. The countersubject breaks down first, the harmony collapses into electric diminished-7th chords, and a sizable new episode makes frantic diversions to stave off new entries.

Four bars freeze around a diminished-7th chord on C♯—until C♮ decisively contradicts and sets up marching canons on the *middle* of the subject. C is winding up like a crossbow about to shoot at the stars; now the longest of the upward surges goes up C–C♯–D–E–F–G–A to transfix D minor (the key of the climactic entry) in a frightening show of power. Motivic material, taken from the very *beginning* of the main subject, stands out all the better now that the triplet figuration has been dropped.

In this episode, it looks as though Beethoven methodically picked over the end, middle, and beginning of the main subject to use as the basis for episodic development—a process that is less surprising than the nature of the development itself. The destruction of the subject in D minor, the "frozen" passage, the dramatic deflection to C, and the march up to the huge cadence—these actions belong in a Beethoven sonata movement, not in anybody's fugue. But the next move is a grandiose effort to reassert fugal hearing. With only a few perfunctory sequences, the tonality flips calmly back to the tonic B♭ for new expositions, as though the D-minor establishment were a matter of no moment whatsoever. This is to flatten tonality into the dispassionate aesthetic of an earlier century. Bach characteristically introduces major sections of movements by such calm shifts from mediant or submediant to tonic—in the very first fugue of *The Well-tempered Clavier*, for example.

Example 140

The rest of the B♭ Fugue is content to seek intensity by means of thematic transformations. A third subsection opens with a new exposition of two entries, compressing the subject-pair slightly but tellingly from 4 bars to 3½ (bars 110–14, in the above example). Countersubject:

squeezed into mordant syncopations which give the piece a new violent rhythmic tic from here on to the end. Subject: divided between two instruments, presumably in order to stress the change which makes the subject symmetrical by pulling its internal cadence a beat sooner. After two entries, when Beethoven wants to launch another developmental episode, he seizes on the new figure which makes the change. It is marked with a bracket in the example.

This long episode is orthodox, if sticky, consisting mainly of circle-of-5ths sequences, the honorable staple of fugal development since Bach's time and before. The circle rolls as far as A♭—significantly, in view of the over-all key plan. Methodically, once again, Beethoven constructs these harsh sequences out of ½-bar, 1-bar, and then 2-bar elements, to gain an obvious sense of breadth. The anapaest figure which turns up with the transformed subject-pair has more personality than the earlier triplets, but peters out even sooner. Perhaps its function was mainly to point up the syncopation.

The gaps in the syncopated countersubject have long been crying out to be filled. This takes place in a fourth subsection when a new transformation of the subject-pair compresses the original 4 bars to 2 (bars 138 ff.):

Example 141

Countersubject: mauled badly at each appearance—and rather arbitrarily, one would think, until a very definite sequence emerges using exactly the final mauled form (bars 147 ff.). Subject: smoothed into triplets, ingeniously resuming and rationalizing the triplet motion of the second subsection. Again the main subject doubles itself in 3rds and 6ths; strong parallel 10ths continue all through the emergent sequence, and through the rapid upward surge into the last powerful arrival:

Example 142

This of course freely recollects the main subject in its original, noncompressed, nontriplet form (and the countersubject is left aside). A fine sense of climax is achieved by the towering height of the violin and by the newly solid root harmonies of the cello. Yet the gritty vigor of the Fugue is mollified by some expressive touches—by a new triplet idea, and by chromatic details in the melody itself. Themselves not entirely without precedent, these details prepare in turn the abrupt cello G♭, which vaults over the dominant F to initiate the next movement, the G♭ *fugato, Meno mosso e moderato.*

This last subsection of the B♭ Fugue is almost as laconic as the first subsection: four rapid regular entries, a small diatonic sequence, and the truncated final entry by way of summary. The B♭ Fugue, as the first link of a chain, lacks the leisure for heavy perorations, which will come naturally and as a matter of duty to the last one.

Qua fugue, the G♭ movement is certainly a curious production; safer to consider it a *fugato.* It spends more than half of its time on a serene, meandering exposition, the greater part of which neglects to be even contrapuntal, let alone fugal. A flowing new subject full of yielding *appoggiaturas* is first highlighted against a very elementary, noncontrapuntal, pulsing accompaniment (bars 160–5, p. 286). After the strenuousness of the B♭ Fugue, the effect is of an almost blinding innocence. The simple homophony turns into simple species counterpoint as the subject is introduced to the basic theme of the Great Fugue, pressed into even notes; this suave combination slowly displays itself in the tonic and then in the dominant. But Beethoven pretends that a true modulation has taken place —which is of course quite contrary to fugal thinking; hovering on the dominant, the subject is allowed to flow silently once again over its shimmering homophonic bedrock, a second ineffable vision of a world without counterpoint. Two further fugal entries (with suspiciously noncontrapuntal new voices) swing again from tonic to dominant. The four voices are in. After a moment, a fifth entry in loose *stretto* moves upward with the theme in the sharp direction.

This singular "exposition" gradually enriches its material harmonically; perhaps that is the essential point. The flowing subject started out over naïve pedal harmonies, tonic to dominant to tonic. At the first properly fugal entries, rich secondary diminished chords emerge. Only at the fourth fugal entry does root harmony consummate the harmonic intention:

Example 143

as though Rameau's *basse fondamentale* has crept in as the final countersubject. Root harmony had just been intimated by the concluding entry of the B♭ Fugue; and the loose *stretto* grows richer yet. At the risk of some oversimplification, it might he said that the B♭ Fugue, the G♭ *fugato*, and the A♭ Fugue concentrate respectively on rhythmic, harmonic, and melodic potentialities of the basic theme.

An even more expressive sequence moves mildly back in the flat direction, with some very exquisite inversion effects on fragments of the flowing subject (see below, bars 205–9). In conclusion, the subject-pair appears twice—the second time freely—over long high tonic and dominant pedals. These seem calculated to recall the "exposition," with its ethereal homophonic visions. The basic theme now emerges on top of the double counterpoint, and inasmuch as its cadence, in the high octave, is by its very nature more assertive than yielding, Beethoven needs to soften it—by means of a downward sequential extension:

Example 144

This warm and eminently cadential idea recurs on the very last page of the Great Fugue. But the G♭ movement ends, as it began, with the flowing theme alone—now presented with an unexpected touch of iron: a sudden flare to *forte*, a stark deployment in four octaves, a new stiffening modification in the cello.

The simple dancelike section in B♭ follows. The blatancy of its return to the original tonal area is accentuated by its incongruity of tone. No less violent is the intrusion of the A♭ Fugue.

As acrid and furious and extensive as the B♭ Fugue, and as incessantly loud, the A♭ Fugue far exceeds it in contrapuntal complexity—and in modulation. This movement engages most seriously with the basic theme, and that means, for Beethoven, following out the modulations implied by the theme's distorted chromatic line. Attention is not allowed to stray to countersubjects. In method, the two large fugues differ greatly. The B♭ Double Fugue returns frequently to full entries of its subject-pair, keeping its episodes rather various and clearly subsidiary. The much more novel A♭ Fugue scarcely once repeats its full subject (let alone its countersubjects) after the opening exposition—there is one important exception—and builds itself up out of successive treatments of fragments of the subject. Technically these might be called "episodes," but they have the much more integral feeling of new, derived subjects being handled single-mindedly for a while and then abandoned. Of ordinary fugal development there is none; everything sounds momentously and monolithically thematic.

The one even vaguely predictable feature of this A♭ Fugue is the exposition that kicks it off. Two spasmodic countersubjects, one of them very free, are derived from fragments of the basic theme in diminution and double diminution. Some all-important details had been prepared in the dancelike section: the trill which agitates the end of the subject, and the iambic $\frac{6}{8}$ rhythms into which the main countersubject is pressed. This virtuoso triple-counterpoint combination is used more as a store of motivic material than as a real fugal building-block. Unlike the double-counterpoint combinations of the B♭ Fugue, it never returns (not even freely) as a later stanchion for the essential structure.

The exposition is barely over before a strident low C in the cello jolts the harmony to III. The earlier sections of the Great Fugue, it will be recalled, wait a good time before heading seriously away from the tonic; this C shocks. The cello initiates a discussion—which seems too obsessive to count as merely "episodic"—of a fragment consisting of the first four notes of the subject:

Example 145

(The second note is now spelled "D♭" instead of "C♯," i.e., 2♭ instead of 1♯—compare line 3 of the paradigm on p. 281. C♯ would point toward the ii triad, D minor—which, to be sure, the full subject would outline if it were all there. But since the subject stops after only four notes, the note D never actually appears, so the climactic note A might as well be a part of the IV triad as part of the ii triad.) D♭, appropriately harmonized, points not toward ii but toward IV, and this harmonic pointer is followed as the fragment swings from instrument to instrument around the circle of 5ths, from C to F to B♭ to E♭.

Here a cursory gesture is made to stabilize the tonality, but instead a new smaller fragment shears off, this time from the end of the subject (violin, bars 324–7, etc.):

Example 146

This spins out of control around the circle from A♭ to D♭ to G♭ = F♯ to B to E to A to D to G and all the way back to C. As though hypnotized by this insane spiral, the countersubject fragments, which had been getting grittier and grittier, pulverize until practically nothing thematic remains except the terrifying trill. At last Beethoven applies the brake, a stiff formal half-cadence on C as the dominant of F.

A second subsection is sharply demarcated by this cadence, and by the advent of new reckless figuration in continuous eighth-notes. (This figuration derives from the subject, once again, but its main effect is rhythmic intensification, as in the second and fourth subsections of the B♭ Fugue.) The second subsection seems to try again—for it brings a new fragment of the subject closely resembling the first fragment, starting from C and circling C–F–B♭–E♭, all just as before. Now Beethoven succeeds in stabilizing the key, with a vengeance:

Example 147

What is established is B♭ minor, the supertonic of A♭, the nub of the subject itself. B♭ is also the original key of the Great Fugue, of course, and G♭—this shattering G♭!—the key of the quiet *fugato*. Over G♭, treated as the heightened dominant of B♭ minor, the subject shrills through its entire length for the one and only time past the exposition—all the more savagely, it seems, on account of a new compression. When the low G♭ sinks to F with a great triumphant bite, the high G♭ in the violin trills downward to meet new mounting canons which develop on the newly truncated subject. This great chain of canons in the cello and the viola, a superb contrapuntal inspiration, rings with the strength of perfect inevitability.

All this is sonata action, once again, not fugue, a fantastic powerhouse effect of the sort that Beethoven had made his hallmark after the *Eroica* Symphony but was now excising from his actual sonata movements. Under such pressure, strong themes wilt: one of the notes of the subject gets fused into a grace note, and the $\frac{6}{8}$ figuration is shattered into frantic little spurts. The significance of these details for the sequel appears in the following paradigm:

Example 148

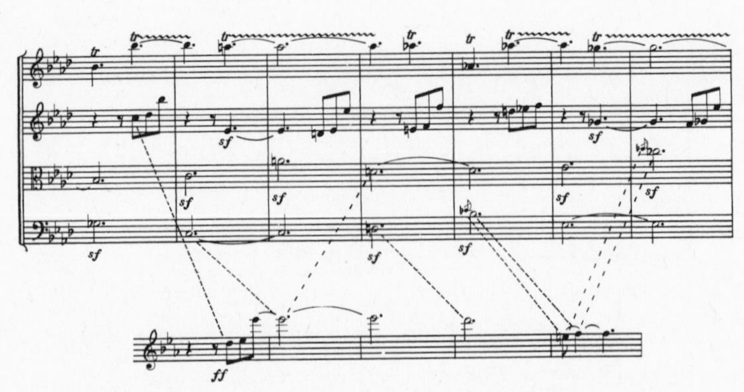

This thematic transformation may be the most extreme prior to Schoenberg, a magnificently quirky, unassailable bit of ultimate violence. Once introduced in this way, melodic inversion of the subject plays a large role in the remaining climactic passages.

Though the trills and the canons were converging clearly upon B♭, the harmony deflects to a tentative-sounding subdominant cadence. Suddenly two bars marked *piano* break the pounding *fortissimo* specified for all the rest of the A♭ Fugue. Somewhat embarrassed by all the quiet, and somewhat chastened rhythmically, the main motif of the B♭ Fugue makes a hopeful little bid for inclusion. This presages a systematic confluence of all the main melodic features from earlier in the composition. Motifs from the B♭ Fugue are accepted as countersubject in an exposition (four entries, in E♭) of the menacing inverted fragment illustrated above. This fragment is soon dropped, after setting in motion an irresistible downward scale passage re-establishing A♭, at which solemn juncture the traditional climax of weight is afforded by a section of dense *strettos*. The subject as a whole would not lend itself to *stretto*—but the subject as a whole has been almost forgotten. Three-note fragments suffice, both the right way up and inverted, with continuing flickers of various motifs from the B♭ Fugue.

The *stretto* section emphasizes B♭, significantly, next to A♭, and concludes with yet another splendid long downward scale passage. These solid down-the-scale cadential preparations typify the A♭ Fugue, just as tense up-the-scale preparations typify the B♭ Fugue. The ultimate statement uses material from the *Meno mosso*—not the actual subject-pair but a free derivative thereof, which is broadened into an 8-bar cadential phrase stretched out past the octave and enriched by a simultaneous melodic inversion of the central theme. The broad cadential phrase is repeated directly, in contrapuntal inversion, hammering out the long-awaited close in A♭. The main motif of the B♭ Fugue, or something very like it, is still at work.

"To make a fugue requires no particular skill," Beethoven remarked in a well-known statement some years before. "In my student days I made dozens of them. But the fancy also wishes to exert its privileges, and today a new and really poetical element must be introduced into the old traditional form." [6] I should like to understand the "new and really poetical element" as meaning in fact the total coherence of the form. If so, it was indeed something that had to be introduced, in the Great Fugue. The problem of its over-all form was not treated as a "fugal" problem at all.

He does not appear to have wished to disturb too far the sense of those two rough diamonds, the B♭ and A♭ Fugues, glistening in an equally rough and ponderous setting. The continuity proceeds by shock tactics—as is guaranteed by the hooligan *Overtura.* The B♭ Fugue is cut off abruptly by an inserted G♭ initiating the G♭ *fugato,* the end of which returns just as abruptly to B♭ for the violently contrasted dancelike section in $\frac{6}{8}$ time, jig time. This thoroughly unfugal section mocks the self-serious contrapuntal pretensions of the basic theme by exposing it as a cadential seesaw. The A♭ Fugue interrupts—enraged, in tempo, like the crack of doom; but after it has hammered out its own overwhelming A♭ cadences, an extraordinary passage of obfuscation twists once again to B♭. The dancelike passage returns verbatim as the beginning of a very long concluding section.

Despite the almost glib recapitulatory effect of this beginning, the concluding section differs wholly in spirit from a traditional recapitulation, to say nothing of a traditional coda. It throws out a whole series of new comments on the basic theme, new possibilities mentioned almost contemptuously and almost contemptuously abandoned. Strange slow harmonizations of the basic theme glance in improbable directions; a witty compartmentalization splits it between two voices; new reference is made to the *Overtura* (p. 278); an irreverent little piece of quick-march, near the end, recalls the military parade in B♭ of the Ninth Symphony Finale. There is a pressing sense of fancy freed, after earlier severities. To this brilliant whimsy, the transformations of the basic theme provide an ironic referential background.

Some critics talk about the Great Fugue in terms of sonata form—

[6] Thayer, p. 692.

the B♭ Fugue and the G♭ *fugato* counting as stable structures in contrasting keys, the A♭ Fugue modulating widely, and the last six pages dilating stably upon B♭ once again. Sonata form is for them an abracadabra phrase begging the real question of coherence, just as for other critics any large piece built on one basic idea turns into a similar talisman. We may be equally unmoved by the frank assault of Daniel Gregory Mason, who considered the work "non-sequacious," "hybrid," a "*pot-pourri*" (and even "repellent"). "We gradually lose the sense of its having any necessary sequence"—but some of us do not lose anything of the sort. The formal conception is radical here, as elsewhere in the quartet to which the fugue belongs, but Beethoven's grip on the continuity is perfectly convincing.

B♭ is the tonic key, and the B♭ dance provides a vise for the form, coarse but unmistakable. The very crudity of the initial approach to B♭ from the G of the *Overtura* presages equally crude returns to the tonic at later junctures. Beyond this, the tonal dynamic has its sturdy features. At the entrance of the A♭ Fugue, the cataclysmic step B♭–A♭ sounds like a reversal of the intrinsic urge of the theme from B♭ to C; and the corresponding pressure of the A♭ subject toward the central tonic (A♭–B♭) inspires what is perhaps the most impressive formal feature of the entire composition. A preliminary parallel step, G♭–A♭, is implicit between the *Meno mosso* and the A♭ Fugue.

From the thematic point of view, the sections engage more and more deeply with the material; this constitutes a felt dynamic, up to the point of release at the long concluding section. The steady probing of the basic theme and its always lively response produce a kind of growing exhilaration—from the Double Fugue to the lyric *fugato* to the formidable modulatory course of the A♭ Fugue. This seems to me more important than the system of thematic confluences, that is to say, the systematic return of subjects from the B♭ and G♭ sections at the climax of the A♭ Fugue. The confluences do not sound genuinely structural; they sound like paradoxical evidence of the fact of thematic transformation. Only one of them makes a real summation and resolution: the one in which the rhythmic subject of the B♭ Fugue joins the basic theme in even notes, running into the warm, memorable cadential extension of the G♭ *fugato* (see p. 288). Appropriately enough, this is the last event in the piece, at the end of the big concluding section. The atmosphere is totally different from that of the B♭ Fugue, as Radcliffe remarks: "There we are immediately aware of a sense of conflict between two exceedingly different personalities; here everything is lyrical and harmonious and its effect, coming at the last stages of a highly eventful and dramatic work, is curiously moving." [7]

There is necessary sequence here, and a "poetical element"—for not everything poetical must necessarily be smooth and songful and minutely knit. To be sure, Beethoven does little to settle the celebrated discontinuities that were heard within earlier movements of the B♭ Quartet and in the joints between those movements. It is possible that he wished to confirm them.

· 5 ·

The Great Fugue serves, or originally served, as termination for Beethoven's most dissociated composition. The C♯-minor Fugue heralds his most perfectly integrated one. The subject of the Great Fugue pushes up the scale to the supertonic. The subject of the C♯-minor Fugue droops down the scale to the minor sixth degree and past it. From these two sets of opposite facts the opposite characters of the two compositions evolve.

The fugue subject gives the Quartet in C♯ minor its taste of the famous 4-note configuration that had been used in the A-minor Quartet and that had been transposed up to provide the subject of the Great Fugue. Here the four notes relax into their traditional tonal position, though they are shuffled into a distinctive order. The first half of the subject moves through 5–7–8–6 (G♯–B♯–C♯–A) and the second half can be viewed as quietly circling and decorating 6–5 (A–G♯). In this view, to be sure, some notes are ignored—but they are notes also ignored by Beethoven in the final distillation of his material. In bars 111–17, the subject omits decorations and dwells on the basic 4-note configuration 5–7–8–6–5.

The energy of the fugue seems to center on one note—the *sforzando* A, the minor sixth degree, which divides the subject in half and provides its longest resting point. The fact of the matter is that constant reinterpretation of this note lies at the very heart of Beethoven's conception. The automatic harmonic underpinning for the minor sixth degree is the subdominant triad, and this, as will be seen in a moment, has its own inestimable force for the progress of the piece. But the composer searched over and over again for other triads, new 7th-chords, or fresh chromatic combinations to vitalize and newly illuminate this kernel note of the subject. There are as many as ten distinct solutions before the fugue is over. (I cannot resist tabulating them, transposed for ease of comparison, and

[7] P. 138.

labeled with bar numbers so that they may be checked against the music examples below.)

Example 149

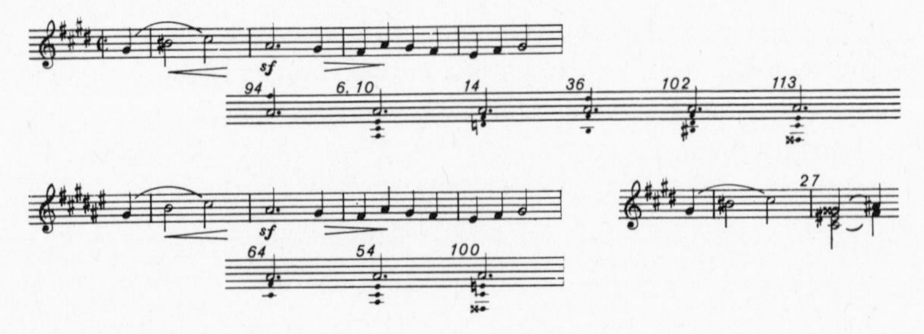

The importance lies not in the number, of course, but in the fact of variation and in the new dimension of feeling that each new chord seems to bring with it. This fugue lacks a countersubject; that very circumstance presages flexibility of harmonic treatment. But no earlier fugue had ever made harmonic variation of its subject into an exhaustive principle and a major means of expressivity. In its own way, the C♯-minor Fugue explores the idea of thematic transformation as deeply as the Great Fugue itself.

The other important point about the Fugue is its unusual tonal arrangement. In the opening exposition, the answer—a "real answer"—is made not on the dominant, but on the subdominant, F♯ minor; the answer, that is to say, wholeheartedly adopts the subdominant bias of the subject itself. Such an answer would not be so remarkable—Bach has examples, in *The Well-tempered Clavier* and *The Art of Fugue*—if Beethoven did not carry through its implications so faithfully. In the key of the subdominant, the minor sixth degree is D, which acts in C♯ minor as the Neapolitan degree ♭II. The coloring thus arrived at affects not only the rest of the fugue but the later movements of the quartet as well. Even more: the answer droops all the way around to B, the "subdominant of the subdominant." A B-minor triad cannot be construed in C♯ minor at all; it speaks only in F♯ minor. Consequently this exposition emanates not only a particular softness and sadness, if you will, but also a particular shifting ambiguity. (Things are made even more exquisite by an incidental G♮ touching the Neapolitan harmony of the subdominant key—hopelessly bleak, hopelessly remote from C♯ minor.) The subdominant key, F♯ minor, is constantly being heard as a kind of double image on top of the tonic; cannot even the original subject be heard in F♯ minor? As Daniel Gregory Mason pointed out, all this allows a wonderful freshness to the dominant modulations which, inevitably, ensue. It also sets up a very serious instability, one that is ultimately resolved in a passage of magnificent integrative power.

This resolving passage—to skip to the end of the Fugue—stands clearly demarcated from the rest of the composition. Throughout, *stretto* is the chief "fugal device" employed, touching most of the interior statements of the subject and even one transitory point within the original

Example 150

exposition. I view the resolving section as consisting of three very free *strettos:*

Stretto 1 (viola, violin 2) already mollifies the subject with a *tierce de Picardie*, an E♯ in bar 96 looking ahead to the ultimate cadence. More importantly, this *stretto* also begins to mollify the subdominant answer. Although the second violin still strikes the Neapolitan D, it no longer settles around the even more aberrant degree B, but dissolves instead into the rich, murmuring imitations that have been providing a cover for the entire action.

Stretto 2 (violin, cello), the strictest and most impressive *stretto*, confirms Beethoven's concern in this matter. Beginning with the answer, the high violin turns luminously not to the subdominant, but to the dominant. It makes in fact a subtle variety of "tonal answer"; the cello has to stretch splendidly to meet it. As the great cello augmentation stakes out the tonic in giant steps, a profound weight is lifted—some giant security has been attained—that allows the violin to assert D♯, not D♮, in bar 100, and to assert B♯, not B♮, in bar 102. These are the regular notes of the tonality, not notes shaded to the subdominant.

Stretto 3 (violin 2, cello) retraces *Stretto* 1—veiled and stretched out by means of imitations and repetitions of both halves of the subject. By now the subdominant answer is distilled down to its essence in the four-note configuration C♯–E♯–F♯–D–C♯, so that the note B never ensues, and D♮ can sound unequivocally like a Neapolitan degree of C♯ minor, not as a subdominant of F♯ minor. Harmonically, *Stretto* 3 differs from *Stretto* 1 in the same crux of B and B♯. In place of the murmuring B's of bars 95–6, B♯ arrives with incomparable weight on the cello open string (bar 113), along with the most impressive variation in harmony ever applied to the central note of the subject. The note B♮, pointing away to the subdominant, has ceded step by step to B♯, pointing in to the tonic. Finally, in bar 116, even the Neapolitan D♮ is softened into the regular second degree D♯—and the minor third, E, is softened into the *tierce de Picardie*, E♯.

Between the subtle, ambiguous exposition and this superb passage of resolution comes a stately discourse on every aspect of the subject. Rarely does a fugue deal so fully with its basic material, or so imaginatively sift the details of its subject. The process is overseen by emotional single statements of the subject as a whole, or almost as a whole—for strictly speaking, past the exposition the subject never appears verbatim, not even in the concluding passage of resolution. The interior statements are generally intensified by *strettos*, but always *plutôt libres que recherchés*. They are all arranged so as to sound rather impressive, but all except the last are also kept unstable and in some sense incomplete. Entering rhetorically, they tend to merge into the expressive flow.

The first interior statement (after the four statements that make up the exposition) emerges out of a very beautiful sequential episode treating the first half of the subject. This statement really belongs in the major mode, in III, E major, but—passionately loath, it seems, to admit to its modality—suffers a hint of *stretto* to press it back to C♯ minor.

The next statement, in the dominant, G♯ minor, deflects with an almost theatrical tremor into a pedal, halting the action first on F♯, then on D♯, and then on A♯ (Beethoven writes B♭). This sounds like a suspi-

Example 151

ciously definite, unfugal type of modulation to the "dominant of the dominant," D♯; but with all that subdominant emphasis in the exposition, the ploy was doubtless well advised. In any case, the F♯ pedal proves the better prophet, for the next and strongest statement arrives, after a recurrence of the sequential episode, in B major (VII).

A free *stretto* in diminution, now, three octaves higher, indicates a new measure of warmth, activity, and anticipation. (It is this diminution idea which returns to provide the rich cover for the concluding section of the fugue—in the minor mode, considerably saddened.) With much help from the diminution figure, the B-major statement surges up and up to prepare for another assertion, a statement of the subject markedly different from the previous ones. The texture suddenly and for the first time becomes aberrant, with everything extremely high in the strings—a white, straining, disembodied effect aided also by the reversal of accents in the subject. In spite of this, the texture seems in some mysterious way calculated to stress the fact of stability, at last. For this time the subject is quite complete, and solidly enough entrenched over its pedal A to promote an untroubled new episode in the same key (A, VI) directly afterwards.

This famous two-part canonic episode, preserving the delicate reversed accents of the A-major statement as long as it can—until obliged to catch its breath—evidently constitutes a very special event in the fugue. Its unique amalgam of timelessness, tranquillity, and poignancy is quite new and unexpected. It feels like a *B* section or a trio, almost, rather than like a fugal episode. Certainly it does not develop, simply repeating itself in dialogue a 5th lower, in D major—the Neapolitan degree, ♭II. Now it only remains to prepare the concluding tonic passage of *strettos* by means of a leisurely, determined dominant. For this Beethoven had pedals all ready, introduced after one of the earlier statements.

After the B-major statement of the subject—the statement with the burgeoning *stretto* in diminution—the fugue has moved slowly and inexorably again and again to the subdominant by the circle of 5ths, from B through E to A and D, and then to G♯ and C♯. This is of course the standard modulatory rut for fugues, one which the Great Fugue, it may be thought, had ground into unusability with its spiked iron caissons. Yet there is a special beauty in the employment of this age-old pattern in the C♯-minor Fugue, which lives on its subdominant preoccupation and on the Neapolitan thrust of its exposition. The great irregular culminating turn of the wheel, from the Neapolitan D to G♯ preparing the tonic C♯, projects that harmonic detail into a quietly commanding pillar of the total form.

One wants to go on: the quartet—Beethoven's greatest quartet—is just beginning to find its stride. The final gesture of the fugue, an upward octave of infinite strength and quiet which seems to concentrate the first two notes of the subject; the piercing and still unresolved memory of the ethereal canonic episode; the whole thrust of the harmonic action—all this looks ahead to the flowering of the next movements and then to the consummation of the great Finale. Just as the essential coherence of the Great Fugue turns out to be not a purely fugal matter at all, so the essential meaning of the C♯-minor Fugue devolves upon something much larger than itself, its ramification into the Quartet in C♯ minor, Op. 131, as a total art form. In its own way each fugue, I am afraid, shows up something artificial in the unspoken premise that underlies the present chapter. For in spite of Wendell Kretschmar, the ironic, stuttering mouthpiece for Thomas Mann (and many others), there really is no special problem of "Beethoven and the Fugue." The problem was to integrate fugue as a form into the larger structure of the cyclic work, and to integrate fugue as a style or principle into Beethoven's wider stylistic world.

If we do not at least (or at last) shake ourselves free of that unspoken premise, we are likely to get ourselves trapped, like Daniel Gregory Mason, into deeply meaningless comparisons. Mason was much concerned with these pieces. The C♯-minor Fugue he loved very much, the Great Fugue not at all.

> If greatness lie more in quality than in quantity, this [the C♯-minor Fugue] rather than Opus 133 would seem to be properly the "great fugue." Its comparative brevity is achieved by exclusion of all irrelevance, by masterful concentration. While it makes plentiful use of such *recherchée* devices as inversion, augmentation, diminution, stretto, they never seem pedantically "sought out," as in the earlier work, but spontaneous, irresistible, the flowering of its inner expressiveness. Its episodes are not bits of sonata style inserted into the fugal texture, but aspects of the fugue itself, so that its "poetical element" is not "introduced," but native. Best of all, its deep sincerity of feeling is completely free of rhetorical overemphasis; it never swells out its chest in pompous unisons; it is too deeply in earnest to be flamboyant.[8]

Yes, very well: one can go even further and characterize the C♯-minor Fugue as an even more exhaustive study of its material than the Great Fugue. In modulation, for instance, the piece dwells with stately regularity on all possible related keys: i, iv, III, v, VII, VI and finally also ♭II, the Neapolitan relationship which is central to the whole composition, but which is only an optional part of the tonal system of the minor mode. This thoroughness makes for a special richness in the total impression,

[8] Pp. 240–1.

even apart from the organization of the harmonic action. Then in the matter of breaking down the subject for episodic treatment, the C♯-minor Fugue must go further than any other fugue three times its length; Beethoven's ingenuity in this matter is really beyond praise. As Mason very truly remarks, the fragmentations of the subject never seem "sought out . . . but spontaneous, irresistible, the flowering of its inner expressiveness." Not much has been said about this in the analysis on the previous pages, but repeated listenings will reveal more and more details of the subject permeating and enriching the progress at every point.

About the Great Fugue, however, Mason quite misses the point. The Great Fugue is a finale; that is the point. Rhetorical emphasis—let us not speak of "overemphasis"—is the business of finales; the Finale of the C♯-minor Quartet has its unisons too, plenty of them, though perhaps they will not strike us as pompous or flamboyant. In deciding to use a fugue as the initial statement of a cyclic composition, Beethoven set himself a new set of conditions. His task was not emphasis or summary, but laying ground for the coming work in its entirety. That he carried out this task particularly well, and more easily than he solved the problem of the fugal finale, is clear—and characteristic: last movements had always strained and sometimes eluded Beethoven's imagination. It could hardly be said that strain and sweat remain as aesthetic factors in the C♯-minor Fugue. Despite its very great originality and freedom, it emanates a very strong sense of normality, to such an extent that one really wonders if an intrinsic "problem" of fugue can have existed at all. Such a perfect harvest seems to belie the labor that made it possible.

One wants to go on. The radical differences in character between the two fugues, which Mason could only put invidiously, will be found indicative of equally radical differences between the Quartets in B♭ and C♯ minor. Which will hardly come as a surprise. It is doubtless time to turn our attention away from technical aspects of fragments of pieces to the whole pieces themselves. Fugue was a technical preoccupation in the third period, but Beethoven's deepest study, then as always, was the totality, the integrity of the individual work of art.

10

DISSOCIATION AND INTEGRATION

Quartet in B♭ Major, Op. 130
Quartet in C♯ Minor, Op. 131

We have observed—to recapitulate for a moment—an underlying parallelism between the first two quartets for Prince Galitzin, the Quartets in E♭ and A minor. While these works differ extremely in character, they share some distinct features of general plan. Both include dance movements that are extended and contrapuntally involved; both locate their centers of gravity in great *adagios* and proceed to relatively simple finales dissolving, at the very end, into an evanescent ether. Beethoven planned things differently in the next two works, the Quartet in B♭, written to conclude Galitzin's commission, and the Quartet in C♯ minor, written (we may suppose) to conclude something within himself. These are the two quartets containing fugues. The dance movements shrink and become strikingly popular, even childlike in tone. The slow movements no longer feel so central—for there are now two slow movements in each quartet—and in consequence the finales are treated with new complexity and emphasis. Or put it the other way around: these quartets drive to climax in their finales, and in consequence tend to keep the earlier movements less weighty than before. This is most obviously the case with the original version of the Quartet in B♭ ending with the Great Fugue, but less obviously it is also true of the Quartet in C♯ minor.

These two works differ in character too, quite as extremely as do the almost continuously lyrical Quartet in E♭ and the now tormented, now transcendent Quartet in A minor. If one cannot articulate the difference so clearly in terms of affect, that is because the sense of affect is constantly elusive in the B♭ Quartet: a mercurial, brilliant, paradoxical work, toying with the dissociation of its own sensibility and toying with the listener's limping powers of prediction. Force jostles with whimsy, prayer with effrontery, dangerous innocence with an even more dangerous sophistication. The Quartet in B♭ is the most problematic of Beethoven's great compositions, a fact that he himself was almost the first to acknowledge, with his deeply equivocal behavior toward the finale. As a result of the separation of the Great Fugue, it does not suffice for the critic simply to deal with the complexities of the preceding movements, and hope to come to some understanding of their internal and mutual coherence. Ideally each set of relationships has to be held up against a formidable double image, the Great Fugue of 1825 and the new Finale composed late in 1826.

In the B♭ Quartet the play of contrast is pushed even further than in the A-minor, to a point at which the sense of continuity becomes, if not a matter of doubt, at least a recurrent subject of ironic inquiry. The problem of continuity comes up both among the movements and also within certain movements—such as one that we have already seen, the fugal Finale, with its violent contrasts and its amazing transitions. The same problem is present and pressing within the opening movement. As usual, this sets the stage for everything that follows.

Like the *Scherzando vivace* of the E♭ Quartet and the first movement of the A-minor Quartet, this is one of those late Beethoven movements that work to maximize contrast—as is proclaimed at once by the intimate confrontation of its *adagio* and *allegro* sections. But whereas with the earlier pieces the dialectic of contrast and its control settled into impressions of pointed humor, or of pain and frustration, here there is something faceless about the endeavor, something purely technical. The movement is an endlessly fascinating one—but the first movement of the Quartet in A minor is over and above that a moving one. To get behind the whimsy in the B♭ Quartet is sometimes extremely difficult. And one really wants to get behind; for whimsy implies that we do not quite follow the composer's line of thought, even though we are keeping faith with it.

That Beethoven wanted to cement that faith seems indicated by the great number of interconnections of one kind or another that he proposed among elements within or across the movements. In this respect the piece probably counts as his most advanced, and it has certainly proved a happy hunting ground for analysts, such as Rudolph Reti, with a special concern for "organic unity." Inevitably, some have undertaken to trace all the thematic material of the quartet to a limited number of germ motifs; Hugo Leichtentritt did this in 1921, and Deryck Cooke in 1963—each finding, of course, a different set of motifs. So this brings us on another level to the eminently problematic nature of this quartet; the relevance and indeed the very presence of such interconnections is the subject of continuing and in practice rather hopeless controversy. What one critic or analyst calls subtle another calls arcane or plain illusory. Delicate as it may be to "prove" any single point, however, the general matrix of relationships cannot be ignored without ignoring Beethoven's special concept of coherence in this work. To be sure, it is a kind of coherence now that is less instinctual than constructed, less direct than refined, less normal than paradoxical: in a word, less sure.

Also less responsive to ordinary efforts at elucidation. Let me attempt to bring out a few of these paradoxical relationships, as I perceive them, within the opening movement of the Quartet in B♭.

· 2 ·

On the basis of the first page, one would probably never predict that the development section which eventually ensues will use material from the *Adagio* introduction. Suppose one did predict; which of the *adagio* motifs will be used, and how? Take ten, twenty guesses. The answer is the 2-note cadence of bar 4, treated not as a rising sequence—as in bars 4–7—but

Example 152

simply as murmuring figuration. The derivation is so tenuous and paradoxical that Beethoven has to lead the listener very firmly by the hand (see p. 310). After bar 100, the 2-note cadence-figure is separated off, repeated three times, and somehow construed as *espressivo*. After such signaling, we will not miss any route it takes.

Consider further that rising sequence in bars 4–7. This early in the piece, are we to hear it in relation to the rising sequence that also happens to underpin the *allegro* theme—the second violin etching out the 4ths B♭–E♭ | C–F, while the first violin shoots down in sixteenth-notes, first from D and then from E♭? I think not; yet in the coda of the movement this is the very relationship that Beethoven wishes to force. Between the *adagio* bars (214–17, 219, 221), which are retracing the rising sequence

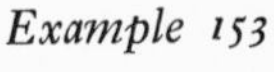
Example 153

of bars 4–7 now intensified by chromatic inflections and by off-beat echoes, he inserts *allegro* bars retracing the first-violin sequence of bars 15–18.

A third case: the distinctive anapaest motif of bar 8 (heralded in bar 6) will hardly be felt as a precedent for the omnipresent sixteenth-note figure of the *Allegro*. Yet in melodic terms, the early motif is undoubtedly beginning to mark out the descending 3rds (G–E♭–C) which grow so insistent later (D–B♭–G–E♭–C | E♭–C–A–F–D; see bars 15–18). Again Beethoven draws the connection in retrospect. The bridge passage of the exposition refers back unequivocally to the anapaest rhythm of of bar 8, only now the 3rds are whisked all the way around the circle, D–B♭–G–E♭–C–A–F–D, after which the rhythm is dissolved directly into the characteristic continuous sixteenth-note motion.

Once the demonstration is accomplished, Beethoven quite loses interest in the rhythmic motif that seems to be emerging, the anapaest idea. In the recapitulation, the motif finds place in one bar only, where it works pretty innocuously around a triad.

These situations involve the subsequent elucidation of paradoxes. There is even something paradoxical about the nature of the motivic saturation produced by the sixteenth-note figure, as compared with the equally dense but much more earnest motivic saturation in a work such as the Quartet in A minor. The figure arises ambiguously out of the *Adagio* (or so I have suggested) and comes into its own during the first group and the small bridge section. In the second group, it first pokes itself owlishly into the lyric flow, then truncates itself with mock ominous solemnity, and then sweetly fades into the scenery as figuration behind a new quarter-note idea—but soon takes over and drowns out the other material in forceful dialogue. The figure drops in to the development section once or twice, making arbitrary monosyllabic comments on the rest of the proceedings.

Paradox has to proceed from norms: suspiciously normal features jostle with abnormal ones all through the Quartet in B♭. The initial *Adagio*, to begin with, behaves like a traditional slow introduction—and like a rather mild example at that, with its routine harmonic deflections and with its dominant and tonic cadences balanced according to the classic norm. After 14 bars, the *fermata* certainly lulls us to expect the advent of a fast theme making a bright contrast (see p. 306). But we certainly do *not* expect the weird disturbance that actually flashes across the screen at this point. Too disjointed to establish itself at once, the *allegro* theme screeches to a halt on a half cadence after a mere five bars. Normal enough in contour—indeed, the second-violin motif with the 4ths is almost pat—the theme astonishes by the perverse dynamics on alternate bars (*forte*, *piano*, *forte*, *piano*), by the frantic speed and range of the first violin, and by the odd *appoggiatura* effects undermining the little hushed stops in bars 17 and 19. The skeetering sixteenth-note passage in the first violin looks like a domesticated version of the scream that prefaces the main theme in the A-minor Quartet.

The *Adagio* starts up again in the dominant—in the hope, perhaps, that the hopped-up double-counterpoint combination will simply go away if no one pays it any attention. In this statement, the *Adagio* is enriched by new imitative gestures which underline the opening interval B♭–A, a descending semitone step with important work in store for it in the sequel. But after four bars of *Adagio*, the *allegro* theme tries again. Without reaching any firmer conclusion, at least it stays in tempo, and a third attempt back in B♭ does succeed in solidifying itself. By this time, after the three thematic statements have fallen into a classic I–V–I pattern, the ambiguous failure of the theme to conclude seems like nothing more serious than a device for joining phrases on a local level.

However the recapitulation treats the ambiguity somewhat differently, and the coda turns it into this witty conclusion for the movement:

Example 154

Here the nonconcluding "open" sequence B♭–E♭ | C–F is modified into the neatly concluding "closed" sequence B♭–E♭ | F–B♭.

The bridge passage of the exposition sounds normal too, indeed suspiciously normal—up to its very last gesture:

Example 155

In spite of the *diminuendo*—a characteristc irony for this quartet—this *staccato* unison chromatic scale is the most devastating event yet in the composition. For nothing so far, not even the hinting at chromaticism, has prepared us for so mechanistic a move to D♭. When D♭ is coolly treated as the 5th of G♭ major, the second key for the movement, the tonal situation appears utterly precarious; normally Beethoven would never dream of establishing a contrasting key-area, let alone a remote key (♭VI), in so dissociated a fashion. One thinks rather of Schubert, in the Unfinished Symphony and the String Quintet in C. But the point here has to do with the grotesquerie of the second-group material, or at least of its beginning. A caricature of a lyric phrase, complete with trite-sounding harmonies, it is only able to proceed at all—after being instantly interrupted by the sixteenth-note figure—by transforming itself into something quite different. The clumsy interval of a 6th which initiates the lyric phrase has just been traced out parodistically by the chromatic scale. Some analysts go further and derive the whole lyric phrase from the first seven notes of the *Adagio*, a perception which certainly enhances the grotesquerie.

More fantastic yet is the treatment of the chromatic scale in the recapitulation. The viola carries it down, not up, accumulating saccharine harmonies as a nonchromatic, nonmodulating cello scale fans out above it:

Example 156

This is preparing a boldly dissociated double image of the second theme. The lyric phrase comes first in D♭, with its harmonies made even more saccharine. It comes a second time in B♭, with its harmonies made over into an astringent, lucid diatonicism. And since the beginning of the recapitulation was undercut, this marks the really decisive return of the tonic key.

Example 157

After the development worked around a circle of 5ths from D to G to C to F, the return of the first *allegro* theme in the recapitulation ran hurriedly (in six bars) from B♭ further around the circle, to a lengthy stretch in E♭, after which the circle continued rolling via A♭ to D♭, for the second theme. So the key of B♭ lends the second theme at its next and final appearance paradoxical new dignity. Simple imitative gestures, soaring upward by 6ths to the very high B♭, even manage to smother those self-multiplying little interruptions by the sixteenth-note figure.

From here on the recapitulation proceeds like the exposition—to the discussion of which we should now return. After the second theme, a very pleasant new idea in G♭ major combines light marching quarter-notes with the sixteenths, in a superbly executed instance of classic *obbligato* counterpoint. (The quarter-notes bear a resemblance to a characteristic

figure of the third movement, which features this style brilliantly nearly all the way through.) The sixteenths grow more and more top-heavy, stopping only at the final cadential idea, a unison bearing a resemblance to the unison that terminates the *Meno mosso e moderato* section of the Great Fugue. Like that passage, this one modulates back from G♭ to B♭—for Beethoven directs a full repetition of the exposition, starting all the way back at bar 1. The cadential unison contains descending steps which, as appears in Example 157, above, can lead easily and pointedly into the unison step at the beginning of the *Adagio:* either the step B♭–A of the repetition or G♭–F in the sequel (bar 93).

The second ending stays for a moment in G♭, in which key the *Adagio* seems to articulate a distinct new section. Very suddenly and very quietly, the key shifts to D major, a tonal dissociation as violent as the shift from B♭ to G♭ accomplished by the chromatic scale. Indeed F♯–D (G♭–E♭♭) corresponds exactly to B♭–G♭ and therefore exactly reduplicates the tonal movement; the scheme involves trisection of the octave into the augmented triad B♭–G♭–D–B♭. If the breach B♭–G♭ had opened a Pandora's box in the exposition, the breach F♯ or G♭–D initiates even more exotic happenings in the development proper.

For use in this section, we have seen how carefully Beethoven set up the basic *ostinato* figuration, drawing it step by step out of a relatively obscure fragment of the *adagio* material. Despite this nod in the direction of normality, this development remains the most eccentric Beethoven ever wrote, and doubtless the most disruptive contrast he ever used in a sonata-allegro movement. The famous interruption of the development in the A-minor Quartet may give a momentary effect of absurdity, but in the B♭ Quartet the entire development section exists in a trance, as though somehow another movement has got going without our quite noticing how. In and around the basic figuration, which stays absolutely regular and flat for 28 quiet bars, tiny fanfares mold the ascending 4ths of the *allegro* theme. Alternately, a far-fetched derivative of the second theme appears, an ugly duckling dream-transformed into a graceful arching element which still, however, exhibits much ambiguity in the matter of continuation. Sometimes the element does not even cadence. How the phrases fit together is never altogether clear.

A curious arbitrary air emanates from this development, in fact—from its random irregularity of phrasing; from the chance encounters with the sixteenth-note figure; from the tendency of the figuration to start little things going off in a corner (the rocking contrary-motion idea of bars 119–22, the 6-bar D–C *ostinato* following bar 123); and from the marvelous cold glow of C major in bar 127, coming out of C minor and then inexplicably turning right back to C minor. And everything sounds at once relaxed and crystal-clear and strangely unsubstantial, thanks to systematic undercutting of the strong beats. At the recapitulation, the swift resolution to the tonic B♭ seems deliberately indecisive. Full tonic solidity waits until the astringent version of the second theme, as we have seen. (But the triumphant recapitulation is only a dormant idea with Beethoven, not a dead one.)

The recapitulation is appreciably changed, at least up to the point of real tonic solidity. The coda has not much to do, beyond returning to the opening thematic material in manipulations that have already been mentioned. One is the extraordinary forced wedding of the *adagio* and *allegro* themes, which places the disruptive underlying contrast of the movement in maximum relief (p. 306). The other is the rather ordinary ironing-out of the sequence of 4ths in the *allegro* theme (p. 308). So the movement ends on a characteristic note of dissociation: normality sharply placed against a conception of startling novelty and imagination. One cannot say that a sense of purposeful strain emerges, but simply a sense of fascination, whimsy, enigma.

A sudden furious whisper in B♭ minor—what is *this* doing in the middle of a great string quartet, one which indeed is supposed to culminate in an exhaustive, learned fugal exercise? Short-breathed, crusty, astute—the opening "doublet phrase" was quoted on page 203, along with its peasant brothers. But the effrontery is less a matter of tone than of the drastic simplicity of the total structure. All we hear is a rapid, short dance (16 bars, 32 with repeats) starting out with a doublet; a *maggiore* trio extending a new doublet just a little further; a small explosion; and a decorated *da capo* which shoots by before we can focus attention on the decorations. Ten bars of coda resume the original doublet phrase, and the *Presto* is over with a snarl. *Bagatelle!*

That is just what Beethoven called such pieces, at least when he wrote them for piano. But there is a half-serious point; besides making its tacit contemptuous comment on the airs and complexities of the opening movement, this one also makes a gesture at collecting up some of the loose ends. These loose ends appear to be harmonic ones, as usual. The much-repeated doublet phrase keeps grumbling around the note G♭, in both its top and bottom lines, a detail whose importance is vouched for by a flash of Beethovenian temper just before the *da capo:*

Example 158

Directly after the doublet is first played, the music shifts to D♭ and back again; and as for the *maggiore* trio, to the extent that its *perpetuum mobile* ever settles at all, it settles in D minor. G♭, D♭, and D—albeit D major, not D minor—were the major points of harmonic arrival in the opening movement.

The third movement, *Andante con moto, ma non troppo,* strikes a less immediately impressive attitude than the slow movements of the other late quartets. That is because a second, and slower, slow movement is in the offing, the *Cavatina.* (Something similar happened in Beethoven's other B♭ Quartet, Op. 18, No. 6, with *La Malinconia,* if the reader can adjust his thoughts back that far.) But what this *Andante* lacks in solemnity it more than makes up in freshness and grace, and it yields to no other music of the last period in sensitivity of response. For Theodor Helm it was the *Lieblingssatz* of the Quartet in B♭, and from it Daniel Gregory Mason could well take four bars in autograph as frontispiece for his study, to stand as emblem or epitome of Beethoven's art.

The first bars, marked "*Preludio*" on one of the sketches, serve both as an integral element of the movement and also as a link to other movements —perhaps the richest link of any devised by Beethoven, even in these last years when he was so concerned with connections between one stage and another of the cyclic composition. The piece starts as though in B♭ minor, the key of the preceding *Presto.* An arresting 2-note figure in the first violin, B♭–A, sounds like a quiet, intense sigh. The identical step B♭–A started

Example 159

the first movement of the quartet too, and grew in significance at the hinges between the exposition and the development, and between the recapitulation and the coda. Underneath the slow step in the violin, an undulating counterpoint stresses another reminiscent note, G♭; the step is repeated, intensified by means of the register, and carried down B♭–A–A♭, as the harmony begins to slip. At once everything clears up.

In D♭ major, a lilting theme emerges a little darkly in the viola, and with it a sonata-type movement which, for all its remarkable fecundity of material, will maintain remarkable uniformity in its mood of delicate and spirited play. D♭ major, then, is the tonic key. In retrospect, the piece seems to have begun with a remote sentiment and on a remote harmony, on vii of vi going to I. But in bar 3 the smart cello figuration still reminds us of B♭ . . .

Uniform in mood, except for two prominent recurrences of the *Preludio* or link-figure—prominent because they move so much slower than the rest of the music. The first recurrence, just prior to the recapitulation, was cited in Chapter 7 (p. 198) because of its similarity to the analogous point of the *Cavatina*—a forward link as arresting as the backward link to the opening unison step of the first movement. Once again a harmonic slippage is involved, though a different one: instead of vii of vi–I, II (or V of V)–I. There is a further parallel here to the magical C-major sonority at the analogous point in the opening movement.

The second, more significant recurrence comes within the long coda

Example 160

of the movement. Expanding the passage, Beethoven brings the basic step in three directly successive statements. And starting from the vii_7-of-vi chord, which is of course a diminished-7th, he makes of the passage the most expressive of all his *tours de force* with such chords, a suitable climax to the long line starting with *La Malinconia*. The first statement weights B♭–A as heavily as possible by underpinning A with its tonic triad. The second does the same for the composite step B♭–A♭; but neither of these amazing, and gorgeous, progressions provides anything like a resolution. The third statement, nearly restating the harmonies of bars 1–2, spells out the melodic progression in full, B♭–A–A♭, carrying the chromaticism on. Instead of any slipping harmony, there is the amplitude of a full circle of 5ths from III to I:

B♭ A A♭ G G♭ F

F B♭ E♭ A♭ (D♭)

The step-figure has not been sounding like a sigh, but more like a deep breath, a pause for meditation, a mature reflection on the play. This wonderful passage is the one Mason chose for his frontispiece.

It is extraordinary what potential Beethoven could still find in the conventional progression of the circle of 5ths; we have seen many fine examples among the last quartets, and will see many more. The present instance has a Mozartian, bittersweet flavor. As the stages of the circling motion are supported ultimately by major 9th chords rather than minor 9ths, the original cloud is perfectly dispelled. Not that Beethoven is through with the sixth degree, vi, and its veiled suggestion of the B♭ tonality of the earlier movements. B♭ returns at a surprising deceptive cadence in bar 80 (see above). Here the D in the first violin, if I do not deceive myself, prefigures the great chasm between D♭ at the end of this movement and the G-major tonality of the next—G major with D♮ in the first violin. The relation may seem strained, but what I think is being strained is our aesthetic sense, not our perception or our interpretation of Beethoven's intention.

As for the main body of the movement, it offers such a spontaneous flow of musical notions, so perfectly disposed and so brilliantly scored, such an enchantment of intelligence and warmth and airy poise, that analytical formulations seem somehow helplessly beside the point. The reader may well glare in disbelief at this statement, coming in this book, but it cannot be helped; this beautifully ordered cascade of melody, dance, and sheer sonority really does not want to be separated. The lyricism distills the *Volkston* that obsessed Beethoven's last years to a point at which there is nothing simple, patronizing, or parodistic left—only pure spring. The piece is also one of his most imaginative in texture, polishing like an intricate cluster of diamonds the *obbligato* openwork that he had come upon earlier, in Variation 2 of the slow movement of Op. 127 and in the *Neue Kraft fühlend* sections of Op. 132. This sound plane had been touched on, tangentially, in the development section of the opening movement. In terms of texture, the Great Fugue comes as close as can be imagined to being its antithesis.

Subtleties of structure can of course be pointed out and dwelled upon: a second subject beginning on the subdominant of the dominant, and a long bright second-group digression in VI of the dominant (rather than ♭VI, as would be more usual). This digression includes a reference to the link-figure and a canon on (of all things) the first theme; it duly returns at the recapitulation in VI of the tonic key, that is to say, in B♭ major. This key always seems to be hiding around the corner. But there is a quality of graceful nonchalance about all the structural modulations in this piece, as there is about the constantly burgeoning sequence of thematic material. The tonal dynamic is approaching that of fugal style, in which the composer can move from one key to another without raising deep urgencies or expectations. Into this conception the harmonic slips of the link-figure and also the penultimate deceptive cadence fit very naturally indeed. Everything seems calculated to facilitate the inspired flow of lyric ideas.

The very beginning of the movement Beethoven marks *Poco scherzoso;* we are asked not to take the sigh very seriously. Somehow the movement is above joking, though, even in a curious way above humor—up to the ultimate cadence, with its fast scale salvaged from the miniscule development section, its rushing harmonic rhythm, its teasing *fermata* rest, and its *subito forte* chord of final resolution (so *subito*, in fact, that its grace-notes are still to be played *piano*). This cadence recalls the *Allegretto scherzando* of the Eighth Symphony, the movement based on the joke about the Mälzel metronome. Beethoven had a way of realizing his unfulfilled conceptions. The quartet helps clarify what, in 1812, had been dimly and much less beautifully present in his mind.

· 3 ·

As though anxious to restore the earthy sources of lyricism that were refined away by the *Andante con moto*, Beethoven placed after it a blunt dance movement, *Allegro assai: Alla danza Tedesca.* (He had the term in

French—*à l'Allemande*—a few years earlier for one of the Bagatelles of Op. 119.) In structure this dance is even more childlike than the *Presto*, which at least hiccups one 7-bar phrase in the course of its trio section:

TEDESCA		TRIO				TEDESCA		CODA	
first doublet		second doublet	second doublet	second doublet (variation)		(partly in variation)			
|: A :|	|: B A :|	|: C :|	|: C :|	|: C :|		|: A :|	|: B A :|	A′	A″
8	8 8	8	8	8	4 × 2	8	8 8	8 + 4 + 2 + 8	
I		I	IV	vi————		————I		(IV)	

Minimizing contrast, the trio here follows in exactly the same key and tempo as the dance proper. Like a number of earlier trios, it flounders disingenuously when called upon to extend itself; all it seems able to do is repeat its simple-minded doublet in different keys. This all adds up to an easy, benign classic parody, a descendant of the *allemande* Finale of the early B♭ Quartet, Op. 18, No. 6. It is not easy to think of another Beethoven movement that transcribes a popular dance model so precisely; which may be what he was trying to explain or excuse by means of the title.

The fascination of this movement lies not in melody, shape, or texture —though in the trio, counterpoint begins to get busy—but in details of the rhythmic figuration and the dynamics. During the first doublet, the accompanying instruments rock in hemiola, or cross-rhythms of 3 × 2 beats cutting across 2 × 3; in this way they dreamily undercut half of the strong beats and spice half of the weak ones. This feature is maintained in the coda, and also in the half-variation of the *da capo* (which, by the way, employs some square-dance fiddle effects like those in the trio of the second movement of Op. 132. That movement too, it will be recalled, shakes up the regular pulse dictated by the dance prototype.) As for the dynamics, Beethoven had some fantastic ideas for inflecting his innocuous doublet phrases. The first of them has a seasick pattern applied to it rigorously; the second is made to *crescendo* harshly eight times, quite out of proportion to its intrinsic slenderness. The dynamics—they are given under the music on page 203—should be performed very scrupulously, and if anything, with exaggeration (though D'Indy cautioned the exact opposite). The piece will begin to sound surreal. One has the sudden idea that if Beethoven had conceived of serial organization, he certainly would have thought of serializing dynamics.

This is not such a crazy thought, in face of the notorious passage at the start of the coda in which he starts to permute bars within the theme:

Example 161

Directly after the rather soporific concluding statement of the first doublet phrase—let us number its eight bars 1 2 3 4 | 1 2 5 6—we are treated to 6 5 2 1 | 1 2 3 4. This is rather delightful, but just what Beethoven was driving at is very hard to penetrate.

The dance ends suavely and strongly on an off-beat, with a sort of double feminine cadence promoted by the hemiolas. For the first time since the trio, the dynamic mark specifies a *forte*. A second slow movement, *Adagio molto espressivo*, ensues, a long heartfelt song in E♭: the *Cavatina*. Then the titanic Fugue. These are very wonderful pieces; the reader has already seen analyses of them in some length. The question at this point, however, is not one of their individual integrity but of their roles within the entire cyclic work. How are we to comprehend the order or aggregate of the six movements in the early, or "Galitzin" version of the Quartet in B♭?

It is an obligatory and natural question, I take it, after the Quartets in E♭ and A minor, and, for that matter, all the others since the "Razumovsky" set twenty years before. In many ways the Quartet in B♭ is problematic, but the heart of the problem lies in the quite radical attitude it embodies toward the balance, confrontation, or sequence of the movements.

Ordinarily, as one senses in a general way, the movements of the cyclic composition are made to fall together into some kind of coherent emotional pattern. The progress from stage to stage is not always direct, but indirections can be experienced as digressions which presently return to the main track; the *Alla marcia* of the Quartet in A minor may feel at first like a deflection, but it soon explains itself as a foil for the recitative which guides fatefully toward the Finale. Like a passionate messenger in a Greek play, the recitative forces attention once again on the central action. But the sense of a central action, in some sort of analogy with the drama, is precisely what seems so deliberately shunned by the Quartet in B♭. One would be hard pressed to isolate a feeling of direction or destination at many points. The digressions assume a life of their own, and the life of the whole piece becomes the life of the "digressions."

The continuity, then, becomes a matter of ironic inquiry, or more particularly a challenge to fresh perception. The piece celebrates dissociation, forced by the play—or rather the war—of contrast. Indeed I am inclined to trace the essential character of the quartet not backward from the Fugue, as Romain Rolland and others have done, but forward from the dissociated opening movement. Beethoven's central concern for contrast, all through the late quartets, here thrusts hard toward the breaking point; once the fragmented imagination had assumed control in the opening movement, paradox and indirection were destined to stay with the piece to the end. More than any other of his great compositions, the Quartet in B♭ bears in its very blood the seeds of disruption: physical disruption, as the event proved.

The most direct means used to force or maximize contrast was of course simply multiplication of movements, from the standard group of four up to six (or even more, if the Great Fugue is construed as consisting of several movements). Except for the *Andante con moto*, all the movements are in one way or another extreme; more than that, something essential about their character resides exactly in their extremity. Among sonata-allegro movements, the first movement of the Quartet in B♭ is Beethoven's *most* contrasty and enigmatic. Among the various scherzo or dance types, the second movement stands out as his *most* precipitous and ill-behaved, the fourth movement as his *most* innocently dance-like. The *Cavatina* is his *most* emotional slow movement—so at least the composer himself felt, if we can credit his admission that the piece brought tears to his eyes every time he so much as thought about it. As for the Finale, the Great Fugue, it not only beggars superlatives but obviously was written with the express purpose of beggaring superlatives (which is not to say that this was its exclusive purpose). Beethoven had never assembled a more recklessly individualistic group of workmen for a putative common task.

Then taking these members, he threw them together in an arrangement calculated to stress their individual extremities and mutual incongruities. Something of this process has already been seen with the second movement, the *Presto*. In the matter of its placement and reference, the piece is beholden to the scheme of the Ninth Symphony, which points its second movement backward, as a sort of epitome of the first. But whereas the granite of that symphony could withstand any little electric storms, the shifting sands of this quartet certainly cannot. As epitome, the second movement turns out to be scurrilous and destructive. Trivial in itself, the *Presto* further unsettles an already dangerously unsettled situation.

Later, the emotionality of the *Cavatina* also comes as a very great shock, for no hints in any of the earlier four movements had prepared for so deep a resource of feeling. If Beethoven had deliberately set out to make it sound as sentimental as possible, he could hardly have chosen a better placement. This shock, however, is nothing compared to that occasioned by the Great Fugue, with its retching *Overtura* and the overpowering violence of its two major fugal sections—a violence likewise entirely out of the range of experience predicated by any earlier movements of the quartet. Now, when a very strong finale is in the offing, Beethoven's rule is to space it off from the slow movement by means of a minuet or scherzo, as much in order to shelter the lyric movement as to smooth over the change of mood. The Third, Fifth, and Seventh Symphonies can be mentioned in this connection, as well as two of the "Razumovsky" Quartets. But in the B♭ Quartet, which boasts of a slow movement more defenseless and a finale more terrible than ever before, the *Alla danza Tedesca* coolly stands aside. Beethoven slips it into the line-up *before* the *Cavatina* rather than after it.

In this position, furthermore, it makes a sensational harmonic rupture with the preceding *Andante con moto:* G major clashing with D♭ major in the relation (or rather nonrelation) of a tritone. Composers are of course not known to be at all timorous of remote clashes. A good example is the confrontation of F minor and D major between the first and second movements of the Quartet in F minor, Op. 95—that extraordinary signpost to the late quartets. But normally such cases are designed to set in relief some particular mystery or trouble in the clashing event—not to introduce an easygoing essay in studied naïveté, whose claim to sit at table with the *Andante*, the *Cavatina*, and the Fugue would never be allowed, if truth be told, without Beethoven's express card of admission. The key of the *Alla danza Tedesca* does not even re-establish some previously important key-area after tonal digressions. It comes simply as a whimsical bolt out of the blue.

And the Great Fugue, Schindler's "*Monstrum aller Quartett-Musik*" —who would have thought of yoking this giant with a midget like the *Presto* second movement? Not even Beethoven, outside of his most dissociated composition. In spite of the confident testimony of some critics, the role of the Fugue within the Galitzin version of the Quartet in B♭ must be allowed to be as problematic as everything else about the quartet. Clearly Beethoven wished to forgo the dynamic of dissolution which had served him so well in the finales of the two (indeed, the three) previous quartets, in favor of a climactic, triumphant termination. Perhaps this was a "precompositional assumption"; to this extent, and no further, I could accept

Rolland's idea of the Great Fugue as a germ of the entire work. On the contrary, the Fugue seems to strive fantastically to make up for the fantastic discontinuities of the early movements. But if anything it confirms, rather than resolves, the previous dynamic of disruption—with its violent system of shocks joining the various great sections, and its cryptic *Overtura* and concluding section. Paradox is its essence, the paradox of different forms of the note-set existing in the same sound-world. At the same time, this great compulsive tantrum seems to pulverize memories into a new organic structure built from the ground up. The Great Fugue burns with its own special flame, pursuing to the point of self-absorption its own retrospective ideal of contrapuntal rigor, and its own proleptic ideal of continuing variation.

Generally one can intuit (although one can articulate only very vaguely) some fairly tangible relation in feeling between a Beethoven finale and the first movement of its composition, or else between the finale and the whole complex of the earlier movements. The finale will act in some sense to resume, or resolve, or reinterpret, or transfigure. But vague as these terms may be, they are not so vague as to seem at all adequate to the situation here. One would not even want to say that the Great Fugue transcends the early parts of the quartet: it wipes them out. There is a sense in which this Finale trivializes the journey which it means to terminate, and there is also a sense in which the Great Fugue orbits upon a private musical sphere of its own, needing no other sounds, needing no other universe.

It is all a matter of degree, of course. I can agree with those who prefer the quartet in the Galitzin version, with the Great Fugue as finale, and who feel the Fugue to be lacking without the backdrop of the quartet. At the same time, I can hardly think of another Beethoven finale that could so much as be imagined as an independent opus, even for a moment. Nor on the other hand can I think of any other important composition of his that ends so problematically as the Galitzin version of the Quartet in B♭.

In all this, it seems to me indicated that Beethoven was working toward some new idea of order or coherence in the cyclic composition, an order markedly different from the traditional psychological sequence that he had developed in the earlier music. This new order is not easy to comprehend, because on the evidence of the Quartet in B♭, the idea was not entirely realized. In the few works that were now left for him to compose, he did not pursue the new conception but reverted to more traditional ideas of order. That something new was in the wind, however, may also be indicated by a slightly earlier composition, in a genre that has come to mind a number of times in connection with the quartet. The Six Bagatelles for Piano, Op. 126, of 1824, shows signs of cyclic unification on some level —though very definitely on a more tenuous level than was ordinarily understood by the composer (or his publishers, who were quite frigid about pieces of this sort). "*Ciklus*," Beethoven wrote on one of the sketches for Op. 126, and the tonal sequence of the completed set—to look no further than tonal sequence—does appear too coherent to have arisen fortuitously as a simple miscellany. The chart below gives the six tonic keys and (below, in parentheses) subsidiary keys or degrees of any importance:

Andante $\frac{3}{4}$	Allegro $\frac{2}{4}$	Andante $\frac{3}{8}$	Presto [and Trio] ¢	Quasi Allegretto $\frac{6}{8}$	Presto—Andante ($\frac{3}{8}$)—Presto
G	G minor	E♭	B minor and major	G	E♭
	(B♭, C)		(G)	(B, C)	(B♭, A♭)

Oddly enough, this aggregate of keys even recalls the second part of the quartet, which reaches B (C♭) for its most emotional passage of all, the passage in the *Cavatina* marked *beklemmt*. The keys also recall *An die ferne Geliebte*, the song cycle written in 1816, an earlier experiment with six small pieces joined in some new vision of total unity. Perhaps these experiments can be thought of as preparing ground for the Quartet in B♭, which also contains its conspicuous *Kleinigkeiten*.

And in the quartet, certainly, something very interesting is going on with all the links and interconnections among themes and movements. As was remarked at the outset, they constitute a special feature, a special problem in this particular work. A number of them have already been mentioned—notably the link from the first bars of the D♭ *Andante* both backward to the opening movement and forward to the *Cavatina*. Even the "bolt out of the blue" of the G-major entrance of the *Alla danza Tedesca*, after the D♭ movement, has its precedent in a deceptive cadence toward the end of that movement. Once G is rudely asserted, it assumes considerable responsibility for associating the last three movements; indeed, the main harmonic breach comes between the first three movements (in the keys of B♭, B♭ minor, and D♭) and the last three (G, E♭, and B♭). G serves as a common tone between the end of the trio of the *Alla danza Tedesca*, in vi, and the *da capo* of the main dance—a rather surprisingly Baroque sort of linkage. G is a centrally important note in the *Cavatina*. G marks the apocalyptic initial announcement of the *Overtura* introducing the Great Fugue, before the actual tonic is reached at all. The fugue subject itself continues to levitate around the 5th C–G, until the great climactic unison near the end of the entire quartet strikes as its melodic high point G once again.

As for the constant upward semitone steps of the fugue subject, they make their hard ironic reference to the downward step B♭–A of the early movements. The Double Fugue in B♭ makes its only big modulation to D minor, before jolting abruptly into G♭ major for the lyric *Meno mosso e moderato* section; G♭ and D were centrally important in the first and second movements—both of which handle G♭ no less roughly than the Fugue. The whimsical shunting from the *Meno mosso* section of the Fugue into the half-comic dancelike passage in B♭ makes a contrast worthy of the *Presto* after the opening movement. Thereafter the modulating A♭ Fugue still keeps the key of B♭ in evidence, rather as the *Andante con moto* shaded its D♭ tonality with recollections of B♭. In the long concluding section of the Great Fugue, the weirdest deflection of all makes an attenuated cadence in A minor—which is the one tonality of all twelve that has never yet been touched in the course of all the six movements.

The relevance of this fact remains obscure, at least to the present writer, who will also confess to misgivings about the meaning of many of the others. He is unable to share the happy confidence of writers like Deryck Cooke in this area, and he is unable to learn much from them since they will not talk about aesthetic relevance. Each individual analyst, I believe, is likely to perceive and value such relationships in his own way. Nevertheless, the shadowy matrix of interrelationships exists; that does not seem arguable. Beethoven was working, on a threshold of perception, toward a new vision of the cyclic whole; critics who want to follow him still find the way hemmed by ambiguity and controversy. (I am speaking of critics who are not disposed to dismiss his effort as merely disjointed.) The ultimate order that he envisaged is perhaps a rather different thing from the provisional order that he established here. As far as I can see, neither has much to do with the deeply instinctual sense of psychological progress that serves to organize the Quartets in E♭ and A minor, and the great majority of earlier compositions. The Quartet in B♭ is a truly radical conception, *the* truly radical work of the third period.

It was also the most rapidly composed of the quartets for Prince Galitzin, though the lengthiest; Beethoven may well have felt in a hurry to complete the long-drawn-out commission. Sketches fall in the months August to November 1825, though some ideas were set down beforehand. It was some time until the first performance, in March 1826. The second and fourth movements were of course much appreciated—wildly applauded—encored. The Finale of course worried everybody: the players, the elite audience, Beethoven's friends, very definitely the publisher, and by implication the composer himself. Before trying to consider his own response, however, we shall do better to take up the works composed while the worry simmered, the Quartets in C♯ minor and F major. Beethoven's renewed attack on the problem of the B♭ Quartet can be properly understood only from the standpoint of the synthesis reached in these new works.

· 4 ·

The Quartet in C♯ minor, composed between November 1825 and July 1826, is the one Beethoven quartet discussed at any length by Sir Donald Tovey. In an essay written on no less signal an occasion than the centennial of the composer's death, "Some Aspects of Beethoven's Art Forms," Tovey proposed to show, with the *Grande Sonate* in B♭, Op. 22, "the uniqueness of this most normal of Beethoven sonatas," and then "the fundamental normality of his most unique work, the Quartet in C sharp minor." [1] In spite of its brevity, the analysis—indeed the whole essay—is one of Tovey's finest. I do not think that "unique" was really the word he wanted—can one really uphold the Quartet in C♯ minor as "more unique" than the B♭? But "normal" very definitely was the word he wanted. Some years later he came to argue the proposition that normality must be the main criterion for art, rather than "originality," "correctness," common sense, or—Tovey's recurring bugbear—any specific theory of harmonic progress. Whatever may be the general merits of the argument, with the Quartet in C♯ minor something very essential certainly seems to be subsumed or capable of being subsumed under a concept of normality.

In what sense is the word to be taken, though? Tovey's Romanes Lecture "Normality and Freedom in Music" does not go far in answering this question, unfortunately. A basic insight is there, but little to probe or refine a concept that might be critically viable. In his delight in and emphasis on a doctor's definition—"We must not confuse the normal with the usual. Only under specially happy conditions is it usual to reach and to maintain the standard which a doctor regards as normal; but this normality is a real and practical standard, not an unattainable theoretical ideal"—Tovey is at his most Victorian, and in the sequel his use of the word is more incanta-

[1] *Essays*, p. 288.

tory than thoughtful. Perhaps this sentence can help: "All art involves conflict. . . . The normal solution of all conflicts will be mutual service, and here alone shall we find perfect freedom." [2] For here is a starting point, however elementary: the uniqueness of this quartet lies exactly in the mutual dependence of its contrasted parts, or as some will prefer to put it, in their organic interrelation. Freedom, normality, and the solution of conflicts may surely be bound up with this. The Quartet in C♯ minor is the most deeply integrated of all Beethoven's compositions; in which respect it stands at the very opposite end of a spectrum from the Quartet in B♭.

An immediate sign of this interrelation is Beethoven's establishment of an express rhythmic continuity through all movements of the work. This counts as an altogether "original" idea—and one that has not been followed much, even in a hundred and fifty years. But Tovey would rightly call it also an altogether "normal" idea, in that it realizes an artistic premise implicit in Beethoven's work from the start. Like all the other novel ideas in this quartet, and there are very many, it seems inevitable and unproblematic once it has been worked out in the composer's own terms. To stress the novelty of his conception, Beethoven actually numbered all the movements "No. 1," "No. 2," and so on, up to seven—as though they were a level series of bagatelles: and he quite terrified the publisher by writing to him in jest that the piece was put together out of plagiarized odds and ends. (The description would apply better to the Quartet in B♭, as Romain Rolland remarked.) But the movements do not really resemble bagatelles, not even No. 3, which consists merely of an 11-bar transition, nor No. 6, a 12-bar tune with plain repeats. The rest are fully rounded independent movements of the traditional sort—this in spite of their unparalleled "mutual service" to one another. As a slow movement and as a scherzo, Nos. 4 and 5 are much more "normal" than the corresponding movements in even so serene a work as Op. 127.

However, Beethoven carefully avoided writing the customary thick double bar between any two of the movements. To be quite precise about it, the players are required to move in strict rhythm from No. 2 to 3, 3 to 4, and 6 to 7, and are required to move directly after a *fermata* note or a *fermata* rest from No. 1 to 2, 4 to 5, and 5 to 6. These *fermata* rests breathe high expectancy; they take next to no time at all. There must be no break of attention, no catching of breath, no coughs or tuning or uncrossing of legs.

[2] *Essays*, p. 183, 184.

At least since Op. 18, the sense of continuity had been growing in Beethoven's cyclic works. What happens now is that the confrontation between the contrasting members becomes explicit; and confrontation—facing—means a start toward resolving the conflicts. Actually the novelty consists only in involving all the parts, for Beethoven had often joined certain selected movements of the cyclic work—generally the last two. Of the eleven quartets from Op. 18, No. 6, to Op. 135, all but three make some such confrontation with the finale, by means of a special link passage to the previous movement or a new slow introduction to the finale. (Even the three other quartets bring in their finales circuitously, that is to say, unstably, off the main key. These are Op. 59, No. 2; Op. 127; and Op. 130 in both versions.)

This sense of continuity in respect to the movements is exactly what raises the main problem with the Quartet in B♭. By contrast, in Op. 131 the intimate facing of the movements extends from the last two members of the cycle back to the middle and to the beginning. Movement No. 1 prepares No. 2 and runs into it as integrally as, say, the *Heiliger Dankgesang* of Op. 132 runs into the section marked *Neue Kraft fühlend.* When No. 2 dies down rather suddenly at the end, it is immediately roused by No. 3, which as a transition ushers in No. 4 with considerable ornament and ceremony. After No. 4, a slow movement of traditional cast, there comes indeed the cleanest break anywhere in the quartet; but No. 5 begins with a special little explosion designed to confront it in a pointed, jocular, ironic fashion—ironic, because the explosion boldly resumes a climactic detail from No. 4 itself. A dramatic gesture leads from No. 5 to No. 6:

Example 162

One can almost hear Beethoven's voice—a deaf man's harsh peremptory shout—commanding an end to this and a new beginning. Indeed, the two sets of octaves have a real operatic flavor, like the orchestral accompaniment to some decisive pronouncement in recitative, some heroic command. Recitative is evoked explicitly in No. 3 and also in No. 6

as it plunges into the Finale. After the Ninth Symphony and the Quartet in A minor, of course, recitative links into a finale were nothing new.

With the movements more integrated rhythmically than ever before, the sequence of keys from one to the next naturally assumes greater sensitivity and greater aesthetic importance. Generally, two main keys suffice for the movements of a classic composition. However the four movements of the "Harp" Quartet, Op. 74, employ—or perhaps the word should be "require"—three different keys, and the six movements of the Quartet in B♭, four. The seven movements of the present quartet employ six. Far from contributing to any suspicion of dissociation, as in the earlier work, this diversity is another sign of the integrative powers that Beethoven brought to bear on the Quartet in C♯ minor. The most profound level on which its coherence is expressed is the perfectly articulated tonal plan supervising all seven movements and every aspect of the work as a whole.

Again Beethoven simply perfected tendencies present in his writing from the beginning. In the quartets starting from Op. 18, No. 3, we have repeatedly seen melodic details projected into structural harmonic features, and these features arching the total cyclic form. In this matter, too, Tovey could well take the Quartet in C♯ minor to expound his paradox of uniqueness and normality.

Certainly there is something schematic, if not perhaps quite rigorous, at work here. The six keys cover almost exhaustively every tonal area that relates directly to the original tonic, C♯ minor; and what is more, even in momentary detail the quartet scarcely ever goes outside that immediate orbit to "indirectly related" key areas. That is a very striking limitation. As usual with Beethoven, this schematic plan is involved with an aesthetic end that is not merely schematic. The tonal exhaustion has something to do—whether as cause or effect I do not think we are permitted to know—with the extraordinary opening of this quartet, not with a movement in sonata form but with a fugue. For it seems clear that under the aesthetic of continuity asserted in so many ways here, the keys of the opening movement are bound to resonate later in the composition. An opening movement in sonata form could only have singled out one or two keys, dramatically stressed and nervously highlighted: the Neapolitan, let us say, plus the sixth degree. But a fugue can (and this one does superbly) map out with dispassionate authority an entire terrain, the whole circumscribed tonal field of the minor mode. Some keys will be slightly less pronounced than others, but in principle all seven related keys are on a par, equal oracles for the future.

In order, the opening Fugue surveys these keys:

i (III) (v) VII VI ♭II i

The less strongly established keys—indicated in parentheses—are the simplest ones, III and v; Beethoven devotes greater care to VI, because the sixth degree is the expressive hinge of the fugue subject, and to the Neapolitan ♭II, because ♭II is the reflection of VI in the fugal answer. Also to VII, on account of the aberrant seventh degree which follows after the Neapolitan in the answer and bends the Fugue in the subdominant direction. Then the seven movements employ the following keys—parentheses now indicating the slighter movements:

No. 1	No. 2	(No. 3)	No. 4	No. 5	(No. 6)	No. 7
i	♭II	(vii)	VI	III	(v)	i

From this scheme the subdominant, iv, is only apparently missing. It will be remembered that both the exposition of the Fugue, No. 1, and the great concluding *stretto* section involve subdominant answers. These throw a serious ambiguity over the entire movement, which is poised half in the tonic, half in the subdominant. An exactly parallel ambiguity shadows the closing movement, too. So the subdominant has its substantial innings.

In view of the new close continuity established by means of rhythm and tonality, it may not be surprising that Beethoven should have taken another unprecedented step—should actually quote or near-quote the main theme of the Fugue, No. 1, in the Finale, No. 7. What a unique, original, sensational stroke *that* was! Even Tovey, who was a great disbeliever in analytical theories of thematic interconnection, called this "an emphatic and unmistakable allusion" of the Finale to the first movement. For a third time, I should be inclined to speak of the originality as a normality, in that it carries through more frankly, and more beautifully, a technical procedure suggested again and again in earlier compositions. Perhaps, indeed, Beethoven here makes "normal" for the first time an artistic device that has hitherto been problematic or tendentious. Perhaps he brings it for the first time to expressive clarity. Tovey might not have wished to put the matter in these terms; for him, there was a clear difference in kind between "an emphatic and unmistakable allusion" and

> long-distance resemblances, where the composer has no means of enforcing his point. . . . I shall never believe that Beethoven in-

> tended the transition passage to B♭ in the first movement of the Ninth Symphony to foreshadow the choral finale which comes three-quarters of an hour afterwards. If he had meant anything by the resemblance, he could have made his meaning clear in the introduction to his finale, where he calls up the ghosts of the previous movements. But here, in the C♯ minor Quartet, he goes out of his way to accentuate his point; the point refers to the very beginning of the work, and not to some transitional passage heard only twice in its course; and not only is the point thus explicable but it has no other explanation.[3]

This has a good common-sensical ring, and the point about the Ninth Symphony may be conceded. But Tovey never committed himself on the subject of more problematic resemblances among movements in, say, the Quartet in B♭. That is hardly the work one would select to demonstrate normality. Does a composer always make his meaning clear?

The difference between a difference of kind and a difference of degree, someone has observed, is one of degree.

· 5 ·

"The lengthy opening Adagio, surely the saddest thing ever said in notes, I would term the awakening on the dawn of a day 'that in its whole long course shall ne'er fulfil one wish, not *one* wish!' " The inner quotation is from *Faust,* the sentence as a whole from another centennial study: *Beethoven,* Richard Wagner's philosophical-cum-historical-cum-nationalistic paean in the year of the fall of Paris. So begins the most famous tribute ever written to the work at hand.[4] It is a curious and not a very satisfactory tribute.

Wagner's frame of reference, of course, causes alarm nowadays. We are likely to prefer Tovey's somewhat overstated disclaimer about his own study: "this essay deals with form, and therefore does not profess to discuss emotional contents." "True form is as inseparable from emotional contents as the plot of a play," but I am under no illusion that the form-analytical plot-scenario at the end of Chapter 9 does any kind of justice to the emotional effect (or content) of this most moving of all

[3] This and later quotations from Tovey are from "Some Aspects of Beethoven's Art Forms," *Essays,* pp. 288–97.
[4] *Prose Works,* V, 97.

fugues. *Molto espressivo,* Beethoven marked it, simply enough, and for many listeners I think it is fair to say that the piece adds a quite special dimension to that term. The Fugue strikes me as less depressed than Wagner evidently felt it: bleak indeed is the beginning, Kareol-bleak, but later there are distinct stirrings of vital energy, and an ethereal vision unmatched even at the serene high point of Tristan's "Delirium." Was Wagner especially taken by the insidious chromaticism of Beethoven's first few lines? This chromaticism cedes gradually to a clearer harmonic palette. Bleaker yet is the matchless place where the canons on A and D turn to the dominant for the resolving section of *strettos* beneath the grieving diminution figure. Yet strength, not grief, is the final impression conveyed by the great authoritative cello augmentation and, ten bars from the end, by those open-string B♯'s. They plumb still another element in the fertile well of continuous, quiet variation. Everything has been encompassed—every tonality, every thematic implication, every harmonic nuance—yet an infinity is kept in reserve. The sense of *grip* at the end of the Fugue seems to me dominant. This is a piece effortlessly in control of itself and effortlessly in control of its limited universe of tonal materials. The resoultion, the encompassment, the effortlessness, the control—surely that is enough fulfillment for any one day's wish.

However this may be, it is a fact that the Fugue changes or evolves in feeling more radically than would have been anticipated from its placid exposition. Its universe may be described as limited, because the conflicts of the sonata world lie outside its scope, but as Tovey pointed out, it "has subtle signs that it is part of a work in sonata style, though the hard dramatic facts of that style are not allowed to disturb its quiet flow." Among these signs are the heavy dominant preparation for the resolving *stretto* section; the ethereal two-part canonic episode; the whole exploratory dynamic of continuous harmonic variation; and the binding memory of subdominant and Neapolitan tropism. The great machine comes to a perfect rest on bearings that are frictionless, but only a feather stroke is required to reactivate the modulatory momentum.

The end slows down into a single note, C♯, meditating and then rising very quietly up the octave. This octave has the amazing quality of distilling and resolving the opening upward 3rd leap of the fugue subject. After a *fermata,* it is answered just as quietly by a rising octave D—and the new movement has begun in D major, the Neapolitan key that was so important in the Fugue. The theme of the *Allegro molto vivace* dances delicately over an unsubstantial pedal, but the crux of C♯–D is unshakably planted.

Example 163

Tovey's scenario for the second movement deserves quotation at some length.

> The rising octave, a semitone higher, begins a lively self-repeating eight-bar tune, pianissimo. . . . The viola repeats the tune, which the violin resumes at the fifth bar and continues with another eight bars that overlap into a new theme, evidently destined to be a transition theme. We are unquestionably moving in sonata style and have left the fugue behind us. Now what will become of the sonata form in these extraordinary circumstances? From the fact that the movement is in this strange key, we may expect that it will not modulate very widely, for fear of losing its bearing or damaging its special key-colour by reminding us of the C♯ minor which is so firmly established by that great and solemn fugue as the key of the whole work. Again, the development of a sonata-form movement is bound to be argumentative: and here again the fugue has forestalled us. Accordingly this D-major movement, which has started with a rondo-like tune, sets out at bar 24 with a highly organized transition theme which expands until at bar 44, having overshot A major (the dominant), it finds itself poised on a chord of C sharp major, dangerously near the key of the fugue.

The danger, it may be added, is increased by a repeated motif harping on the crux notes C♯–D–C♯.

> After a pause the situation is saved by the bold stroke of playing the first theme again actually in E, the dominant of the dominant. This is "dominant preparation" with a vengeance; and four more bars lead safely into A major, where (at bar 60) a lively second subject begins. But it behaves like the second subjects of Beethoven's rondos and allied types of finale, and soon shows a hankering for the tonic and for a return to the first theme. At bar 84 the theme does return. . . .

Two points specially interested Tovey: that the second movement introduces the quartet at last to "the hard dramatic facts of the sonata style," and that it does so nonetheless in a decidedly restrained fashion. The piece can be categorized as a "sonata form without development," for what happens now is simply a tonic return of all the previous material. (In this quartet, real sonata form *with* development is being saved—for the Finale.) And although this *Allegro molto vivace* adopts many of the simple habits of a rondo finale—but its form stays simpler than that of any respectable Beethoven rondo—intrinsically it has more the personality of a scherzo or dance movement. It is a nearly monomotivic or monorhythmic piece, the first and second subjects and the transition theme all moving in much the same dancing rhythms. Indeed, the 4ths of the transition theme derive from a detail right in the middle of the first theme (see p. 332—a detail that disguises the underlying "doublet" structure of that theme). The dominant gait ceases only at the danger spot which skirts C♯. This near-*perpetuum mobile* feels more like a curiously gentle scherzo than an opening sonata-allegro, even one of the most lyric persuasion.

The lack of serious modulation, contrast, or development, and the whole rhythmic situation, contribute to one underlying quality: flatness. The Fugue is flat in its own way, the way of all fugues; the *Allegro* is flat in another way. Contrast was a touchy matter because the piece could not risk "losing its bearings or damaging its special key-colour"—the key-color on which its very life and character depend. The matter can also be considered otherwise. Dissatisfaction with the dynamic of sonata form had caused Beethoven to deflect or undermine it, in one fashion or another, in such opening movements as those of Op. 127, 132, and 130. Finally he has come to the point of dropping sonata form altogether for the opening large statement. But there remained a fundamental need for conflict to fructify the work as a whole—to get it, as it were, off the ground. Conflict could not come out of the Fugue, nor does it come out of the *Allegro* (though that might have been arranged: then the Fugue would have shared the same key as the *Allegro* and sounded like its slow introduction). Instead the conflict comes *between* movements that are "flat" in themselves—between the deliberate *Adagio* tread of the Fugue and the ephemeral dance of the *Allegro*, and particularly between the tonalities of C♯ minor and D. The whole idea was only made possible by the new sense of continuity posited by the Quartet in C♯ minor. Every aspect of this amazing work serves mutually with every other.

A brief but surprisingly strong coda flares up in octaves built on the transition theme with the 4ths. (This theme had been skipped in the recapitulation.) *Fortissimo* is indicated for the first time in the quartet; then everything dies down abruptly. Just as the Fugue had its subtle signs of belonging to a larger work, so the present movement too, in its coda, hints to the future. In fact the coda is echoed at a later point in the quartet. The *Allegro molto vivace* might almost be conceived of as an independent movement within some less continuous matrix—almost, but for the coda.

One gropes, again, for a way to characterize this movement—at once so straightforward and so strange, at once lucid and elusive, with its evaporating octaves everywhere and its pedals (even the second theme has a superior pedal), its shimmering rhythms and its dreamlike false security in the Neapolitan region. Wagner got hold of quite a jelly: "The inward eye then traces the consoling vision (*Allegro* $\frac{6}{8}$), perceptible by it alone, in which that longing becomes a sweet but plaintive playing with itself: the image of the inmost dream takes waking form as a loveliest remembrance." For the next movement, No. 3, he had a slightly better idea: "And now (with the short transitional *Allegro moderato*) 'tis as if the master, grown conscious of his art, were settling to work at his magic. . . ." At first square and humdrum, the *Allegro moderato* turns deliberate and ceremonial in a warm *Adagio* recitative which seems indeed bent on settling down to business. The evanescent quality must be dispelled, so that the slow movement, No. 4, can have its feet firmly on the ground. Another purpose for the transitional movement, I believe, is to forestall the clear dominant relationship that would otherwise obtain between No. 2, in D major, and No. 4, in A. Dominant relationship is being saved for a later juncture. No. 3 manages to make the lyric slow movement sound subdominant—as is, indeed, most "normal."

The voice is direct and unconstrained. In the variation tune, lyricism unfolds with perfect freedom, simplicity, and certainty. I suggested that we identify this tune—this was on page 213—as a sister of the variation melody of the Quartet in E♭, Op. 127: a younger sister, less soulful and serious-minded. She is Dorabella rather than Fiordiligi, *Andante* rather than *Adagio*. Perhaps she wears a species of Mona Lisa smile, like the doublet tune of the *Allegro molto vivace* before her. The lyric quality is popular in the best sense of the word, and captures Beethoven's aspiration perfectly: "*ohne Kunstgepräng' erklungen*," as the poet says in

An die ferne Geliebte, art without the adornments of Art, the illusion of art concealing art.

The movement as a whole has less need to be weighty, for unlike Op. 127 (or Op. 132), this quartet locates its center of gravity not in the middle but in the end. Consequently these variations avoid modulation entirely; even the tune avoids establishing the dominant between its two simple strains. The variations give the impression of a brilliantly diverse series of revelations, a chain with the heaviest link at Variation 6, the hymn-variation. Such an order differs radically from the architectural design of the modulating variations of Op. 127. Like every other movement in Op. 131 before the Finale, this *Andante* has its special restraint, its special flatness, its special responsibility to the larger organism.

Variation 1 holds motivically to the tune and keeps its original meter and tempo. It ornaments the tune in a mood of continuous free burgeoning characteristic also of Variation 4 (and of the early variations in Op. 127). Variation 2, *Più mosso*, evokes another of those rustic dances that keep flashing through Beethoven's late compositions; A major was his particular rustic key. Here the opening motif turns into a new figure involving an upward 4th, and the end of the dance burgeons with surprising strength into an octave passage based on this figure. The flaring up and the melodic contour involving the 4th both recall the coda of the *Allegro molto vivace*, No. 2.

Variation 3 recalls the ethereal two-part canonic episode of the opening Fugue—though with very mixed feelings, in a very strange frame of mind. Now Beethoven treats the repeated strains of the variation tune rigorously; there is no free burgeoning at all. Each strain consists of an unaccompanied two-part canon at the 2nd between cello and viola; then in the repetition of each strain, while another pair of instruments has the identical canon, new contrapuntal material is added by the instruments left over. In the repetition of strain 1, the new material amounts to a quaint *cantus firmus* underpinning the canon. In strain 2, the new material is generated in 3rds and 10ths out of the canonic lines themselves, which appear to have been contrived in simultaneous invertible double counterpoint at the 10th and 12th, more or less. It is the old schoolroom smell, once again—but perfumed in a quite indescribable way. Beethoven's description is *Andante moderato e lusinghiero*, that is, seductively or coaxingly. Curious coaxing, with those carping trills and *sfp*'s and hair-raising dissonant clashes in the repeated second strain.

Tovey pointed out a very interesting parallel between this canonic variation and the canonic *Benedictus* in the *Missa solemnis*.

The next two variations form a contrasted pair. Variation 4 ornaments the tune as lushly as possible, and with new solemn grace determined by the *Adagio* $\frac{6}{8}$ time. Between the strains, double-counterpoint inversion is manipulated beautifully; the off-beats are shot through with great sonorous repeated-note *pizzicatos*. The next link in the chain, an *Allegretto*, is a liquidation variation *par excellence*, like the final variation of the "Harp" Quartet, Op. 74. Under its shifting $\frac{2}{4}$ syncopations, melody and ornament wither almost completely into a mere harmonic skeleton of the tune. This variation handles the repetitions of the strains most mechanically; strain 2 is simply marked with repeat marks.

Variation 6, on the other hand, treats the repetitions of the strains most dramatically—which is quite a paradox, in view of the fact that this is the hymn-variation and undoubtedly the spiritual center of the entire quartet. The first strain bespeaks earnest contemplation, not drama, with its long series of absolutely even note-against-note quarters. One almost thinks of the *Heiliger Dankgesang* of Op. 132. The elementary texture is sprung apart and strained in a remarkable way, with thick sounds in the lower instruments and the melody soaring in the very ether above. As in other slow movements of this period, Beethoven gets a characteristic serene quality by undermining the subdominant harmony. However, at the repetition of the first strain the tune is moved up in

Example 164

register as though expressly to accommodate a striking new sixteenth-note figure in the low cello. Doubtless something was needed to forestall rhythmic monotony, but this muttering figure assumes a great deal more responsibility than that. The cautionary indication *non troppo marcato* is soon forgotten, as the extraordinary sound rasps furiously at the very beginning of the second strain and, during repetition of the second strain, erupts up into the melody itself. For a moment the harmony contorts itself violently. An unforgettable dramatic note of menace is introduced into the atmosphere of prayer.

An extra bar of transition, and there follows a "half-variation," running through the first 8-bar strain only, without repeat. It bears the seed of its own incompletion, for each of the instruments in turn seems to play a little improvisatory cadenza; the improvisatory tone not unnaturally breaks the variation down into glowing trills.—Now all six (or six and a half) variations have by design avoided not only modulation but even change of mode from A major to A minor. As though in compensation for this lack, Beethoven brings four bars of the tune as a rather tentative *Allegretto* in C major, so that C♮ and F♮, the two distinguishing notes of the key of A minor, can at least put in an appearance. The coda thus initiated soon brings the same nervous *allegretto* fragment in F major, dissolving into further cadenza work for the first violin. As Tovey says, these *allegretto* passages make "the only modulatory purple patch in the whole quartet, by going outside the circle of directly related keys" (related to C♯ minor). The purpose of the second passage, I believe, is not only to balance the C-major purple, but also to maneuver into a position from which the note A can be highlighted:

Example 165

As the third degree of F major, A is repeated as in bar 4 of the tune—and then repeated seven more times with increasing excitement. This anticipates the celebrated final gesture of the movement, which again introduces F♮ as preface to a repeated A in high, ethereal *pizzicatos. Ma semplice:*

Example 166

The repeated A echoes back over the whole extent of this wonderful *Andante*. The tune itself had a tendency to repeat notes: see bars, 2, 3, 4, 5, 9, 17–18, 19–20, and so on (p. 213). During the original statement of the tune, the cello, playing *pizzicato* for the first time in the quartet, worked out a repeated-note figure of its own by way of accompaniment. A more insistent repeated-note accompaniment underlies Variation 2. *Pizzicato* repeated chords and repeated notes clangorously punctuate Variation 4. Note-repetition is at the heart of the conception of the climactic hymn-variation, No. 6.

And I take it, too, that the jocular contradiction of the *Andante* by the next movement, shown in the example above, echoes back to the unforgettable cello figure in that climactic variation. The jocularity is helped by the square dominant relation, E major after A.

The E-major *Presto*, No. 5, is perhaps the most childlike of all Beethoven scherzos. You could say that the *Alla danza Tedesca* of the B♭ Quartet runs it a close second (though of course it cannot quite qualify as a scherzo); if its main dance does even less in the way of phrase structure than the main dance of the *Presto*, with the two trios there is certainly little to choose between the bare repetitions of the *Tedesca* and the giddy folk medley of the present *Presto*. This medley was discussed and illustrated on page 201. Furthermore the *Scherzo* is quite innocent of that subtle play of texture, rhythm, and dynamics that gives a special air of refined parody to the *Alla danza Tedesca* and to most other movements of this type. There is really very little "refinement" about it; it is Beethoven's most childlike scherzo in his most mature and complex work of art.

Considered as a separate entity, the piece would have to be judged faceless, if pleasant. But it cannot be so considered; it plays its special role in the total drama of the C♯-minor Quartet. Beethoven brought himself to make a genuine resting point in the total journey, a moment (but a timeless moment) of play before the *Adagio* in G♯ minor will lead back to concerns broached by the opening Fugue. Contrast is minimized to the extent that the trio follows in the same key and tempo as the *Scherzo* proper, and uses much the same motivic material. And besides this negative role, it has a positive one: as may well be supposed, the *Presto* is integrated harmonically into the total scheme. Its main (almost its only) modulations or passing modulations single out iii (G♯) and IV (A)—A major is the key of the preceding *Andante*, No. 4, and G♯ minor is the key of the coming *Adagio*, No. 6. In the terse lament of No. 6, furthermore, the step A–G♯ emerges very subtly, triggering a world of recollection in the Finale.

(What will be recollected is the Neapolitan crux D–C♯ of the first and second movements, and acting as an upper reflection of this, the step A–G♯ will inspire much of the thematic material of the Finale, No. 7. Indeed, the configuration D–C♯–A–G♯ could be said to function more seriously in this quartet than the set B♯–C♯–A–G♯ which Bekker and others want us to carry over in the ear from Op. 132. For what it is worth, the first important notes of the variation tune happen to be A G♯ D C♯—or, remembering the repeated notes, A A G♯ G♯ D D C♯ C♯.)

G♯ and A are almost the only modulations in the whole *Presto*, though in addition the *Scherzo* does approach the plain dominant, B major. When it gets there, it fusses inordinately, slows down, expostulates with this key and persuades it (against its better judgment) to try being G♯. This little comedy forms, in fact, the one element of diversion in the *Scherzo*—the one deflection from a dancelike regularity comparable to that of the *Alla danza Tedesca*. Like a child repeating a joke, Beethoven makes us go through the process five times identically—for the full alternation scheme is

Scherzo	Trio	Scherzo	Trio	Scherzo	(Trio)	(Scherzo)
with repeat				with repeat		

The third *Scherzo* changes dynamics to include a lot more *pianissimo*, and after the trio in parentheses (a mere recollection of 14 bars), the last *Scherzo* in parentheses rushes to a stop in an astounding passage of *pianissimo sul ponticello* writing for all the instruments, mostly on their highest strings. Was this a sound Beethoven had actually heard, back in the days when he was hearing, or did he *make up* the sound for the first time in 1826? Beethoven deaf was quite capable of "hearing" or imagining or inventing not only relationships between notes but also sonorities pure and simple.

The instruments conclude in abrupt octaves on E and G♯—functional notes (p. 327). Reproachfully the viola begins a beautiful mourning song in G♯ minor, *Adagio quasi un poco andante*, the miniscule movement No. 6. For a moment the simplicity of the tune and its unabashed emotionality suggest a new *cavatina*. (There is a real parallel between the large ending sequence of the Quartets in B♭ and C♯ minor: the childlike dance or scherzo, the heartfelt song, and the concluding statement of unprecedented intensity—unprecedented, that is to say, in terms of the piece so far.) However, the present tune is probably too slight to make a real *cavatina* or a full movement of any sort. A most interesting detail in the articulation of its tiny *a a b a b a* form (with everything in 4-bar members) concerns the gradual introduction of Neapolitan harmony into the cadences of the successive *a* phraselets. The first of them (p. 327) has no such flavor, but in bar 9 the Neapolitan A♮ is substituted as a passing note for the normal second degree A♯; in bar 17, A♮ appears also on the first beat, as an inner voice right in the harmony; and in bar 25, A♮ is tellingly reiterated. Then in bar 27 the Neapolitan A-major triad

Example 167

comes frankly in root position. The rich sonorities here begin to suggest the opening Fugue. The harmony swings decisively toward C♯ minor and the Finale.

> At this point [says Tovey] we must survey the keys which have been heard in the course of the work. The fugue may be taken to have established C♯ minor with a firmness beyond the power of any mere introduction. The "allegro molto vivace" was then able to maintain itself in D major, the flat supertonic, but could not venture far afield, and so had a finale-like second subject that speedily returned to its tonic. The slow movement, in A major, was confined to the key of its theme. . . . The scherzo was confined to E major and A major.
>
> Now, at last, in the introduction to the finale we have heard the dominant of C♯ minor. And now at last it will be, at all events theoretically, possible to cover a wide range of key and have some expansive and argumentative development.

In other words, the point has come at last for Beethoven's most characteristic, "normal" musical process: a movement in sonata form. The whole ingenious scheme of the quartet has been leading up to this. The Finale crowns the composition in practically every way: in force of expression, intellectual intensity, breadth of action, and integrative power over the composition as a whole.

At a number of not unexposed places in the present study, finales have certainly seemed to be causing trouble. I have gone so far as to postulate a "problem of the finale" in Beethoven—with scant warrant, some readers may have felt like complaining. The best I can offer by way of warrant is the Finale of the Quartet in C♯ minor, which provides a standard of what a finale can be and do. If we keep the notion of a "problem," it is Beethoven's most nearly perfect solution; if we do not, it simply ranks as his greatest finale. Success was achieved, furthermore, under the particularly severe conditions of mutual service posited by this particular work of art—so that the Finale has to deal not only with its own conflicts but also, more richly than ever before, with those of the quartet as a whole. This double task (which Beethoven had just invented for himself) was met magnificently by the movement at hand.

The piece is also in some sense Beethoven's most "normal" finale. For all its strenuousness, it altogether lacks strain—the strain evident in many an impressive concluding statement in Beethoven: among the quartets, in the Great Fugue and in the half-fugal Finale of the C-major "Razumovsky" Quartet. (I should also like to add here, *sotto voce*, the Finale of the very first quartet, D major, Op. 18, No. 3.) Beethoven has arranged things here so that he can strike frankly with his best weapons —themes in strong contrast and in arresting juxtaposition, exciting modulations, "expansive and argumentative development," triumphant returns, and great summary codas. Sonata form is treated without rigidity and yet (what is rare in finales) with full emphasis and amplitude—with perfect freedom, Tovey could say. There is no more flatness, but instead the sharpest head-on confrontation of ideas. After a series of experiences rather carefully muted in sentiment, the Finale rends all through Beethoven's formidable range of violence and passion.

In fact, the mood of the C♯-minor Finale heightens and purifies the famous C-minor mood of Beethoven's early years. The great accomplishment lies in preserving all the force and innocence and heroic thrust while discounting any suspicion of overextension of feeling. When Beethoven finally rises to the pretensions of the C-minor mood, they are no longer pretensions. This is another index of the essential normality of the Quartet in C♯ minor.

The very aspect of the main theme seems to look back twenty years to the days of defiance after the Heiligenstadt Testament. In mood and in specific technical detail, it resembles the finale theme of the E-minor

Example 168

"Razumovsky" Quartet. But in the earlier time, Beethoven with all his attainment could never have constructed such an admirably tensile instrument. There are two rhythmic motifs and four 4-bar phrases—Phrase A using the first (anapaestic) motif, and Phrase B, C, and D using the second (iambic) motif in two configurations, one going up and the other going down:

	up down	up down	down down	down down
A_i	B_i	C_v	D_{-i}	$D'_{(N)}$

The real life of this scheme, as is implied by the subscript numbers on the diagram, comes from the pistol-shot modulation to the dominant in Phrase C, and from the balasting turn to the Neapolitan degree in the repetition of Phrase D (D′). Phrase A, it has often been observed, resumes the note-set of the subject of the opening Fugue, namely 5–7–8–6–5. More particularly, Phrases B and D as well as A stress the sixth degree and the step 6–5, A–G♯. This has been specifically foreshadowed by the three preceding movements.

What has not been foreshadowed is the violence of the main theme, its pent-up emotion, its wildness. This is new to the quartet—yet conceivably it *has* been hinted at, by the savage little link between movements Nos. 5 and 6 (p. 327. In one sense No. 6 amounts to a digression, for the link could have led directly into No. 7; Phrase A has something of its same angry, operatic gestural quality.) In Phrases B, C, and D, the abruptness of Phrase A is steadied into the harsh driving of both theme and accompaniment. This violence Beethoven rationalizes into the total conception by means of extraordinary braking action in Phrase D′: the catch in the rhythm, the *piano*, the *legato*, the pathetic turn to the Neapolitan. The Neapolitan recalls the first movement of the quartet in a sudden flash of memory—and there immediately follows a new theme, still in the tonic, which confirms the memory. Without duplicating the original fugue subject, this theme retraces its line, performs a sort of inversion or transformation upon it, and thrusts it deeply into the present action.

In feeling, however, the new theme greatly simplifies the rich *espressivo* of the Fugue into pathos, by means of its innocent doublet construction, its augmented-2nd steps, and its inverted *strettos* which haunt the cadences (see p. 203). Until the coda, this new doublet theme acts as a check or corrective to the turbulence of the Finale. Here at the beginning, after the doublet is duly (if loosely) repeated, the turbulent main theme returns to do the office of a bridge:

	up down	down down	down
A_i	C_v	$D_{-i^6_4}$	D′ canons→

Phrase A adopts a continuous iambic rhythm as accompaniment, thus smoothing over its own disruptive energy. With modulation in mind, Beethoven omits Phrase B; he undercuts the tonic "return" in Phrase D by means of a $^6_4$ chord; and he uses the repetition of Phrase D (D′) to run right in to modulatory canons. These lead very abruptly to the second key, E major, III.

The contrast is little short of unnerving; the E-major theme is lyric innocence itself. Four times in dialogue, the upper instruments repeat the same 4-bar phrase—only it sounds like a 2-bar fragment in double-slow tempo because the harmony changes only once every two bars. Beethoven is really dealing with a sharp confrontation of *allegro* and *adagio* sections, comparable to that in the opening movements of the Quartets in E♭, A minor, and B♭. The fragment itself consists of a great scooping downward scale, recouped by a positively Straussian upward leap into a *ritardando.* The sense is again of an evocation of the human voice, though in a more personal context than that of conventional opera as Beethoven knew it.

Four *ritardandos*—what a comment upon the Dionysian frenzy which the iambic motif seemed to be working up for the movement as a whole! Marked and often systematic *ritardandos* are a feature of all the main movements of the quartet except the Fugue. A pathetic continuation modulates as abruptly as ever to F♯ minor for a full-scale return of the main theme. In the abruptness of all its transitions, this Finale brings to mind the Quartet in F minor, Op. 95, though the characteristic quirkiness of that composition has been—again—somehow normalized.

A full-scale thematic return at this point certainly follows no standard formal prescription; it gives the movement something of the character of a rondo. Yet the key of this return—the subdominant, F♯ minor —would be as out of place in a traditional rondo as in a traditional sonata-form movement. For all that, its serves perfectly here. The theme assumes almost its original form, up to the point at which Phrase D′ gathers a whole-note *cantus-firmus* scale accompaniment and launches into stormy developmental action:

Example 169

A double *fugato* emerges, quite strict except for the fact that the answer comes in the subdominant: the very same anomaly as in the Fugue of the opening movement of the quartet. After four entries, the *fugato* bows to the inevitable and swings to the subdominant of F♯, B minor. Two more entries—there are no episodes—bring the total up to 24 bars of rising whole-notes for the *cantus firmus;* if we allow Beethoven octave transposition, he has stomped up a scale extending for almost three octaves (including, by the way, some fine augmented-2nd steps). And the scale lands him on D, the crucial Neapolitan degree. First treated as the third degree of B minor, D soon becomes a temporary tonic in its own right.

Only so strong a paroxysm as Phrase A could halt the huge scale; and once introduced, the anapaestic rhythm of Phrase A now supplies material for the rest of the development. Modulations follow the circle of 5ths: B–E–A–D–G♯ laying ground for the tonic key, C♯ minor. All this seems normal enough. But the plan also happens to correspond with that of the opening Fugue, from the point of its strong B-minor entry through the A-major and D-major two-part episodes to the same irregular culminating turn of the wheel from Neapolitan to dominant, D–G♯.

As in the Fugue, a comparatively extended passage of dominant preparation precedes the return. But the passage here is an immensely dynamic one, employing in fact a favorite device of Beethoven's most ambitious sonata and symphony movements of the second period, a thematic breakdown. Everything collapses away except dominant harmony, which shudders themelessly up and down from *piano* to *pianissimo* for nine bars before exploding, in another three, to the recapitulation.

The recapitulation, too, revives a tradition from Beethoven's earlier symphonic writing, the expanded, triumphant return. Only the Ninth

Example 170

Symphony can match this place for power and conviction. In the nature of the case, such returns work best with an orchestra handy; among the string quartets they occur only in two of the earliest pieces, Op. 18, Nos.

2 and 3, and in one of the most symphonic, the E-minor "Razumovsky" Quartet. Yet I think it would never occur to a listener to notice the absence of orchestral forces in the C♯-minor Quartet, the return is so shattering. Beethoven rewrites the theme radically, the texture being thickened and complicated almost beyond belief. Phrases C and D′ are omitted entirely—because the turn to v in Phrase C would have disturbed the required stability, and the turn to ♭II in Phrase D′ would have anticipated the really functional turn to the Neapolitan coming up. Instead, a new Phrase B′ appears as a complement to Phrase B, both of them rocking back and forth over a new thundering *cantus firmus* three whole-notes long. The tremendous distension of texture is not only a matter of this *cantus firmus*, which migrates methodically up through the four instruments, and of the steely violin trill held over from the retransition. In addition, the anapaestic motif rings through all the spaces in Phrase A—along with the iambic—and in Phrase B the upward iambic motif mirrors itself in contrary motion:

		up down	up down	up down	up down
		down	*down*	*down*	*down*
A_i	A_i	B_i	B'_i	B_i	B'_i

Both the new *cantus firmus* and the trill stress the notes 6–5 once again.

Wagner's characterization seems to apply, if at all, best at this point: "the dance of the whole world itself: wild joy, the wail of pain, love's transport, utmost bliss, grief, frenzy, riot, suffering; the lightning flickers, thunders growl: and above it the stupendous fiddler who bans and bends it all, who leads it haughtily from whirlwind into whirlpool, to the brink of the abyss. . . ."

After such a return, there is something deeply and doubly pathetic about the entrance of the doublet theme—the theme which recalls the Fugue—not in the tonic key but in the subdominant. And it is the mighty grasp of the new 3-note *cantus firmus* that has turned it in the new direction. A shorter analogue to the original bridge slips headlong in the flat direction, in preparation for Beethoven's most sensational coup, recapitulation of the second subject in the Neapolitan tonality. To quote Tovey for the last time:

> The wheel has come full circle. The whole quartet is a perfect unity, governed by the results of the initial event of that modified first movement [No. 2] which maintained itself in the flat supertonic after the opening fugue had firmly established the key of C♯ minor.

> Hence the restraint in the matter of modulation, even in the Finale, where Beethoven was free to expand in argumentative development. His power of modulation is really unsurpassed even by Wagner, but this fact is generally ignored or disbelieved, because the occasions on which Beethoven exercises the power in any obvious way are very rare.

The maintenance of the *Allegro molto vivace* in D major was made possible by the Neapolitan thrust of the Fugue; Neapolitan harmony has reasserted itself in movement No. 6 and at various points in the Finale—already in Phrase D′ of the exposition and in the goal key of the development section. Lest there be any doubt as to the significance of the D-major color at this recapitulation of the second theme, Beethoven almost immediately juxtaposes it with C♯ major and with the lyric second theme again. It is not hard to rehear—it is hard not to rehear—the octave C♯ and the octave D linking movements Nos. 1 and 2. There are still superb Neapolitan touches to come in the admirably drafted coda.

This section does not return to the main theme as a whole, only to individual phrases and motifs, but it does bring the doublet theme again, safely home in C♯ minor. The theme bursts right out of its doublet shell, in such a way as to clarify even further its reference to the fugue subject:

Example 171

Compare bars 290–1, for example, with bars 26–7 on page 299. But Beethoven's idea here was not simply to clinch a point with Tovey. In the recapitulation, as in the exposition, the doublet theme was a pathetic shadow of the past thrown like a cautionary restraint over the strenuous, passionate assertions of the Finale. In the coda, at last, restraint is thrown aside—from within. Even the Fugue joins the dance with Wagner's *ungeheuer Spielmann.* Beethoven even offers to trace the derivation of the driving iambic rhythm from the first notes of the doublet theme in diminution (that is, from the fugue subject ultimately); a tall story, which will be credited only in the rapture of the moment.

Between rapture and pathos, between the extremes of exaltation and tragic grief, the coda rages back and forth from one matchless inspiration to another. This inversion of the development *fugato*, for instance:

Example 172

The penultimate cry of strength from the upward iambic motif—which has always been rather overshadowed by the downward motif—coincides with the strongest *cantus firmus* yet. The tied whole-note is adamant. The dynamics here look like the Great Fugue, and indeed much of the same intensity burns in both of these late quartet finales, though in this one the conflagration is much more sternly under control. A themeless *non ligato* scale in D major transfixes the Neapolitan harmony. A poignant extension of the doublet theme runs down the scale to a hush preparing this last idea:

Example 173

The new 3-note *cantus firmus* of the recapitulation is quenched back to a 4th instead of its original powerful 6th. It shuffles to a halt in an *ostinato* (sevenfold!), along with remnants of the downward iambic motif and the anapaestic motif together.

Meanwhile the whole scene clouds over ambiguously with subdominant harmony; and this ambiguity simply provides the last great binding force of organic interrelation. For from the moment it suffered its answer in the subdominant, the opening Fugue was similarly clouded. In both movements, subdominant bias accords with the functional emphasis on the Neapolitan, and also with the unusual prominence of the seventh degree, B. (Choice of B minor for movement No. 3 formed a definite part of Beethoven's total integrative scheme.) The ultimate page of the quartet finds itself poised half in the tonic, half in the subdominant —until six bars sweep up five octaves in still another abrupt gesture of assertion. The question is closed; and with it the seven movements complete their perfect mutual trajectory.

So closes the quartet which, if Karl Holz is to be believed, Beethoven finally said was the greatest of his last compositions. Like any composer, he did not much like the inquiry. Which was the greatest? "Each in its way. Art demands of us that we shall not stand still. . . ."

"You will find a new manner of voice treatment," Beethoven is supposed to have added, "and thank God there *is less lack of fancy than ever before*."[5] Holz's reply is not recorded, but if there was one occasion when that cool, irrepressible character ever allowed himself to be awed by the great man to whom he had attached himself, this should have been it. "*An Phantasie fehlts, Gottlob, weniger als je zuvor.*" Less lack of fancy. That is an understatement to leave us all speechless.

[5] Thayer, p. 982.

11

BEETHOVEN IN 1826

Quartet in F Major, Op. 135

Beethoven was fifty-five. He had just recently moved into the last of his very many apartments, on the third floor of the *Schwarzspanierhaus* in the Alsergrund district of Vienna. There he composed the whole of the Quartet in C♯ minor, and there he spent the last year of that disarray which, with Beethoven, passed for ordinary living. There, at the end, he was tapped and drained and physicked and hayseed-bathed and narcotized with Rhine wine and frozen punch. Snow lay outside the house as he died, his fist clenched and raised against a great violent spring thunderstorm. Truth can sometimes be more romantic than fiction.

In music—in the string quartet in these last years—Beethoven ordered what he was so pitifully unable to order in any other aspect of his existence. Outside of his art, the disarray of his life was practically total, extending to objects, appearances, dealings with the world of affairs, and human relationships both deep and superficial. The mess in his rooms was legendary, in spite of the presence of live-in servants and solicitous friends. His appearance was such that to be seen on the streets with him was an embarrassment; there is a story about him unwittingly causing a cattle stampede. In the area of ordinary dealings or arrangements, he had learned to rely heavily on one special friend or famulus who relieved him of responsibilities. This person would take care of matters ranging from multiplication sums and the procurement of pens, fish, and medicines, to negotiations with publishers (under Beethoven's eye) and withdrawals from the cumbersome banking system of those days. He stood ready to accompany the composer on his tavern journeys; he was expected to offer continual practical advice, which was very frequently ignored. This role was now filled by a young man in his twenties, Karl Holz, a minor government official who was also a keen musical amateur. As Holz was then serving as second violinist of the Schuppanzigh Quartet, he was closely involved with Beethoven's artistic life as well. Thayer characterizes him as a "cheery companion" and a man of some sense and backbone, if not perhaps of any overdue sensitivity.

Beethoven enjoyed company, and would appear to have been a fascinating person to visit or have a drink with. But one entered into personal relations with him only at the price of suspicion, exploitation, and ill-treatment. His paranoiac tendencies really passed the bounds that can be ascribed, conventionally, to deafness. Actually Holz suffered less on this account than most of Beethoven's associates, such as the tenacious Anton Schindler, who resumed the office of famulus when Holz retired to get married. If Beethoven's gallery of friends contains few appetizing portraits, the reason is that few self-respecting people who were not obliged to deal with him chose to put up with his demands and his lack of consideration. They simply drifted away after a time. A special category of persons was constrained to deal with him, the publishers; and as is only too well known, Beethoven's dealings with publishers were often less than frank or even honest. To be sure, most (not all) of the publishers were hardened to this, and kept pressing him for contracts to the very end.

Something else was involved here, of course: money. Unquestionably Beethoven had solid grounds for financial worries. Not to speak of the scars of an impoverished childhood, he was obviously unfitted for a salaried post and could live only from his pen; illness was a spectre. He had seen the annuity given him by Princes Kinsky and Lobkowitz and Archduke Rudolph wither away, and he had shivered through the panic of 1825. Nonetheless, his attitudes and actions concerning money assume an obsessive, irrational quality that is not contradicted by other traits of his personality. The same financial neurosis that seems to be revealed by his business dealings appears in the way he was now doling out the allowance for his nineteen-year-old nephew, Karl, and spying on his every purchase. Then the preoccupation of his last weeks was accumulating cash in order to keep his bank shares untouched as a legacy for Karl. It seems likely that as he saw Karl striving for independence, he thought subconsciously of holding on to him by this pecuniary means.

Karl was of course another person who was constrained to deal with Beethoven, his legal guardian. Beethoven's emotional attachment to his "son," as he always called him ("adopted son," on more formal occasions), was not only inordinately deep, but also the only commitment he now cared about—the only one left for him to care about. His monumental inability to order his own passion in this matter led by slow, harrowing steps to disaster. The relationship very nearly killed Karl, who in this year attempted to put a couple of bullets through his head; and though he recovered, it may very well be said to have killed Beethoven. Schindler said as much, and Drs. Editha and Richard Sterba also speak quite directly of "the long tragedy of love which the great master underwent with his nephew and which finally killed him." [1]

Their detailed reconstruction of the relationship, which forms the heart of their psychoanalytical study *Beethoven and his Nephew*, can be abstracted here very briefly. They make the case that Beethoven's irrational possessiveness toward his brothers (which was attended by great hostility to both their wives) transferred itself perforce to the nine-year-old nephew who was left his ward in 1815. He worked himself into a barely sane lather of hatred against the mother, who was the joint guardian, sank himself in litigation to gain the sole guardianship, and made demands on the child's love that were as tyrannical as they were poignant. These Karl was less and less able to tolerate as he grew to manhood; Beethoven on the other hand was able and ready to apply intolerable pressure. By the act of suicide, according to the Sterbas, Karl freed himself psychologically from this senseless domination. It was now only a matter of time before he broke away. Beethoven could not—anyhow, he did not—survive the wound caused by the destruction of his one great remaining emotional tie.

Things did not happen all at once. The year 1826 begins with Beethoven ill again and depressed, and tormented by a general worsening of all the old points of conflict. He thinks Karl is purposely avoiding him, denigrates the moral character of the boy's friends and his mother, and accuses him of borrowing and lying about money and worse. Karl may have been seriously in debt, but if so, the fact does not emerge in all the frank talk after the suicide attempt. This step was taken after long consideration, so he told the police, "because my uncle harassed me so." This was around the first of August. For a few days he was in real danger; Beethoven was horrified and mortified, but certainly still far from completely crushed. While Karl lay two months in the hospital, through August and September, Beethoven planned for his future and made sure that he would not go back to his mother. To this end, he whisked Karl

[1] P. 302.

away on his release to the little hamlet of Gneixendorf, a two days' trip up the Danube, near Krems. Here his brother Johann van Beethoven had his estate, which Ludwig had heretofore refused to visit, despite several invitations.

The stay at Gneixendorf was supposed to be quite short, a "vacation" or a "period of reconciliation" prior to Karl's joining his regiment—for an extremely reluctant Beethoven had consented to his enlistment in the imperial army. But there are indications that the unhappy man was dreaming of settling down for good in the country with Karl. In any case, life there was a martyrdom, full of new scenes between uncle and nephew. Johann's ménage must have been a sufficiently depressing one; as he explained to Ludwig in an effort to coax him to come, his wife Therese "has surrendered her marriage contract and entered into an obligation permitting me to drive her away without notice at the first new acquaintance that she makes." "You will scarcely see the woman. She looks after the housekeeping and works." Beethoven resented this sister-in-law as fanatically as the other.

The visit dragged on for two more months, through October and November, till finally Karl and everyone else insisted that there could be no further postponement. Therese had just left for Vienna in the one carriage—Beethoven, according to the Sterba's guess, having refused to ride with her—so he and Karl had to travel in the rain in some kind of cart. He reached Vienna ill with pneumonia.

Yet a few days later he has the pathetic fantasy of following Karl to the regiment in Moravia! That could not be; he was, as the event proved, already on his deathbed. "Thus the beloved youth slipped from his grasp and Ludwig was forced to recognize that he had no more power over him. Thereupon he collapsed." [2] Karl finally got away at the very end of the year, after assisting at Beethoven's first operation, and after doing some proofreading of the last quartets. He did not write many letters, perhaps not understanding how hopeless the illness had become —and understandably, the entourage at the *Schwarzspanierhaus* would have been in no great anxiety to enlighten him. Beethoven did not die until the end of March. For almost four months he had done little more than take a sketchbook in hand: four months deprived of music, haunted instead by everything that he could not control: including finally life itself.

[2] Sterba, p. 295.

· 2 ·

With all this, in terms of composition 1826 has to be counted one of Beethoven's surpassing years. The Quartet in C♯ minor, begun shortly before the beginning of the year, was completed by July—that is to say, before the suicide attempt. In and around February, work on it was interrupted by serious illness, as had been the case with the A-minor Quartet ten months earlier. The Quartet in F, Op. 135, though sketched in part earlier, was composed mainly during the grim months of August and September, with Karl in the hospital and Beethoven agonizing over everything about him: his health, his legal status, his growing hostility, the pressures to have him sent away from Vienna, and the likelihood that he was seeing or about to see his mother. At the end of September, Beethoven took the quartet sketches along with him to the retreat at Gneixendorf, but within a couple of weeks he is reporting the piece ready, except for the copying.

And up to the end he is full of the most diverse plans: an opera with Grillparzer dealing with the fairy Mélusine, who was half snake on Saturdays; an important overture on the notes B A C H; oratorios in Handel's manner; and the Requiem Mass which he had long been considering. Holz claimed repeatedly that Beethoven had pieces "completely sketched in his head," whatever that means: two movements of another C-minor Symphony, the first part of an oratorio *Saul* using Hebrew modes (!), and the first movement of a string quintet.

The Mélusine project is especially fascinating and curious from more than one point of view. This was to have been a full-fledged Romantic opera to rival *Der Freischütz* and *Euryanthe;* indeed objections were raised because of the similarity of the story to that of the De la Motte Fouqué–E. T. A. Hoffmann *Undine*. But the work that Beethoven in fact produced, the Quartet in F, has nothing whatsoever to do with any Romantic stirrings. On the contrary, the first movement of this quartet is his most successful evocation of the style of Haydn and Mozart. It is a thoroughgoing neoclassic investigation, of a kind that seems to have fascinated Beethoven now and then at every stage of his career: one thinks of the Quartets in G and A, Op. 18, Nos. 2 and 5, parts of the C-major "Razumovsky" Quartet, and the Eighth Symphony. The F-major Quartet turns sharply back, not forward, more so than any other major work in a decade.

This self-conscious classicism has not attracted much attention among commentators, but it seems to me plain at every step of the opening *Allegretto* movement. It appears in the initial thematic statement, for instance, with its network of chiseled motifs in smart juxtaposition:

Example 174

A short mercurial motif, beginning the piece away from the tonic, spoiling for trouble—that is a characteristically Haydnesque point of technique. A parallel can be drawn with the theme of an early Haydnesque essay by Beethoven, the Quartet in G (see p. 46). Both themes begin with a pair of alert, inquisitive 2-bar phrases ending on the dominant (in the G-major Quartet, two different phrases; in the F-major, the same one repeated with a lively *sforzando* the second time). The pair is answered by a genuinely melodic phrase working up the scale archly, and then down again—a phrase starting squarely on the tonic so as to resolve that dominant. The phrase also ends squarely on the tonic so as to balance in a funny way, which sounds much too conclusive, much too soon. In both works, Beethoven indulges in the standard paradox of allowing this phrase to make the really conclusive cadence at the very end of the movement.

The quality of tonal movement in the F-major Quartet is also purely classical. After the *cantus-firmus* theme in bars 10–14—one of the most pleasant and original ideas in the piece: how solemn to plumb its genial little enigma for traces of the mantic 4-note configuration of the Quartet in A minor!—after the *cantus-firmus* theme, the dominant is emphasized at once, in bars 15 ff.; but this is not yet the true modulation to the second group. Having made this preliminary reconnaissance Beethoven returns to the tonic and from there launches a highly formal bridge passage—a cautious, leisurely double approach to the dominant key, of a type that occurs commonly in Mozart's work, rarely in Beethoven's. The difference from the abrupt plunges that have passed for modulations in his recent works—in the first movement of the B♭ Quartet, the Finale of the C♯-minor, and for that matter the Finale of the present F-major—hardly needs comment. The bridge closely resembles that in the first movement of the "Pastoral" Symphony. The second subject, alternating tonic and dominant bars, recalls the "Pastoral" and also an old cliché of Beethoven's first period. There is the customary small harmonic cloud after the second subject, and then self-repeating cadential phrases, all according to the best classical models.

And the development section centers around a quite explicit *hommage* to Haydn—a "false recapitulation," which again counts as a considerable rarity in Beethoven's work. A vaguely fugal passage has opened the development, making an admirable double-counterpoint combination out of the *cantus firmus* and the opening 2-bar inquisitive motif. The end of this episode, where the *cantus firmus* goes to A♭ in the second violin, is illustrated below (bars 74–8. The triplet flashes, incidentally,

Example 175

derive from the second subject). It will be observed that the 2-bar motif is posing its questions rather insistently from E♭ (bars 73, 74, 78, and 79); and sure enough, this *seems* to be answered by a recapitulation in bars 81–3. Yet one knows enough to feel uneasy about it: it comes too soon, it has not been properly prepared, and it appears to have mistaken the key (which is B♭). But then what do we think when the next bars, 85–6, offer to rectify the mistake and bring the theme in the tonic key? This is a witticism exactly in Haydn's manner. After an expectant (and, to be frank, also a more or less expected) moment of hesitation, the harmony shifts toward A minor, and the development can continue with a second good-sized episode. When the recapitulation finally arrives, it is acting quite smug about the tease.

Earlier in this study—it was in Chapter 5—a distinction was drawn between two poles or types of sonata-form treatment, which Beethoven was already capitalizing on in the Op. 18 Quartets and sharpening in the "Razumovsky" series. The first movement of the F-major "Razumovsky" Quartet exemplifies the "progressive" type, and the first movement of the E-minor, with its balancing repetitions, the "symmetrical." The present *Allegretto*, even though it lacks any repetitions, adheres very frankly to the symmetrical, architectural, or Mozartian ideal. The development is discreet, and the recapitulation is in no way functionally altered; the one outstanding modification, flexing the *cantus-firmus* theme with chromatic *appoggiaturas* in eighth-notes, serves as decoration only. Then the coda mirrors the recapitulation, opening with a similar passage in double counterpoint (but on the decorated version of the *cantus firmus*) and actually encompassing the "false recapitulation":

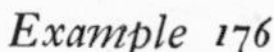
Example 176

The joke flips back on itself, for this time the tonic harmony in bars 189 ff. has to be taken absolutely at face value (compare bars 85–6). The paradoxical ending, making a really conclusive cadence out of the uncomfortably premature one of bar 10, compounds the witticism.

In his early years Beethoven may well have felt a need or an ambition to emulate the classic masters, to catch the secrets of their technique and the refinements of their expressive visions. This may lie behind the Mozartian modeling of movements of the A-major Quartet, Op. 18, No. 5, and the outspoken rough humor of the G-major. Perhaps it is fanciful to imagine this ambition still lurking subconsciously at the time of the *Eroica* Symphony and at the time of the Great Fugue; perhaps not. But it would be hard to imagine or understand the urge outlasting the Quartet in F; this first movement at last matches and outmatches Haydn and Mozart on their own ground. One would hesitate to say that Beethoven had done this before. Wit, intelligence, effortlessness, high style—the perfection of the writing here is complete. If this was what Beethoven meant, in his celebrated remark to Holz, by "a new method of voice leading," he was guilty of yet another understatement.

Why does the movement seem, in its way, to be as tranquil as the *Lento assai, cantante e tranquillo* in D♭, the beautiful third movement of this quartet? All sense of conflict seems to have been eliminated, though how this has been done is not at all easy to analyze. Beethoven does not employ contrapuntal or fugal styles, *ostinati* or monorhythmic effects, nor does he pinch on normal sonata procedures—to mention some of the means employed to minimize contrast in other movements of the late quartets. Here the technique is quintessentially classical, and in many places reminiscent of Haydn, the real specialist in contrast and its manipulation. But the spirit is so different; lacking is Haydn's ceaseless enthusiasm, that down-to-earthness which (for all that it can also grow tiresome) assures his sense of involvement with his musical procedures. For Beethoven, wit is an urbane stylistic reflex, not really a source of fun, as for Haydn, or even a source of private esoteric satisfaction, as often for Mozart. The whole vision is too abstracted—or abstract—to count as "humorous." Something dispassionate, even *désengagé* about the Quartet in F resembles Haydn less than Mozart in the incredibly lovely, incredibly unruffled "Prussian" Quartets of his last years.

That certainly sounds like an unusual set of qualities to ascribe to a major work by Beethoven. Certainly the first movement of the Quartet in F is not straining at the frontiers opened up by the Great Fugue and the Quartet in C♯ minor. Perhaps then it should not be called a major work; but it is so very beautifully composed.

The second movement, on the other hand, stands in the main stream of technical, stylistic, and expressive exploration carried out by the late quartets as a group. Since the third movement, the *Lento assai*, is going to be so quiet, the scherzo assumes a special responsibility for dynamism (as also happens in the two E♭ Quartets, Op. 74 and Op. 127). This responsibility the present *Vivace* fulfills in a perfectly fantastic way, from the odd "doublet phrase" in triple counterpoint that makes up its *a* phrase, to the rupturing tattoo that make up its *b* phrase, and to the apocalyptic trio. The piece is as swift and quirky as a bagatelle, a fact that should not obscure its very ominous undertones.

I call the original doublet odd because the relative weight of its contrapuntal members remains so elusive, thanks to the cross rhythm (and I count the counterpoint as triple by including the pedal C, which originally comes in the middle and later comes on the top and on the bottom). The *b* phrase does nothing but hammer at an utterly discon-

Example 177

certing E♭—disconcerting, unless you hear the E♭'s of the first-movement coda still echoing—in the following weird cross-rhythmicization of a "regular" 8-bar module:

8 1 2 3 4 5 6 7 8 1
2 3 2 3 2 3 2 3 2 3 2 3 2 3 2 3 2 3

THEME

1 1 3 5 1 3 5 1 4 1 1 1
2 3 2 4 6 2 4 6 2 3 5 6 2 3 2

dim. *p* *pp* *cresc.*
F E♭———————————————E F/C

(This movement is not one of those which the composer of *Le Sacre du printemps* calls "pedestrian.") The thematic statement indicated at the right of the chart is the one with the pedal C on the bottom, and so it acts not as a true return, but as a dominant preparation—an effect assisted by the liberal application of V-of-V sounds. Then the actual return comes in two contrapuntal voices only. The original violin part now lies below the original cello part, causing well-calculated grinding clashes; this is Beethoven's last rustic parody, his last broad joke at the expense of the counterpoint books, heir to the raucous trios of the E-minor "Razumovsky" Quartet and of Op. 74. The miniscule form of the present *Scherzo*—so far all we have got is |: 8 :| 8 8 8—is slightly extended by cadential phrases which continue to repeat themselves in invertible counterpoint.

The material of the *Scherzo* proper is all extremely confined. Not to speak of the *b* phrase, but only of the two main ideas of the double counterpoint, one of them simply vacillates around A, G, and F, while the other works mechanically up and down the scale to the sixth degree. The trio changes all that. Starting in the same key and tempo as the *Scherzo* (as is Beethoven's habit in the last years), the main phrase of the trio races upward for two octaves and stamps when it arrives at the peak. After a repetition, the piece makes an effort to stabilize itself, using developments of a small rapid turn-motif. Instead, the music shunts up the scale from F major to G major, where the scale shoots for the stars again, twice 8 bars. There is a new sense of iron purpose to the sequence of events.

In some considerable excitement, another step is taken, and the scale works through its twice-8 bars in A major; then suddenly the heavens burst. An absolutely wild, shattering climax comes in the very last place that might have been anticipated, namely in the trio of a scherzo. The three low instruments grind the turn-motif into A over and over again, nearly fifty times without any interruption, while the violin screams a wild triumphant leaping dance above. *Fortissimo* is required for the first time in the entire quartet. A major is Beethoven's rustic key, and certain details here recall the folklike trio of the A-minor Quartet—but it is Wagner's *ungeheuer Spielmann* who is deploying the doublet phrases now, tearing at the square-dance fiddle over the bagpipe drone. Walter Riezler found this passage to be even more extreme in its fury than the Great Fugue, for there "the fugal form is still perceptible beneath all the tumult," whereas here "the tumult comes, divested of all art, like a bolt from the blue into the calm and unconstrained ease of the movement, which is only now and then disturbed by moments of tension." Riezler adds: "Even when Beethoven seems to have lost all self-control, and to have worked himself up into the wildest frenzy, he sees the world with eyes that are as clear as ever. But he is not afraid to draw aside the curtain that veils the abyss. He knows no fear of chaos, out of which matter is made form, because he is aware of his power to give form to all that his eyes have seen." [3] Perhaps

[3] Pp. 243–4.

this clarity of vision is expressed by the eventual calming of the tumult, in this remarkable passage of return to the *Scherzo* proper:

Example 178

Beethoven whittles away at the turn-motif, accidental by accidental, until it no longer lives in A major but in F, and is shown to spell out the numb configuration A–G–F with which the *Scherzo* will begin its *da capo*. Thus Beethoven "gives form to all that his eyes have seen." And it has been pointed out by Roger Sessions that the steps marking the tonal centers of the trio—F major, G major, and A major—"compose out" this same configuration. At the return passage, Beethoven marks *ppp*. It is indeed the still voice after the hurricane.

The *da capo* is literal, up to the 6-bar coda in pure hemiola:

8 1 2 3 4 5 6
2 3 2 3 2 3 2 3 2 3 2 3

1 1 3 5 1 3 5 1 3
2 3 2 4 6 2 4 6 2

dim. p più p pp f

F C/F ————————————

This all comes on the tonic triad, not on E♭. But the tiny explosion at the very end (*f*) holds to the pedal C which has been a feature of the movement.

Stiller yet is the *Lento assai, cantante e tranquillo* which follows. Its deeply serene tonality of D♭ major (♭VI of F) is established gently upward from the common tone of F (see p. 219); D♭ sounds in reference to the previous pedal C. In discussing this movement, I have tried to indicate the sophistication beneath the simplicity and to present it as a logical conclusion of Beethoven's exploration of the principle of variation, which had occupied him throughout the third period and had produced some of its finest monuments. How to employ variation form for a new vision of tranquillity? This movement is as original in its way as the *Scherzo*. One really must not treat the Quartet in F as though it shirked the stylistic and expressive adventure of the last quartets—as an "evasion," in Romain Rolland's unfortunate term.

Then the notorious Finale: another quartet piece with a title, to go along with *La Malinconia* and the *Heiliger Dankgesang eines Genesenen an die Gottheit, in der lydischen Tonart*. Like the earlier works, this one involves a particularly gross contrast. Beethoven annotates the beginning in this style:

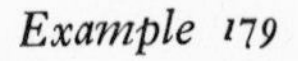
Example 179

—like a "Sphinx" in Schumann's *Carnaval*. Presumably he did not mean to have the sphinxes actually played or sung prior to the Finale, but the urge to get his quartets talking was certainly carrying him a good way.

There is a comic canon by Beethoven using the *Es muss sein!* tag, and an anecdote to go along with it. A certain Ignaz Dembscher, who held quartet parties in his house, had not subscribed to the première of Op. 130 in March 1826. So Beethoven refused to lend him the parts until he paid up. When Dembscher heard this, he moaned "*Wenn es sein muss!*"; the remark caught Beethoven's fancy, and he tossed off a feeble canon with the words "*Es muss sein! ja ja ja ja! Heraus mit dem Beutel!*" Thayer suggested that the quartet theme might have been in his head already, and the words clicked right in with it. However, the form of the theme in the quartet differs from that in the canon, and improves upon it.

And there is another comic canon tied up with a major work by Beethoven, as everyone knows: the canon about *Lieber Mälzel* of metronome fame and the *Allegretto* of the Eighth Symphony (another F-major composition, another conspicuous classical evocation). No metaphysical overtones have been discerned in that movement, so far as I know, in the way that this has been done with the present Finale. Rolland put the case with circumspection and charm:

> It is a common tendency of the German mind to wring a sententious and general signification out of an ordinary word in some daily use (I noted this in *Jean-Christophe*): so—your good German, when his servant brings him the mustard after dinner is over, and when he says —simply enough—"Too late," catches himself and adds philosophically (I have heard him!) "Too late: as ever in this life!" Beethoven re-read that "*Es muss sein!*" under a much more general interpretation. And the trivial response evoked the serious question, in an altogether different tone of voice—a question that surged from the very depths of the Beethovenian soul: "Should it be? Must it be?" Must *what* be? —all that you desire; all that commands your thought and weighs upon it; "the difficult decision," the order of Destiny, the acceptance of life. . . .[4]

Who is being the good metaphysical German here, though—the author of Op. 135 or the author of *Jean-Christophe?* If a choice were required, I would think that those sections of the movement which develop the *Muss es sein?* motif sound more like a farcical depiction of an old miser's discomfiture than like any deep serious speculation. Rolland admits that the resolution of the question, in the sections using the *Es muss sein!* motif, offers "no character of accepted Necessity, not even of 'the difficult decision' according to the title, but of a gay determination. . . ." Beethoven makes light of all previous decision-making perplexities.

The slow introduction to the Finale, a 12-bar section marked *Grave, ma non troppo tratto*, offers but a single scene: the cello and viola in stiff octaves dragging the *Muss es sein?* motif up an odd, chromatically distorted scale:

G A♭ C D♭ D♭ E E F F G
E A♮ B♭ C D

To my ear the image is operatic enough: a recitative for Pantalone, punctuated first by dubious stirrings (Mélusine, perhaps?) and then by blustering chords in the upper instruments (the Spanish Captain Spavento?). The scoring suggests an opera orchestra, but in a gauche way that has to be understood as parodistic (or self-parodistic: Beethoven could have been thinking of the Ninth Symphony). Mock orchestral effects are exaggerated in a second, quite similar *Grave* which introduces the recapitulation (this movement exemplifies "symmetrical" sonata form with a venge-

[4] *Les Derniers Quatuors*, pp. 299–300.

ance). None of this is very funny, perhaps—with Beethoven, the broader the joke the less effective—until *Es muss sein!* timidly acknowledges the piteous roar in the low instruments. For a moment Pantalone and Brighella inch up the odd scale together, in lockstep counterpoint.

To this comedy the *Allegro* offers no serious answer. As in one of those deft demonstrations in analytic philosophy, the question is rephrased and shown never to have amounted to a true question in the first place. *Es muss sein!* as a diatonic inversion of *Muss es sein?* has to move down the scale instead of up:

Example 180

To arrive so clearly at a thematic subdominant is a very quiet move for Beethoven; and then to have the subdominant stressed further, by means of the urbane little winding-motif of bars 17–18, would also be much more characteristic of Mozart. The urbanity is compounded by the fact that the winding-motif is a sort of free variation of *Es muss sein!* itself. A suggestion of canon, almost unnoticed in bars 19–20, proves to be an extremely good prophet, and we can probably prophesy on our own that sooner or later the glaring holes in the theme are going to be filled by echoes or compressions of some kind. This happens first when *Es muss sein!* returns as a cadence theme at the end of the exposition.

Further statements of this motif, compressed together and forced upward in slightly chromatic 3rds, open the development by knocking roughly out of the second key (which is A major). This is another Mozartian recollection—of the well-known stroke which opens the development in the Finale of the Symphony in G minor. Thereafter *Es muss sein!* and winding-motif canons are joined together in double counterpoint, unobtrusively but very neatly indeed. The combination moves dutifully down the scale for six degrees:

G	F	E	D	C	B♭	A
E D	D C	C B	B A	A G	G F	F E

Next comes the charming fairy march of a second subject, which has been cited on page 203 along with all the other half-popular doublet phrases.

The theme is hardly developed at this juncture, but it is scored and harmonized even more seductively than in the exposition. It really belongs in *A Midsummer Night's Dream.* Fresh canons continue the development deferentially, almost reticently, until the second *Grave* section arrives to prepare the recapitulation.

Here the two exclamations of *Es muss sein!* and the winding-motif are all compressed together without leaving any air at all. As is appropriate in

Example 181

a recapitulation, the tendency is even more clearly to the subdominant (notice all the E♭'s) and even more systematically downward:

|: C B♭ :| (F E♭ D C) A G F E♭
A G G F D C C B♭ B♭ A A G F E E D D C C B♭

The bridge goes to D major, as though to balance A major, which was the second key of the exposition. (A major is more or less permanently seared on the eyeballs as the climactic key of the second-movement trio.) However, as D major already accommodated the second theme in the middle of the development section, it would be redundant here, so after the proper gesture Beethoven can slip around directly to the tonic again.

Example 182

The recapitulation proceeds quite symmetrically. At the end of it Beethoven coolly directs that the second half (including the *Grave*) may be repeated or not, *a piacere*. Then in the coda, the anticipated mirror image of the gruff opening of the development becomes fantastically clouded. What makes the magic of this brief 6-bar section—the new hint of chromatic uncertainties back of *Es muss sein!* reminiscent of *Muss es sein?*—or the dreamlike texture, or the halting unpredictability of the upward progressions? or is it the evocative set of key-centers hinted at—A major and D major, and then E♭, the "sore" note of the first two movements and the note that has been edging us toward the subdominant all through this one? A delightful *pizzicato* catches up the second theme again, in the same harmonization as was used in the development. Finally *Es muss sein!* runs down the scale in a further rhythmic compression:

C B♭ A G F
A G G F F E E D C

With no further ado the movement ends with the last phrase of the cadence theme, *unisono* and *fortissimo*. It ends, in fact, just as humorously as the first movement.

The piece includes one extra-special joke, a quotation from the E-major *Scherzo* of the Quartet in C♯ minor (!):

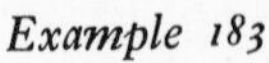
Example 183

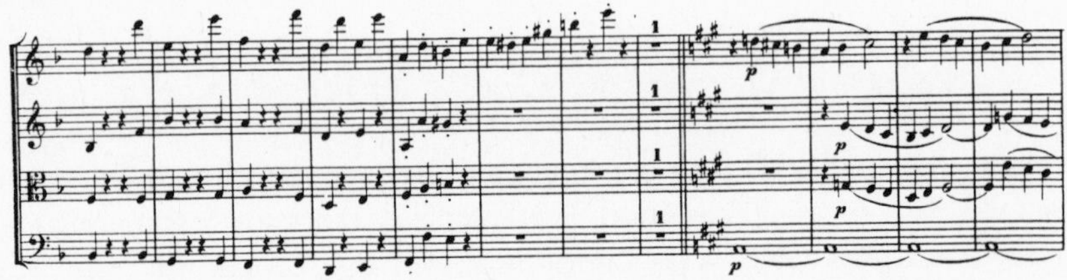

I expect Beethoven noticed a certain analogy between *Es muss sein!* plus the winding-motif, and the fugue subject of the earlier quartet. I should not, however, use this to support theories about "threads that cross . . . lines of demarcation and connect one Quartet with another"—Riezler's phrase—and an attendant lack of individuality in the late quartets. (The thread would also have to cross to the orchestral *fugato* in the *Dona nobis pacem* of the *Missa solemnis*.) In *Die Meistersinger*, Hans Sachs can quote from *Tristan und Isolde* without detracting from his own individuality or that of the world he inhabits.

Laughter, spontaneity, verve—these are the characteristics of this marvelous little *Allegro*. By comparison, even the Finale of the Quartet in E♭, Op. 127, seems studied. If we try to characterize it as elegant or brilliant, it will smile back at us playfully, without quite understanding. For all of its classic references, and for all of its perfection of shape and procedure, the piece is too unbuttoned and elusive and natural to count as a classic evocation like the first movement of the quartet. That quality has been modulated—after the tumult of the *Scherzo* has given way to the serenity of the *Lento assai*—into something more earthy and more ethereal, both qualities at the same time and both in the very highest degree. Romain Rolland spoke of "*un gai vouloir.*" Something like the essence of gaiety is what Beethoven captured, at Gneixendorf, in the last movement of the last of his quartets.

· 3 ·

That dismal retreat in the waning autumn of 1826 served him for the completion of another project: a new finale for the Quartet in B♭, Op. 130, as a substitution for the Great Fugue. It was certainly a less lucky undertaking; in recasting the quartet according to this prescription, Beethoven's motives must be owned to have been unclear, and his success at least questionable. And in supplying two alternate routes through the single work of art, he posed (for us, at any rate) a neat aesthetic problem which does not resolve itself without some difficulty.

The difficulty lies less in the general nature of the problem, perhaps, than in the extremity of the attendant circumstances in this particular case. When a mature artist has produced and promulgated a work of the calibre of Op. 130, he does not ordinarily change his mind about it, within a year, in such a drastic way. Certainly Beethoven had provided no precedent for such an action. Other movements are known to have been omitted or switched very late in the process of composition, but before the first performance and the publication—for example, the *Andante favori* originally intended for the "Waldstein" Sonata. Then there are the revisions of *Fidelio* in 1805–6 and 1814—but opera is a law unto itself in the matter of revisions, and was in any case a field in which Beethoven was feeling his way. The Quartet in B♭ was completed, sold to a publisher, dispatched to Prince Galitzin, performed before an audience of Viennese connoisseurs, and actually all engraved before Beethoven changed the finale.

And of course the change amounts to much more than a "revision," as the term is ordinarily conceived. The work of art was turned upside down: the severe, apocalyptic, utterly radical Fugue supplanted by a quiet, sunny, Haydnesque *Allegro*. This can look like a capitulation. Why did Beethoven undertake to rewrite the piece? what events led up to his decision to do so? It would be nice if the circumstances of the case shed light on at least some aspects of the aesthetic problem.

Often, though, it seems to work just the other way around. The facts being far from unequivocal, their interpretation is influenecd by the position the critic happens to take on the relative merits of the two versions of the quartet. Partisans of the new version will probably come down hard (and rest) on the ostensible fact that the quartet with the new finale does represent Beethoven's ultimate decision. But was he entirely master of himself in this matter? Partisans of the Great Fugue, and especially those who see a "triptych" in the late quartets, will probably stress the considerable evidence that Beethoven was not.

The most elaborate argument from this position has been put together by Ivan Mahaim, in *Beethoven: Naissance et Renaissance des Derniers Quattuors.*[5] It makes an interesting story, starting with the first performance of the quartet, in March 1826. The *Presto* and the *Alla danza Tedesca* were applauded and encored, but the Fugue met with resistance—the audience puzzled, Beethoven's friends disconcerted, and the composer himself irate: "And why didn't they encore the Fugue? That alone should have been repeated! Cattle! Asses!" But no one, perhaps, was more upset than the publisher, Matthias Artaria. He had already paid the unprecedented sum of 80 ducats for the quartet, and now found himself facing the prospect of an unmarketable commodity. The first intimation of a tangled future for the Great Fugue involves Artaria, in a discussion with Beethoven and Holz. "People on all sides are demanding a piano four-hand version of the Fugue," Artaria writes in a Conversation Book, shortly after the premiere. "Will you authorize me to publish it in that form? . . . We will publish score, parts, and four-hand version all at the same time."

"What was behind this machiavellian intervention?" Mahaim wants to know, and Artaria's gambit may be admitted to be pretty disingenuous. As the event proved, demand for the four-hand version of the Fugue was so slow that a second edition waited until 1964! There is no record yet of a plan of replacing the Fugue, simply of arranging it and issuing it separately for piano. Beethoven agreed to have someone make a transcription, but this displeased him, and he engaged in four months of "passive resistance" (as Mahaim sees it) before supplying Artaria with his own arrangement. The publisher had to pay twice. His relations with the composer grew strained.

Twenty-five years later, Holz remembered how Beethoven "held tight to the Fugue, and was persuaded only with difficulty to separate it from the quartet [*sie davon zu trennen*]." He also claimed that Artaria "charged me with the terribly difficult mission of convincing Beethoven to write a new finale. . . . Beethoven asked to think about it, but already the

[5] Pp. 419–37.

next day I received a letter giving his agreement. . . ." From all this, and other material, Mahaim draws a picture of Artaria working on Beethoven by gentle steps in two separate "interventions," both of them of course smoothed by financial assurances. In April, Artaria and Holz innocently offer to publish the Fugue as a separate item, presumably *in addition* to its inclusion within the quartet. In August or September, Holz alone, but acting for Artaria, broaches the idea of a substitute finale. By this time, Beethoven was presumably conditioned to thinking of the Fugue as a separate item; anyhow it will not be lost. The first specific reference to the new Finale comes up in Conversation Books of September.

This construction accounts for Holz's use of the word *trennen* (separate) rather than, say, *entsetzen* (substitute). He was thinking of the first intervention—which was sufficiently painful and difficult. It also explains his assertion that the job of bringing Beethoven around was given to him, Holz, even though it is known that Artaria himself took the lead in April. Here Holz was thinking of the second intervention. Finally, the theory accounts for the striking fact that as late as mid-August, when the quartet was finally engraved, it still contained the Great Fugue as finale.

With all this reluctance, why did Beethoven agree? Money would be part of the answer. He received 12 ducats for the piano arrangement and 15 for the new Finale; 15 ducats was about enough for him to live on for a month. Beethoven's feelings about money have been spoken of above. But over and above this consideration, Mahaim stresses the particular time of the second intervention and "capitulation": after Karl's suicide attempt, in August or September.

> What did it matter to him now, a few months before his death, if he separated the Great Fugue from his Quartet and substituted another finale? The future which would see the Fugue live again in the concert hall, and resume its authentic place, seemed to him distant and uncertain. The present, for him, was the period of "reconcilation" before the departure of his beloved "son" . . . a departure which signified the bankruptcy of his most imperious emotional aspirations. . . . He would compose a pastiche-finale for them, those "cattle," those "asses." . . .[6]

There is much that is persuasive about the argument. But as usual, external evidence of this sort tends to stop short of the really interesting questions. For example: was or was not Beethoven satisfied with the Great

[6] P. 427.

Fugue as finale for the quartet? Even if everything went exactly as Mahaim says—the intrigue, the pressure, the prevarication, the profound reluctance—we are still not justified in taking Beethoven's attitude at face value as fundamental devotion to the original form of the quartet. It can be taken as a sign of self-doubt and self-exasperation and resentment that other people kept telling him what he knew better himself. Beethoven's outer behavior was much too erratic to allow easy deductions from it about his motives or his feelings. Although the amount of information available about him in the last years compares very favorably to that available earlier, it still amounts to very little for the purposes of subtle analysis.

In this whole matter of replacing the Fugue, I do think we should hesitate to charge the composer with artistic irresponsibility. This is, in plain terms, what the onus of Mahaim's evidence is seeking to establish. Those were bad times, and unusual pressures—and a very unusual composition; but there is also the matter of precedent in Beethoven's lifelong inner self-righteousness where major works are in question. A concept of "responsibility" here does not require that he undertake to revise every past composition about which he may entertain some small reluctant doubts. It does assume that when for once in his life he does undertake such a revision, it is for some better reason than cupidity, depression, cynicism, or (as J. W. N. Sullivan quite insufferably suggested) lofty indifference.

In short, I am inclined to take Beethoven's replacement of the Fugue as an acknowledgment (however reluctant, bad-tempered, greedy, etc.) that he saw something wrong with the way it sat in the quartet. But I also take it that the problem could not be met at all so simply. It ran much deeper than the finale. The second version of the quartet is also unsatisfactory—the standard for "satisfactory" being provided by the other late quartets, and most particularly by the newly completed Quartet in C♯ minor.

One tries, gingerly, to put oneself in his position. Although his B♭ Quartet was less than a year old, others composed in the meantime had already brought him within sight of new horizons. He had reached a new stage of ascent, one is tempted to say, a stage which transcended the very terms of previous problems. The drama of dissociation and integration had played itself out in the Quartets in B♭ and C♯ minor, at least temporarily. The C♯-minor Quartet could not have taught Beethoven how to make up the discontinuities of the B♭, but only how not to have written them in the first place, or how to have written them in another way. From his later standpoint, the problem he had wrestled with so awesomely in the Great Fugue may very well have seemed quite remote.

In any case, what Beethoven tried to do was view the Quartet in B♭ in the light of still another fresh artistic experience, that of the Quartet in F, Op. 135, which was just finished. He proposed a sunny, gay, classicizing, Haydnesque conclusion; and that too, obviously, provided no true solution.

The new Finale delighted Artaria, however, as well it might. Although it is not a standard rondo at all, it does have a rondolike tune, a darting, *pianissimo* little *a b a′* structure with regular repeats and with more than its share of sophistication. As its first (by no means its only) Haydnesque feature, this tune begins with a "Clock"-Symphony viola ticking out an accompaniment figuration—but on G (VI) rather than on the tonic; the tonic arrives via the circle of 5ths only at the end of the 8-bar *a* phrase. Pure Haydn, too, is the history of this anomaly in the sequel:

1. Exposition:	*G* . . .	G————C–F–**B♭**		G–C–F–**B♭**
2. Development:	*C* . . .	C (–**E♭**?)–F	*stop!*	
3. Recapitulation:	D . . .	D (–**F**?)–G B♭-**E♭**		G–C–F–**B♭**

This diagram means to show, first, that after the ticking figuration on *G* . . . the *a* phrase of the tune traces the circle G–C–F–B♭, and is immediately repeated. Second: that when, considerably later, after a new episode, the ticking starts on *C*, and so leads us to expect the harmony to circle toward E♭—especially since the episode was in A♭—that at this point something else happens. Beethoven stops at the first turn, F minor, and with a flip of the mode begins his development as conventionally as you please on the dominant, F major. Third: that at the recapitulation, when the violin starts on *D*—not knowing at all what to make of all the fracas, just going about its own business—we expect the harmony to circle toward F major. Using sustained harmonies in the lower instruments as a kind of veil, Beethoven switches the anticipated circle D–G–C–F into D–G B♭–E♭. He has started recapitulating the *a* phrase too far in the dominant direction (on D), and finished it too far in the subdominant direction (on E♭); but he can recoup very neatly by means of the original *a* phrase in place of a literal repetition.

Here the bow to Haydn seems even deeper than in the first movement of the Quartet in F because Beethoven seems to be getting so much more pleasure out of these Haydnesque manipulations. The F-major first movement is also recalled by the aspect of the modulation in the present exposition: a leisurely double approach to the dominant key, once again, and an extremely formal—even vacuous—bridge section. However, the really striking parallel with the Quartet in F involves the *Scherzo:* the extraor-

Example 184

dinary 16-bar unison passage illustrated above, before the recapitulation, comes from the same tumultuous well as the climax of the trio in the earlier composition. There is the same sense of unknown energy flaring without notice, of turbulence suffered and controlled—the same whiff of the Great Fugue. In technical terms, there is the same whittling away of accidentals to make the modulation in a *decrescendo*, and the same rigid vise of 4-bar phrases. The passage provides the new Finale with its most individual moment, as well as with a quite unexpected and terrible climax of intensity.

To return briefly to the main tune: by opening on G and working around the circle of 5ths to the tonic B♭, the tune preserves the exact sequence of the so-called *Overtura* which opens the Great Fugue, the original finale. I find that I can formulate only two other ideas carried over from one finale to the next—and even these I should hesitate to consider as obligatory "requirements" in the composer's mind, as aspects uniquely determined by some "necessity" in the earlier movements. One specific idea must have been to include a sharply differentiated episode in the unusual (but not unprepared) key of ♭VII (A♭), comparable to the great A♭ Fugue in the original. The other more general idea was simply to have a substantial piece, appreciably longer than a normal finale, at any rate longer than would result naturally from the theme that Beethoven settled on.

Combining these two prescriptions, he invented a special drawn-out structure for the movement, which can be outlined as follows:

Exposition (sonata form, but : using a rondo tune) :	Episode: second rondo tune	Development	Recapitulation	Second tune	Coda
(2) |: 8 :|: 14 :|	|: 8 :|: 8 :|: 8 :|				
(G) B♭ F	A♭	(C)F→	(D)B♭	E♭–B♭	B♭

It is perhaps worth saying that this structure, though probably unique, does not on that account rank with Beethoven's great imaginative creations of musical form, such as the first movement of Op. 132 or the second movement of Op. 59, No. 1. The present Finale makes its accommodations on a much more relaxed and pragmatic level. The very fine second tune in A♭, being quite self-contained, gives the movement a rondolike spread, over and above its contribution of 48 bars on two separate occasions. (The inevitable "doublet phrase" with which this tune begins may be seen on p. 203 once again.) The coda, too, is exceptionally long, brilliant, and powerful—by analogy to the extended B♭ section that ends the Great Fugue, perhaps.

Artaria's satisfaction with the new version of "his" quartet has not been shared by sterner spirits in the twentieth century. It would be interesting to know what Beethoven's later reaction—or action—might have been, if he had lived to attend the new premiere. There is of course a third position on the two versions, besides partisanship for the Great Fugue and partisanship for the new Finale: in the opinion of Walter Riezler, "the present Finale is not, as is often maintained, a mere make-shift, forced upon him by his publishers' opposition and lack of understanding on the part of the public. Two possibilities are inherent in the previous movement: to increase the tension to the limit of human endurance and shift the climax to the end of the whole work, or to relax it and finish in a mood of quietness and serenity. . . . Both endings are 'organic', and both are in keeping with the 'idea' of the work. . . ." [7] Considering when and where he wrote, in Munich in 1936, Riezler was probably being bolder to recognize the simple fact of multiple possibilities in a work of art than to plump for some kind of one-track "necessity."

Yet this is not quite satisfactory either. What is the "idea" of the Quartet in B♭? The piece celebrates dissociation—that is determined once and for all by the opening movement. The sense of sequence is thoroughly problematic, within the movements and among them. In the

[7] P. 239.

previous chapter, it was suggested that Beethoven was working toward a new concept of order, a concept that was not entirely realized or, apparently, at the moment pursued. Whatever it was, it seems to have departed from the instinctual psychological model which holds for most of his music, and which was to reach its most subtle articulation in the Quartet in C♯ minor. So if we are speaking of tension, relaxation, and so on, plenty of possibilities for the Finale were, if not "inherent," open.

Beethoven turned the piece upside down, something that would have been inconceivable with any one of the other late quartets. The Great Fugue had tried almost desperately to dress down the conflicts and discontinuities of the previous movements by means of an exhaustive, self-obsessed renewal. In its own violence, it reflects and indeed magnifies those discontinuities; it caps, but scarcely resolves, the prior sequence—caps it superbly, overpoweringly. Beethoven's idea at that time, here and in the C♯-minor Finale, was to weight the cyclic composition extremely heavily in the direction of the conclusion.

This idea, I believe, had now become quite remote to Beethoven. The new Finale assumes the easier, more symmetrical plan of the Quartet in F. Consequently, the center of gravity in the new version of the Quartet in B♭ is shifted from the end to somewhere else—just where, is hard to say; the other movements seem a little lost without the Great Fugue to dominate them. The Fugue runs the danger of trivializing the experience of the other movements, but the new Finale runs the danger of seeming trivial itself. This nimble and certainly not inconsiderable conclusion glosses over, but scarcely resolves, the problematic sequence of the earlier movements.

As for the "relaxation," we are perhaps obliged to ask, with Stravinsky, whether this may not have been pursued a little too enthusiastically—in such passages as the bridge in the exposition and recapitulation and the brief contrapuntal development section (before the passage of tumult preceding the return). The line between simplicity and blankness is not always easy to draw, but in this case the F-major Finale can serve as a standard. There is some "pedestrian" writing here, no question about it, along with some very good writing.

· 4 ·

The most problematic of all his compositions harassing him to the last, demanding a second equivocal resolution: this strange episode of the substitute Finale for the Quartet in B♭ terminates a survey of the Beethoven quartets. The surveyor, who has stepped back frequently enough to gaze at the individual peaks and valleys, may still find himself overwhelmed by a view of the total panorama. It is one of the most magnificent in the entire territory of music; it has a way of shutting out other prospects.

It is not—to return to a point made earlier—something that would have been expected simply on the basis of familiarity with the terrain. Only the initial impetus was predictable. Under the Viennese classicism of the 1790's, in the tradition of Haydn and Mozart, Beethoven was bound to start writing quartets, just as men are impelled to climb mountains. But it took a great imaginative leap to see, beyond this, how the quartet could be used to accommodate his rapidly evolving and thoroughly unclassical thought over the next three decades. After the Op. 18 Quartets of 1798–1800, the genre offered him an expressive range that seems actually wider than that in any other branch of musical composition. Perhaps the most dramatic witness to the range would be the set of minor-mode quartets, the Quartets in E minor, F minor, A minor, and C♯ minor; in no other areas are the particular dark passions of the minor mode explored so deeply and variously. But much more broadly, the quartets encompass music that is serene as well as passionate, extroverted as well as disturbed, normal as well as radically experimental, esoteric as well as "available"—each of these things, one is driven to say, in some kind of superlative degree. The record of this should be traceable in the previous course of this survey, if it has lived up at all to its intentions.

The range is not without pattern, though the tendency to neaten up the panorama had better be kept in check. From the present vantage point, and in a certain light, the three last compositions stand out significantly. The Quartets in B♭, C♯ minor, and F, Op. 130, 131, and 135, sum up three characteristic aspects or energies of Beethoven's artistic activity, energies which may also be seen to inform many of the earlier compositions.

"Art demands of us that we do not stand still," he said, but that was only the beginning of it. In his *grandes époches créatrices*—the phrase is Romain Rolland's—he would not stand still and he would not probe ahead in any deliberate, circumspect fashion. He insisted on rushing ahead from exploration to exploration—as appears even in the Op. 18 Quartets. The process had to involve some stumbling or at least some breaking of pace. Overreaching themselves, some of his greatest compositions court disruption; paired with them, and perhaps prepared by them, other compositions create whole new models of internal coherence. One perspective in which Beethoven's art (and perhaps his life) can be viewed is as the outcome of these opposite drives toward integration and dissociation.

The Quartet in B♭—a work so disruptive that I have allowed it to spill into four separate chapters—constitutes an extreme and a climactic case, but not an isolated one. A previous instance is the Quartet in C, Op. 59, No. 3. Here each movement—the slow introduction, the A-minor *Andante quasi Allegretto*, the Finale, and the surprisingly rococo *Menuetto: Grazioso*—involves a more hectic exploration, in one direction or another, than most other movements in the two remaining "Razumovsky" Quartets. Again the total effect is of an oddly dissociated personality and of chthonic powers closer than usual to the surface of the work of art. Again the weight of the piece tilts toward the Finale—the half-fugal Finale which amounts to a preliminary vision of the Great Fugue itself. Even before the second period, a broad process of disruption can be seen to set in halfway through the composition of the six Quartets of Op. 18. Op. 130 even finds a parallel in the last Op. 18 Quartet, likewise in B♭ and likewise oriented toward the Finale. Confrontation of *adagio* and *allegro* sections, which is staged again and again in the late music, exists in a primitive form between the precocious *La Malinconia* and the equally precocious dance Finale.

The Quartet in C♯ minor has its full share and more of unprecedented features, and one would hesitate to describe it as "less exploratory" than the Quartet in B♭. But more contained, less reckless in its explorations it certainly is; in Beethoven's *œuvre*, this work stands out as the paradigm of expressive coherence and "mutual service" among all parts and all elements. Among the middle-period quartets, the E-minor "Razumovsky" is the most heavily unified, imposing certain restraints on itself by comparison with its more reckless companions: all four movements hold to the same tonality, for instance, and a single blunt harmonic relationship crops up arrestingly in each one. In some ways, its Finale actually resembles that of the Quartet in C♯ minor rather closely. Perhaps the line can be traced back even further, to the single minor-mode quartet in Op. 18—but only foggily with a piece as crude and unconscious as Op. 18, No. 4. There, too, all the movements hold to the same key, and three of them certainly cleave together by means of the famous "C-minor mood" of Beethoven's early years.

The Quartet in F, Op. 135, belongs to another tradition. In addition to works of art that can be roughly categorized as "integrative" or "dissociative," there are also those that I might style "nostalgic"—elusive spiritual "parodies" of an earlier style, evocations of the artistic world of Haydn and Mozart treated somehow as quite remote in spirit if not in technique. Naturally, the matter is hardest to gauge in the first period, when the composer had in fact not departed very far from the older technique. Still, even at that time it seems to me that some works are better understood in this way, rather than as student essays in an "imitative period of composition." A work of this sort—whether or not it comes to full realization—is the Quartet in G, Op. 18, No. 2, and another is the minuet of the Quartet in A, Op. 18, No. 5, one of the perfect creations of the first period. The decidedly nostalgic *Menuetto: Grazioso* of the C-major "Razumovsky" Quartet ought to be mentioned again, as well as the slow introduction and opening *Allegro* of that composition, with their rather uncomfortable burden of relationship to Mozart's so-called "Dissonance" Quartet. The "Harp" Quartet in E♭ is another case, coming directly before the visionary *Quartetto serioso* in F minor—and forming with it the greatest imaginable contrast. Such contrasts are frequent in the sequence of Beethoven's work. The Quartet in F major is finally a transcendent case, which can shed light on the earlier efforts.

Efforts of this sort run all through Beethoven's career, then, rather like his repeated experiments with fugue, a technical principle evocative of an even earlier musical era. For this reason, if for no other, it is absurd to make excuses for the last quartet, for its un-Faustian tranquillity and relaxation. The suggestion has been seriously made that Beethoven wrote it grudgingly, at a time when he could barely summon up the will to live and entertained only one idea, making money. Neither internal evidence, nor some external evidence indicating that at one stage the piece was to have included only three movements, can be made to support this notion. On the contrary, the external evidence points to a characteristic Beethovenian exploration: try cutting down on the number of movements in the cyclic form, just after having tried multiplying them to five, six, and seven in Op. 132, 130, and 131. A few recorded complaints by Beethoven about writing the piece have been taken too literally, as though in his state of mind after Karl's suicide attempt he always knew exactly what it was he was complaining of. Then, of course, we are told that the phrases *Muss es sein?* and *Es muss sein!* depict the composer's reluctance and resignation, respectively, in the matter of finishing up the job.

The line of argument recalls that taken in disparaging the new Finale for the Quartet in B♭. It has even less validity—less, because the Quartet in F is even more beautifully composed. This quartet does not stand out as either a very significantly integrative work or as a dissociated one; Op. 135 is not pre-eminently an exploratory work at all, any more than Op. 18, No. 5, or Op. 74 (though each of these has its exploratory aspects, as I have tried to show). There is no reason to doubt Beethoven's integrity, or to doubt that he was producing a work of integrity, besides accomplishing exactly what the course of his artistic development required at the particular juncture. Something analogous was required at various earlier times, as is perhaps made clear at those times by the context of subsequent work. In the case of Op. 135 the context is lacking, that is all.

That the piece is very different from the Quartets in B♭ and C♯ minor is of course true, excellently true, and it should not be necessary to have to insist on the individuality of these three last quartets. Their individuality, or authenticity, is the measure of their greatness. The quality exists in spite of "threads" traceable between them in the form of a recurring four-note thematic configuration, and threads of another sort traceable (with as much justice) in terms of style and gesture. Each work deals in the characteristic amalgam that I have tried to define for the third period—the duality of solicitation and introspection, the inward-outward, public-private aspect of the art. The "naked human voice," as Thomas Mann put it, confronts the daemonic in the sharpest possible way. On the one hand there are those stammering-shouting recitatives, and music of an instant emotional appeal like that of the *Cavatina*, and medleys of country dances or nursery tunes flitting insistently through one and all. On the other hand there is the cataclysmic Great Fugue and its after-shocks in the retransition of the substitute Finale, in the trio of the F-major *Scherzo*, and—if one can think of cataclysm normalized—in the Finale of the C♯-minor. There are common elements; but what matters is the separateness, the integrity of individual works of art.

In any reasonable critical system, certainly, matters of thread and panorama count as secondary. To neaten things up, by way of conclusion, one could probably pull together all the threads that have been running through this book—such conceptual strands as the balance of exterior and interior context, history and analysis, the "problem of the finale," the developing subtlety of voice and insight, the manipulation of musical contrast, and latterly the rough categorization of "integrated," "dissociated," and "nostalgic" compositions, etc. Other threads, perhaps important ones, exist. But what one really wants to do is pull them all out and leave the works themselves clear and free and immediate to the listener's response. The threads serve mainly to baste together the critical enterprise.

The integrity of a work of art is like the integrity of a person. Mature Beethoven compositions demand that kind of particularity, concern, and intimacy of response; the last quartets, I have suggested, go out and meet the listener half way. In fact, they almost accost him. Perhaps the analogy can be pursued a little farther—not in order to catch, but to suggest how hard it may be to catch, the connections between intimacy of response and conceptual knowledge. Studying human beings, for instance, we can draw on the general terms of history and social science; even rough categorizations can prove useful as a provisional thing; case histories and biographies are prepared, and so are analyses extending to fine psychological nuance. When we really engage with individuals, however, this knowledge is quite possibly put aside as undoubtedly interesting, helpful, true—and yet in a fundamental sense beside the point. It is not the stuff of which personal relationships are directly made.

Likewise with the mass of formulations developed by the critic in treating works of art. As real involvement with the Beethoven quartets grows, all the concepts—whether sophisticated or simple, revealing or trite—become not so much valueless as provisional in their value. The critic, as a dealer in provisionalities, counts himself lucky to make an occasional penetration or illumination. In the last analysis, he hopes exactly to see his work put aside in this sense.

An awareness of these facts does not (as the reader sees) militate against the erection of fairly elaborate critical structures. For although conceptual terms—terms of pattern, thread, and formulation—can never bring us *to* the work of art, the fact remains that they can bring us some way *toward* it. That is the manifest, indeed the necessary, condition of knowing, and it provides a quite sufficient incentive.

However, a keen awareness of the provisionality of criticism and the centrality of the work of art will have at least two salutary effects. First, it will inhibit the cultivation of methodologies, whether historical, analytical, or anything else. Methodologies resemble ideologies in their tendency to lead charmed lives of their own absurdly abstracted from the real world—the world of people and quartets. Secondly, it will encourage talk about the personalities of individual works of art. And while this is an awkward and subjective business, rarely satisfactory to anyone, and to some people trifling and offensive in the extreme, nonetheless it is response on the one level that directly counts. It should not be avoided, and it cannot be, if criticism is conceived and valued along the lines here indicated.

BIBLIOGRAPHY

INDEX OF BEETHOVEN'S WORKS

INDEX

BIBLIOGRAPHY

I · BASIC SOURCES

Ludwig van Beethoven's Werke. Leipzig [1862–1949].

The Breitkopf & Härtel *Gesamtausgabe.* The quartets (Series 6) were edited by Ferdinand David (1810–73), the famous Leipzig concertmaster, quartet leader, and pedagogue for whom the Mendelssohn Violin Concerto was written. No critical apparatus. The music examples in the present book are for the most part reproduced from this edition.

——, *Supplemente zur Gesamtausgabe,* ed. Willi Hess. Wiesbaden, 1959–65.

Vol. VII includes Beethoven's piano arrangement of the Great Fugue, Op. 134.

——, *Werke,* ed. Beethoven-Archiv, Bonn (Joseph Schmidt-Görg, director). Munich, 1961–.

The new *Gesamtausgabe. Abteilung* 6, Vol. III (quartets, ed. Paul Mies, Vol. 1), contains Op. 18, the early version of Op. 18, No. 1, and Beethoven's arrangement of the Sonata, Op. 14, No. 1, for quartet. Critical apparatus and later volumes not yet published, at the time of writing.

The Letters of Beethoven, tr. and ed. Emily Anderson. 3 vols. London and New York, 1961.

Kinsky, Georg, and Hans Halm. *Das Werk Beethovens: Thematisch-bibliographisches Verzeichnis.* Munich, 1955.

Nottebohm, Gustav. *Beethoveniana.* 2 vols. Leipzig, 1872, 1887 (repr. 1925).

Quartet sketches discussed in the following *Aufsätze:* Vol. I, 18, 19; Vol. II, 1, 7, 11, 12, 22, 27, 29, 30, 46, 54, 58.

Several sketchbooks for the late quartets were not described by Nottebohm:

(1) *Madrid.* Op. 132, 130, 133. See Cecilio de Roda, "Un Quaderno di Autografi di Beethoven del 1825," *Rivista Musicale Italiana,* XII (1905), 63–108, 592–622, 734–67.

(2) *Moscow.* Op. 132, 130. See M. Iwanow-Boretzky, "Ein Moskauer Skizzenbuch von Beethoven," *Musikalische Bildung,* Nos. 1–2 (Moscow, 1927), 75–91, with a complete facsimile.

(3) *Berlin.* Op. 133, 131, 135, and the new Finale of Op. 130. See J. S. Shedlock, "Beethoven's Sketch Books . . ." *Musical Times,* XXIV (1893), 530–3.

See also Alfred Rosenzweig, "Ein unbekanntes Skizzenblatt Beethovens," *Melos,* VII (1928), 414–16, on the *Adagio* of Op. 18, No. 2; and Alfred Orel, "Das Autograph des Scherzos aus Beethovens Streichquartett op. 127," in *Festschrift Hans*

Engel, ed. Horst Heussner (Cassel, 1964), pp. 274–80. There is an unpubl. diss. (Bonn, 1951) on the Op. 18 sketchbook by Erna Szabo.

Other sketchbooks are mentioned briefly—and tantalizingly—in such works as Kinsky-Halm and in the inventories of various Beethoven archives. In the edition of Beethoven's sketches currently under way from the Beethovenhaus at Bonn, no quartet material has so far appeared.

Thayer, Alexander Wheelock. *Life of Beethoven*, rev. and ed. Elliott Forbes. 2 vols. Princeton, 1964.

The standard biography, revised and brought up to date. Earlier editors were Deiters and Riemann (1901–17, in German) and Krehbiel (1921, in English).

II · COMPREHENSIVE STUDIES OF THE BEETHOVEN QUARTETS

Helm, Theodor. *Beethoven's Streichquartette*. Leipzig, 1885. 2nd edn., 1910 (repr. 1921). 355 pp.

Expanded from articles in the Vienna *Musikalische Wochenblatt*, 1873.

Indy, Vincent d'. "Beethoven," in *Cobbett's Cyclopaedic Survey of Chamber Music*, ed. Walter Willson Cobbett. London and New York, 1929 (repr. 1963), pp. 83–106.

Newly reprinted. D'Indy's ideas have considerable currency.

——. *Cours de Composition Musicale*. 3 vols. Paris, 1903–33.

"*Les seize quatuors de Beethoven*," II: 2, 225–55. D'Indy's influential (and as I think misleading) analysis of the Great Fugue, II: 1, 95–6.

Marliave, Joseph de. *Beethoven's Quartets*, tr. Hilda Andrews. London and New York, 1928 (repr. 1961). 379 pp.

This well-known book is embalming critical attitudes of the 1870's, for the great body of it consists of direct translation from Helm. The situation was pointed out in a note (due to Professor Martin Bernstein) in the 1928 edition, a note missing from the 1961 reprint.

Mason, Daniel Gregory. *The Quartets of Beethoven*. New York, 1947. 294 pp.

The Musical Pilgrim series:

Hadow, W. H. *Beethoven's Op. 18 Quartets*. London, 1926. 64 pp.

Abraham, Gerald. *Beethoven's Second-Period Quartets*. London, 1942. 79 pp.

Fiske, Roger. *Beethoven's Last Quartets*. London, 1940. 77 pp.

Radcliffe, Philip. *Beethoven's String Quartets*. London, 1965. 192 pp.

The one modern study, and the best.

Riemann, Hugo. *Beethoven's Streichquartette* (*Meisterführer Nr. 12*). Berlin and Vienna [1910]. 189 pp.

Valetta, Ippolito. *I Quartetti di Beethoven*. Rome, 1905. 96 pp.

Program notes written for a performance of the complete Beethoven quartets. There are other publications of this sort, such as Fritz Reitz (Zürich, 1927) and Arthur Shepherd (Cleveland, 1935).

III · OTHER WORKS

Beethoven: Letters, Journals and Conversations, ed. and tr. Michael Hamburger. London, 1951 (repr. New York, 1960).

Beethoven, the Man and the Artist, as Revealed in His Own Words, compiled by Friedrich Kerst, tr. and ed. Henry Edward Krehbiel. New York, 1905 (repr. 1964).

Bekker, Paul. *Beethoven*, tr. and adapted by M. M. Bozman. London and New York, 1925.

Cooke, Deryck. "The Unity of Beethoven's Late Quartets," *Music Review*, XXIV (1963), 30–49.

Czerny, Carl. *Über den richtigen Vortrag der sämtlichen Beethoven'schen Klavierwerke* [etc.], ed. Paul Badura-Skoda. Vienna, 1963.

Ebert, Alfred. "Die ersten Aufführungen von Beethovens Es-dur Quartett (op. 127) im Frühling 1825," *Die Musik*, IX (1910), 42–63, 90–106.

Förster, Emanuel Aloys. *Kammermusik*, ed. Karl Weigl. *Denkmäler der Tonkunst in Oesterreich*, Vol. LXVII. Vienna, 1928.

Grew, Sidney. "The 'Grosse Fuge': an Analysis," *Music & Letters*, XII (1931), 253–61.

Jonas, Oswald. "A Lesson with Beethoven by Correspondence," *Musical Quarterly*, XXXVIII (1952), 215–21.

Kerman, Joseph. "Beethoven: the Single Journey," *Hudson Review*, V (1952–3), 32–55.
On the Quartet in A minor, Op. 132.

Kirkendale, Warren. "The 'Great Fugue' Op. 133: Beethoven's 'Art of the Fugue,'" *Acta Musicologica*, XXXV (1963), 14–24.

Mahaim, Ivan. *Beethoven: Naissance et Renaissance des Derniers Quatuors*. 2 vols. Paris, 1964.
A very detailed and interesting (and uneven) study.

Mann, Thomas. *Doctor Faustus*, tr. H. T. Lowe-Porter. New York, 1948.

Marx, Adolph Bernhard. *Ludwig van Beethoven: Leben und Schaffen*. 2 vols. Berlin, 1859 (many later editions).

Mies, Paul. *Beethoven's Sketches*, tr. Doris L. MacKinnon. London, 1929.

Reti, Rudolph. *The Thematic Process in Music*. London and New York, 1951.

Riezler, Walter. *Beethoven*, tr. G. D. H. Pidcock. London, 1938.
Perhaps the best concise survey of Beethoven's music available in English.

Rolland, Romain. *Beethoven: les Grandes Époches Créatrices*. 6 vols. Paris, 1928–45.
A detailed "life and works" concentrating on the main periods; a major monument of Romantic criticism. See especially Vol. 5, *Les Derniers Quatuors* (1943).

Schenker, Heinrich. "Beethoven zu seinem opus 127," *Der Tonwille*, IV (1924), 39–41.

Scott, Marion M. *Beethoven*. London, 1934.

Sessions, Roger. *The Musical Experience*. Princeton, 1950.

Sterba, Editha and Richard. *Beethoven and his Nephew: a Psychoanalytic Study*, tr. Willard R. Trask. New York, 1954.

Stravinsky, Igor, and Robert Craft. *Dialogues and a Diary*. New York, 1963.
Pages 62–5 on Beethoven and the quartets.

Sullivan, J. W. N. *Beethoven: His Spiritual Development*. London and New York, 1927 (many times reprinted).

Tovey, Donald Francis. *Beethoven*. London and New York, 1945.

——. *A Companion to Beethoven's Pianoforte Sonatas*. London, 1931.

——. *Essays and Lectures on Music*. London, 1949. Published in the United States as *The Main Stream of Music and Other Essays* (New York, 1949).

Wagner, Richard. *Beethoven* (1870), in *Prose Works*, Vol. V, tr. William Ashton Ellis. London, 1896.
It would seem a shame to protect Wagner from Ellis's prose.

Wedig, Hans Joseph. *Beethovens Streichquartett Op. 18 Nr 1 und seine erste Fassung* (Veröffentlichungen des Beethovenhauses, Bonn, No. 2). Bonn, 1922.

INDEX OF BEETHOVEN'S WORKS

INDEX

A NOTE ABOUT THE AUTHOR

JOSEPH KERMAN was born in London on April 3, 1924, the son of an American writer. He attended University College School (London), New York University (A.B., 1943), and Princeton University (Ph.D., 1950). He is now a professor of music at the University of California (Berkeley). Since 1948 he has contributed articles on many musical subjects to Hudson Review, The Musical Quarterly, Partisan Review, Opera News, High Fidelity, *and other magazines. He is the author of* OPERA AS DRAMA *(1956) and* THE ELIZABETHAN MADRIGAL *(1962).*

A NOTE ON THE TYPE

The text of this book was set on the Linotype in Janson, a recutting made direct from type cast from matrices long thought to have been made by the Dutchman Anton Janson, who was a practicing type founder in Leipzig during the years 1668-87. However, it has been conclusively demonstrated that these types are actually the work of Nicholas Kis (1650-1702), a Hungarian, who most probably learned his trade from the master Dutch type founder Kirk Voskens. The type is an excellent example of the influential and sturdy Dutch types that prevailed in England up to the time William Caslon developed his own incomparable designs from these Dutch faces.

This book was designed by Betty Anderson. It was composed and bound by H. Wolff Book Manufacturing, New York, and printed by Halliday Lithograph Corporation, West Hanover, Massachusetts.